SECRETS OF THE KILLING STATE

SECRETS

OF THE

KILLING STATE

THE UNTOLD STORY OF LETHAL INJECTION

CORINNA BARRETT LAIN

NEW YORK UNIVERSITY PRESS

New York

NEW YORK UNIVERSITY PRESS
New York
www.nyupress.org

Library of Congress Cataloging-in-Publication Data
Names: Lain, Corinna, author.
Title: Secrets of the killing state : the untold story of lethal injection /
Corinna Barrett Lain.
Description: New York : New York University Press, 2025. |
Includes bibliographical references and index.
Identifiers: LCCN 2024031969 (print) | LCCN 2024031970 (ebook) |
ISBN 9781479832965 (hardback) | ISBN 9781479832972 (ebook) |
ISBN 9781479833009 (ebook other)
Subjects: LCSH: Lethal injection (Execution)—United States. | Capital punishment—United
States. | Executions and executioners—United States | Justice, Administration of—United
States—Criminal provisions.
Classification: LCC KF9227.C2 L35 2025 (print) | LCC KF9227.C2 (ebook) |
DDC 364.660973—dc23/eng/20240716
LC record available at https://lccn.loc.gov/2024031969
LC ebook record available at https://lccn.loc.gov/2024031970

This book is printed on acid-free paper, and its binding materials are chosen for strength
and durability. We strive to use environmentally responsible suppliers and materials to the
greatest extent possible in publishing our books.

The manufacturer's authorized representative in the EU for product safety is Mare Nostrum
Group B.V., Mauritskade 21D, 1091 GC Amsterdam, The Netherlands.
Email: gpsr@mare-nostrum.co.uk.

Manufactured in the United States of America

10 9 8 7 6 5 4 3 2

Also available as an ebook

Produce your cause, saith the Lord,
bring forth your strong reasons.

—Isaiah 41:21

Contents

INTRODUCTION

Three hours. That's how long it took the state of Alabama to kill Joe Nathan James by lethal injection in 2022, setting a new record for the longest execution in United States history. James's autopsy showed puncture wounds and bruising at the knuckles and wrists, indicating that executioners had tried (and failed) to insert an IV in those locations. It revealed puncture wounds in his musculature, nowhere near the anatomical vicinity of a vein. And it documented a deep, jagged incision that pathologists suspect occurred when James flinched as executioners were attempting to perform a "cutdown"—a surgical incision used to expose a vein for IV access when all else has failed.

James's autopsy told the story of an inept execution and torturous death, but the state of Alabama told a story of success. According to Alabama's spokesperson, "Nothing out of the ordinary" had happened.[1] And the worst part? He wasn't wrong.

In Alabama, horribly botched executions by lethal injection are not, in fact, out of the ordinary. Botched executions—executions that go seriously wrong in some obvious way—happen all the time. Two months after the long and laborious death of Joe Nathan James, Alabama punctured Alan Miller *eighteen times* over the course of ninety minutes in the name of a "humane" death by lethal injection. The state finally stopped the execution, and two months later, it stopped another—the execution of Kenny Smith—when, once again, executioners could not access a vein.

Alabama's governor took the unprecedented step of temporarily halting executions in the state pending a "top-to-bottom review" of lethal injection.[2] Then the state decided to try something new: death by nitrogen gas. Alabama botched that execution too, subjecting the same Kenny Smith to a twenty-two-minute execution in which he gasped for air, writhed, and convulsed so violently that the gurney itself shook. Nitrogen gas is its own train wreck, but let's not forget the reason for Alabama's latest move: the problems with lethal injection.

Other states are struggling too. In 2014, Oklahoma took over forty-five minutes to execute Clayton Lockett, who woke up in the midst of his own execution and tried to get up off the gurney. The next year, it injected Charles Warner with the wrong drug. Those two incidents inspired a six-year break from executions in the state, but Oklahoma broke that fast in 2021 with the execution of John Grant, who went into full-body convulsions and repeatedly vomited on the gurney after being injected with the drugs.

And the list goes on. Arizona conducted three executions by lethal injection in 2022—its first since 2014's botched execution of Joseph Wood, who gulped and gasped over six hundred times as he died—and Arizona botched all three, leading the newly elected governor to halt further executions in the state pending an independent review of lethal injection. Ohio's governor also has put executions on hold, explaining in 2019 that lethal injection was putting public health at risk. The state had been buying drugs for lethal injection on the sly through its Department of Public Health and Addiction Services, and when the companies that sold the drugs found out, they threatened to stop sales to Ohio's state agencies altogether—a move that the governor stated "would put tens of thousands of our citizens at risk."[3] Tennessee's governor has temporarily suspended executions too, this time because of revelations that the state had been violating its own execution protocol since 2018.

Lethal injection accounts for nearly 98 percent of all executions in the United States.[4] This is how states execute—and it is also why they don't. Over the last decade, problems with lethal injection have done more to slow executions than any of the death penalty's other problems, perhaps more than all of them combined.

The irony is thick. What was supposed to be a kinder, gentler, more *humane* way to die at the hands of the state is now responsible for more torturous deaths than any other execution method in our nation's history. And what was supposed to be a way to make executions easier to carry out has now made them infinitely harder.

Why is lethal injection such a hot mess?

This is the question I set out to answer as a death penalty researcher. I couldn't understand why lethal injection—ostensibly the most humane execution method yet devised—kept leading to torturous deaths. We use drugs to euthanize pets every day, and we know how physician-assisted suicide works. If drugs can be used to humanely end life in these other contexts, why are states so breathtakingly bad at doing it here?

The answer ended up being a book—*this book*. But the short answer is that most everything I thought I knew about lethal injection was wrong. Lethal injection is nothing like what people think. This is its untold story.

Botched executions are a part of this story, but they are the tip of the iceberg. They are the suffering that we see. Yet there is also suffering that we *don't* see. A 2020 study of over two hundred lethal injection autopsies found that 84 percent showed acute pulmonary edema—lungs filled with froth, evidence that prisoners had drowned in their own fluids.[5] As one court put the point, we are essentially waterboarding people to death.[6] We're just doing it with drugs under a façade of peaceful slumber.

But the tale told here is even bigger than the executions themselves, for behind the scenes is where it unfolds. Who knew (I didn't) that states were deciding what drugs to use by Google searches. Or that the lethal injection drug combination that every state used for thirty years was made up off the top of some guy's head. Or that the people pushing the syringes aren't doctors. Or that states were getting drugs for lethal injection (at least until the DEA confiscated them) from a drug distributor run out of the back of a London driving school.

States tell us that lethal injection is humane, and when all goes as planned, that is how it looks. The scene is serene and distinctly medical, adding an aura of competence and careful oversight. The white coat enjoys a credibility not associated with the black hood.

But the visual is largely stagecraft—what Pulitzer Prize–winning journalist Garry Wills has called the "dramaturgy of death."[7] The gurney, the scrubs, the fact that executioners swab prisoners' arms with alcohol before inserting the needle that will kill them—it's all just theater. Backstage is a much uglier truth of medicine run amok.

People think lethal injection is a mostly humane execution method that sometimes goes wrong for reasons we can't quite understand. It is not. Botched executions are not random glitches, but rather the spillover effects of a system that is deeply broken. Lethal injection not working well is how lethal injection works.

Why, then, do states stick with it? Granted, a few states are moving to other execution methods—some old, some new. But most have stuck with lethal injection like glue, despite a track record of torturous deaths and a mountain of difficulties at every turn. What explains their dying devotion?

The answer lies in the fact that lethal injection is *special*. Every other execution method—hanging, the electric chair, gas chamber, and firing squad—lays bare the brutality of the state that kills in our name. Lethal injection hides it. With lethal injection, we don't have to deal with the sight of blood, or the smell of burning flesh, or the sounds of suffering—all potent reminders of what the state is actually doing. Instead, we get to tell ourselves that prisoners are just drifting off to forever-sleep, and that has made it easy for us to *not* think about what the state is doing. *Out of sight, out of mind.*

The death penalty in America is a highly symbolic issue whose utility lies more in politics than crime control, as criminologist David Garland has powerfully shown.[8] For most Americans, support for the death penalty is support in the abstract. Lethal injection keeps the death penalty abstract. It allows the political uses to flourish while hiding the brutality that executions entail.

That brings me to what this book is, and is not, about. This is a book about lethal injection—it is a book about *how* we kill, not whether we should be doing so in the first place.[*] To be sure, the two questions are

---

[*] Relatedly, for those wondering why this book is bereft of the terrible crimes that these prisoners have (presumably) committed, it is because the prisoners in lethal injection cases are not challenging their death sentences. Death at the hands of the state is a given. The only question is how it will be carried out.

not unrelated. The revelations in this book have larger implications, and readers may disagree about what those implications are. I have my own thoughts, of course, but I invite you to walk with me first—to see the revelations for yourself and come to your own conclusions before considering mine. For now, it suffices to say that this book makes serious allegations that warrant serious support. Rest assured, I brought the receipts.

The pages that follow pull back the curtain, presenting a view of lethal injection that states have worked hard to hide. These are the secrets of the killing state—all that we know from litigation files, scientific studies, investigative journalism, autopsy reports, research across a number of fields, and statements by the people involved. We are now over forty-five years into the lethal injection era, and most Americans still have no idea what states are doing in their name. It's time they found out.

1

THE EXECUTION OF CLAYTON LOCKETT

One of the top ten news stories of 2014 was Oklahoma's execution of Clayton Lockett, the man who woke up in the midst of his own execution and tried to get up off the gurney.[1] Lockett's execution shocked the public and brought worldwide attention to American executions. But the backstory is every bit as horrifying as what appeared on the front page news, and it provides a rare view of how lethal injection works—and why it doesn't.

Facing a torrent of criticism, Oklahoma's governor vowed to conduct an "independent review" of Lockett's execution to identify what went wrong.[2] But the governor chose a member of her own cabinet to lead it, and that cabinet member was the person overseeing Oklahoma's Department of Corrections (DOC). In fact, that cabinet member had risen from the ranks of the DOC—he was a former DOC employee—and he was present at Lockett's execution.[3] No part of being a material fact witness in the very investigation he was leading said "independent." But the upside of having an insider do the review is that the people he spoke to were candid and conversational, not cautious and close-lipped like in the litigation setting.

All told, this non-independent "independent review" produced more than three thousand pages of transcripts of interviews with the people involved, providing a "boots on the ground" view of lethal injection that we have never seen before, and will likely never see again. Thanks to those transcripts, we have a reconstructed account, from the mouths of the people who were a part of it, of an execution by lethal injection in one of the most death-dealing states in the country.[4] Oklahoma has conducted more executions than any other state except Texas—this is what lethal injection looks like in a state that ostensibly knows what it is doing.

HIGH DRAMA PRELUDE

Our story starts with high drama in the Oklahoma courts. The Oklahoma DOC had initially refused to say what drugs it would use in Lockett's execution, and even after relenting on that point, it steadfastly refused to disclose their source, citing a recently passed state secrecy statute that protected (among other things) the anonymity of lethal injection drug suppliers. Lockett and another condemned prisoner had challenged that law, and a state trial court had ruled it unconstitutional. "I do not think this is even a close call," the judge stated. "To say that no one, not even the court, has access to that information, I think that does deny [the prisoners] access to court."[5]

Oklahoma appealed the ruling, so Lockett filed a motion to stay his execution pending the outcome of the state's appeal. After all, winning at the trial court didn't do him much good if he was dead before the ruling became final and the state had to abide by it. The state opposed the motion, arguing for his execution to proceed. That's when the drama began.

The Oklahoma Court of Criminal Appeals refused to grant Lockett a stay, stating that it lacked jurisdiction to do so. The secrecy statute challenge was a civil action, the court reasoned, and it was the Court of *Criminal* Appeals. Lockett appealed to the Oklahoma Supreme Court, arguing that the court *did* have jurisdiction. A stay of execution could only be issued in a capital case, he argued, and capital cases were criminal matters. Besides, Lockett pointed out, civil courts had no jurisdiction over capital cases, so he could not get relief elsewhere. The Oklahoma Supreme Court agreed, sending the case back to the Court of Criminal Appeals to "reconsider" its jurisdictional ruling, and if *We meant what we said* counts as reconsideration, then the court did as it had been told.[6] For a second time, the Court of Criminal Appeals dismissed the stay request for lack of jurisdiction, so back to the Oklahoma Supreme Court Lockett went.

With Lockett back a second time, the Oklahoma Supreme Court reasoned that it could not be the case that *no* court had jurisdiction to consider his motion for a stay of execution, particularly since being dead would render the litigation moot. "As uncomfortable as this matter makes us," the Oklahoma Supreme Court wrote in its opinion, "we refuse to violate our oaths of office and to leave the appellants with no access to the courts, their constitutionally guaranteed measure."[7] With that, it issued the stay.

What happened next was the stuff of constitutional law legend. The governor refused to honor the stay, stating that it was "outside the constitutional authority" of the Oklahoma Supreme Court,[8] and a state legislator introduced articles of impeachment against the five state Supreme Court justices who had voted in favor of the stay, charging them with "willful neglect of duty and incompetence."[9] As the Oklahoma attorney general candidly conceded, the state was in the midst of a "constitutional crisis."[10]

But the crisis would not last long. A mere two days after issuing the stay, the Oklahoma Supreme Court decided the state's appeal on the merits, ruling that the secrecy statute was constitutional after all, so the execution could go forward. The title of one news article on the fracas told the tale: "Oklahoma Just Neutered Its State Supreme Court."[11]

Oklahoma finally had the green light to execute Lockett, but it had come at the expense of a highly publicized—and overtly politicized—legal fight that had thrust the execution into the spotlight. People were watching. For Warden Anita Trammell, this was an opportunity. "I told my staff this is our time to make [the DOC] director shine, the governor shine, the state shine because of all the publicity surrounding this," Trammell told investigators. But if ever an execution could make a state shine, this would not be it.

BEHIND THE SCENES

While the Oklahoma DOC was fighting to execute Lockett as fast as it could, it was also trying to solve a problem behind the scenes: it didn't have the drugs to conduct the execution. Oklahoma had been using pentobarbital as the first drug in its three-drug lethal injection proto-col,[12] but the pharmacist supplying the drug "fell through," leaving the DOC empty-handed. "As far as looking for drugs, we were all looking for drugs," recalled Mike Oakley, who was general counsel for the DOC at the time. Oakley and his deputies attempted to buy pentobarbital from a number of pharmacies across the state, to no avail. Oklahoma would need a new drug.

At that point, the race was on to find one. "There was pressure from those people who were above us to get it done and get it in place," Oak-ley told investigators. "There were calls from the governor's office," he stated. "There were meetings at the AG's office that I was not—I did not attend them. But after those meetings, we would get word from the AG's office that we better hurry up and do something." He went on to say: "There are people calling daily. Sometimes more than once a day, sometimes more than twice a day, sometimes three times, four times a day, saying 'Is it done yet?' . . . You got an Attorney General who is run-ning for office. You've got a governor who is running for office. You've, there's pressure to get it done . . . a definite push to make the decision, get it done, hurry up about it."

Just four days after announcing that it would need a new drug, the DOC revised its protocol, indicating that it had found one. The state would be using midazolam, a drug relatively easy to get because of the sheer number of companies that sold it.

Oklahoma's lethal injection protocol at the time gave the warden "sole discretion as to which lethal agent will be used for the scheduled ex-ecution."[13] But it wasn't the warden who made the decision to switch to midazolam. That decision was made by the DOC's lawyer, Mike Oakley. Oakley had no medical expertise, so how did he choose midazolam?

"I did my own research, I looked on-line, you know. Went past the key wiki leaks, wiki leaks or whatever it is," Oakley told investigators, "and I did find out that when administered, midazolam would adminis-ter, would render a person unconscious. . . . That's what we needed," he stated, "so we thought it was okay."

When asked about his knowledge of midazolam, Oakley answered: "I will say generally that we knew midazolam had the same properties as pentobarbital as far as sedation goes"—and this would have been a good answer, but for the fact that it was wrong. As we will see in chapter 3, pentobarbital is a barbiturate; midazolam is a benzodiazepine. Those are different classes of drugs, with different abilities to block pain. Whatever it was that Oakley looked at—and who knows what it was because he didn't remember, and he didn't bother to write it down—it either didn't have this critical piece of information, or he didn't take note of it.

Had Oakley done nothing more than read the FDA warning label on midazolam, he would have known that the drug is not approved for use as the sole anesthetic in a painful procedure. Had he called a local pharmacy, he would have learned that midazolam and pentobarbital are different classes of drugs with different properties. Had he picked up the most basic pharmacology textbook (the University of Oklahoma College of Medicine is just down the road from his office), he would have read that midazolam is pharmacologically incapable of achieving anesthesia, and that this had everything to do with its class as a drug.

Oakley did none of these things. He was researching what drug to use to block pain in state executions, and did not even keep a record of the websites he consulted. What lawyer, in what world of professional competence, does this?

Oakley told investigators that he also had a conference call with officials in three states—Illinois, Arizona, and Texas. Illinois had repealed its death penalty back in 2011, so that was a strange place to go for advice, and at that point in 2014, neither Arizona nor Texas had ever used midazolam in an execution (Texas still hasn't). But taking Oakley at his word, he spoke to officials in these three states about midazolam, and also spoke to a DOC lawyer in Ohio, who said that midazolam "took longer than phenobarbital [*sic*] but it didn't take as long as what the news stories were [saying]."

"So yeah, that's how I researched it," Oakley told investigators. "I suppose I could have said 'No,'" he stated, "but what would have been, what would have been the option, and you have to understand too, there is political pressure. This is political."

And so it came to be that a lawyer acting under intense political pressure and with no medical expertise whatsoever chose the drug that Oklahoma would use to execute its prisoners. But Oakley didn't act alone in this regard; he had an assist from a lawyer in the Oklahoma AG's office, John Hadden. After Lockett's execution, the Oklahoma AG's office insisted that the DOC was solely responsible for the protocol; the AG's office had nothing to do with it.[14] This was not true.

Oakley told investigators that Hadden was his partner in the protocol revision process, and that using midazolam "was a joint decision." According to Oakley, Hadden was responsible for "the legal aspects" of the new protocol, and in that capacity, he had read a transcript of expert testimony defending the use of midazolam in Florida. No one consulted that expert (or anyone else) before adopting midazolam in Oklahoma's new protocol. "There was really no need to meet from a legal perspective," Oakley stated, explaining that "as far as the dosage and the amounts that he testified to, he wasn't going to say anything different on the witness stand here."

Again, that *might* have made sense, but for the fact that Oklahoma didn't use the same dosage as Florida. Florida used a 500 milligram dose of midazolam in its executions by lethal injection. Oklahoma used 100.

Did Hadden think using *one-fifth* the dose of the drug that was supposed to prevent pain didn't matter? Or did he just not realize that they were using one-fifth the dose? Hadden and Oakley *wrote* the new protocol, so to think they could not even copy Florida's dosage right is almost unfathomable. But the incompetence is astounding either way.

Prisoners challenging Oklahoma's protocol would later claim that the state's cursory investigation of midazolam was akin to "an approach one might expect of a high school student who waited until the last moment to write a term paper—not the approach one should expect of the State engaging in the taking of human life."[15] It's a good bet that even high school students would have done more than the state did here, but one can at least say this: what Oakley and Hadden did would not qualify as due diligence in *any* area of the practice of law. Not one.

Where was Warden Trammell—the person designated in the protocol to decide the drugs—in all this? "I tried to bring her up to speed, I really did," Oakley told investigators, saying that he "had to make a constant effort to try to bring Anita into the loop because decisions were being made, legal decisions, from a legal standpoint were being made where she wasn't really brought into all those decisions."

"All I can say is that I didn't write the policy," Warden Trammell told investigators. "I don't know anything about the drugs. I was just—I'm told the drugs that's gonna be used. . . . I signed the damn thing," she stated, "I didn't write that policy. I didn't choose those drugs."

THE DAY OF THE EXECUTION

On the day of Lockett's execution, Warden Trammell signed another piece of paper that made it look like the state was following procedures when it wasn't: an affidavit swearing that the drugs were obtained from a licensed pharmacist, that they weren't expired, and that they had been stored properly. Trammell had never been asked to sign something like that before (it came from Hadden in the AG's office) and she mentioned it to her supervisor, DOC director Robert Patton. Patton had signed similar affidavits in his prior position with the Arizona DOC, but that was when "preparing for a lawsuit," he told investigators, "not an hour before an execution." Patton inquired about the purpose of the affidavit, and was told "the intent was to release that document to the media."

Patton asked Trammell about the statements she had attested to in the affidavit. "For example," he told investigators, "the Warden was attesting in this affidavit that the pharmacist was a licensed pharmacist. And I said, 'Warden, have you ever saw [the] license?' And her response was 'no.'" Patton asked Trammell whether she knew the truth of other statements in the affidavit. She did not. Trammell had signed the affidavit, but she didn't know any of the assertions to be true.

Patton told Trammell to verify what she could, then revise the affidavit to omit the rest (which she apparently did). "I mean, in hindsight I wouldn't have signed it. I wouldn't do that again," Trammell told investigators. But she had an execution to conduct, and it was time to assemble the people who would do it.

Warden Trammell insisted that her executioners were prepared. "We practiced hard. I mean hard," she told investigators. "We did everything by policy," she stated, "and that whole policy talks about everything right up to the execution." As a federal court would later find, the entirety of Oklahoma's execution training was *pre*-execution training—training "up to bringing the offender into the execution chamber."[16]

For those who find it unfathomable that Oklahoma's execution training did not include training for the actual execution, the executive summary of the independent review concluded: "There was no formal training process involving the paramedic, the physician or the executioners and their specific roles. . . . The executioners only receive formal training from the paramedic on the day of the execution and informal training from previous executioners during actual executions."[17] As one executioner told investigators: "All's I know is this is who your—you know, call these people, give them a date and we get them over to the facility . . . and we talk about that and that's really it."

Oklahoma used a paramedic to set the prisoner's IV line, and a doctor to declare unconsciousness and pronounce death. Neither knew what to expect with midazolam. "I wasn't briefed, nobody went over anything about what we could expect from this new drug as far as what might be seen," the paramedic told investigators. The doctor had participated in a prior execution, but told investigators that "this was a whole different set of medications" and he also didn't know what to expect.

On the day of the execution, Director Patton told Warden Trammell that midazolam worked "much slower." "It's the first information I received on that," Trammell told investigators. Patton had stressed the importance of a conscious check given the slower effect of the drug, and Trammell relayed that information to the guards who would actually push the plungers on the syringes. "The executioners didn't know anything about it," she told investigators. "No one did."

THE BEGINNINGS OF A BOTCHED EXECUTION

So far, the story has been told as if Lockett's execution was the only execution that Oklahoma conducted that day—and it was. But that is because the state cancelled a second execution scheduled for the same night. Lockett had been joined by another condemned prisoner in his secrecy statute challenge, and when the state prevailed on that challenge, it decided to execute Lockett and the other prisoner the same day. It would be a day of firsts for Oklahoma—first execution using midazolam, and first double execution in over a decade.

Both firsts added stress to an already stressful situation. For Director Patton, the state's double-date with death was "particularly concerning." It was "a new protocol," he explained, "one I was not familiar with really. . . . I have never participated in, nor has many people in the world . . . participated in, two executions in one day," he stated.

The paramedic was stressed too, stating: "There was just a sense—an air of urgency. When you walked in there, you know how you can walk into a room and you can feel stress? . . . The quick, quick. Got to get it done. Got to get it done. And got to make sure that everything is done right. This, knowing this was our first time with this particular drug." Some of what went wrong, the paramedic told investigators, "I blame that on the—the aura of rush. Rush, rush. Get this done. Quick, quick and hurry, hurry . . . that was the atmosphere."

Adding to the paramedic's stress was the fact that the setup was all wrong. The syringes, the saline, the tubing—none of it was right. As the paramedic told investigators: "Previously to this execution I was given syringes of drugs and syringes of flushes and they're 50-milliliter syringes. . . . This time, I was given drugs that were in small 20-cc or 20 milliliter—instead of 50 I was given 20. . . . There was no 50 milliliters of anything, which is normal."

The two guards who actually pushed the syringes, along with the guard who was with them, also told investigators that the size of the syringes was wrong. "I don't think they gave the right amounts," one said. "Just from being around this [the other] times that I've done [executions], I've seen the size of the syringes."

Curiously, the report from the independent review made no mention of the possibility that the state didn't even have the right-sized syringes, despite the fact that all four frontline execution team members—the paramedic and three guards—told investigators that this was the case. Even more striking is the fact that these four executioners believed they had been given the wrong amounts of the drugs, *and yet proceeded with the execution anyway.*

The equipment was messed up in other ways too. The syringes were not labeled like they usually were, and the saline flushes weren't in syringes at all. "The flushes were little bags of saline," the paramedic told investigators. "They were not in syringes so I had to call or had them call down to the infirmary and get me some syringes so I could draw out the flush."

On top of all that, the tubing for the IV was wrong. "The tubing they sent me was suction tubing," the paramedic stated, "so I had to provide the IV tubing that was used . . . because the tubing they sent me was very inappropriate for what it was sent for." She told investigators: "I picked up the suction tube and I said 'what is this for?' He said 'I don't know I guess that's the extension tubing.' I said 'no, this is suction tubing.' This looked like a garden hose and I put it over on the shelf."

After straightening out the equipment as best she could, the paramedic turned to her main task: inserting the IV. She began with the crook in Lockett's left arm, and was able to access the vein on the first try, but didn't have the tape to hold the catheter in place. She told investigators: "I got the vein on the first stick. Now why, I don't know, but I didn't have my tape with me so I was holding it and I had asked . . . I said get me some tape. Well, they didn't pick up on what kind of tape I was wanting. They brought me gauze and they brought monitor tape, but of course by the time I was holding it trying to get secure, it blew."

The paramedic then tried accessing Lockett's vein in two other places on his left arm, telling investigators: "I got it to stop bleeding, the injection site, and I went back into the execution room, got the tape, put the tape on the right hand, took the tape with me to the left hand. . . . I think I stuck him three times on the left arm." In the clinical setting, she would have stopped there. "We have a policy at my service that we only try three times—three sticks," she stated, adding that "many of the paramedics, if they can't get it on the second stick, they're not going to try a third." Perhaps that is why, after three tries on Lockett's left arm, the doctor stepped in to assist.

The doctor first tried the jugular vein in Lockett's neck (that's right, he literally went straight for the jugular). The jugular vein is a particularly bad place for high-volume injections because, as an expert would later explain, "if the catheter fails in the same way this catheter failed, the fluid will collect right next to the airway and . . . could basically strangle the person."[18]

This turned out to be a nonissue, because the doctor was unable to access the jugular vein. "The needles that I had available to me were an inch and a quarter long," the paramedic explained. "That's not very long for a jugular vein."

While the doctor was trying to access Lockett's jugular vein, the paramedic was trying to establish IV access in his other arm. She made three sticks in the same three places on Lockett's right arm as she had made on his left. No luck. Seeing that the doctor was also unsuccessful, she asked, "Do you want to do a cutdown on the subclavian?" "Yeah I guess," the doctor replied, so they turned their attention to the subclavian vein that runs under the collarbone.

A cutdown is a surgical incision that cuts through the skin and underlying layers of tissue, fat, and muscle to expose the area immediately adjacent to a central vein. Because it involves a deep incision, it also involves a good deal of bleeding, and that was a concern for Warden

Trammell, who was in the execution chamber with the doctor and para-medic as they tried to set the IV. "I'm sitting there thinking to myself I've never seen the cutdown so I don't know how bloody it would be and I thought—I purposely did not get up to look because I didn't wanna have a bad reaction to it, you know, fixing to do an execution," Trammell told investigators. She could conduct an execution, but she didn't know if she could stomach the sight of blood.

Because she couldn't look, Warden Trammell didn't know that the doctor didn't actually do a cutdown. "That's pretty traumatic, you know, to cut your chest open and stick a needle in it," the paramedic would later say. She had draped the area and swabbed it, but the doctor decided to try to access the vein from the surface using the landmark method instead. "There's a way to do it on the clavicle to where you go from the shoulder and sternal notch together, put your fingers together and that's where you go in," the paramedic explained. The doctor "tried for quite a while to find it," she stated, estimating that this took a good five to ten minutes. The autopsy showed "at least three distinct needle marks at where the normal entry point would be," an expert would later tes-tify, noting that "each of those needle marks could be used for multiple passes with a needle."[19]

While the doctor was trying to access the subclavian vein, the para-medic turned to Lockett's feet. She tried two veins in his right foot, but was unsuccessful both times. She didn't know the names of those veins, but she could describe them and noted that "the skin on the feet is very tough and it hurts." "It was kind of a bloody mess," Warden Trammell told investigators, "and the offender was in some pain." But Lockett "was taking it like a man," she stated. He never complained, "not one time."

But Warden Trammell was stressed. "I was just getting nervous about what all I was seeing and the difficulties that they were having," she told investigators. She was also confused. "The doctor was struggling and said, 'I can't, you know, I can't get it,'" she stated, but "I thought the cut down was a sure way of getting it, you know? I thought that was pretty much the last resort." Trammell thought a cutdown had been done, so she didn't understand why it wasn't working. "I thought the final—if all else fails you could do the cut down. Cause I thought it was fool proof that you do a cut down and you're, you know, you're in."

But they weren't in, not by a long shot. The paramedic had done at least eight sticks—three in the left arm, three in the right, and two in the foot ("at least" because the autopsy found even more puncture marks in those places).[20] And the doctor had done six sticks—three in the jugular, and three in the subclavian—for a total of at least fourteen needle punctures. All that and they were no closer to IV access than when they started. "Let's go for the femoral," the doctor told the paramedic. So that's what they did.

Inserting an IV in the femoral vein, which is located in the upper thigh, is a complicated procedure requiring a level of skill that general medical professionals lack. "Surgeons, cardiologists and other specialists would be trained in starting such IVs," one anesthesiologist explains, "but it would not be the sort of training I would expect a primary care physician to have."[21] The doctor in Lockett's execution practiced in an emergency medicine setting, so presumably he had been trained in setting femoral lines.[22] But the paramedic had not. "I don't do femorals, period," she told investigators. "That's not something I've just ever been trained on. Most paramedics have not been trained in femoral arteries or veins."

But what the paramedic knew about femoral IVs would turn out to be important: they required a longer needle. The femoral vein is buried deep below the skin's surface, so one of the challenges is reaching it. "I went . . . to see if I had a 2 and ½-inch 14 gauge. That's what you're going to need for a femoral," the paramedic later stated.

She didn't have one. "All I had was the inch and a quarter and I told him three times, all I have is an inch and a quarter." The paramedic distinctly remembered the doctor's response: "Well, we'll just have to make it work."

"This is a pretty horrendous error in judgment," a doctor would later testify, explaining: "This is a catheter that was not designed for femoral use. That's obvious to anybody who has ever placed a central catheter. This is a catheter that was designed for use on the peripheral extremities or somewhere . . . where the blood vessels are close to the surface of the skin."[23] He went on to say: "A one-and-a-quarter-inch catheter would never be used in this way. It's simply not long enough to reach the femoral vein in a reliable fashion for any length of time," making it "extremely predictable that this catheter was going to fail."

"I just didn't understand how we were going to be able to do it with the short needles," the paramedic told investigators. She was relying on the doctor. But the doctor had never tried to access a femoral vein with a needle that short.

The paramedic cut Lockett's scrubs to access his upper thigh. The doctor didn't have an ultrasound to guide him, so once again he used the landmark method, finding the femoral artery, feeling the pulse, and aiming just inside of that. The doctor "couldn't get it" and kept "kinda jabbing, trying to get that vein," Warden Trammell told investigators, "There was blood everywhere."

Finally, the doctor was able to access Lockett's vein. "Looks good, looks good," Warden Trammell remembered him saying. But it wasn't good. The entry point was more toward the abdomen than it should have been, which meant it was not the shortest path to the femoral vein. "The reason you place a catheter in certain sites is to ensure that you're taking the best possible route towards your target vessel," a doctor would later explain. "In this case, by going a little more superiorly or upward, the femoral vein would be a deeper structure, making it even less likely for an inch-and-a-quarter catheter to be able to reliably reach that area."[24] The doctor had stuck a wrong-sized needle in the wrong place.

Right away, it was apparent that the catheter wasn't stable. It was functional only when held in a certain position, a condition referred to in the clinical setting as "positional." The catheter "was real positional because the needle was real short," the paramedic told investigators, "so we had to prop it up and tape it down." At first, "it wasn't flowing right," she explained, but "we would twist it this way and it would flow right, so . . .

whichever position it needed to be in that's what we maintained it in and then we tried to tape it down in that position and when it was taped it was still flowing properly."

After nearly an hour of trying to set the IV, it was finally time to inject the drugs, but not before one last critical misstep: covering the IV injection site. "I mean, you know from where they put that [catheter] you could see his privates," Trammell later explained, so "we covered it up for his dignity."

Warden Trammell saw the choice as between a dignified death and a monitored one, but a third option would have been to do a makeshift screen that allowed for observation on one side. "In Arizona, we did what we called a tent when we did a femoral," Director Patton told investigators, explaining: "You basically brought over a medical tray . . . and you drape the tent over it so the warden still has a visual of the groin area. So you always have a visual on that IV line." Apparently, Patton did not share this pro tip ahead of time.

The paramedic then left the execution chamber—"I don't watch the patient. That's not my job," she told investigators—which left just the warden and the doctor in the execution chamber with Lockett, and someone from the governor's office listening in by phone. Warden Trammell was tasked with monitoring the execution, but she couldn't see the one place she needed to watch. Meanwhile, three guards waited in a small anteroom adjacent to the execution chamber, where two would push the syringes while a third monitored the execution through a window between the two rooms. The scene was set for an execution about to go haywire.

THE EXECUTION

While Warden Trammell monitored an injection site that she couldn't see, guards in the adjacent anteroom started pushing the drugs. Midazolam was first. Ordinarily, lethal injection drugs travel around 92 inches—over seven feet—to get from the anteroom to the execution chamber, but in Lockett's case, the paramedic had added two 20-inch sections of extension tubing when trying to set an IV in his foot, and then had neglected to take them off, so the drugs had to travel 132 inches—eleven feet—instead. Despite the added risks of this arrangement, the guards were confident in the delivery of the first drug. (They were wrong, but they were confident).[25]

Upon injecting the midazolam, a five-minute wait began. Prior lethal injection litigation had resulted in a settlement agreement requiring Oklahoma to do a conscious check five minutes after injecting the first drug, so the state had to wait. Warden Trammell told investigators:

> I was watching his face and his expressions and nothing was happening. I mean nothing was happening. Nothing. You know, he was trying to be real patient. It was obvious. He was laying there with his eyes closed and I mean, it just looked like nothing was happening for a while. And then he'd open his eyes and he'd kinda look around and at one point he looked over at me like what—what's taking so long . . . then he started, he closed his eyes and his breathing slowed down just a little bit but I mean, I knew he was still conscious at that five minute mark. . . . it was apparent.

At the five-minute mark, the doctor did the obligatory conscious check, opening Lockett's eyes to check for eye movement and "kind of thump[ing] on his chest." One media witness told investigators that the doctor may have said, "Mr. Lockett are you unconscious." But the witness wasn't sure. "He may have said 'Mr. Lockett is unconscious,' it was one of those two," the witness recalled, "and at that point, Lockett opened his eyes and said 'no, I'm not.'" The doctor said something to the warden, and the warden announced: "The offender is still conscious." They would give it a few more minutes.

Two minutes later, the doctor checked again. By that time, Lockett's eyes were closed and his jaw had gone slack, leaving his mouth slightly open. He looked like he was asleep. The doctor repeated the tests and saw no response, so he declared Lockett unconscious.

At that point, the warden gave the green light for executioners to push the next two drugs. "I don't know what they were," the doctor said of the drugs, adding, "I didn't really care to know what they were. They started infusing them."

That's when the chaos began. Executioners were pushing the second drug when they heard a moan. Whoever was listening to the execution from the governor's office also heard "a muffled moaning noise," which the doctor later confirmed came from Lockett.

Lockett began writhing under the restraints, arching his back, and clenching his jaw as his body buckled. He then started quivering all over and kicked his foot, pushing hard against the restraints in an apparent attempt to get up off the gurney. One media witness described the scene as follows:

> He's strapped down, so he can only move his shoulders and his head forward . . . and he mumbles "something is wrong." . . . He's grimacing, lifting his head and shoulders off the gurney, and then he lifts his up-per head and shoulders with a lot more force. It just seemed to get— his jerking up off the gurney seemed to be getting more forceful. And I heard him say "man." Like "oh man." . . . Because he was strapped down his movements were restricted, but it was like he was using all the force he had to try to lift up . . . against the strap, just trying as hard as he could. . . . He was squeezing his eyes tight and tightening his muscles and his mouth as if he were grimacing in pain.[26]

"This shit is fucking with my mind," witnesses heard Lockett say. Some also heard him mumble something to the effect of "the drugs aren't working."[27] Onlookers gasped.

Warden Trammell didn't know what to do. "I was kind of panicking," she told investigators, "Thinking oh my God. He's coming out of this." She looked to Director Patton, who was sitting in the front row, for direction. Nothing. She then turned to the doctor, who got up, looked under the sheet, and confirmed her worst fear: there was a problem with the IV.

Then Lockett made what one witness described as a "gigantic, really large pronouncement jerking forward, shoulders off the gurney, head moving forward, grimacing." She later testified, "I don't know how far up the restraints were on him, but I mean he, he was pretty powerful."[28] So powerful that Lockett's autopsy would later find bruises on his body from those lurches against the restraints, identifying them as injuries from blunt force trauma.[29]

"Ladies and gentlemen, we're going to temporarily close the blinds," Warden Trammell announced.[30] She made that decision, she told investigators, because it was clear that Lockett "was no longer unconscious when he should have been. . . . You've got a guy here moving who shouldn't be moving." From that point on, everything that would happen would be out of public view.

Back in the adjacent anteroom, the executioners were still pushing the drugs. "It's tough to push the plunger right now," one of them stated. They were halfway through pushing the third drug when the blinds in the execution chamber came down. "They're lowering the blinds," the guard observing the execution from the anteroom told the others. "They're putting the blinds down and he's trying to get off the table," he stated. "They've stopped the execution."

The executioners stopped pushing the drugs and the paramedic was summoned to the execution chamber. At that point, the sheet covering Lockett had been pulled back so the IV insertion site was visible. Warden Trammell saw "a clear liquid on top of his groin area . . . and blood," and the paramedic noted that the needle was "tilted to the side" despite being taped in place. There was also a distinct swelling underneath the skin, which the doctor described as "smaller than a tennis ball but larger than a golf ball."[31] A bulge of that size, or even half of that size, surely would have been noticed had someone been monitoring the injection site. But that would have required the injection site to be visible, and it wasn't.

Lockett mumbled incoherently, and "was a little bit more aggressive" than before the blinds were lowered, one of the guards from the anteroom told investigators. "I did go over and hold him down, just so he wouldn't buckle," the guard stated. As he did so, the paramedic was telling Lockett to take deep breaths. The doctor said something to the effect of "I've never used this drug before" and "I–I don't know what to say."

Warden Trammell did not know what to do. "We don't have anything in the policy that tells us what to do. Nothing. . . . There's no direction or anything," she told investigators, "Our policy doesn't tell us what to do when something goes south." The only contingency planning in the protocol was for a cutdown if they had trouble inserting the IV, but the situation at hand was well beyond that.

At this point, the question was whether to help Lockett live, or help him die. Should they try to resuscitate him? *Could* they? "Do you want me to try?" the doctor asked. "But then we are going to have to take him to the ER," he stated, and someone in the room said, "No we can't do that." The protocol provided that in the event of a stay, life saving measures would be administered. But "we didn't get a stay," the warden reasoned. "We just had a malfunction."

Warden Trammell decided to try to finish the execution. "I mean, that was our goal," she explained. "Our instructions was to execute that offender and that's, that was what we were doing." The paramedic agreed. "I thought, how strange," she told investigators, "Why would we take him to the ER? You know, the drugs are working. I mean, they're doing the—it's not the best one we've ever done but obviously the drugs are working because he's dying."

And he was. Lockett was starting to succumb to the effects of the second and third drugs—his heart rate fell and he began to settle as the drugs seeped into his bloodstream. The question then became whether enough of the drugs were absorbing into his system to finish the job. "How am I supposed to know if there's enough drugs to absorb?" the doctor snapped. He didn't even know what the second and third drugs were.

There was a little more of the third drug that they could inject, but first they needed to reestablish the IV. The doctor went to work on Lockett's other femoral vein—the left femoral as opposed to the right—and asked the paramedic to get a needle. "That's all I have is those inch and a quarters, still," she said. "Okay," he answered. "We'll just have to do the best we can."

The doctor inserted the needle, and blood started backing up into the IV line. "You've hit the artery," the paramedic told him. "Well, it'll be alright," the doctor told her. "Go ahead and get the drugs."

"No, we can't do that . . . It doesn't work that way," the paramedic stated. "I wasn't trying to countermand his authority," she told investigators, but she knew that in order to work, the drugs had to go to Lockett's heart, and that required a vein.

The doctor pulled out the needle, and as he did, "blood squirted up and got all over his jacket," Warden Trammell recalled. She remembered the doctor's response. "He was complaining about that," she told investigators, saying he's "gotta get enough money out of this to go buy a new jacket."

By this time, it was apparent that Lockett would eventually die on his own. He was unconscious, and his heartbeat was growing increasingly irregular and slow. Director Patton informed the warden that the governor was "stopping the execution." But there was nothing to stop. All they could do was wait.

Clayton Lockett died forty-three minutes after executioners started pushing the drugs, and an hour and forty-seven minutes after the paramedic started trying to set an IV, in one of the longest executions in United States history.

THE AFTERMATH

In the immediate aftermath of the execution, Oklahoma officials stated that Lockett died of a "massive heart attack," a narrative that persists today.[32] But two autopsies were performed on Lockett's body—one by the state and one by an independent lab—and neither concluded that Lockett died from a heart attack. Lockett's heart showed no signs of organ damage, leading both autopsies to the same conclusion: Lockett had succumbed to the combined effects of the lethal injection drugs.[33]

"I went home that night and on the TV it said he had a massive heart attack and I thought where'd that come from," Warden Trammell told investigators. "It's not like at 7:06 he had a massive heart attack and died," she stated. "He was dying the whole time. . . . It was just taking a lot longer because it was absorbing into his system instead of going directly into his vein." Trammell had watched Lockett's heartbeat grow progressively weaker until it stopped. She didn't know medicine, but she knew what she saw. That was no heart attack.

Oklahoma officials also stated that the execution did not go as planned because Lockett's vein had "blown" or "exploded."[34] This, too, was patently false, this time as a matter of basic anatomy. The femoral vein is one of the largest blood vessels in the entire circulatory system, and although it is not impossible for the femoral to collapse, the scale of damage for it to do so would have to be tremendous. "To this day I still say [the doctor] said the vein exploded," Director Patton told investigators, then added: "Looking back on it, I just believe [the IV] popped out. . . . a femoral vein doesn't explode or collapse."

Over time, the state's story morphed from *The femoral vein collapsed/exploded* to *Lockett just had bad veins*, which also explained all the sticks it took to get IV access in the first place. The state claimed that Lockett had been dehydrating himself so that his veins would be hard to access. But the state's autopsy found "no evidence of dehydration,"[35] and the independent autopsy noted "excellent integrity of peripheral and deep veins for the purpose of achieving venous access."[36] Moreover, DOC medical personnel had checked Lockett's veins in the days leading up to his execution and indicated each time that his veins were "good" (including once with an exclamation point!).[37] DOC medical personnel also checked Lockett's veins on the morning of his execution, and reported that they were "'good' and acceptable for IV access."[38] Lockett's veins weren't the problem.

The problem, as a federal court would politely put it, was "ineffective application of medical implements."[39] As medical experts noted, there was simply no other explanation for the seventeen puncture wounds found on Lockett, each of which represented an attempt at venous access on a man whose veins were by all accounts easily accessible.[40] The problem was not bad veins. The problem was the exceptionally inept performance of the people trying to access them.

Oklahoma officials made a third patently false claim—that Lockett "remained unconscious" during the course of his execution—and this claim was especially important because it went to whether Lockett had suffered at the hands of the state.[41] If Lockett was unconscious the whole time, then the state could plausibly maintain that he did not suffer. And if Lockett did not suffer, then even if the execution did not go as planned, the state could not be accused of a torturous death.

John Hadden, the lawyer from the Oklahoma AG's office whose haphazard work was partly responsible for the state's adoption of midazolam, typified this stance. Hadden, who attended the execution and saw what happened firsthand, told investigators, "It wasn't as if he was in my interpretation he was in pain where he was trying to . . . I don't know get out of [the restraints] or escape or anything like that." Whatever Hadden saw, it was *not* Lockett in pain, and *not* Lockett trying to get up off the gurney. As for the movements that witnesses saw, those must have been involuntary seizures.

But the witnesses to Lockett's execution, and the doctors who read the eyewitness accounts of what happened, would have none of it. "If someone is having a seizure, by definition, they can't speak," one doctor explained.[42] "People who are asleep don't make efforts to speak to you. They don't rise up off the gurney," another doctor stated, adding, "Surgery would not proceed very far if anesthetized patients ever did that."[43]

Witnesses to Lockett's execution were equally sure about what they saw. When a person has a seizure, "everything is limp and the body is doing its own thing but he was fully in control," one witness told investigators. Another stated that she knew Lockett was conscious "because of the statements he made, the slurred statements and the deliberateness of his movements off that gurney."

But how can anyone *really* know what Lockett was experiencing, the state argued in the litigation that followed. "You're not a doctor, you have no medical background, you're not an EMT or a nurse, so this was merely your lay opinion of what you were seeing?" the state pressed one witness at trial. "It was consistent with other people I have seen in great pain," the witness answered.[44] Time and again, witnesses insisted that what they saw was not involuntary seizures. It was the sickening sight of a man waking up in the midst of his own execution.

But the federal court that presided over the litigation sided with the state. According to the court, it was impossible to know whether Lockett was actually in pain. "Any such conclusion is laden with an element of speculation," the court stated, and Lockett's statements on the gurney were not what "one would have expected Lockett to make if he was feeling the searing pain that he certainly would have felt if he had been conscious."[45] So he probably wasn't.

In the end, the prisoners lost their legal challenge, and the "independent review" largely absolved the state of wrongdoing, finding that "the protocol was substantially and correctly complied with throughout the entire process."[46] What happened to Lockett was treated as just an isolated mishap.

Except it wasn't.

Welcome to the world of lethal injection.

2

FAUX SCIENCE

We know how to euthanize beloved pets—veterinarians do it every day. And we know how physician-assisted suicide works—it is legal in several states. If drugs can be used to humanely end life in these other contexts, why is it so difficult in the death penalty context?

The answer is one of the best-kept secrets of the killing state: lethal injection is not based on science. It is based on the *illusion* of science, the *assumption* of science. "What we have here is a masquerade," one lab scientist says. "Something that pretends to be science and pretends to be medicine but isn't."[1] Consider first the birth of lethal injection.

THE BIRTH OF LETHAL INJECTION

In 1976, the Supreme Court gave states the green light to resume executions after a decade of legal wrangling over the constitutionality of the death penalty,[2] and Oklahoma was eager to get started. The only hitch was how to do it. Oklahoma's electric chair was dilapidated and in need of repair, but more importantly, it was widely viewed as barbaric and inhumane. The state was looking to try something new. A state legislator approached several physicians about the possibility of death by drugs—a lethal injection. They wanted nothing to do with it, but the state's medical examiner, Dr. Jay Chapman, was game. "To hell with them," the legislator remembered Chapman saying. "Let's do this."[3]

Chapman had no expertise in drugs or executions. As Chapman himself would later say, he was an "expert in dead bodies but not an expert in getting them that way."[4] Still, he said he would help and so he did, dictating a drug combination to the legislator during a meeting in the legislator's office. Chapman first proposed two drugs, then later added a third. *Voila.* In 1977, the three-drug protocol that states would use for the next thirty years was born.

The idea was triple toxicity—a megadose of three drugs, any one of which was lethal enough to kill. The first drug, sodium thiopental, would kill by barbiturate overdose, slowing respiration until it stopped entirely. The second drug, pancuronium bromide, would kill by paralyzing the diaphragm, preventing it from pumping air into the lungs. And the third drug, potassium chloride, would kill by triggering a cardiac arrest. The effects of the second and third drugs would be excruciatingly painful, so the first drug did double duty by blocking pain as well.

How did Chapman come up with his three-drug combo? "I didn't do any research," he later confided in an interview. "I just knew from having been placed under anesthesia myself, what was needed. I wanted to have at least two drugs in doses that would each kill the prisoner, to make sure if one didn't kill him, the other would." As to why he added a third drug, Chapman answered, "Why not?. . . . You wanted to make sure the prisoner was dead at the end, so why not add a third drug," he said, asking: "Why does it matter why I chose it?"[5]

This is how the original three-drug lethal injection protocol came to be: a man working outside his area of expertise and who had done no research just came up with it. "There was no science," says law professor Deborah Denno, one of the leading experts in the field. "It was basically concocted in an afternoon."[6] As another lethal injection expert, law professor Ty Alper, put the point, Chapman "gave the matter about as much thought as you might put in developing a protocol for stacking dishes in a dishwasher."[7] For the careful dish stackers among us, it's fair to say he gave it less.

But that was good enough for Oklahoma, which adopted the new execution method without subjecting it to a shred of scientific scrutiny. No committee hearings. No expert testimony. No review of clinical, veterinary, or medical literature. The state was embarking upon an entirely new way to kill its prisoners, and did none of the most basic things.

Texas followed Oklahoma's lead the next day, and then other states did too, carelessly copying a protocol that had been carelessly designed in the first place. "There is scant evidence that ensuing States' adoption of lethal injection was supported by any additional medical or scientific studies," a court reviewing the historical record wrote. "Rather, it is this Court's impression that the various States simply fell in line relying solely on Oklahoma's protocol."[8] As Deborah Denno observes, the result was an optical illusion—states touted a "seemingly modern, scientific method of execution" without an iota of science to back it up.[9]

Jay Chapman was as surprised as anyone by other states' adoption of his protocol. "I guess they just blindly followed it," he later stated, adding, "Not in my wildest flight of fancy would I have ever thought that it would've mushroomed into what it did."[10] "I was young at the time," he explained. "I had no idea that it would ever amount to anything except for Oklahoma."[11]

Over time, every death penalty state in the country would adopt Chapman's three-drug lethal injection protocol—not because they had studied it, but because in the absence of studying it, there was nothing to do but follow the lead of other states. "I didn't have the knowledge to question the chemicals," one warden explained, saying that he had "no reason to because other states were doing it."[12] "It wasn't a medical decision," an official from another state explained. "It was based on the other states."[13]

Sociologists have a name for this, a term of art for fads based on a faulty assumption. They call it a "cascade to a mistaken consensus," and lethal injection is a textbook example.[14] States had come to a consensus in adopting the three-drug protocol, but it was based on the assumption that other states knew what they were doing. They did not.

ENTER SCIENCE

The fact that the three-drug protocol wasn't based on science is not to say that science on the drugs didn't exist. All three drugs were FDA approved, so there were studies and FDA warning labels saying what each drug did. The problem was that none of that science could predict what would happen when the drugs were used in lethal injection.

Lethal injection is an "off-label" use of a drug, and although doctors use drugs for off-label purposes all the time, they aren't trying to kill people, so their off-label use doesn't come anywhere close to the use of those drugs as poison in lethal injection. Lethal injection uses drugs in amounts that no one has ever prescribed, let alone studied in a research setting. It delivers the entire dose of a drug at once—a practice known as "bolus dosing"—rather than delivering the drug in an IV drip, as is typical for large doses in the clinical setting. And it uses combinations of drugs that are simply unfathomable in the practice of medicine, giving rise to the possibility of "profound physiological derangements" (science-speak for freakishly weird results), as overdoses of different drugs affect the body in different ways.[15]

Who knew what was going to happen when all three of these perversions came together. No one did, and the studies to find out had not even begun. In the biomedical research setting, a baseline showing of scientific support is required for testing on animals, and the three-drug protocol didn't even meet that threshold. As one lab scientist quipped, "You wouldn't be able to use this protocol to kill a pig."[16]

But states weren't killing pigs. They were killing people, so they forged ahead, undaunted by the unknowns. Yet over time, the executions that followed created data points of their own, and those data points drew scientists. If states would not go to the science, science would come to them.

Granted, the data was thin. In some states, the problem was secrecy. "There is an enormous amount of information from executions (autopsies, toxicology, ECG recordings, EEG recordings, execution logs, and photographs)," one expert explained, "but most of it has been kept secret."[17] In other states, the problem was poor record-keeping. In still others, it was a state's decision to stop keeping records altogether. For example, Texas—which conducts more executions per year than any other state—stopped conducting post-execution autopsies altogether in 1989. "We know how they died," a state spokesperson stated when asked about the reason for the no-autopsy policy.[18]

That said, the raw data that scientists did manage to get was enough to raise serious concerns about the three-drug protocol. State officials were making "scientifically unsupportable" claims about lethal injection, researchers stated, so they decided to look at the data to see what it showed. In 2005 and 2007, researchers published two peer-reviewed studies on lethal injection, the first major studies of their kind.[19]

In the first study, researchers obtained toxicology reports from forty-nine executions in Arizona, Georgia, North Carolina, and South Carolina.[20] (Texas and Virginia, the two states with the most executions in the country at the time, refused to share their data.)[21] Because they had no other way to determine whether prisoners were anesthetized when they were injected with the second and third drugs, researchers measured the postmortem amounts of sodium thiopental (the first drug) in the blood, finding that most prisoners had amounts lower than what was necessary for anesthesia, and some had only trace amounts in their system.[22]

To be sure, using data from dead bodies to surmise what was happening in live ones was hazardous in its own right. "Extrapolation of ante-mortem depth of anesthesia from post-mortem thiopental concentrations is admittedly problematic," the researchers conceded. Still, the wide range of sodium thiopental amounts in prisoners' blood suggested gross disparities during their executions as well. "It is possible that some of these inmates were fully aware during their executions," the researchers stated, but their conclusion was more modest: "We certainly cannot conclude that these inmates were unconscious and insensate."[23]

Vigorous debate ensued. "You can't take these post-mortem drug levels at face value," one forensic pathologist stated, explaining that the amount of a drug in the blood dissipates after death, just as it does in life, and most autopsies in the study were conducted around twelve hours after death, so the postmortem measurements didn't say much about the sodium thiopental in a prisoner's blood during the execution.[24] The study's authors shot back with point-by-point responses to the criticism, but the damage was done.[25] The so-called "*Lancet* study," named for its publication in one of the most prestigious medical journals in the world, would forever be tainted by skepticism.

Had the first study been the only study of the three-drug protocol, one might have said that the science was inconclusive. But a second study was published two years later, and its findings were far less subject to dispute. In the second study, researchers examined execution logs in California.[26] California's expert had testified that the effects of sodium thiopental were well understood. Within sixty seconds of receiving the overdose, "over 99.999999999999 percent of the population would be unconscious," the state's expert stated, and "virtually all persons [would] stop breathing within a minute."[27] But when researchers examined the logs from California's eleven executions by lethal injection, they found that this was not the case. In six of the eleven cases—54 percent—the logs showed that the prisoner "continued to breathe for up to nine minutes after thiopental was injected."[28]

This was alarming not only because it showed that the state's expert was wrong, but also because it suggested that the prisoners had died torturous deaths. In the absence of a trained professional assessing anesthetic depth, the cessation of breathing provides a rough proxy for adequate anesthesia.[29] Thus, the fact that over half the prisoners continued breathing was an ominous sign that they had not been fully anesthetized prior to injection of the drugs that would cause slow suffocation and cardiac arrest. Executioners had recorded prisoners' vital signs, but had not understood what they meant.

California's execution logs revealed another problem as well: the same six prisoners who continued to breathe did not go into cardiac arrest after injection of the third drug, potassium chloride, which the state's expert had said would kill within two minutes.[30] Given the massive dose of potassium chloride, how could this possibly be?

The answer was one of the "profound physiological derangements" that no one saw coming, at least not until researchers documented it:

the bolus dose of sodium thiopental had depressed circulation so dramatically that it blunted the bolus dose of potassium chloride. Prisoners' hearts raced in response to the potassium chloride, but not enough to induce cardiac arrest, leaving them to die by slow suffocation from the paralytic instead.[31]

The findings from California's execution logs led a federal court to invalidate the state's lethal injection protocol in 2006. "The evidence is more than adequate to establish a constitutional violation," the court stated, noting that it was "impossible to determine with any degree of certainty whether one or more inmates may have been conscious during previous executions or whether there is any reasonable assurance going forward that a given inmate will be adequately anesthetized."[32] The governor has since declared a moratorium on executions in the state, and it remains in place today.

Looking back, it's fair to say that for the first thirty years of lethal injection, states used a three-drug protocol without understanding how it actually worked. State experts made claims and stated them with confidence, but what they said didn't turn out to be true. Sodium thiopental didn't do what states said it would do, and potassium chloride didn't do what states said either—largely because no one accounted for the possibility that a bolus dose of the first drug would blunt the bolus dose of the third. States had no idea what their toxic drug combinations would actually do. They were slowly suffocating prisoners to death, and they didn't have a clue.

WHY NOT JUST COPY HOW WE EUTHANIZE PETS?

While states were executing prisoners with a three-drug protocol that they didn't understand, veterinarians were euthanizing pets with a one-drug protocol that was long established and FDA approved. The standard protocol for euthanizing cats and dogs is a bolus overdose of the barbiturate pentobarbital. The same one-drug protocol is also used for physician-assisted suicide. Why didn't states just use the protocol that these humane deaths used?

The answer starts with lethal injection's creator, Jay Chapman. Chapman didn't tell states to use the one-drug protocol. He gave them the three-drug protocol instead. Maybe he didn't think to ask, *How do we put down pets? How does physician-assisted suicide work?* If one were trying to devise a humane death by drugs, it is hard to imagine not asking these questions—but maybe he didn't. Or maybe he *did* ask (or already knew) and intentionally chose not to go with the one-drug protocol. Either way, one can only conclude that Chapman wasn't trying to copy how we euthanize pets, because he easily could have done so, and that's not what he did.

Why is hard to say. But Chapman's reaction to the possibility that his protocol had resulted in torturous deaths offers a window into his thinking. He stated:

> Perhaps hemlock is the answer for the bleeding hearts who completely forget about the victims—and their suffering—Socrates style. The things that I have seen that have been done to victims is [*sic*] beyond belief. And we should worry that these horses' patoots should have a bit of pain, awareness of anything—give me a break."[33]

Those are not the words of a man trying to copy how we euthanize pets.

Scouring the historical record reveals other possible explanations as well. One state—Texas—appears to have considered the one-drug protocol and rejected it because, in the words of its prison system medical director, "people would think we are treating people the same way that we're treating animals."[34] Apparently, it did not occur to him that this would have been an improvement.

That said, Texas appears to be the only state that seriously considered the one-drug protocol. In other states, it does not appear to have been part of the conversation around lethal injection at all. So what was?

In fairness, support for lethal injection was not about any one thing. Different people favored it for different reasons. But pouring through the comments of legislators who sponsored lethal injection bills in their state, a curious theme emerges. In state after state, advocates of lethal injection were talking about how executions *looked*.

Consider, for example, the pitch for lethal injection by the author of New Jersey's lethal injection bill: "If you're on the jury, the thought of some guy in that chair sizzling is going to bother them. This way, with lethal injections, it might ease their conscience when they come up with a verdict."[35] Or this, from the legislator who sponsored New Mexico's lethal injection bill: "It should make the death penalty easier for everyone to swallow. You just take and stick it to 'em until they're dead."[36] Or this, from the Texas prison chaplain at the time: "I would like to see this carried out in a nice clean room, something that doesn't look like a prison. Certainly not a death cell. I can conceive of how this could be handled in such a way that it could be considered gentle, humane, if done with care."[37]

For many, the allure of lethal injection was a visually palatable execution that would be easier for the public to accept. In fact, the sponsors of lethal injection bills in a few states made clear that their interest was *not* a humane death. The sponsor of Tennessee's lethal injection bill, for example, told his fellow legislators, "We should draw and quarter those suckers who commit these heinous crimes, but that ain't constitutional."[38]

All this is to say that there is substantial evidence in the historical record that lethal injection was less about a humane death, and more about a humane-*looking* death, which helps explain why the locus of legislative energy wasn't the humane induction of death in animals. A humane-looking death was humane enough.

Upon reflection, this makes perfect sense. Executions by electrocution and lethal gas were ghastly affairs; lethal injection was clean and tidy. The country had not seen an execution in ten years, and people had grown squeamish about displays of state violence. If states were going to start executing again, they needed clean and tidy.

This was especially true because a federal court had just recognized the right to televise executions (it wouldn't last, but no one could have known that).[39] The sponsor of the Texas lethal injection bill introduced the bill explicitly in response to the ruling, stating that he was "repulsed by the idea of an electrocution taking place in someone's living room."[40] The sponsor of Oklahoma's lethal injection bill just passed around photos from an electric chair execution instead.[41]

Perhaps most tellingly, lethal injection's visual appeal explains the *timing* of its adoption. States had been euthanizing pets with pentobarbital since the 1930s. If lethal injection was really about a humane death, the technique had been around for decades. Yet states didn't think to use it as an execution method until the mid-1970s. Lethal injection wasn't on anyone's mind until states started sweating over the optics of executions.

Over time, it became increasingly clear that the one-drug protocol that states were using for animal euthanasia provided a much more humane death than the three-drug protocol being used for executions. This prompted condemned prisoners to sue states, demanding to be executed veterinary-style, and that turn of events gave rise to yet another reason why states didn't adopt the one-drug protocol: courts didn't make them.

In Tennessee, for example, prisoners claimed that they were entitled to be executed under the state's Non-livestock Animal Humane Death Act (they were animals, after all, and they weren't livestock). The court rejected the challenge, finding that the legislature did not intend for the state's animal euthanasia statute to apply to humans.[42] *Fair enough.* But the fact that prisoners were suing as members of the "non-livestock" class was a testament to the embarrassing reality that the induction of death in animals was way more humane than the induction of death in humans, who (at least in theory) had constitutional rights protecting them from being executed however the state wanted.

In 2008, the Supreme Court decided its first lethal injection case— *Baze v. Rees*—and a plea to use the one-drug protocol was part of the prisoners' legal challenge.[43] As it turns out, the second drug in the three-drug protocol, the paralytic pancuronium bromide, is explicitly forbidden for use in animal euthanasia in most states, and that included Kentucky (the state in *Baze*). As the prisoners noted, Kentucky law actually required use of the one-drug protocol for the humane death of animals. It just didn't extend the same courtesy to humans, leading Justice Stevens to wryly observe, "Kentucky may well kill petitioners using a drug that it would not permit to be used on their pets."[44]

But the prisoners lost their legal challenge. "No other state has adopted the one-drug method," the Supreme Court wrote, and the prisoners had "proffered no study showing that it is an equally effective manner [of execution]."[45] As for the fact that the one-drug protocol was based on long-established veterinary science and decades of experience euthanizing pets, the court stated that "veterinary practice for animals is not an appropriate guide to humane practices for humans."[46] Never mind the fact that the three-drug protocol had no science behind it whatsoever, and that death veterinary-style would have been a vast improvement over the death that prisoners would otherwise get. *Baze* told states that they didn't have to adopt the one-drug protocol, so they didn't. But fate was about to intervene.

In 2009, just a year after *Baze* was decided, a shortage in the raw ingredients needed to produce sodium thiopental (the first drug in the three-drug protocol) sent states scrambling for a replacement, and the drug they could most easily get their hands on was pentobarbital—the drug used for animal euthanasia and physician-assisted suicide. That caused states to pivot on the one-drug protocol. After fighting tooth and nail *not* to use the protocol that veterinarians used on pets—after insisting in case after case how disastrous it would be to use the one-drug protocol in executions—a number of states adopted the one-drug protocol on their own when the sodium thiopental shortage threatened to stall their executions.

For those about to breathe a sigh of relief, not so fast. As we'll see, pentobarbital executions are torturous in their own right. Understanding why requires understanding more about the drug, so I save that discussion for the next chapter. Here, our focus is the science behind the drug choices that states make, and there is more of that story to tell.

When the supply of sodium thiopental ran dry, not all states turned to the one-drug protocol. Some stuck with the three-drug protocol, and just looked for a replacement for the first drug. When the dust settled, that replacement was the drug midazolam, ushering in a whole new era of faux science. This new era was more sophisticated, but its essence was the same. What state experts said would happen didn't turn out to be true, and states had no idea what their drug combinations would do.

MEET MIDAZOLAM

Midazolam is a sedative in the same family of drugs as Valium and Xanax. Anesthesiologists call it "a martini in a syringe."[47]

We don't know the backstory of how midazolam was initially chosen for use in lethal injection. Florida was the first state to adopt it, using it in an execution that went awry in 2013.[48] In the wake of that execution, a reporter asked a Department of Corrections (DOC) spokesperson why Florida decided to use midazolam in the first place. The spokesperson refused to say, stating, "Those decisions are exempt from public record because they could impact the safety and security of inmates and officers who are involved in that process."[49] How Florida's decision-making process for choosing a lethal injection drug could jeopardize "the safety and security of inmates and officers" she didn't say.

The following year, Ohio used midazolam in the nation's first *two-drug* lethal injection protocol, combining midazolam with the opioid hydromorphone. The state's expert (the same guy who was wrong about various aspects of the three-drug protocol) stated that midazolam would act "synergistically" with hydromorphone, creating a multiplier effect that would "knock the patient out and stop his breathing," causing death within a few minutes.[50]

But the state had nothing to back up that claim. No one had ever tried to induce death with an overdose of those two drugs, so no one really knew what would happen. The prisoner who would serve as the guinea pig in this execution experiment, Dennis McGuire, sued.

In addition, Ohio was considering an intramuscular (IM) injection of the drugs, since IV access was a recurring problem. "I do not believe that any method of execution ever proposed in the United States is as slow as this one," McGuire's expert testified, predicting that the protocol would lead to "a terrible, arduous, tormenting execution."[51] The state's response was to dismiss the expert, an anesthesiologist at Columbia University, as "uninformed on this topic."[52]

Both sides could only speculate as to what would happen when the two-drug protocol was used, and that was enough for a court to reject McGuire's challenge. The court stated:

> There is absolutely no question that Ohio's current protocol presents an experiment in lethal processes. The science involved, the new mix of drugs employed at doses based on theory but understandably lacking actual application in studies, and the unpredictable nature of human response make today's inquiry at best a contest of probabilities. To pretend otherwise, or that either of the experts or this Court truly knows what the outcome of that experiment will be, would be disingenuous.[53]

"But as odd as it sounds," the court went on to say, "this is not a problem until it is actually a problem." Until prisoners could show that a new protocol *wouldn't* work, the law required courts to assume that it would.

Soon thereafter, McGuire's own execution provided the proof he needed. McGuire began to show signs of struggle five minutes into his execution, clenching his fists, straining against the restraints on the gurney, and gasping loudly for air. "There were powerful choking sounds that were wracking up his body," one media witness said.[54] "I was aghast," another witness stated, reporting: "Both of his fists were clenched the entire time. His gasps could be heard through the glass wall that separated us. Towards the end, the gasping faded into small puffs of his mouth. It was much like a fish lying on the shore puffing for that one grasp of air that would allow it to breathe."[55] A prison official reportedly mouthed "I'm sorry" to McGuire's family members.[56] It took twenty-six minutes for McGuire to die, setting a record for the longest execution in Ohio's history.

Subsequently discovered emails revealed that Ohio officials knew the risks of their newfangled protocol all along. One state official expressed concern that "administration of midazolam and hydromorphone IM may result in the condemned gasping for air in a hyperventilating fashion, with eyes still open," adding: "This scenario would create the appearance, at least, of suffering, which would upset witnesses and inspire litigation."[57] For those wondering whether states care more about a humane death or the appearance of one, here is one state's answer.

Undaunted by Ohio's 2014 execution fiasco, Arizona decided to use the same two-drug protocol six months later when it executed Joseph Wood. The result was disastrous again.

Wood started gasping for breath shortly after the drugs were injected. "He gulped like a fish on land," one reporter stated, writing: "The movement was like a piston: the mouth opened, the chest rose, the stomach convulsed."[58] The reporter counted the number of times this happened. Wood gasped for breath more than 640 times.

Wood's execution lasted one hour and 57 minutes—long enough for his lawyer to ask for (and get) a telephone hearing with a judge to try to stop it. Wood's execution was the longest execution in US history, at least at the time. Execution logs later revealed that in the state's desperation for Wood to die, executioners had injected him with the two-drug protocol *fifteen* times.

Wood's execution unleashed a torrent of public criticism, and since then, no state has used the two-drug midazolam-hydromorphone protocol. Nowadays, midazolam is used in the three-drug protocol with a paralytic, or not at all.

Prisoners have sued to stop this too, and in 2015, that litigation became the Supreme Court's second lethal injection case, *Glossip v. Gross*.[59] *Glossip* upheld the use of midazolam in the three-drug protocol, but more important in the context of the current discussion is what the litigation revealed. The litigation in *Glossip* forced the state to show its hand, unearthing just how bad the state's science actually was.

GLOSSIP V. GROSS

In *Glossip*, the prisoners next in line for execution after Clayton Lockett sued, arguing that midazolam would not block the pain of the second and third drugs. Lockett's botched execution was part of their proof. Lockett's autopsy showed that he had more than enough midazolam in his system to render its full effect, yet its full effect was not enough to block the excruciating pain of the second and third drugs. Lockett was asleep. Breakthrough pain woke him up.

Oklahoma's entire defense of midazolam rested on just one expert: Dr. Roswell Lee Evans, dean of Auburn's School of Pharmacy in Alabama. Evans was not a medical doctor or pharmacologist. He was a pharmacist turned higher ed administrator, serving as the pharmacy school's dean for the past twenty years. Evans had never actually used midazolam in the clinical setting. In fact, he had no experience in the clinical setting at all.

Evans also had not conducted clinical research on midazolam or any drug anywhere close to it, and here is what that looked like when he was asked about his expertise under oath:

Q: Have you been involved in research involving the use of midazolam?
EVANS: No.
Q: Have you been involved in research involving the use of diazepam?
EVANS: No.
Q: Have you been involved in research involving the use of lorazepam?
EVANS: No.
Q: Have you been involved in research involving the use of propofol?
EVANS: No.

Q: Have you been involved in research regarding the use of pentobarbital?

EVANS: No.

Q: Have you been involved in research regarding the use of sodium thiopental?

EVANS: No.

Q: Have you been involved in research regarding the use of halothane gas?

EVANS: No.

Q: Have you ever been involved in research regarding anesthetics of any sort?

EVANS: No.

Q: Have you ever published regarding the use of anesthetics of any sort?

EVANS: No.[60]

As late-night talk show host John Oliver said of the exchange: "That guy is not an expert on anything he's supposed to be an expert on."[61]

Evans claimed that Oklahoma's 500-milligram dose of midazolam (the state had upped the dose after Lockett's execution) made it "a virtual certainty that any individual will be at a sufficient level of unconsciousness to resist the noxious stimuli which could occur from application of the second and third drugs."[62] This was so, Evans claimed, because a 500-milligram dose of midazolam was itself lethal, and as it shut down respiration, it would induce a coma, thereby eliminating any awareness of pain. "You're paralyzing the brain," Evans explained, and although "paralyzing the brain" wasn't exactly anesthesia, it accomplished the same thing by blocking the prisoner's ability to perceive pain.[63]

But Evans had nothing to back up his claims. Not a single source said that midazolam would work this way. No pharmacological research. No academic texts. No clinical studies. Nothing in the scientific literature suggested that midazolam could paralyze the brain.[64]

What, then, was the basis for his opinion? Evans cited two sources: drugs.com and a manufacturer's Material Safety Data Sheet (MSDS).

Drugs.com was a general information website, and the MSDS was what OSHA required drug manufacturers to file in order to document hazards associated with the drug—fire and explosion risks, safety precautions, and the like. Neither was the sort of source one would expect to see as support for an expert opinion on how to humanely kill people, and both contained disclaimers—one stating that it was "not intended for medical advice," and the other stating that it was "without any warranty, express or implied, regarding its correctness." On top of that, drugs.com undermined—if not flat-out contradicted—Evans's claim, stating that midazolam "should not be used alone for the maintenance of anesthesia."

Critics had a field day. The chair of one medical department stated that she was "a little horrified" by the sources that Evans was relying on, observing more generally: "These kinds of doses are not given by any clinician. To say that they know what this dose would do? I don't think anyone can say that."[65] The vice chair of another medical school's pharmacology and toxicology department told the press: "As scientists, we use primary literature. . . . We have resources available to use so we would not go to a website of this sort."[66] At trial, an expert testified that he would not rely on drugs.com, "And I would probably not accept a work product from a student that provided me with a report where drugs.com was used as the reference source."[67]

Even more strange was the fact that neither source actually supported Evans's theory—neither said anything about midazolam's ability to paralyze the brain. Evans had made up his theory whole cloth, leading the Actual Innocence Project to file an amicus brief in *Glossip* arguing that the theory was so inherently unreliable that it never should have been admissible in the first place. In fact, Evans's theory was so bizarre that by the time the case arrived at the Supreme Court, not even Oklahoma was trying to defend it. The notion that midazolam could "paralyze the brain" was conspicuously absent in the state's brief.

The oral arguments in *Glossip* paint a vivid picture of just how bad the state's science was. "They . . . conceded, as I read their brief, that it does not work the way the doctor said it worked, that it does not paralyze the brain," Justice Sotomayor stated.[68] "Nobody thinks [this theory] is anything other than gobbledygook," Justice Kagan chimed in, describing Evans's theory as "the thing that . . . you don't defend" and telling the state's attorney, "That's just wrong . . . You know that's wrong."[69]

Justice Breyer was more methodical in his questioning, and more insistent in getting an answer, stating:

> [Evans] said there is an extrapolation from his conclusion that 500 milligrams could cause death, and so if that much is likely to cause death, it's certainly likely to cause a coma. And a coma would prevent the person from—from pain. But his evidence for that was zero. We know that, in fact, lots of drugs can kill people without first putting them into a coma. And so we look to see what is it he thinks that if this kills you will first put you into a coma. And when I looked—or asked my clerks and others to look—we found zero.

The state's attorney did his best to dodge the question, but Justice Breyer interrupted. "Let me put it differently," he stated, then asked pointedly:

> I think what he was driving at, your expert, was that you were in a state such that you would feel no pain. And the reason he thought you were in that state is because 500 mg will probably kill you. And if it's going to kill you, it must, of course, at least first put you in that state. . . . I really want to know where in the record does he provide support for that statement.[70]

The state's attorney pivoted, and other Justices jumped in with other questions. Justice Breyer would leave the exchange empty-handed.

Lost in the shuffle of the takedown of Evans's theory was the fact that even its premise—the notion that a 500-milligram dose of midazolam was lethal—was flat-out wrong. Evans claimed that a 500-milligram dose of midazolam was lethal based on "an extrapolation of a toxic effect."[71] But determining a drug's toxicity is part of the FDA approval process, and it turns out that midazolam's toxicity is astronomically low.

Evans had used midazolam's TD_{LO}—"Toxic Dose, low," the lowest dose known to have produced a toxic effect—as the measure of toxicity, which the literature refers to as "rare fatalities . . . in geriatric patients."[72] But TD_{LO} is not the standard measure of a drug's toxicity. By definition, TD_{LO} is measuring outliers.

The standard measure of a drug's toxicity is its LD_{50}—"Lethal Dose, 50," the lethal dose for 50 percent of a tested population (here, laboratory rats). Midazolam's LD_{50} is 50 mg/kg: 50 milligrams of midazolam for each kilogram of body weight.[73] Using that measure, rather than the lowest dose ever known to have had a toxic effect, one gets a strikingly different picture of what it would take to create a toxic effect with midazolam alone. For an average person who weighs 70 kilograms (154 pounds), for example, the amount of midazolam it would take to create a *halfway* lethal effect (because that's what LD_{50} is—it's the amount that is lethal in half the tested population) is 3,500 milligrams. That's *seven times* the 500-milligram dose used in lethal injection.

The scientific literature repeatedly refers to the "minimal toxicity" of midazolam, a feature of the class of drugs called benzodiazepines more generally.[74] Midazolam is a benzodiazepine, and the literature states that the toxicity benchmark "is very high for benzodiazepines, making them remarkably safe medications."[75] Midazolam is just not that toxic, a rather inconvenient fact for a theory built on its toxicity.

But once again, the prisoners lost. By a five-four vote, the Supreme Court in *Glossip* held that it was the *prisoners'* burden to show that midazolam wouldn't work, not the state's burden to show that it would, and because a 500-milligram dose of midazolam had not been subjected to scientific testing, there was no evidence to support the prisoners' claim.[76] Granted, the prisoners had pointed to existing science—they even had an amicus brief from a group of pharmacology professors saying they were right.[77] But the majority rejected that evidence, stating that existing science had not studied a 500-milligram dose of midazolam and thus had "minimal probative value" as to what a 500-milligram dose might do.[78] As far as the majority was concerned, the prisoners' complete dismantling of Evans's theory was merely an "attempt to deflect attention from their failure of proof."[79]

Glossip v. Gross is widely viewed as one of the most poorly reasoned (and blatantly political) death penalty decisions ever issued by the Roberts Court. As law professor and lethal injection scholar Eric Berger put the point, *Glossip* was not just wrongly decided—"it was *Gross* error."[80] But not even the Supreme Court's ruling could cover what the litigation had exposed. The state's science was a farce. The emperor had no clothes.

Scientists knew the science of midazolam. They knew that states were inflicting torturous deaths under a paralytic that made them look peaceful. So in the aftermath of *Glossip*, they decided to gather the data that hadn't existed, reviewing autopsies to see what they could find. What happened next was a discovery no one saw coming.

THE AFTERMATH OF GLOSSIP

By 2018, scientists had reviewed the autopsies of twenty-seven of the nation's thirty-two executions using midazolam (for a sense of perspective, those thirty-two executions were around a third of all executions nationwide since states started using midazolam in 2013). In all of the executions with midazolam, "the lungs were heavy with fluid," a pathologist testified in a 2018 lethal injection trial in Tennessee.[81] A normal lung weighs 400–450 grams, he stated, but the lungs in the autopsies from midazolam executions were more than double that. In twenty-three of the twenty-seven cases, the autopsies showed acute pulmonary edema, indicating that prisoners had drowned in their own fluids. People suffering from this condition experience "terror, panic, drowning, asphyxiation," the pathologist explained, describing it as "a medical emergency" for which patients would receive morphine in the clinical setting "because they are in such a state of panic."

The prisoners also brought a new voice to the courtroom: Dr. David Greenblatt, the pharmacologist responsible for the earliest studies of midazolam that formed the basis of its FDA approval. Greenblatt was the nation's preeminent expert on midazolam—he had authored just short of eight hundred peer-reviewed articles on midazolam and benzo-diazepines more generally, and that work had been cited over sixty-five thousand times worldwide.[82] No one knew more about the drug than he did, and his explanation for why execution autopsies were showing pulmonary edema was something that *neither* of the parties' experts had fathomed.

Midazolam had to be mixed with hydrochloric acid to make it water soluble, Greenblatt explained, and the capillaries in the lungs had "a the very thin and delicate membrane" that was "very sensitive to acid."[83] The acid in the bolus overdose of midazolam was destroying the membrane in the lungs, making them "leaky," he stated. "So the lungs acquire fluid, and that makes air exchange difficult if not impossible." Hence the acute pulmonary edema.

It is worth pausing to appreciate the fact that it took the country's most knowledgeable expert on midazolam to even understand what was happening. The litigation in *Glossip* had been about whether midazolam could block the excruciating pain of the second and third drugs. The scientists said it couldn't. The Supreme Court said it could. But the working assumption all along was that it was the *paralytic* that was making prisoners gasp and heave. It didn't occur to anyone—at least not until Greenblatt explained it—that midazolam was the culprit. In a cruel twist of fate, the drug that was supposed to spare prisoners from excruciating pain was the very drug inflicting it.

"The inescapable conclusion is that states have almost certainly been torturing people to death in their execution chambers," a reporter covering the Tennessee trial wrote for *The Intercept*.[84] But the court rejected the prisoners' challenge, reasoning that the Supreme Court was "aware of the risk of midazolam" in *Glossip* and yet had ruled it constitutionally permissible.[85] Besides, the court held, the prisoners had failed to provide the state with an alternative way to kill them, a new requirement from the ghastly *Glossip* case. With that, the court ruled that the next execution could go forward, and it did. The prisoner was Billy Ray Irick, who coughed, choked, and gasped for air as he died, his face turning dark purple and his body jolting and convulsing against the restraints in his twenty-minute-long execution.[86]

Since then, lawyers for condemned prisoners have filed suits in other states to remedy the "scientific inaccuracies that cry out for reevaluation" regarding midazolam's use in lethal injection.[87] Of these, two are worth noting here. One is a 2019 case that went to trial in Ohio. The court in that case wrote a 148-page opinion, noting that "the case against midazolam is now much stronger," and that there was now "good evidence that midazolam will cause the 'waterboarding' effects of pulmonary edema."[88] Every medical witness to testify agreed that pulmonary edema induced "a sense of drowning and the attendant panic and terror, such as would occur with the torture tactic known as waterboarding," the court noted. Thus, if Ohio were to execute a prisoner with midazolam, the court concluded, it would "almost certainly subject him to severe pain and needless suffering."

"Reading the plain language of the Eighth Amendment, that should be enough to constitute cruel and unusual punishment," the court went on to say, but the Supreme Court in *Glossip* had imposed "a wholly unprecedented obligation" upon prisoners to identify an alternative means for their own execution, and this was something that the prisoner had not done.[89] The court had no choice but to dismiss the case. "This is not a result with which the Court is comfortable," it stated.

A federal appellate court affirmed, but in a shockingly short six-page opinion, it disagreed with the trial court that pulmonary edema was a constitutional problem in the first place. "Suffocation does not qualify as 'severe pain and needless suffering,'" the appellate court stated.[90] Ohio could do as it pleased.

Yet the trial court's findings rattled Ohio Governor Mike DeWine, who as a state senator had helped write the state's death penalty law, and who as state attorney general had pushed Ohio to adopt a lethal injection secrecy statute (which it did). "Ohio is not going to execute someone under my watch when a federal judge has found it to be cruel and unusual punishment," DeWine stated, declaring an unofficial moratorium on executions in the state.[91] Ohio's courts might allow torture, but its governor would not.

The other case of note was a 2022 lethal injection trial in Oklahoma. In that case, a federal court ruled that midazolam could reliably "render the inmate insensate to pain."[92] That trial court was the same trial court that found Evans and his theory credible on its way to the Supreme Court in *Glossip*. In fact, that trial court was the same court that refused to find that Lockett had suffered during his execution, stating that any such finding was "laden with an element of speculation."[93] Even the name of the 2022 case was partly the same, as Richard Glossip was once again the lead plaintiff. (Oklahoma still hasn't executed Glossip, who raised such powerful evidence of innocence that the state's attorney general conceded error and asked for the conviction to be overturned, to no avail.)[94]

In parallel fashion, the prisoners in both the 2015 and 2022 *Glossip* cases pointed to spectacularly botched executions to bolster their claims. In the 2015 *Glossip* case, they had pointed to the botched execution of Clayton Lockett. In 2022, they pointed to the botched execution of John Grant, who repeatedly convulsed and vomited on the gurney in 2021. "As the convulsions continued, Grant then began to vomit," one media witness reported. "Multiple times over the course of the next few minutes, medical staff entered the death chamber to wipe away and remove vomit from the still-breathing Grant."[95] Grant's autopsy showed that the combined weight of his lungs was a whopping 1,390 grams.[96] He had suffered from acute pulmonary edema as he died.

Today, it is not quite right to say that states have no idea what midazolam does or how it works. States know what the autopsies show, and they have seen with their own eyes the suffering that midazolam executions entail. And yet they insist upon using it.

BUT WE CAN'T DO EXPERIMENTS . . .

One response to faux science is to say this is a problem inherent in the execution enterprise. It's the nature of the beast. After all, we can't do experiments on people to see how well they die. As one medical journal put the point: "No ethical researcher would propose a study to establish such procedures, no ethical reviewers would approve it, and no ethical journal would publish it."[97] This was also Jay Chapman's response to the critique that his three-drug protocol was untested. "How did they want [it] tested?" he scoffed. "Did they want someone to go out and take a bunch of prisoners and see what happens?"[98]

Well, no, except this is *exactly* what states did. As one doctor says, "There's no medical or scientific basis for any of it. It's just a series of attempts: obtain certain drugs, try them out on prisoners, and see if and how they die."[99]

But could it have been any different?

The answer is yes, in two ways. The first goes back to the early 1980s, when a group of condemned prisoners sued the FDA to force it to oversee the drugs used in lethal injection.[100] The FDA argued that its authority was limited to regulating drugs in the interest of public health, and using drugs to kill people was pretty much the opposite of public health. A federal trial court agreed, but the appellate court reversed, noting that the FDA had already claimed regulatory authority over drugs used for animal euthanasia as a matter of public health. If drugs used in animal euthanasia posed a conceivable threat to public health, the court reasoned, "then certainly drugs used to kill human beings pose such a threat."[101]

Had the ruling stuck, the FDA would have had to examine the science behind the three-drug protocol, and that almost certainly would have forced states to adopt the one-drug protocol that was already FDA-approved for use in veterinary euthanasia. But the ruling did not stick. The Supreme Court reversed, holding that the FDA's enforcement authority was discretionary, so the agency could do as it pleased.[102] With that, the only regulatory authority that could have required states to support their lethal injection drug choices closed its doors for business.

The other road not taken is one we can also lay at the feet of our Supreme Court. The Supreme Court requires prisoners challenging an execution method to show "a substantial risk of severe pain"—a risk that is "sure or very likely to result in needless suffering."[103] The burden is not on the state to show that its execution method *won't* result in needless suffering. The burden is on the prisoner to show that it *will*.

Here's how that plays out. The state adopts a new drug combination and claims it is humane. Then when prisoners say it isn't so, the Supreme Court tells them to prove it. But there is no science on whatever the state just made up, so there is no way to prove it and the prisoners lose, destined to become the very thing they needed: evidence of a torturous death.

A federal judge explained it this way:

If the science does not yet exist when an inmate's appointed time comes, we say "alas, you have not shown a likelihood of suffering, maybe the next guy can." And then we say the same thing next month. The upshot is that an inmate staring down the barrel of the new protocol will only be able to show a likelihood of unnecessary suffering if someone ahead of him has suffered unnecessarily. Until the unthinkable happens, we charge ahead unthinking.[104]

When states have no burden whatsoever to show that their drug combinations are minimally reliable, they don't have to test them on guinea pigs before trying them out on humans. The condemned prisoners *are* their guinea pigs. States can do whatever they want.

Indeed, lethal injection is now so wildly experimental that there is a whole side debate raging over whether executions constitute human experimentation in violation of federal law and international human rights treaties. Critics say that executions by lethal injection are essentially biomedical experiments on humans, but without any of the required protections: a solid foundation in the scientific literature, reliance on animal and clinical studies, independent expert review, monitoring and recording of data, evaluation of the data to test the original hypothesis, and informed consent.[105]

Yet even if the claim is wrong—even if executions aren't the type of biomedical experiments that regulations and human rights instruments have in mind—the fact that states aren't doing any of the things that make for good science is a problem in its own right. As a factual matter, lethal injection *is* human experimentation, and it's bad experimentation at that—the kind that would clearly be illegal if it weren't so off-grid. In our system of federalism, we like to say that states serve as "laboratories of experiment."[106] But not literally. Not like this.

Apropos the point, any discussion of faux science would be incomplete without mentioning one last thing: history is repeating itself. Ever the leader in execution ingenuity, Oklahoma adopted the nation's first statute authorizing executions by nitrogen gas in 2015, while awaiting the Supreme Court's decision in *Glossip*. "There wasn't much debate that I can recall," one legislator said of Oklahoma's nitrogen gas bill. "We all bought in pretty much right away."[107] To the extent there was opposition to the bill, another insider told the press, it was because some legislators "didn't want the inmate to feel good while dying. They wanted pain."[108] Thus far, three other states— Alabama, Mississippi, and Louisiana—have followed Oklahoma's lead, and Alabama conducted the nation's first execution by nitrogen gas in January 2024.

Execution by nitrogen gas kills by forcing a prisoner to breathe pure nitrogen, depriving them of oxygen and causing death by suffocation. Death by nitrogen gas is "fast and painless," the sponsor of Oklahoma's nitrogen gas bill stated. "You just sit there and a few minutes later, you're dead."[109] "It's foolproof," he told the press.[110]

Ah, the confidence. Such optimism for once again having nothing to back up that claim. Oklahoma's statute was based on an unpublished fourteen-page paper (double-spaced) written by three liberal arts professors at East Central University in Ada, Oklahoma, who have no medical training and no scientific backgrounds. "We probably talked about it for three hours," one of them stated. "We just did the best we could."[111] As Deborah Denno observes, "The paper is so poorly written, sloppy, hastily assembled, and typo-ridden that even the name of one of the authors on its cover is misspelled."[112]

Asked why he decided to get involved, one of the professors answered: "Now [lethal injection] is like an experiment every time. Here's some drugs and maybe we'll have a paramedic administer it and let's see what happens. Maybe this will kill 'em. It's kinda haphazard, and I think it's only going to get worse."[113] He wasn't wrong, except for the fact that this has been true of lethal injection since Day One.

The fourteen-page report acknowledged the "lack of scientific literature" supporting nitrogen gas as an execution method, but surmised that it would be humane based on what is known about deaths by nitrogen gas in other contexts—industrial accidents, scuba diving accidents, suicide, that sort of thing. In those contexts, the person just passes out, then dies.

Doctors are less sanguine. "There's a huge difference between someone accidentally (or intentionally) breathing pure nitrogen, versus forcing them to breathe it," one doctor says, adding: "Have you ever seen someone struggling to breathe? They gasp until the end. It's terrifying."[114]

In January 2024, Alabama proved him right.

In litigation clearing the way for Alabama to use nitrogen gas, the state repeatedly stated that its new execution protocol would work within seconds. "The state's method will rapidly lower the oxygen level in the mask, ensuring unconsciousness in seconds," the attorney general had promised.[115] This was the basis for Alabama's claim that execution by nitrogen gas was "the most painless and humane method of execution known to man." In legal filings, the state had claimed: "In all likelihood, hypoxia will cause unconsciousness in a matter of seconds, rendering [the prisoner] unable to feel pain."[116]

But that is not what happened. Five media witnesses were present to bear witness to what they saw in the twenty-two-minute execution of Kenny Smith, the same Kenny Smith who survived Alabama's botched attempt to execute him in 2022. The accounts were consistent. For a good four minutes, Smith heaved and writhed and thrashed against the straps on the gurney, convulsing so violently that the gurney itself shook. Smith was retching inside the mask and gasping for air, violently jerking his head in a desperate attempt to escape the slow suffocation that would kill him. Even after the first four minutes, Smith continued to gasp for breath. "I have never seen such a violent reaction to an execution," one veteran reporter stated afterward.[117] And that's just what the reporters saw from the viewing room.

Jeff Hood, Smith's spiritual advisor, was in the chamber with Smith when he died. "I want to make something perfectly clear: Anyone who claims that this was anything short of torture is not just mistaken, they are a dangerous liar," Hood stated afterward.[118] "The gurney wasn't supposed to move. Yet, move it did," Hood wrote of the account. "Kenny was shaking the entire gurney. I had never seen anything so violent." He recalled: "Veins spider-webbed in every direction. . . . I kept wondering if his bulging eyeballs were going to shoot right though. Saliva, mucus and other substances shot out of his mouth. The concoction of body fluids all started drizzling down the inside of the mask. . . . I could see the horror in his eyes. In fact, I'll never forget it."[119]

Alabama called the execution "textbook" and insisted that nothing had gone wrong. "Our proven method offers a blueprint for other states," state attorney general told the press after the fact.[120] "Alabama has done it, and now so can you."

3

TORTUROUS DRUGS

Tennessee allows prisoners to choose how they will die at the hands of the state, and five of the seven people it has executed since 2018 chose to die by the electric chair rather than lethal injection. By all accounts, death by electrocution is a ghastly affair. It cooks the organs and chars the skin, permeating the death chamber with the sickly smell of burning flesh. Death by electrocution is the only execution method that states themselves have found unconstitutional, with Nebraska's Supreme Court finding that "electrocution will unquestionably inflict intolerable pain," and Georgia's Supreme Court pointing to the "specter of excruciating pain" and "certainty of cooked brains and blistered bodies."[1] Yet prisoners are choosing this over lethal injection. Why?

The answer is that death by lethal injection is *worse*. As we will see, death by lethal injection is every bit as torturous as death by electrocution; it just takes longer. Death by electrocution takes under five minutes, usually bringing death within two or three. Death by lethal injection takes anywhere from ten to twenty minutes, and that's if it goes according to plan. This is why Tennessee's prisoners chose to die by the electric chair rather than lethal injection: they knew both deaths would be torturous, so their best move was to make it quick.[2]

Lethal injection projects the image of a painless, peaceful death, but here we'll see the ugly reality of what these drugs actually do. Our journey starts with the only drugs that have stayed more or less constant over time: pancuronium bromide and potassium chloride (the second and third drugs in the three-drug protocol). It then turns to the ever-changing first drug in the three-drug protocol—as well as the one-drug protocol—to show how they are torturous too.

THE PARALYTIC: PANCURONIUM BROMIDE

The second drug in the three-drug protocol is the paralytic pan-curonium bromide (or one of its über-close variants).[3] In the clinical setting, pancuronium bromide is used to keep patients still during surgery, and for trivia buffs, this is the synthetic version of *curare*—the drug that the indigenous tribes of the Amazon used on arrows to paralyze their prey. Pancuronium bromide works by relaxing the body's muscles and then preventing their ability to contract. It first causes motor weakness, then paralyzes the limbs, and then finally paralyzes the diaphragm and other muscles in the body's core. Because the diaphragm is what pushes air into the lungs, pancuronium bromide stops breathing—hence the need for a ventilator when patients go into surgery.

For rather obvious reasons, states don't put prisoners on a ventilator when executing them, so if prisoners are conscious when injected with pancuronium bromide, they will experience death by slow suffocation, straining to draw increasingly shallow breaths as paralysis of the diaphragm sets in. "The experience in onset and duration and character would be very similar to that of being suffocated by having one's nose and mouth blocked off," one doctor explains.[4] "Not being able to breathe . . . is one of the most powerful, excruciating feelings known to man," another doctor says, explaining: "It is nearly impossible for most untrained human beings to hold their breath voluntarily for more than 1 minute. . . . Panic and terror, and the attempt to fight take over. Even human beings who are underwater will reach such a level of agony that they will be compelled to take a 'breath' within about 1 minute."[5] This irrepressible urge to breathe is known as "air hunger," and it only grows more intense as the seconds pass without taking a breath.

Worse yet, pancuronium bromide couples the inability to breathe with the inability to struggle. By the time pancuronium bromide gets to the diaphragm, prisoners are "locked in"—they cannot scream or fight or even writhe in pain. "The thought of being chemically entombed and unable to breathe or cry out is terrifying," one doctor says.[6] "It would be like having the worst night terror imaginable," another explains. "You would experience oxygen hunger from being unable to breathe but be unable to move, all while being fully conscious."[7] Pancuronium bromide's effects are a horrific combination—unspeakable suffering in the most literal sense.

But it's even worse than that, because pancuronium bromide not only prevents the expression of pain, but also projects the expression of peaceful slumber. Pancuronium bromide is a muscle relaxant. It works by relaxing muscles and then freezing them that way. As one doctor explains, "Any person or animal who'd been given pancuronium, they are going to appear serene and tranquil and peaceful and comfortable, regardless of whether they are awake and in agony."[8] Witnesses see a soft drifting off to sleep, oblivious to the fact that it is just a chemically created façade. Sometimes ignorance really is bliss.

For a sense of just how impenetrable the façade of pancuronium bromide is, it's worth noting that even in the surgical setting, where the drug is routinely used, medical professionals don't always know when a paralyzed patient has come out of anesthesia and is experiencing pain. The phenomenon is called "anesthesia awareness," and for those already nervous about surgical procedures, not to worry, the occurrence is rare—less than one percent of all surgeries. Still, that works out to between twenty-six thousand to fifty-six thousand cases a year, enough for several medical associations to issue a "practice advisory" cautioning surgical teams to take extra precautions when using pancuronium bromide because signs of consciousness and distress are nearly impossible to detect.[9] (As a point of comparison, survivors of anesthesia awareness describe their ordeal as "the worst terror that I've ever experienced," "unbearably severe," and "the most traumatizing experience of my life"—and they were on a respirator).[10]

All this is to say that pancuronium bromide both *causes* excruciating pain and *conceals* it. This is why the vast majority of states—forty-two of fifty—explicitly prohibit its use in animal euthanasia.[11] The contrast is striking: the animal welfare community has prioritized a death that is *actually* humane, whereas executing states have prioritized a death that *looks* humane, but at the risk of being torturous instead.

And for what? That's the kicker—the paralytic isn't even necessary. Pancuronium bromide does nothing to anesthetize the prisoner—that's the job of the first drug. And it's not needed to induce death—the third drug does that, and there's no point in slowly suffocating someone to death when they are about to die by cardiac arrest. Pancuronium bromide is superfluous in the three-drug protocol. It literally inflicts "gratuitous pain," and since that is what prisoners must prove to make an Eighth Amendment claim, one would think that the drug would be prohibited for use in lethal injection just as it is for putting down pets.[12]

But that is not the case, which brings us to *Baze v. Rees*, the Supreme Court's first major lethal injection ruling.[13] As we know from chapter 2, the prisoners in *Baze* challenged the three-drug protocol, proposing to be executed veterinary-style with the one-drug pentobarbital protocol instead. Here we turn to the prisoners' alternative proposed ruling in the case: prohibit the paralytic.

The Supreme Court rejected this alternative too, and that's why states can (and do) use a paralytic in their protocols today. According to the Court in *Baze*, pancuronium bromide served two legitimate purposes. First, it stopped breathing, "hastening death," and thus serving the state's "legitimate interest in providing for a quick, certain death."[14]

This justification was all but ignored at oral arguments in the case, presumably because it just wasn't true. Death by slow suffocation is not a quick death. It takes a good ten minutes, and the drug that immediately follows it, potassium chloride, is supposed to kill in just two.[15] That was the very point of the prisoners' challenge—that the paralytic did not in fact hasten death. The paralytic dragged it out, and if prisoners weren't anesthetized, the drug would subject them to the excruciating pain of slow suffocation along the way.

But hastening death wasn't the real reason for the paralytic anyway, as Kentucky itself acknowledged. The real reason was to render death "dignified for the inmate, dignified for the witnesses."[16] As the lawyer for Kentucky told the Supreme Court during oral arguments in the case, "The purpose it serves is the purpose of dignifying the process for the benefit of the inmate and for the benefit of witnesses." Justice Stevens repeated it back just to make sure he heard the lawyer right: "The interest in protecting the dignity of the inmate and of the observers is the justification for the second drug?" The state's answer: "Yes."[17]

Kentucky argued—and the Supreme Court in *Baze* agreed—that states had a legitimate interest in preventing the possibility of involuntary muscle spasms in the dying process. For the record, experience has shown that the concern about muscle spasms was just another example of faux science—states using the one-drug protocol don't use a paralytic, and no one complains about muscle spasms today.[18] But even back when *Baze* was decided, the first drug in the three-drug protocol was a barbiturate *anti-convulsant*, so the justification didn't make sense.

Especially galling was the state's claim that the paralytic was for the benefit of the prisoners they were executing. Executions are hard to view as anything other than inherently undignified deaths—they are planned killings with people filing into a room to watch—and at the end of the execution, the prisoner is dead, so whatever dignity they may have lost, they aren't around to miss. Moreover, the very fact that prisoners were suing to stop the state from using a paralytic in their executions was a good indication that promoting the dignity of their death at the risk of it being a slow, torturous one was not a trade-off they were willing to make.

What "dignified for the inmate, dignified for the witnesses" really meant was dignified *for the executing state*. It was the state that benefited from an aesthetically pleasing death, no matter what the prisoner was actually experiencing. And it was the state that stood to lose if the reality of a torturous death came to light.

In *Baze*, the state argued that a purely cosmetic function was sufficient to justify the risk of excruciating pain, and the Supreme Court agreed. For those still wondering what lethal injection is about, here is your answer. Lethal injection is not about a humane death. It is about a humane-*looking* death, and the comfort that this provides is not just for execution witnesses. It's also for you and me.

One might even say it is *especially* for you and me. Conspicuously absent from Kentucky's reasons for using a paralytic was the biggest benefit to the state of all: the ability to portray lethal injection as a serene, sleep-induced death, solidifying in the public's mind the notion that executions are humane (so prisoners should stop their whining). As lethal injection scholar Deborah Denno explains, "We don't want executions to look like what they really are: killing someone."[19] We want executions, but only if they look like something else.

The paralytic gets us that, but it comes at a steep price, and prisoners aren't the only ones who pay it. You and I pay it too.

We pay for it in the loss of democratic accountability. States don't conduct public executions like they used to, so we rely on witnesses— particularly from the press—to provide the public scrutiny that executions in the town square once did. Executions are the government at its most powerful moment, and if we don't know what is happening in that moment, then we cannot hold the government accountable for what it does and doesn't do in our name. But how are witnesses to perform this critically important democratic function when states are using a drug whose very purpose is to prevent them from seeing what is happening? The paralytic turns public scrutiny into a perfunctory function— witnesses are present, but by the state's own hand, there is nothing for them to see.

We also pay for it in the loss of our constitutional rights. The Eighth Amendment's "cruel and unusual punishments" clause offers more limited protection than one might think. Under current doctrine, prisoners must show that an execution protocol is "sure or very likely to cause . . . needless suffering" to prove a constitutional violation.[20] But how are prisoners supposed to make that showing when states use a drug for the very purpose of hiding suffering? As we know from chapter 2, pointing to existing science won't do.[21] Prisoners need evidence from actual executions, and the paralytic makes sure that there isn't any.

Then there is what this lack of democratic and legal accountability gets us: states acting with impunity, using drugs that they would never dream of using if the world could see what they actually do. A prime example is midazolam. We know from chapter 2 that states used midazolam in two executions without a paralytic; both were grossly botched, triggering a torrent of public outrage.[22] Yet in the wake of those botched executions, states didn't stop using midazolam. They just stopped using it without a paralytic. The paralytic is a proverbial "get out of jail free" card, exempting states from the legal and political consequences of visibly botched executions. As one doctor puts the point: "The paralytic covers a lot of sins."[23]

In this regard, what Justice Sotomayor wrote in 2015's *Glossip* dissent is still true today. "The states may well be reluctant to pull back the curtain for fear of how the rest of us might react to what we see," she wrote. "But we deserve to know the price of our collective comfort before we blindly allow a state to make condemned inmates pay it in our names."[24]

THE ROAD SALT: POTASSIUM CHLORIDE

The third drug in the three-drug lethal injection protocol is potassium chloride, a naturally occurring salt in the human body that can also be extracted from salt water and various minerals. In the commercial setting, potassium chloride is used as road salt to melt ice on roads, and it is also used as a substitute for table salt to lower the sodium level of processed foods. In the clinical setting, potassium chloride is administered in miniscule amounts for any number of reasons, including managing high blood pressure and treating heart conditions.

In the lethal injection setting, potassium chloride is used to trigger cardiac arrest, which would be painful enough if that's all the drug did. But that's not all the drug does. Potassium chloride is a highly caustic agent, so the other thing it does is chemically burn the veins as it makes its way to the heart. This "would feel like someone was taking a blowtorch to your arm," one doctor says,[25] while another describes it as "a grotesquely painful experience" that "feels like injecting liquid fire."[26] As a point of comparison, a woman who had anesthesia awareness and had been administered potassium chloride said it felt like "fires of hell flowing through my veins"—and she wasn't given anywhere near the dose used in lethal injection.[27]

BEFORE TURNING TO THE FIRST DRUG . . .

Understanding what pancuronium bromide and potassium chloride do is the key to understanding why the first drug in the three-drug protocol is so important. Without the anesthetizing effect of the first drug, the second and third drugs would cause an excruciatingly painful death—one that the state in *Baze* conceded would be "constitutionally unacceptable."[28] As such, it is worth spending a moment to clarify two concepts before turning to the first drug.

One is the difference between anesthesia and unconsciousness. Anesthesia means that a person is insensate—they have no sensation, so they can't feel pain. (For trivia enthusiasts, the term *anesthesia* comes from the Greek word *anaisthēsia*, meaning "absence of sensation.") This is why general anesthesia is also called a "surgical plane of anesthesia"—because it blocks even surgical-level, cut-your-chest-open pain.

Unconsciousness, by contrast, is just a state of not being conscious. In anesthesiology circles, this is known as "deep sedation," and patients who are deeply sedated retain the ability to feel more than minimal pain.[29] As one doctor explains, "A patient asleep might not awaken to calling their name, or the stroke of the eyelashes or a pinch to the finger, but would certainly awaken to a blowtorch applied to the skin."[30]

For the big picture perspective, sedation is a continuum. A person could be minimally sedated and able to respond normally, or moderately sedated and responsive to most stimuli, or deeply sedated and arousable only in response to painful stimuli.[31] The American Society of Anesthesiologists (ASA) has a chart on its website that lays this out clearly:

FIGURE 3.1. American Society of Anesthesiologists Chart on Continuum of Depth of Sedation

	Minimal Sedation Anxiolysis	Moderate Sedation / Analgesia ("Conscious Sedation")	Deep Sedation / Analgesia	General Anesthesia
Responsiveness	Normal response to verbal stimulation	Purposeful** response to verbal or tactile stimulation	Purposeful** response following repeated or painful stimulation	Unarousable even with painful stimulus
Airway	Unaffected	No intervention required	Intervention may be required	Intervention often required
Spontaneos Ventilation	Unaffected	Adequate	May be inadequate	Frequently inadequate
Cardiovascular Function	Unaffected	Usually maintained	Usually maintained	May be impaired

As the ASA chart shows, anesthesia is the deepest level of sedation; it is what happens when a person is so deeply sedated that they have become insensate.[32] Thus, a person who is under general anesthesia is necessarily unconscious, but a person who is unconscious is not necessarily under anesthesia. As one doctor told a court: "If I went into my ICU tomorrow and said, 'This patient appears unconscious, I'm not going to worry about their pain,' the nurses would run me out on a rail, and rightfully so."[33]

Here's why all this matters. A prisoner could be unconscious and unresponsive to minor stimuli like pinching the arm or rubbing the sternum, but then be jolted awake once they can't breathe or start to experience the searing pain of potassium chloride. Unless the person is fully anesthetized, the fate that awaits them is the horrifying scenario of waking up in the midst of their own execution—gasping for breath and reeling from the intense burning sensation of potassium chloride, all while witnesses watch them die a seemingly peaceful death.

The question, then, is not whether the first drug in the three-drug protocol will make prisoners unconscious. The question is whether it will make them so deeply unconscious that they have reached a state of anesthesia, because that is the state needed to avoid a torturous death.

Here is a fitting place to address the tired trope in the Supreme Court's lethal injection cases (and parroted by lower courts) that prisoners are not entitled to "a painless death."[34] No one is arguing that. No one is even suggesting it. One searches in vain for prisoners in any case, in any state, at any level, saying they are entitled to a painless death. The claim prisoners are making is that they are entitled to a death *that is not torturous*—and that requires anesthesia because the second and third drugs in the three-drug protocol are torturous drugs.

The other concept to clarify up front is the meaning of the phrase "induction of anesthesia." One might think that a drug approved for the induction of anesthesia can actually get a person to that state, and this is the claim that executing states have made. As an example, the solicitor general in Oklahoma's 2022 lethal injection case told the court: "Midazolam is approved to induce general anesthesia, and general anesthesia means no pain."[35]

But that's not what the term "induction of anesthesia" means. "Induction of anesthesia" is a term of art within the field of anesthesiology, and it refers to the process that gives rise to anesthesia but is not the state of anesthesia itself.[36] In fact, when a state of anesthesia has been reached, the induction phase has come to an end, and the next phase of anesthesia, the "maintenance" phase, has begun. Tellingly, surgeons don't ever (as in never, ever) do their handiwork during the induction phase of anesthesia.[37] They have to wait to get to the maintenance phase before they can cut skin.

An apt analogy (with thanks to the anesthesiologist who explained this to me) is the on-ramp to a highway. You enter the ramp, but that doesn't mean you're on the highway. Same thing when you accelerate your speed and turn on your turn signal. Those are things you do to get on the highway, but doing those things doesn't mean you're there. The on-ramp is just how you get to the highway, and where you are at the beginning is not where you are at the end. At the end, you're on the highway—and that also means you've just left the ramp.

Induction is the on-ramp to a state of anesthesia. In the induction phase, medical professionals do all sorts of things to prepare patients for surgery. They give antianxiety drugs to relax the patient so their body is more accepting of the next steps. They give amnesiacs so the patient won't remember any traumatic experiences that may occur. And they use drugs to get the patient off to sleep so they can do various presurgical procedures (like insert a breathing tube). In each of these instances, they are using drugs approved for the induction of anesthesia, but that doesn't mean that those drugs can actually achieve that state. If they could, they'd be approved for more than just the induction phase. They'd be approved for the maintenance phase of anesthesia too.

All too often, courts have missed these important distinctions. In part, this is because the medical literature is not exactly a paragon of clarity. Medical professionals sometimes use the terms "unconscious" and "insensate" interchangeably, relying on the larger context of the discussion to provide the clarity otherwise lacking.[38] Experts for executing states have contributed their fair share to the confusion as well, capitalizing on ambiguities in the literature to attribute qualities to the drugs that are neither supported nor actually asserted in the literature itself.[39] And then there's the fact that the Supreme Court used the term "unconscious" to mean "insensate" in its first lethal injection case, *Baze v. Rees*, conflating the two concepts for lower courts forevermore.[40] Now that we have clarity on these key concepts, we're ready to turn to the first drug in the three-drug protocol—all *five* of them.

THE ORIGINAL FIRST DRUG: SODIUM THIOPENTAL

Sodium thiopental is the original first drug in the three-drug lethal injection protocol, and it is still listed in the protocols of thirteen of the twenty-seven death penalty states.[41] That said, sodium thiopental hasn't been used in an execution for over a decade because states can't get their hands on the drug. We'll spend an entire chapter talking about the lethal injection drug shortage—that's chapter 6—but here, it's worth noting that states are still trying to buy sodium thiopental, and if they succeed, the drug may well be back in business. In short, sodium thiopental is down, but not out, as a lethal injection drug, and that means it still matters.

Sodium thiopental is considered the gold standard for the first drug in the three-drug lethal injection protocol. It is a barbiturate classified as an "ultra-short-acting" drug, with an onset of action around thirty seconds and full effects occurring in around a minute.[42] In the clinical setting, sodium thiopental is used with other drugs to achieve anesthesia for longer procedures, and is approved as the sole basis of anesthesia for short procedures lasting fifteen minutes or less (although nowadays, doctors use propofol instead).

In the clinical setting, the dosage of sodium thiopental tends to run between two hundred and five hundred milligrams, with factors like age, weight, health status, anxiety level, and a history of alcohol or drug abuse determining the proper dose.[43] In the lethal injection setting, states were injecting two, three, and even five *grams* of the drug—ten times the clinical range—which experts said would reliably achieve anesthesia and render irrelevant the individualized considerations that normally come into play.[44] And that should be all there is to say.

Except. We know from chapter 2 that sodium thiopental often didn't work as states said.[45] States said that within sixty seconds of receiving a bolus overdose of sodium thiopental, prisoners would stop breathing, a rough-and-ready indication that they were under anesthesia. But that didn't happen in over half the executions in California. Why not?

Veterinary science provided one explanation. Like lethal injection, veterinary medicine uses bolus dosing (administering the entire dose of a drug at once), and it routinely used bolus injections of sodium thiopental back when the drug was widely available. Turns out, the bolus dosing for large animals scales well across species, providing an instructive benchmark for humans.[46] (Fun fact: swine in particular are considered an excellent model of human cardiovascular and cardiopulmonary physiology, with comparable brain size and cerebral blood flow. *We're built a lot like pigs, who knew.*)[47]

This led a team of scientists to examine the veterinary guidelines for producing anesthesia in large animals using sodium thiopental. They found that in the veterinary setting, the therapeutic dose for short procedures lasting fifteen minutes or less was 18-22 mg/kg.[48] That's eighteen to twenty-two milligrams of sodium thiopental per kilogram of body weight.

Then the scientists looked at the body weights listed in forty execution autopsy reports from North Carolina. They found that the three-gram bolus "overdose" that North Carolina was using wasn't an overdose at all. When scaled to body weight, the median dose for prisoners was just 20.3 mg/kg—the midpoint that veterinary science used for a *therapeutic* dose of the drug.[49] In fact, for some prisoners (those who weighed the most), the three-gram bolus overdose equated to just 11.2 mg/kg—an amount far below the therapeutic range used in veterinary medicine.

Scientists also ran the numbers for the two-gram dose of sodium thiopental that most states were using at the time, and the results were even more alarming.[50] "On the basis of execution data and clinical, veterinary, and laboratory animal studies, we posit that the specified quantity of thiopental may not provide surgical anesthesia," the study concluded. "Thus, some inmates may experience the sensations of pancuronium-induced paralysis and respiratory arrest."[51]

The fact that states were not actually using a massive overdose of sodium thiopental also meant that two concerns that had been taken off the table were now back on it. First, factors known to impact the effectiveness of sodium thiopental were back in play. Prisoners on death row were highly likely to have a history of alcohol and/or substance abuse, which meant they were highly likely to be resistant to sodium thiopental and would need a larger dose for effect.[52] Prisoners about to be executed were also highly likely to have elevated anxiety levels, triggering the release of stress hormones that likewise increased resistance to the drug.[53]

The second concern goes back to the fact that sodium thiopental is an "ultra-short-acting" drug—it works quickly but only for a short time. The duration of sodium thiopental's effect is dose dependent, so a massive overdose would reliably provide anesthesia for the duration of a standard execution. But we now know that two and three grams are not a massive overdose. Thus, aside from the question of whether the dose of sodium thiopental was enough to anesthetize prisoners in the first place was the question of whether it was enough to anesthetize them for the duration of the execution. If the duration of anesthesia was short, or the execution ran long, the prisoner would awaken to a torturous death.

If there was a bright spot in the data, it was that the five-gram bolus overdose that a few states were using came close to the massive overdose that states professed to be administering all along.[54] That said, even the five-gram dose is only so reassuring given how states came to it. Texas was the leader in using the five-gram bolus overdose, and to the extent other states used it too, they appear to have been following Texas. And why did Texas use five grams of sodium thiopental? A corrections department lawyer from another state testified that she had asked her Texas counterpart that very question. The conversation, she said, went like this:

> I said, 'Every other state I have spoken to is using two grams of sodium thiopental. Why are y'all using five?' And he started laughing and said, 'Well, you see, when we did our very first execution, the only thing I had on hand was a 5-gram vial. And rather than do the paperwork on wasting 3 grams, we just gave all five.'[55]

To the extent that Texas was using a dose of sodium thiopental that would reliably ensure anesthesia, it was by sheer happenstance.

THE ONE-DRUG PROTOCOL: PENTOBARBITAL

Less than two months after the Supreme Court upheld the three-drug protocol in *Baze v. Rees*, an Ohio court struck it down as a matter of *state* law, ruling that it created "an unnecessary and arbitrary risk that the condemned will experience an agonizing and painful death."[56] If Ohio wanted to conduct executions, it would need to do so using the one-drug protocol that veterinarians used to put down pets. Shortly thereafter, a shortage of sodium thiopental forced states that were still using the three-drug protocol to look for a new drug as well. The obvious choice was pentobarbital.

Pentobarbital is a barbiturate like sodium thiopental, but unlike sodium thiopental, it is classified as a "short-acting" (rather than "ultra-short-acting") drug. In the clinical setting, pentobarbital is used to treat epileptic seizures and reduce cerebral swelling in the wake of traumatic brain injuries. Pentobarbital is also the drug used in animal euthanasia and physician-assisted suicide.

At first, states (other than Ohio) used pentobarbital as a substitute for sodium thiopental in the three-drug protocol. This was plainly problematic, as pentobarbital's slower onset and peak effect—onset in around a minute, deep sedation in three to five—meant that prisoners would feel the suffocating effects of pancuronium bromide and the intense burning of potassium chloride before pentobarbital produced its anesthetic effect.[57]

But in relatively short order ("relatively" meaning a couple of years and a couple dozen executions later), states stopped using pentobarbital in the three-drug protocol on their own. Pentobarbital was the drug used in animal euthanasia, and buying one drug was easier than buying three. Once Ohio debuted the one-drug protocol in an execution in 2010, states using pentobarbital in the three-drug protocol quickly moved to using just the one drug.

Today, eight states and the federal government—just under a third of the twenty-seven death penalty states—use the one-drug pentobarbital protocol for lethal injection.[58] These jurisdictions tend to have active execution chambers, which explains why the one-drug protocol accounts for half to two-thirds of the nation's executions each year.[59] Texas, for example, uses the one-drug protocol—it abandoned the three-drug protocol in 2012 when its supply of the second drug ran dry—and Texas conducts more executions, by far, than any other state. In fact, Texas alone is responsible for around a third of all executions in the United States over the past forty years.[60]

The one-drug protocol offers a number of distinct advantages. It is simpler, eliminating the need to manage the sequence and timing of multiple drugs. It results in states chasing after one drug rather than three. It allows witnesses to see what is actually happening. And most importantly, it reduces the risk of excruciating pain by removing the two drugs that cause it.

Presumably, this is why Jay Chapman—the "father of lethal injection"—later stated that if he were to do it again, he would not recommend the three-drug protocol for which he is famous. He would use the one-drug protocol instead. "Hindsight is always 20/20," he said.[61]

The one-drug protocol has a problem of its own—we'll turn to that at the end of this chapter—but given its advantages, why don't all states use the one-drug protocol? In the early years, state experts said that the one-drug protocol would cause muscle spasms, and that death would take a long time, if it came at all. "Electrical activity in the heart may persist for a very long time, in healthy people almost certainly for more than half an hour," one expert warned. "Everyone involved will have to wait a very long time for the heart to stop."[62]

But none of that was true. No one has survived an execution with the one-drug protocol (although, as we'll see, several executions have had to be called off because executioners could not access a prisoner's vein). No one is talking about unsightly muscle spasms with the one-drug protocol (although witnesses *are* talking about prisoners gasping for breath, a sign that they are in respiratory distress). And no one is waiting a good half-hour on average for prisoners to die from the one-drug protocol (although a 2020 study showed that compounded pentobarbital, which states are now forced to use, has extended the average execution time for the one-drug protocol to almost nineteen minutes).[63]

Nowadays, the reason states give for not using the one-drug pentobarbital protocol is that they can't get the drug—and that may well be true. But it's worth noting that Texas and other states manage to get pentobarbital, and states have a long history of both buying lethal injection drugs from out-of-state suppliers and sharing their execution drugs.[64] That leaves just one other reason why states don't use the one-drug protocol: they don't have to. The Supreme Court has upheld the three-drug protocol three times now, so for states that prefer the guaranteed good look of a paralytic, there's no need to do anything else.[65]

THE MARTINI IN A SYRINGE: MIDAZOLAM

When states started using pentobarbital in lethal injection, the companies that manufactured the drug took steps to stop executioners from accessing it, and that left states with two options. One was to get pentobarbital from a compounding pharmacy rather than manufacturer (more on that in chapter 6). The other was to find yet another first drug. For states that chose the second option, the new drug was midazolam.

Florida was the first state to adopt midazolam in the three-drug protocol, using it in a 2013 execution in which witnesses said the prisoner had "more body movements after losing unconsciousness" than when pentobarbital and sodium thiopental were the first drug.[66] The next year, two states—Ohio and Arizona—tried midazolam in a two-drug protocol, and as we know, both executions were so badly botched that the drug has not been used since without a paralytic.[67] Today, five states use midazolam as the first drug in the three-drug protocol, accounting for around a third of all executions annually.[68]

We already know a little about midazolam from chapter 2, which examined expert testimony defending the drug to make a point about faux science. Here we'll dive deeper, examining what the science says about midazolam (as opposed to what it doesn't). Midazolam is the battlefield where the war over lethal injection drugs is currently being fought. As such, we're going to park right here for a bit to sort out the truth about midazolam. This is where a clear understanding of the terms becomes important—because if you understand the terms, then you'll understand the science, and if you understand the science, then you'll understand why midazolam is a horrifying choice as the first drug in the three-drug protocol.

Midazolam is not a barbiturate like pentobarbital and sodium thiopental; it is a benzodiazepine in the same class of drugs as Valium and Xanax (hence the moniker "martini in a syringe").[69] In the clinical setting, midazolam is used for the induction of anesthesia, relaxing patients before surgery and relieving their anxiety. In fact, its clinical use has included administration to prisoners several hours before their execution to give them "an anxiety-free mind."[70] Midazolam is also an amnesiac used to prevent surgical patients from remembering traumatic events that may occur, and in high doses, it is used to put patients to sleep (sedate them to the point of unconsciousness) so that minor procedures like colonoscopies can be performed, although even then, it is typically paired with a narcotic to ensure that the patient does not awaken from pain.[71]

Like pentobarbital, midazolam is classified as a "fast-acting" drug. Its onset of action is two to three minutes, and according to its FDA label, it can achieve sedation in three to five, although its peak sedative effect takes around fifteen minutes.[72] This makes midazolam wildly inappropriate for use as the first drug in the three-drug protocol for the same reason that pentobarbital was so plainly problematic—even if it worked the way states say it does, it would work too slowly to protect prisoners from the excruciating pain of the second and third drugs.

But the biggest problem with midazolam is not that it works too slowly, but rather that it doesn't work the way states say it does *at all*. States say that midazolam will render a prisoner insensate. That is not true, and we know it's not true because producing anesthesia is not something that midazolam has the chemical capacity to do.

Like all benzodiazepines, midazolam has a single mechanism of action: it works by binding with a neuron inhibitor called GABA (gamma-amniobutryic acid). But the amount of GABA in the body is limited, so when the GABA that midazolam can bind with has maxed out, so has midazolam's sedative effect. "If there is more midazolam than there are places for it to bind on GABA receptors," one doctor explains, "that extra midazolam can't do anything. Increasing the dose of midazolam simply produces extra midazolam floating around the brain with nothing to do."[73] As another doctor puts the point: "It doesn't matter if you give the person 500 additional doses or five million doses. It won't have any more effect."[74]

This is what is known as a "ceiling effect"—the maximum effect that a drug can have because it has maxed out the mechanism by which it works. "The ceiling effect of midazolam and other benzodiazepines is not controversial and is portrayed in many introductory pharmacology textbooks," one expert explains, quoting study after study "so that it will be obvious that a ceiling effect is documented and pervasive in the scientific and pharmacological literature."[75] *Lawyers can be so obtuse.*

Importantly, midazolam and other benzodiazepines hit their ceiling effect *before* they can produce anesthesia, a pharmacological fact amply documented in the authoritative texts in the field. Consider, for example, Brenner and Stevens's *Pharmacology*, which states that benzodiazepines cause unconsciousness "not reaching the depth of general anesthesia needed for loss of reaction to painful stimulus. . . . Because benzodiazepines work only in the presence of GABA," the text explains, "benzodiazepines exhibit a ceiling effect whereby greater doses do not produce significantly greater effects and do not depress the brain to the point of anesthesia and death."[76] Midazolam may be used to *induce* anesthesia, but that is not to say that it can *produce* anesthesia. Those are two different things.

Goodman and Gilmann's *The Pharmacologic Basis of Therapeutics*—dubbed "the holy book of the pharmacology discipline"—is equally clear on this point. "Benzodiazepines do not produce the same magnitudes of neuronal depression produced by barbiturates," it states, adding: "Although the clinical literature often refers to the 'anesthetic' effects and uses of certain benzodiazepines, these drugs do not cause a true general anesthesia . . . and a failure to respond to noxious stimuli sufficient to allow surgery cannot be achieved."[77]

Anesthesiology texts say the same thing, although it is often the *absence* of midazolam in their discussion of anesthesia-producing drugs that is most telling. Miller's *Anesthesia* states: "In the clinical practice of daily anesthesia, midazolam is often used immediately before induction of anesthesia."[78] Conspicuously absent in this anesthesia text is any claim that midazolam can produce anesthesia. Reves et al.'s *Anesthesiology* is explicit on this point, stating: "Midazolam cannot be used alone, however, to maintain adequate anesthesia."[79]

Dr. David Greenblatt, who as we know from chapter 2 is the nation's preeminent expert on midazolam, does not mince words about midazolam's inability to produce anesthesia. "No matter what dose is given," he says, "midazolam can only produce a degree of sedation that is insufficient to render a person insensate."[80] "Will midazolam make a person 'unconscious'? Yes, it will," he explains, "but only to a certain level, and that level is not deep enough to effect insensateness."[81] "Keep in mind the distinction between being 'unconscious' and 'insensate,'" Greenblatt cautions. "Just because an inmate is 'unconscious' does not mean he is insensate."[82]

For those who like numbers, two are worth noting here. The first pertains to a device called a BIS monitor (BIS is short for "bispectral index score"), which anesthesiologists use to help them assess whether a patient has reached anesthesia or is just in a state of deep sedation. The lower the score on the BIS monitor, the deeper the sedation. On a BIS monitor, the range for anesthesia is forty to sixty. Studies put the score produced by midazolam at around seventy.[83] Bodies are weird and react to drugs differently, so this is not to say that a person could *never* hit the forty-to-sixty range with midazolam. It's just to say that if they did, they'd be the random outlier.

The second important number is the dose at which midazolam reaches its ceiling effect. Greenblatt is clear on this point too. "Studies demonstrate there is a point in the range of 15–40 mg at which there is no further sedative effect created by additional doses of midazolam," he says, pointing to his own work and that of others.[84] That puts midazolam's ceiling effect at less than *one-tenth* the five-hundred-milligram dose that states are using in lethal injection, which means all that extra is for naught.

"No matter how much you give of it, it's still a benzodiazepine," one pharmacology professor says, and that's the rub.[85] The problem isn't the dosage, it's the drug. The problem is that even an exceptionally high dose of midazolam cannot produce an effect that the drug is pharmacologically incapable of producing.

This is why midazolam is not FDA-approved for use as the sole drug in anesthesia. "Believe me, the drug companies that invented it and made it would have loved for it to have been granted by the FDA the moniker as a general anesthetic," says anesthesiologist David Lubarsky. "But it didn't get that, because it doesn't do that," he says, explaining that in clinical trials, even large doses of midazolam "failed . . . in terms of blunting the effect of surgery."[86]

Lubarsky spent nearly two decades as chair of University of Miami's department of anesthesiology, and a number of those years as the chief medical officer of the University of Miami Health System as well (he now has a very long title at UC Davis).[87] In that capacity, Lubarsky estimates that he has overseen the administration of midazolam in some form or fashion around a *million* times, so he speaks from the voice of experience when he says that midazolam "would never be used and has never been used as a sole anesthetic to give anesthesia during surgery. Not ever."[88] "In my entire career," he says, "I don't know of anybody who has ever used midazolam as a sole anesthetic agent for a surgery."[89] Tellingly, state experts can't think of such an occasion either.[90]

Worse yet, midazolam has no pain-relieving properties, which is to say that it is not an "analgesic" any more than it is an anesthetic. (As a point of comparison, analgesics take away the ability to feel pain, whereas anesthetics take away the ability to feel entirely.) This means that what one prisoner's expert said about midazolam—that using it in an execution was like "taking a bottle of aspirin to treat an amputated leg"—is not quite right. Midazolam doesn't even rise to the level of a bottle of aspirin.[91]

And it's even worse than that, as studies show that in certain populations—primarily patients with a history of aggression, substance abuse, and psychiatric disorders (so, pretty much all of death row)—midazolam is known to cause a "paradoxical reaction," which is an effect other than what is intended, and usually just the opposite.[92] Instead of reducing anxiety, for example, midazolam can increase it, and another known paradoxical reaction to the drug is "hyperalgesia," which is when a person experiences pain even more intensely than they normally would.[93] That's right, midazolam can "superadd" pain, to use a weird word that is now en vogue at the Supreme Court.[94]

Not to worry, states say, the risk of a paradoxical reaction from midazolam is just one percent, and that is true—in one study.[95] But other studies have put the risk between 10–20 percent, and a study of subjects in the at-risk category showed that over half—58 percent—had a paradoxical reaction to benzodiazepines.[96] Whatever the number, the risk is high enough to merit a warning on midazolam's product label, along with a notation saying that the risk of a paradoxical effect is highest when the dose is "inadequate or excessive."[97] *Which it is here.*

What an absolutely horrific choice for the first drug in the three-drug lethal injection protocol. This is why a group of sixteen preeminent pharmacology professors filed an amicus brief with the Supreme Court when the Court considered the constitutionality of midazolam in its second lethal injection case, *Glossip v. Gross.*[98] *Glossip* was decided in 2015, and, as we know from chapter 2, the prisoners lost—the Court held that they had the burden of proving that midazolam would not produce an anesthetic effect, and because there was no science on a five-hundred-milligram dose, they had not met their burden of proof.[99] But as the dissent in *Glossip* noted, the science was clear that midazolam would not produce anesthesia no matter how much the state injected, and the professors' amicus brief—filed "in support of neither party" and solely in the interest of getting the science right—made the point plainly. "The fact that midazolam does not ever achieve general anesthesia is consistent with, and explains, the clinical uses of the drug," the professors stated, adding: "It is widely recognized in the scientific and medical community that midazolam alone cannot be used to maintain adequate anesthesia for surgery."[100]

In 2017, the professors wrote again. This time their amicus brief was in support of a petition to revisit *Glossip*, and their anger over the "profoundly troubling" use of midazolam in executions was evident. "These are not idle disagreements with a prior court's conclusions, but the opinions of pharmacological experts supported by reliable scientific principles," they wrote.[101] Then they proceeded to answer every question that the Justices had used to support their *Glossip* ruling. *Don't know the dose at which midazolam reaches its ceiling effect? Here it is. Confused about the difference between unconsciousness and anesthesia? We'll clarify that too.* Every single thing that the Justices needed to rectify their ruling in *Glossip* was right in front of them. Reality would not bend to the state's will, the professors warned, writing: "Neither the parties' legal arguments nor the dosage can change the material properties of this drug."[102] *Certiorari denied.* The Justices didn't want to hear it, literally.

At this point, you might be wondering what states are saying to defend midazolam's use in lethal injection. We know from chapter 2 that in *Glossip*, the state's expert said that anesthesia didn't matter because a megadose of midazolam would render prisoners insensate by "paralyzing the brain"—a theory so bizarre that not even Oklahoma stood by it when the case was before the Supreme Court.[103] But that begs the question: What did Oklahoma do to defend its use of midazolam?

One thing Oklahoma did was misstate the science on midazolam. During oral arguments in *Glossip*, Justice Sotomayor confronted the state's lawyer on this very point, saying: "I am substantially disturbed that in your brief you made factual statements that were not supported by the cited . . . sources, and in fact [were] directly contradicted."[104] "I'm going to give you just three small examples among the many I found," she stated, "So nothing you say or read to me am I going to believe, frankly, until I see it with my own eyes the context, okay?" She then proceeded to point out that the state's brief had quoted midazolam's FDA label for the proposition that the drug could reach "deep levels of sedation virtually equivalent to the state of general anesthesia" but had taken out the key words "when taken with other drugs that suppress the central nervous system."[105] And the state had cited a study purporting to say that midazolam could be used as a "full surgical anesthetic" but it had taken out the part that said "But presuming there were no ceiling effect."[106] She never did get to her third example.

Oklahoma's conduct in the 2015 *Glossip* case before the Supreme Court inspired a close look at what the state and its experts were saying in the 2022 *Glossip* case back in Oklahoma. As we know from chapter 2, the judge in 2022's *Glossip* case (who was the same judge that decided 2015's *Glossip* case) once again upheld the use of midazolam in the three-drug lethal injection protocol.[107] In the 2022 litigation, the state of Oklahoma made two claims—both central to the court's ruling—that merit mention here.

One claim goes to the BIS score that midazolam can achieve. Oklahoma's experts claimed that midazolam was plenty capable of producing a BIS score lower than 60—a proposition that the court relied on in its written opinion in the case.[108] But the studies that the state cited for that proposition did not in fact support it. One of the studies concluded that "the maximum effect of midazolam on the BIS is approximately 70," and that "BIS does not decrease further even if plasma concentration increases to levels higher than that required by sedation"—documenting not only midazolam's *in*ability to achieve anesthesia, but also its ceiling effect (the existence of which the state's experts flat-out denied).[109] Another of the state's studies noted a BIS score as low as 56, but that was an outlier—the average BIS score in the study was 69.[110] And the third of the state's studies put the low BIS score at 66, and the average at 71.[111] (For those wondering, *Who are these experts anyway?*, curious readers can find entire exposés about them as part of the "small pool of experts" willing to defend midazolam's use in the three-drug protocol.)[112]

The other claim provides an unfortunate example of what happens when a court does not understand the medical terms being used when talking about these drugs. The court in 2022's *Glossip* case relied on the fact that midazolam is FDA-approved "for the induction of anesthesia" to rule that the drug could actually achieve anesthesia.[113] In a footnote, the court noted that Reves's *Anesthesiology* "treats as unremarkable the proposition that midazolam induces anesthesia," and that is true.[114] But what the Reves's text says is this: "Midazolam may be used intravenously for the induction of anesthesia (table 2). Induction *is accomplished when there is unresponsiveness to command and loss of the eyelash reflex*."[115] Clearly, inducing anesthesia is not the same as producing anesthesia because the text says that induction "is accomplished" when a person is no longer responsive to calling their name or brushing their eyelashes, and those things are *not* indicia of anesthesia. As we know, those things are markers of unconsciousness—"deep sedation," to use the ASA's terminology—and no one questions whether midazolam can produce that.[116] The court in 2022's *Glossip* case conflated unconsciousness with a state of anesthesia, and misconstrued what the term "induction of anesthesia" meant.

To support its ruling, the court also pointed to midazolam's FDA-approved label, which explicitly states that midazolam may be used for the "induction of general anesthesia." But tellingly, what the label says is "For induction of general anesthesia, *before administration of other anesthetic agents*."[117] Midazolam's label does not say that the drug can produce anesthesia. In fact, it presumes that other anesthetic agents will be administered to get from the induction on-ramp to the anesthesia highway.

At the risk of belaboring the point (and only because courts are getting it wrong), two other data points merit mention. The first is Dr. Greenblatt, who says that midazolam was originally intended to serve as an induction agent for anesthesia—a "starting point so you can transition to actual anesthesia."[118] The idea was to use midazolam "at the initial stage of the anesthesia process in which people are made calm and sedate, and to reduce the patient's anxiety, so that they will accept the next step," he explained, adding: "It's not midazolam producing anesthesia, it's the initial stage of induction."[119]

The other data point is the American Society of Health System Pharmacists' *Drug Information*®. The AHFS *Drug Information*® is the most comprehensive evidence-based source of drug information available—it is a massive compendium spanning over 3,500 pages that provides every bit of information anyone would ever want to know about a drug (and then some).[120] Here is what it says about midazolam under the subheading "Induction and Maintenance of Anesthesia":

Midazolam is used IV for induction of general anesthesia *prior to other anesthetic agents*. Induction with IV midazolam results in anxiolysis, anterograde amnesia, and dose related hypnotic effects (progressing from sedation to loss of consciousness) but not analgesia. Midazolam also is used as a component of balanced anesthesia (e.g. nitrous oxide and oxygen) for maintenance of anesthesia during short surgical procedures. . . . *Midazolam should not be used alone for maintenance of anesthesia. . . . Concurrent use of an opiate agonist usually is necessary to maintain adequate anesthesia.*[121]

In the real world—that is, outside the world of lethal injection litigation—there is simply no question about what midazolam can and cannot do. It can relieve anxiety. It can produce amnesia. And it can sedate to the point of unconsciousness. What it cannot do (alone) is block excruciating pain.

Perhaps this is why in the 2022 *Glossip* case, Oklahoma made the novel and astounding claim that even if prisoners could feel the suffocating effects of the paralytic, the sensation wasn't actually painful. "While muscle relaxants may cause sensations of suffocation," the state asserted, "they do not cause physical pain."[122] Faced with the inescapable reality that midazolam cannot block torturous pain, Oklahoma simply declared that torturous pain was not that painful. The same slow suffocation that the state in *Baze* conceded was so torturous as to be "constitutionally unacceptable" is now not so bad after all.

States know the truth about midazolam. They know from the authoritative texts in the field. They know from the studies. They even know from their own drug suppliers. "Here's my concern with midazolam. . . . The subjects may be able to feel pain from the administration of the second and third drugs," a pharmacist who had been solicited as a supplier wrote to the Tennessee DOC. "Consider the use of an alternative like ketamine, or use in conjunction with an opioid," the pharmacist suggested. The DOC point person's response: "I'll pass this info on to the higher ups." A follow-up email from the point person came soon after: "the powers that be" wanted to stick with the protocol they had.[123] Now *that's* saying something—even a random pharmacist knew the truth about midazolam, and this pharmacist was more bothered by the prospect of a torturous death than the Tennessee DOC.

States *know*. And another reason they surely know is that officials can see with their own eyes that midazolam executions are executions marked by *suffering*. Prisoners open their eyes, clench their fists, gasp and heave, and strain against the restraints on the gurney in execution after execution using midazolam (at least before the paralytic takes effect). In Ohio's 2019 trial, prisoners called over twenty witnesses who had viewed executions using midazolam, each of whom provided a detailed account of prisoners struggling to breathe when they should have been asleep.[124]

As a final point, recall that the Supreme Court in *Glossip v. Gross* upheld the use of midazolam in lethal injection based on the lack of studies relevant to a 500 milligram dose. *We just don't know, so, states, you're good to go.* But it turns out, not even that was right. "We actually have extensive experience with overdosage," Greenblatt says, pointing to his own studies involving patients who were brought to the hospital after overdosing on benzodiazepines—one of which involved almost one hundred patients and included overdoses approaching the equivalent of 2,000 mg of midazolam.[125] According to Greenblatt, "The findings from those studies are all consistent. . . . No matter how big the dose is, they get sleepy for a while, they're somnolent, you can still rouse them, and then they wake up and they're fine, uniform experience."[126] Importantly, he adds, patients in the study "were sensitive to painful stimuli when they entered the hospital with those massive overdoses in their systems."[127]

In 2017, two years after *Glossip*, Brenner and Stevens's *Pharmacology* published its fifth edition. At the end of its discussion of midazolam, the text noted that in recent years, the drug had been used in lethal injection, and the Supreme Court had upheld its use. The last line stated matter-of-factly: "It was the first instance that the Supreme Court considered a basic pharmacology question concerning the differences between barbiturates and benzodiazepines; a question they failed to answer correctly."[128] It was a *basic* question. In the halls of learning, as opposed to the halls of justice, the scientists would have the final say.

THE OUTLIERS: ETOMIDATE AND FENTANYL

The last two variants of the first drug in the three-drug protocol—etomidate and fentanyl—are each used by just one state. Florida started using etomidate in 2017 when it ran out of midazolam and couldn't find a new supplier, and it has since conducted just over a dozen executions using the drug. Nebraska and Nevada announced protocols using fentanyl that same year, although Nevada's protocol has been tied up in protracted litigation, leaving Nebraska as the only state that has actually used fentanyl in an execution by lethal injection.

Etomidate is an anesthetic—it can achieve anesthesia, and it is "ultra-fast-acting." But etomidate is also super–short lasting. In the clinical setting, it is known to wear off in as little as five minutes.[129] That's why, in the practice of medicine, etomidate is only used for short, painful procedures like realigning a dislocated joint. Witnesses to executions using etomidate in the three-drug protocol have reported seeing prisoners heaving, convulsing, and gasping for breath.[130] All we know for sure is that etomidate can render a prisoner insensate for a good five minutes. Executions by lethal injection take ten to twenty.

One might think that fentanyl, a synthetic painkiller that is fifty to a hundred times stronger than morphine, would be suitable for lethal injection, as the drug is already responsible for thousands of unintentional deaths in our nation's tragic opioid crisis. In Nebraska, fentanyl is part of the nation's first-ever four-drug protocol. The protocol starts with a shot of valium, then follows the three-drug format, using fentanyl as the first drug. So it's valium, then fentanyl, then the paralytic, then potassium chloride.

Nebraska has executed just one person with its four-drug protocol—Cary Dean Moore in 2018—and what happened there is perhaps the reason why the state has not conducted another execution since. Prison officials told a court that "witnesses reported no complications" during the twenty-three-minute execution, but that wasn't true.[131] Media witnesses reported that right after receiving the fentanyl dose, "Moore coughed, his diaphragm and abdomen heaved, he went still, then his face and fingers gradually turned red and then purple, and his eyes cracked open slightly."[132] Witnesses said that Moore's eyes cracked open right after the injection of potassium chloride, and that within a minute of this happening, a prison official who was in the execution chamber said something into his radio. Seconds later, the curtain closed. It remained closed for fourteen minutes, at which point it was reopened and Moore was dead.

Prison officials did not explain what happened behind the curtain and did not take media questions, so no one knows what actually transpired during those fourteen minutes. But several days after the execution, a prison spokesperson told the press that the decision to close the curtain was not a reaction to anything happening with Moore; the state had planned to close the curtain at that time all along.[133] Media witnesses didn't buy what the state was selling. "Nobody drops the curtain so that you cannot see the moments when the prisoner dies," one reporter said. "That's why you have witnesses, so they can see and report what happens."[134] Whatever happened—and to this day, we still don't know—it was the first and last time that the four-drug fentanyl protocol was used.

THE 2020 REVEAL: ACUTE PULMONARY EDEMA

Before 2020, the story of torturous drugs had just one plotline: the second and third drugs in the three-drug protocol were torturous, and the first drug failed to protect prisoners from excruciating pain. But 2020 brought revelations that the various drugs used as the first drug in the three-drug protocol—as well as pentobarbital, the one-drug protocol—were torturous too. In a perverse irony, the very drugs that were supposed to prevent excruciating pain were instead causing it.

Now we have a second plotline. This one begins in 2016, when an anesthesiologist was asked to examine some execution autopsy reports for drug levels in the blood.[135] The anesthesiologist, Dr. Joel Zivot, was reviewing the toxicology data in one of the reports when something else caught his eye: the lungs were abnormally heavy. The average lung weighs 400–450 grams; these weighed twice that. Zivot checked the other autopsy reports. *Same thing.* Zivot knew he was on to something, so he reached out to Dr. Mark Edgar, an anatomical pathologist who was then his colleague at Emory University Hospital (and is now at the Mayo Clinic). Edgar confirmed what Zivot suspected: the prisoners had suffered from acute pulmonary edema as they died.

As we know from chapter 2, pulmonary edema occurs when fluid seeps into the lungs—that's what makes them heavy. Pulmonary edema can happen for any number of reasons, including when extremely high doses of drugs are administered extremely quickly. Acute pulmonary edema (also known as "flash pulmonary edema") occurs when the pulmonary edema is sudden and severe, developing in seconds and minutes rather than hours or days.

Acute pulmonary edema is excruciatingly painful. "When it begins," Edgar says, "the patients are short of breath. They feel like they can't catch their breath and they breathe a little bit faster."[136] As the condition progresses, he explains, "the work to get air into and out of the lungs increases as the airways progressively fill with water." At this point, "the work of breathing is extreme," Edgar says, "and you may see things like heaving-type respiration, the abdomen protruding in and out because the diaphragm is pushing in a desperate effort to inflate lungs that are still and filled with liquid." Edgar likens pulmonary edema to "drowning from within, having your lungs fill with fluid and not being able to do anything about it," an experience he describes as "severe respiratory distress with associated sensations of drowning, asphyxiation, panic and terror."[137] Other medical professionals are more blunt: the sensation is the same as the torture technique known as waterboarding.[138]

Zivot and Edgar knew what they had found was important, but they needed a bigger data set to confirm their discovery, so they started collecting autopsies. One of the earliest public previews of that work was Edgar's review of the autopsy from Virginia's 2017 execution of thirty-nine-year-old Ricky Gray. Gray's execution, which lasted thirty-three minutes, used the three-drug protocol with midazolam as the first drug. Witnesses reported that Gray started making gasping, snoring, and snorting-type noises shortly after the midazolam was injected. "Once it got going, I saw more labored breathing that I have seen in the past, but I'm not sure of the significance of that," one media witness stated.[139]

Gray's autopsy connected the dots. "Blood-tinged fluid is present from the mouth," Edgar's report stated, and "the upper airways contain foamy liquid."[140] The presence of foamy liquid—froth—in the upper airways occurs in only the most severe cases. It's called "fulminate pulmonary edema," and it happens when the lungs are so full of fluid that the fluid spills out of the lungs and up into the throat and mouth. "I cannot know how the executioners intended or expected the drugs to work," Edgar told the press, but "the anatomic changes described in Ricky Gray's lungs are more often seen the aftermath of a sarin gas attack than a routine hospital autopsy."[141]

By 2018, Edgar had reviewed twenty-seven autopsies from midazolam executions—every autopsy available—and he presented his findings for the first time at a trial in Tennessee (we talked about those findings in chapter 2).[142] But Edgar had focused solely on midazolam. It would be another two years before the world would learn that the problem was not just midazolam. The problem was inherent in all lethal injection drugs.

In 2020, National Public Radio reported the findings of a study of over 200 execution autopsies collected from states across the country and reviewed by a team of experts in the field.[143] The study found that 84 percent showed pulmonary edema, and the phenomenon was found in every lethal injection protocol. The findings for executions using midazolam were not a surprise—30 of 36 documented pulmonary edema. The surprise was that pulmonary edema also showed up in 98 of 122 executions using sodium thiopental, 4 out of 4 executions using etomidate, and 49 of 58 executions using just a single shot of pentobarbital. Why was this happening?

The answer has to do with our body's pH balance, which runs between 7.35 and 7.45. Benzodiazepines like midazolam are highly acidic; their pH runs between 2.5 and 3.5, and that tsunami of acid is what damages the delicate membranes of the capillaries in the lungs, causing pulmonary edema, as we saw Greenblatt explain in chapter 2.[144] But barbiturates like pentobarbital and sodium thiopental are problematic in their own right—they are highly alkaline with a pH between 10–11, and that makes them caustic, which *also* destroys the delicate membranes of the capillaries in the lungs.[145] When these drugs are injected in small amounts, their pH isn't a problem because the body is very good at restoring pH balance. But lethal injection doesn't use small amounts, and the body can't buffer that pH fast enough to neutralize it before the drug reaches the lungs and starts doing its damage.

Turns out, pulmonary edema is a well-known complication of opioid and barbiturate overdoses more generally. "If we increase a dose of almost any medication and give it intravenously, you may have a thousand drugs capable of causing pulmonary edema when given at a higher than therapeutic dosage," a pulmonologist who has spent decades studying the relationship between drugs and damage to the lungs explains.[146]

The suffering associated with pulmonary edema isn't an issue when death comes almost immediately, as with animal euthanasia. Suffering takes *time*. And pulmonary edema doesn't occur when a drug is ingested orally, as with physician-assisted suicide, because when a drug enters the body through the stomach, the mechanism of absorption is vastly different than when it is injected directly into the bloodstream.[147] But we don't make prisoners drink the poison that will kill them. We strap them down and inject them with it instead, and that causes pulmonary edema.

Once the NPR study hit, prisoners began using it to challenge the one-drug protocol, and this is where the federal government makes a cameo appearance in our story. For the most part, the story of lethal injection is a story about executing states. But the waning days of the Trump administration brought a slew of federal executions, and the federal government chose the one-drug protocol to conduct them, so litigation over that protocol is a part of our story too.

In the 2020 litigation, prisoners presented yet another review of execution autopsies, this one focusing on executions using the one-drug pentobarbital protocol. Of the twenty-seven autopsies reviewed, seven failed to report on the lungs altogether, but of the remaining twenty, all twenty showed pulmonary edema. Indeed, in half of those twenty autopsies, the pulmonary edema was severe, and in three-fourths of the severe cases, the pulmonary edema was fulminate, with fluid in the upper airways.[148] "Flash pulmonary edema is a virtual medical certainty in any execution carried out under the federal government's pentobarbital protocol," the doctor who reviewed the autopsies wrote in her report.[149]

A federal court granted the prisoners a stay of execution, finding that they had "amassed an extensive factual record" that the one-drug protocol caused pulmonary edema and would inflict excruciating pain.[150] But the Supreme Court lifted the stay, allowing the federal government to execute the prisoners before their challenge to the protocol could go to trial, thus ending the litigation because the plaintiffs were dead.[151]

Two days after the Supreme Court lifted the stay, the United States executed Wesley Purkey. Officials stated that the execution was "humane" and "without any pentobarbital-related complications."[152] But Purkey's autopsy begged to differ. His lungs, which should have weighed 800–900 grams together, weighed over 1,100 grams *each*, and frothy liquid was found in his windpipe.[153] Purkey suffered from fulminate pulmonary edema as he died.

What are states—and the federal government in this instance—saying in response to the revelations of pulmonary edema? One thing they've said is that we don't have to worry about pulmonary edema because by the time it develops, the prisoner is dead. This is what the federal government's experts (who were also Oklahoma's experts) said in the 2020 litigation over pentobarbital, and the Supreme Court pointed to this claim when lifting the lower court's stay.[154]

But aside from duping the Supreme Court, this response hasn't gotten much traction, and for good reason: it is physically impossible to form froth in the lungs of a body that is dead. Froth is just a bunch of tiny air bubbles situated in fluid—it's a mixture of fluid and air—and as doctors have been quick to point out, if the person is dead, there's no air trying to get past the fluid to form froth in the first place.[155] For the body to form froth, air must be passing through the lungs, and not just once or twice. Froth can only form if the person is trying to *breathe*.

Another response—and this one is specific to litigation over midazolam—is that *something* is causing pulmonary edema in these executions, but it's not midazolam. Here we see a hodgepodge of alternative explanations. *It's the paralytic that's causing the problem, and we already knew that was a torturous drug.* Or, *It can't be midazolam causing pul-*

monary edema because we see it in pentobarbital executions too. Or, *The prisoner was choking on his tongue.* Or, *Nothing.* Just a claim that there's enough blood in the body to buffer the acid, such that "midazolam is not likely to produce pulmonary edema via an acid effect."[156] *It just won't.*

But these responses also haven't gotten much traction. We know that midazolam is the drug causing pulmonary edema because the second drug (the paralytic) stops breathing, and, again, you need breathing to make froth.[157] The fact that other drugs cause pulmonary edema as well does nothing to change that, nor does the fact that a prisoner was choking on his tongue (and apparently he was, but are we really to believe that all these prisoners were just choking on their tongues?). At this point, there is no serious debate about whether these drugs cause pulmonary edema, and no serious debate about whether it happens when the prisoner is still breathing.

The debate now has shifted to whether prisoners can feel it. State experts say that prisoners are "unconscious" by the time the pulmonary edema develops, so they are incapable of feeling pain.[158] But aside from the fact that unconscious does not mean insensate, state experts have it exactly backward—it's pulmonary edema that develops immediately, and the drugs that take time to reach their peak effect.

We've already talked about the time it takes for drugs like midazolam and pentobarbital to reach peak effect, but lest there be any doubt as to which happens first—the drug's effect or pulmonary edema—the science is unequivocal. "Lung injury starts immediately," Dr. Greenblatt says, explaining that when a drug is injected into the vein, it travels straight to the heart and then to the lungs, where it "will immediately begin causing irritation and damage to the pulmonary capillaries and lung tissues. . . . It will take at least a few circulations for that acid to mix and get buffered back to a 7.4 pH," Greenblatt says, but once the damage to the capillaries is done, it's done, so even after the drug is buffered, the lungs will continue to take on fluid.[159]

Worse yet, Greenblatt explains, the fact that the body has to buffer the pH of midazolam in order to absorb it means that "the sedative effect of midazolam will be delayed during that buffering process as well."[160] "The higher the dose, the greater the delay," he says, citing studies that document the phenomenon.[161] And what is true of midazolam because it is a strong acid is also true of pentobarbital because it is a strong base.[162] In both cases, a drug that is already too slow to meet the onset of pain will have an effect that is even slower.

Now we know why prisoners are gasping and heaving, coughing and convulsing, and showing other signs of respiratory distress on the gurney—and why we see this not only in midazolam executions (that is, before the paralytic shuts down breathing) but in pentobarbital executions too. Death penalty scholar Austin Sarat has documented over seventy accounts of prisoners suffering from severe respiratory distress in lethal injection executions across the country between 2010 and 2020 alone.[163]

In the 2020 litigation over pentobarbital, the federal government tried to deny that accounts of respiratory distress were in fact accounts of respiratory distress. The government's expert characterized what media witnesses were reporting as violent chest heaves as "hyperventilation due to the anxiety associated with impending death" that had "no relevance to pulmonary edema whatsoever."[164] The Associated Press did not let the claim go unanswered. One of its reporters had witnessed ten of the federal government's thirteen executions in its 2020 execution spree, and stated that as to the execution in question, the "stomach area heaved uncontrollably *immediately* after the pentobarbital injection [for] about a minute," and that this "distinctive jerking and jolting was visible in at least half the executions" he had witnessed.[165] Those violent heaves weren't just pre-execution jitters, the reporter insisted. They were an obvious and immediate response to the injection of a bolus overdose of pentobarbital.

As a fallback position, states say that even if prisoners are in fact heaving and gasping from pulmonary edema, they are doing so unconsciously. *Not to worry, it might look bad before the paralytic kicks in, but they can't feel a thing.* But we know that's not true either. Witnesses report seeing prisoners' eyes pop open and even seeing tears in their eyes. "It gave me the creeps," an anesthesiologist said upon reading one such account. "It's a classic sign of an anesthetized patient being awake."[166] They hear prisoners groan—at least where the sound hasn't been turned off in the execution chamber, as the federal government did with its 2020 executions—and they see prisoners grimace, clench their jaws, move their fingers and toes, and strain against the straps on the gurney.[167]

But even when we don't see prisoners struggling, that doesn't mean they are insensate any more than not seeing gasping and heaving means that they didn't suffer from pulmonary edema. The science is clear that people drugged to oblivion can consciously experience pain but be too sedated to express it, even without a paralytic.[168] Greenblatt says this is what is happening when an execution looks like it went smoothly but the autopsy says otherwise, insisting: "Any assessment that these executions were problem-free is incorrect as a matter of indisputable scientific fact."[169]

Perhaps this is why states have offered one final response to the mounting evidence that prisoners are consciously suffering from the waterboarding effects of pulmonary edema as they die: *so what*. "Even if inmates were conscious of the pulmonary edema later found in their autopsies," lawyers for Oklahoma argued in 2022, "the evidence is still insufficient to show they were sure or very likely in severe pain."[170]

Here, then, is the official response to revelations of pulmonary edema from lethal injection:

Pulmonary edema isn't a problem because the prisoners are already dead.
And if they aren't dead, the drugs we're injecting aren't the problem.
And if they are the problem, the prisoners can't feel it.
And if they can feel it, well, that's okay too.

States could have saved us all a lot of time by just owning their torturous executions in the first place.

And that goes for courts too, several of which have found that torturous pain isn't torturous enough. In the 2018 litigation in Tennessee, for example, the court found that "whatever pain the inmates felt did not last long enough to count as unconstitutional torture."[171] Similarly, the court in Oklahoma's 2022 *Glossip* case found that *if* in fact John Grant (the person who repeatedly threw up on the gurney) "did experience conscious pain and suffering as he was executed, the interval within which he would have experienced pain and suffering would have been very short—less (probably quite a bit less) than five minutes." The court went on to say:

> To be sure, the "pain and suffering" would have been more than negligible, mainly because, being strapped down in a supine position, Grant would have had no way to stop or otherwise alleviate the combined effect of simultaneously regurgitating and struggling to breathe. But the court concludes that pain and suffering of that duration and magnitude, if it occurred at all, falls short of the severity required, for Eighth Amendment purposes.[172]

More than negligible. As anesthesiologist Joel Zivot likes to say, "The easiest pain to bear is someone else's."[173]

Apropos the point, what one federal judge wrote in a 2008 Virginia lethal injection case is worth repeating here. He stated:

> From the comfort of a judicial bench, five minutes may pass quickly and without note. However, when in the course of five minutes a lethal chemical navigates a person's veins, rendering him incapable of breathing, let alone crying out in anguish, followed by a second deadly chemical, a salt that excruciatingly scorches the membrane of every blood vessel it touches as it travels the length of his circulatory system until finally stopping his heart, that same five minutes becomes a drastically longer period of time.[174]

Five minutes is a *long* time when you're being tortured to death, and executions by lethal injection take way longer than five minutes. We have now come full circle to the reason why prisoners are choosing to die by electrocution instead.

Would the American people authorize states to slowly suffocate prisoners to death, or burn them alive, or waterboard them as they die? It's a legitimate question, because that is exactly what states are doing with lethal injection. They are inflicting the modern equivalent of these horrific deaths. They're just doing it with drugs instead.

4

AN EXCEEDINGLY DELICATE, ERROR-PRONE PROCEDURE

In 2009, Rommel Broom became the first person in sixty years to survive his own execution.[1] For over two hours, executioners poked and prodded Broom to access his veins, sticking him with a needle eighteen times. Blood ran down Broom's arm, and one of the sticks hit his ankle bone, causing him to scream in pain. An executioner rushed out, answering "No" when asked if she was okay.[2] Broom, a former drug user, did his best to help, pointing out what he thought were good veins, flexing his arm and tugging on the rubber tourniquet to tighten it. Later he wept. Executioners were circling back to places they had already tried, inserting needles into bruised and bloody sites. Finally, they gave up. Executioners doubted they would be able to access a vein and were fatigued from trying. Broom died of COVID-19 before the state could try again.

Fast forward to 2022, when Alabama set a new record for the longest execution in US history and had *two* back-to-back failed attempts at executions by lethal injection. Problems accessing a prisoner's vein in Alabama and other states led *The Guardian* to dub 2022 "the year of the botched execution."[3] But those problems aren't new. Nor are they the only reason why states struggle to conduct executions by lethal injection.

Turns out, lethal injection is hard—as in *really* hard—to do. Lethal injection retains the delicacy of a medical procedure, with its demand for precision and attention to detail, but adds some things and takes away others, resulting in a Frankenstein version of the medical model. The result is an exceedingly delicate procedure that is also exceedingly error prone. The combination is a killer.

This is why lethal injection has the highest botch rate of any execution method in United States history. The average botch rate for other execution methods hovers around three percent. The botch rate for lethal injection is seven to eight percent—and that's just measuring the mishaps we can see.[4] To borrow from one executioner's articulation of the point, "Shit does happen."[5] Yes, yes it does, and here are the reasons why.

PREPARING THE EQUIPMENT

Lethal injection requires a number of medical instruments, so the first step in any execution by lethal injection is preparing the equipment. Departments of correction (DOCs) typically ask pharmacies to provide the equipment they need and may not tell them the purpose for which it is to be used, so any number of things can go wrong with even this most basic task. As we saw in chapter 1, the saline for Lockett's execution arrived in bags rather than syringes. The tubing was the wrong kind. The syringes weren't the right size, and neither were the needles, which played a key role in the disaster that was about to unfold.

We don't know how often these sorts of mistakes happen—Lockett's execution provided a rare insider's view. But the historical record documents a long list of errors when executioners are preparing the drugs. Some drugs arrive at the DOC in syringes, some don't. It depends on the source, and it depends on the drug. Therein lies the hitch: some lethal injection drugs don't come premade. They have to be mixed.

A prime example is sodium thiopental, the original first drug in the three-drug protocol. Sodium thiopental has to be mixed, and its use in lethal injection over the course of three decades left a well-developed record of what happens when prison personnel are charged with this task. As we'll see, prison personnel are still mixing lethal injection drugs today. We just don't have the same record of what is happening behind the scenes, so we'll use sodium thiopental as a case study to make the point.

Sodium thiopental comes in a powder that has to be reconstituted, a process that involves mixing it with a "diluent" (here, sterile water) to create a standard 2.5 percent injectable solution.[6] State experts said that reconstituting sodium thiopental was "as easy as mixing Kool-Aid."[7] But if the reconstituted solution was too diluted, prisoners would receive an underdose of the all-important first drug, and if it was too concentrated, the dose that prisoners would receive would be oversaturated, which likewise would prevent the drug from having its full effect. In Goldilocks fashion, reconstituting sodium thiopental had to be done *just right.*

Mixing sodium thiopental also required guarding against potential contaminants, which time would show to be their own cause of botched executions.[8] "Extreme care in preparation and handling should be exercised at all times to prevent the introduction of microbial contaminants," sodium thiopental's package insert stated, cautioning that the stability of the reconstituted drug "depends upon several factors, including the diluent, temperature of storage and the amount of carbon dioxide from room air that gains access to the solution."[9] That's not like mixing Kool-Aid.

Further complicating matters was the fact that some lethal injection protocols had their own instructions for reconstituting sodium thiopental, and they were different from the instructions on the package insert of the drug. For example, Tennessee's lethal injection protocol at one point called for five grams of sodium thiopental to be mixed in a fifty milliliter solution, resulting in a concentration of the drug that was 10 percent—*four times* the concentration designated in the packet insert for the drug.[10] When asked to clarify the state's process for reconstituting sodium thiopental— *Were executioners in Tennessee actually doing that?*—the warden answered, "Yes. Yes. There were 5 grams of sodium [thiopental] in one 50 cc syringe. Yes."[11] For those wondering whether sodium thiopental was even injectable at that concentration, the answer is apparently yes, although one shudders to think what prisoners in Tennessee were experiencing as a result.

Missouri's experience was disastrous in a different way. Missouri's lethal injection protocol called for a dose of five grams of sodium thiopental, but the chemical dispensary logs from executions showed that only 2.5 grams were being used. The prisoner next in line for execution sued. Attorneys for the state assured the court that five grams were being used, writing: "Defendants have stated consistently that 5 grams of sodium pentothal are used in executions in Missouri. Five grams are in fact used. The reference to the 2.5 grams noted in the drug log is not correct. . . . (Defendants are attempting to run down the source of the error in the record, and continue to do so.)"[12]

But the next day, the state wrote again to walk back that assertion. In a letter to the court, counsel for Missouri stated: "Upon further review, defendants have just determined this afternoon, contrary to previous representations, that 2.5 grams of sodium pentothal was prepared and used at the last execution (not 5 grams) and that 2.5 grams was prepared for use at the execution of plaintiff." The state understood the gravity of its mistake, writing: "Defendants and their counsel apologize to the Court and the parties for providing incorrect information."[13]

This led the court to allow a limited deposition of the doctor who prepared the drugs, who stated under oath:

> I determined to use 2.5 grams of sodium [thiopental]. This determination occurred because of the difficulty in dissolving the powder, obtained from a new supplier, containing more than 2.5 grams in the liquid that could be accommodated in a syringe. . . .
>
> I have to stick a needle through this plastic and inject my own diluents, which I know will give me no more than 50 ccs for the final product, which is what I'm aiming for in the final injection. We have encountered problems trying to mix more than three or four grams using this method, mainly because of an inert substance possibly put in by the manufacturer to prevent mis-mixing, which I know several drug companies do. . . . So right now we're still improvising.[14]

It's hard to say which is more frightening—the fact that the person preparing the drugs for lethal injection was "improvising," or the fact that he was using half the amount of the anesthetic on purpose because more than that wouldn't mix well.

On top of that, the doctor was reconstituting sodium thiopental at the wrong concentration. He was reconstituting 2.5 grams in a 50-milliliter solution, which yielded a 5 percent concentration of the drug rather than 2.5 percent.[15] Missouri was using *half* the dose of sodium thiopental called for in its protocol, at *twice* the concentration called for in the drug's package insert.

These sorts of mixing errors led courts in the early to mid-2000s to invalidate several state lethal injection protocols. In Missouri, for example, the fact that the state was improvising the amounts of lethal injection drugs led a federal court to rule that until remedial measures were taken, lethal injection was constitutionally impermissible.[16] In California, a federal court cited the state's improper mixing of lethal injection drugs as one of several reasons for finding a constitutional violation, explaining that "team members' admitted failure to follow the simple directions provided by the manufacturer of sodium thiopental further complicates the inquiry as to whether inmates being executed have been sufficiently anesthetized."[17]

Likewise, in Tennessee, a federal court ruled that the state was "deliberately indifferent" to the risk of excruciating pain in part because of the DOC's lackadaisical approach to mixing lethal injection drugs.[18] Turns out, the executioner with the most experience mixing sodium thiopental in Tennessee had learned by watching an executioner in Texas. A blue-ribbon committee appointed by the governor recommended that the DOC "employ a 'qualified person' to show the executioners how to mix sodium thiopental . . . a pharmacist, a nurse, or an anesthesiologist."[19] But the Tennessee DOC had ignored the recommendation, which then ripened into a constitutional violation.

Then came *Baze v. Rees* in 2008.[20] In *Baze*, the prisoners pointed to a litany of mistakes mixing sodium thiopental, but the Supreme Court was unmoved, finding "minimal risk of improper mixing if the manufacturers' thiopental package insert instructions were followed."[21] *Baze* single-handedly ended challenges to the mixing of lethal injection drugs, deciding once and for all (and against a mountain of evidence to the contrary) that the task was within the competence of prison personnel.

This is why the record on mixing lethal injection drugs is stunted outside the context of sodium thiopental: *Baze* shut down these claims. As a case in point, an appellate court in Tennessee vacated the trial court's finding of "deliberate indifference" in the wake of *Baze*. "Although medical experts testified that the State should employ an expert to advise the execution team on the mixing of the lethal injection chemicals," the appellate court wrote, "*Baze* rejected this requirement, noting that this task was not difficult."[22]

That brings us to 2023, when Tennessee's lackadaisical approach to mixing lethal injection drugs was once again in the news. An execution snafu had led Tennessee's governor to put executions on hold while an outside review of the state's lethal injection procedures was conducted, and that review revealed problems with the preparation of lethal injection drugs. Two decades later, history was repeating itself.

From the report produced by the outside review, we know that Tennessee's vecuronium bromide (the paralytic) comes "in a powder which would require reconstituting" and that the state's midazolam is compounded rather than manufactured, which requires storage at below freezing temperatures, then transfer to a refrigerator twenty-four hours before use, and then finally requires mixing with saline solution in a syringe.[23] All this, done by prison guards.

The report noted that those storage requirements were not being followed, and the only guidance that executioners received for preparing the drugs was a set of instructions from the pharmacy and a phone call with the pharmacist.[24] What happened on that call we don't know, but it was notable enough to make the report, which simply stated that the pharmacy's "impression from that phone call was that the members of the execution team they spoke with were inexperienced in preparing syringes for injection."[25] Four decades into lethal injection, prison personnel are still charged with reconstituting lethal injection drugs—controlled-substance injectables that require precision and careful handling—and they still don't know what they are doing.

Aside from all that, executioners have to calculate the right amount of powder to get the right dose of the drug, and then get that amount into the right syringes. Again, sodium thiopental provides an illustrative example. Sodium thiopental was available in kits that supplied the proper amount of diluent along with the powder, but even assuming that states used those kits and followed their directions (of note, Missouri did not), how many kits of sodium thiopental powder did it take to produce a two-, three-, or five-gram megadose for lethal injection? The package insert couldn't tell executioners that; they had to figure it out for themselves. A three-gram dose of sodium thiopental required six of the standard five-hundred-mg sodium thiopental kits, whereas a five-gram dose required ten, but how many kits a state needed varied with the amount of sodium thiopental in each kit and the amount designated in the protocol. Just imagine the opportunities this created for human error—error in calculating the correct number of kits, error in mixing one or more of those kits, error in transferring the solution from that number of kits into some other number of syringes.

And how does one go about filling the syringes? By and large, these are corrections department people. They don't know. Over time, they have learned by on-the-job training—a horrifying prospect in its own right—which is also to say that the early years of lethal injection were especially disastrous in this regard. To give just one example, executioners on several occasions tried to put two drugs in the same syringe. "It looks like the two drugs just don't mix," a state's DOC spokesperson stated in the wake of one such incident, adding that the drugs "get tacky and don't flow when they come together."[26]

This is what happened in the first execution by lethal injection in the United States: the warden put the first two drugs in the same syringe, and they promptly "coagulated to form a jelly-like substance."[27] Critics lambasted executioners for not knowing the basics of "IV 101." But a source familiar with the fiasco stated: "You know, give him a break! You've got a man who doesn't know anything about medical procedures and here he's doing something—he's totally out of his element."[28] That was 1982. But it could have been 2022 instead.

One last point about the syringes—lethal injection requires a lot of them. One might think, as I did, that the three-drug protocol takes three syringes. *One, two, three—how hard could this be?*

But that is not the case. Massive overdoses of drugs require massive amounts of volume to inject them. Most lethal injection protocols call for the large fifty- and sixty-milliliter syringes, but even then, the three-drug protocol requires nine to fifteen syringes, and the one-drug protocol requires at least two to three, and maybe as many as six, depending on the amount of pentobarbital being injected and the size of the syringe being used.[29]

Part of the reason for the hefty number of syringes in the three-drug protocol is that the drugs coagulate when they come into contact with each other, so executioners also need saline flushes between the drugs. To minimize confusion, a number of states color-code the syringes—a rather terrifying approach given that nearly ten percent of the male population has some degree of color blindness.[30] In practice, the color-coding system looks something like the picture in Figure 4.1, which came from the Oklahoma trial court's opinion in the 2022 *Glossip* case.[31] But the reason it was there is that prison officials had mislabeled one of the slots on the shadow board, and then used the mislabeled board in

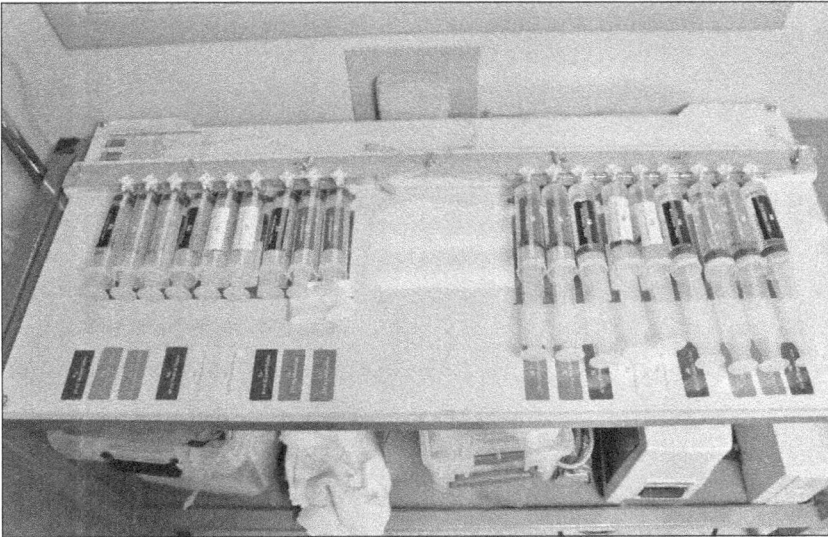

FIGURE 4.1. Oklahoma "Shadow Board"

three executions (maybe four). The device designed to prevent confusion had instead created it.

To be clear, the number of syringes used in lethal injection isn't a problem of its own. It's just an amplifier, multiplying the opportunities to get one or more of those syringes wrong—measured wrong, filled wrong, labeled wrong, ordered wrong, pushed wrong. The opportunities for error abound, and we're just getting started.

ACCESSING A VEIN

Once the equipment is ready, the execution can begin, and it begins by accessing the prisoner's vein. Executioners get IV access by inserting a catheter—a thin tube connected to a needle—into the vein and then removing the needle, leaving the tube in place. A catheter is the reason why executioners don't have to establish IV access each time they make an injection. With a catheter, they just have to do it once.

But inserting a catheter for lethal injection is notoriously difficult to do. Stories are legion of prisoners being pricked with a needle a dozen times or more in long, drawn-out attempts to access their vein.[32] Back in 1997, a Florida commission tasked with examining lethal injection reported that "difficulty locating a viable vein to establish an intravenous connection" was a common problem in executions by lethal injection.[33] Twenty-five years later, that is still true. A 2019 review of execution autopsies found that over half showed evidence of IV placement problems.[34]

But people do this every day—why is it so difficult in the lethal injection setting? Part of the difficulty owes to the stress of the situation. IV team executioners are under tremendous pressure. The entire execution hinges on their ability to set a proper IV, and if they don't do it right, the prisoner will suffer a torturous death. So the stakes are high, and people are watching—literally and figuratively. As we know from Clayton Lockett's execution, that sort of pressure can lead to mistakes (like forgetting the tape to secure a catheter in place), and even little mistakes can have big consequences.

For rather obvious reasons, prisoners about to be executed are stressed too, and that has physiological consequences of its own. Stress and anxiety cause a condition called "vasoconstriction"—constriction of the blood vessels—which makes finding a vein, and accessing it, difficult under any circumstances. (For those wondering why the people who take their blood are always so nice and conversational, a perusal of their training materials reveals that this is partly just business; fighting vasoconstriction with small talk is something they are trained to do.)[35]

But the main reason for the difficulty goes well beyond that. Condemned prisoners are often former IV drug users, and they tend to have poor general health from years of hard living, giving them notoriously weak and compromised veins. In addition, the death row population is aging, and their veins are more frail—a condition referred to in the medical literature as "age-related degeneration of connective tissues."[36] Now add the fact that morbid obesity, extreme muscularity, and heavily pigmented skin (all of which are common on death row) are widely recognized in the clinical setting as reasons why veins can be hard to find and access, and one begins to get a sense of just how challenging the task of setting an IV in the lethal injection setting can be.[37]

But nothing drives the point home like a good example, so consider Ohio's 2017 botched execution of Alva Campbell, the second person ever to survive an execution by lethal injection.[38] Campbell was sixty-nine years old at the time and suffered from lung cancer, prostate cancer, and respiratory problems, among other ailments. He received oxygen treatments four times a day, used a colostomy bag, and had to be brought to the death chamber in a wheelchair. Executioners even gave Campbell a pillow to prop up his head so he wouldn't have trouble breathing while they executed him. Lawyers had warned that Campbell's health was too poor to support an IV for lethal injection, but Ohio went forward with the execution anyway. Executioners spent an hour examining Campbell's veins in an effort to avoid failed attempts to find a suitable site, then spent another half-hour trying to insert a catheter, patting Campbell on the arm and shoulder to comfort him while they repeatedly stuck him with a needle. Finally, they gave up. Ohio set a new execution date, but, like Broom, Campbell died on his own before the state could kill him.

The same thing happened in Alabama the next year (that's right, Alabama's two failed executions in 2022 were not its first). In 2018, Alabama tried to execute sixty-four-year-old Doyle Lee Hamm. Hamm's lawyer warned that his veins were severely deteriorated from advanced cancer, hepatitis C, and years of drug use, and that it would be next to impossible to set an IV line, presenting medical testimony to back up the claim. But the state's doctor disagreed, going so far as to say that establishing IV access would be a "piece of cake."[39] It was not. For two and a half hours, executioners tried to find a vein, sticking Hamm eleven times. In the process, executioners almost certainly punctured Hamm's bladder, as he urinated blood for most of the next day, and almost certainly punctured his femoral artery as well, as Hamm bled profusely from one of the sticks to his groin area, soaking the pad and requiring a new one. Finally, executioners gave up. A DOC spokesperson told the press: "I wouldn't necessarily characterize what we had tonight as a problem."[40]

The same scene has played out time and again in completed executions too, and for a poignant example, consider Arizona's execution of Frank Atwood in 2022. "I have witnessed life. And I have witnessed death," one media witness wrote. "But nothing could have prepared me for the surreal spectacle I witnessed during the execution of Frank Atwood."[41]

Atwood, who was sixty-five years old and suffered from a degenerative spinal condition, had to be brought to the execution chamber in a wheelchair and propped up with a medical pillow while lying on the gurney. After some unknown number of attempts to insert a catheter, Atwood asked, "Could you try the hand? They have been able to go in there before." As relayed by the media witness: "The IV team members looked at each other, looked at Atwood, looked at each other again, and said, 'Sure, we'll give that a try.'"[42] It worked.

After the execution, the reporter tweeted: "THE EXECUTION TEAM MEMBERS RELIED ON ADVICE FROM THE MAN THEY WERE TRYING TO EXECUTE."[43] He later wrote: "I have looked behind the curtain of capital punishment and seen it for what it truly is: a frail old man lifted from a wheelchair onto a handicap accessible lethal injection gurney; nervous hands and perspiring faces trying to find a vein; needles puncturing skin; liquid drugs flooding a man's existence and drowning it out."[44] Having reviewed dozens upon dozens of accounts of executions, that sounds about right.

What emerges is a sense of the sheer futility of lethal injection—it is hard to imagine a more ill-suited way of executing a bunch of aging, ailing former drug users than a method that requires successfully tapping into their *veins*. Jay Chapman stands by the execution method. "But you have to have some skills to do it," he says. "You have to have the ability to find a vein and mix the drugs, because [some] come as a powder."[45] *So noted.* We'll come back to this point in the next chapter, when we talk about the skills that executioners *don't* have.

For now, it merits mention that back in 1954, Great Britain's Royal Commission on Capital punishment considered—and rejected—the idea of lethal injection largely on the basis of "anatomical difficulties."[46] If states had done any research at all before adopting lethal injection, perhaps they would have seen that report. Or perhaps they would have figured out for themselves that lethal injection is an especially ill-advised way of executing the demographic of prisoners on death row. But they didn't. So here we are.

What, then, are executioners to do when they have tried and failed to access a prisoner's vein? One option is to declare the execution a bust, and let the prisoner live to die another day. Ohio, Alabama—and as of 2024, Idaho—have all called it quits in the midst of an execution.[47]

The other option is to abandon the peripheral veins and attempt to access a central vein instead—typically the femoral vein in the upper thigh, next to the groin. Central veins are bigger and stronger, so they can withstand the trauma of a catheter insertion more easily. But there's always a hitch, and the hitch here is that central veins are buried deep under the surface, which makes accessing them even harder to do.

There are just two ways of accessing a central vein. One is a "cutdown." As noted in chapter 1, a cutdown cuts through the skin and underlying layers of tissue, fat, and muscle to expose the area immediately adjacent to a central vein so that a catheter can be inserted in much the same manner as it would be in a peripheral vein.[48] Because the incision is deep, cutdowns cause a good deal of bleeding, which in the clinical setting is controlled by the use of a ligatory suture (a fancy sewing-type maneuver) or cautery (a burning technique using chemicals or electricity to seal wounds from blood loss).[49] Cutdowns aren't something that just anyone—or even any doctor—can do. They are surgical procedures that require surgical skills and tools.

These days, cutdowns are rarely, if ever, used in the clinical setting, and a few years ago, one might have said this was true in the execution setting too. Then came 2022. The autopsy of Joe Nathan James (the man whose death at the hands of Alabama's executioners set a new record for the longest execution in US history) revealed "telltale signs of a cutdown," as well as telltale signs of pain: a jagged incision, suggesting that James had flinched as executioners cut him to access his vein.[50]

In addition, Arizona used a cutdown when it executed Clarence Dixon in 2022. Dixon was Arizona's first execution since its nearly two-hour long execution of Joseph Wood in 2014 (the man who was injected with the two-drug protocol fifteen times).[51] For twenty-five minutes, witnesses watched executioners try to access Dixon's veins, to no avail. Then they watched as executioners used a cutdown to access the femoral vein. "I did see what appeared to be some cutting into the groin," one media witness stated after the fact, adding, "They did have to wipe up a fair amount of blood."[52]

That said, most states have abandoned the cutdown in favor of a less bloody alternative: a catheter long enough to access a central vein from the surface. This kind of catheter—a "central line"—is the reason why cutdowns in the practice of medicine have become largely obsolete. A central line requires a bigger needle, a guide wire, and a number of extra steps.[53] Even in the clinical setting, placement of a central line is considered to be an exceedingly delicate procedure, with complications occurring 5 to 20 percent of the time (depending on the operator's experience and expertise).[54] Not surprisingly, complications occur more often in cases of "challenging patient anatomy," which, as we know, highly correlates with the population on death row.[55] "Central venous line placement is not to be undertaken lightly as a substitute for difficult peripheral venous access," one medical task force report cautions, noting that "the procedures involved usually require a high level of operator skill."[56]

And that's just the skill to insert the central line—we haven't talked about the skill required to find a central vein in the first place. How is an executioner supposed to know where to insert the needle when a central vein is too deep to feel or see? Surface anatomy can give the presumed location of a central vein, and doctors sometimes use the "landmark technique" to identify a central vein's location. But even in the clinical setting, the complication rate for that is 10 to 20 percent, which is why central line placements typically use an ultrasound to identify the location of a central vein and guide the needle, wire, and catheter placement.[57] But execution chambers aren't generally equipped with ultrasounds, and in any event, it turns out that using an ultrasound to place a central line requires substantial skill of its own, especially when placing a femoral line.[58]

What happens if executioners miss the femoral vein in their attempt to set a central line? The biggest risk is hitting the femoral artery, which is right next to the femoral vein. We saw this in Oklahoma's execution of Clayton Lockett and Alabama's attempted execution of Doyle Lee Hamm. Other complications include puncturing the bladder (here, again, Hamm's attempted execution is an example), or the bowels, or the femoral nerve. Perhaps this is why Arizona and Alabama went back to a cutdown. It might be crude and bloody and painful, but it requires less finesse than a central line.

Given the challenges of setting a central line, it is striking just how often executioners have resorted to it. In the 2020 review of autopsies noted earlier, a quarter of the autopsies reviewed—one in four—documented use of a femoral line.[59] A separate review of Arizona's executions in 2022 revealed that eleven of the state's most recent sixteen executions—two-thirds—used a femoral line, and six required more than one stick to insert it.[60] A central line is not an executioner's first choice. It is their last resort, and this too tells us something about just how hard it is to access a prisoner's peripheral vein.

Thus far, we have assumed that executioners know when they have missed the vein that they are trying to access. That is why they keep trying. But what if they don't know that they have missed the vein? What if they *think* they are in, but they aren't?

If the mistake is hitting an artery rather than a vein, executioners are going to know, and so will everyone else because it will make a bloody mess. Arteries are how the heart gets blood to the rest of the body—they pulsate blood with each beat of the heart (which is why you press on an artery to take your pulse). That's a mistake that would be hard to miss.

The same cannot be said for IV insertion errors where the catheter does not go deep enough into the vein, so it slips out during insertion, or where a catheter goes so deeply into the vein that it goes in and out the other side. In both instances, the catheter ends up delivering the drugs into tissue, rather than the bloodstream, a problem known as "infiltration." Infiltration is not only exceedingly painful, but also exceedingly problematic for an execution method that relies on drugs coursing through a prisoner's veins.

States say we don't have to worry about infiltration because executioners would know if the catheter is not properly sited in the vein. They claim it would be "obvious to an average person"[61] because there would be fluid buildup around the injection site—and that may well be true (although it also might not be, for reasons we'll talk about shortly). But the question is not whether executioners would know once the problem becomes obvious. The question is whether they would know *before* the damage is done, and the answer to that is no.

Two botched executions in 2006—one of which is among the most famously botched executions in the history of lethal injection—illustrate the point. The first (and less known) of the two is Ohio's botched execution of Joseph Clark. Clark's execution lasted ninety minutes, during which time he was punctured nineteen times (at one point he reportedly asked, "Can't you just give me something by mouth to end this?").[62] Executioners thought they had finally established IV access after trying for thirty minutes, but they were wrong. As the drugs started flowing, Clark started convulsing and raising his head, saying, "It don't work. It don't work."[63] Turns out, the catheter had not been properly sited in his vein. Executioners didn't know. The man they were executing had to tell them.

The other example is Florida's famously botched execution of Ángel Díaz later that same year. For twenty-four minutes of his thirty-four-minute execution, Díaz squinted, clenched his jaw, attempted to speak, and struggled to breathe. "It seemed like Ángel Díaz would never die," one media witness wrote.[64] Florida officials stated after the fact the execution took longer than expected because Díaz suffered from liver disease, and that slowed the effect of the chemicals.[65] But that wasn't true. The state's own autopsy reported that Díaz's liver was just fine, and doctors were quick to point out that if his liver had been diseased, that would have expedited the poisoning process, not prolonged it. What the autopsy did show, however, was that the catheter in each of Díaz's arms had gone in and out the other side of his vein, sending drugs into the surrounding tissue from the start. This caused massive chemical burns on each arm—blisters filled with "watery pink tinged liquid" measuring 12" × 5" on one arm, and 11" × 7" on the other.[66] Díaz had "the kind of injury we see when a kid has fallen into a campfire," one doctor stated, adding that he would have needed skin grafts had he survived.[67] In addition, Díaz's autopsy revealed "bilateral jugular venous distention"—bulging jugular veins in the neck—showing forensically what witnesses already knew to be true: Ángel Díaz was conscious as the paralytic set in, straining to gasp increasingly shallow gulps of air.[68]

Grotesque pictures of soggy, broken flesh falling off of huge swaths of subcutaneous tissue flooded the internet.[69] "Killer's Skin Rips and He 'Chokes for Air' in 'Worst Botched Execution Ever,'" the headline of the UK's *Daily Mirror* blared.[70] Florida put executions on hold, and eventually the outrage subsided. It spiked again in 2014 when *The New Republic* did a feature on the Díaz execution after the botched execution of Clayton Lockett.[71]

Did executioners not see the massive blisters on Díaz's arms? They either didn't see or didn't care (or some combination of both), but the point here is that the catheter was improperly placed from the start and the problem was not apparent until it was literally apparent. By the time these sorts of catheter problems are discovered, it will always be too late.

IV insertion problems cause a *lot* of suffering for an execution method whose brand is a humane death, and it raises a question: How much is too much? At what point do a state's protracted efforts to establish IV access violate the Eighth Amendment? "Is it 10 pokes? Is it 11? Is it 100? Is it one hour?" a judge asked Alabama's lawyers in 2022 as the state pushed for more executions even as it left a trail of botched ones in its wake.[72] Whatever the limit, states apparently haven't hit it yet, as courts thus far have refused to intervene.

This has left states to do as they please, and their response to the challenges of accessing a vein has been twofold. One is Alabama's move in 2022: simply extend the time to carry out an execution beyond midnight on the date of the death warrant, when the state's authority to take a life would otherwise expire. After a review of its procedures in 2022, Alabama gave itself the ability to take as long as the governor allows to execute a prisoner. "More time is worse," one prisoner's attorney told a court. "It could mean unending torture."[73] "You ever hear that expression a death by a thousand cuts?" another attorney asked, adding: "Whatever you call this lethal injection business—it may be worse."[74]

The other move is one that twenty-two of the nation's twenty-seven death penalty states have made: simply hide the IV insertion process from public view. Virginia adopted this policy in the wake of its thirty-minute-long execution of Ricky Gray in 2017, and kept it until the state abolished the death penalty in 2021. Critics called the new policy "outrageous" in light of the questions raised by Gray's prolonged execution, saying that it "clearly related to a desire to prevent the public from seeing what might go wrong."[75] But the Virginia DOC insisted that its decision to change its decades-old practice was business as usual. "The department periodically updates its internal policies," a spokesperson stated, and this happened to be one of those occasions.[76]

From time to time, lawyers have been known to find out what happened during the IV insertion process anyway, and Arizona's execution of Robert Towery in 2012 provides a memorable example. At the time of Towery's execution, witnesses were not allowed to see the IV insertion process (that has since changed), and his lawyer worried about what might happen behind closed doors. The lawyer instructed Towery to ask for counsel if the IV insertion process went seriously awry. Officials had already warned Towery that his microphone would be cut off if he said anything untoward in his last words—another prisoner in another state had blurted out "They butchered me back there!"[77]—so Towery and his lawyer worked out a code. Towery would use the word "mistake" in his last statement if there were IV insertion mishaps, and if he was denied access to counsel, he would mention his attorney by name. When the execution date came and it was time for his last words, Towery stated that he had made "mistake after mistake after mistake" in his life, adding, "Hey Dale, I should have called you."[78] His autopsy revealed nine puncture wounds from the state's repeated attempts to gain IV access, and a cutdown to the femoral vein. It was later learned that it took executioners nearly an hour to set Towery's IV.

INJECTING THE DRUGS

Once executioners have established IV access, they can inject the drugs, and this step of the execution process has given rise to a variety of random mishaps. Executioners have administered the wrong drug. They have administered the right drugs in the wrong order. They have administered the right drugs, in the right order, but without a saline flush between the drugs, causing the drugs to coagulate—this time in the tubing rather than the syringe. Executioners have even administered the right drugs, in the right order, and with a saline flush, but fastened the prisoner's restraining straps too tightly to allow the flow of the drugs.

Lest one think these are just rookie mistakes, Oklahoma alone has made two of these errors within the last decade, one as recently as 2023. In 2015, the state injected Charles Warner with the wrong drug during his execution (and almost did it again, as we'll see in chapter 8).[79] And in 2023, it secured the restraining straps on Anthony Sanchez's wrists so tightly that his fingers "turned a sickening shade of blue."[80] Executioners realized that something was wrong when they injected the drugs and nothing happened. "You could tell there was a little bit of panic setting in. They were scared," one execution witness stated.[81] Perplexed executioners "bustled around" checking this and that, then noticed that Sanchez's hand was blue and loosened the restraint. It worked. After the fact, a DOC spokesperson denied that anything had gone wrong, stating: "The restraints were not too tight on Sanchez, nor did they cut off circulation."[82] But the witness, a spiritual advisor who had also witnessed other executions, vehemently disagreed. Sanchez's hand was *blue*. "I know what an execution, a lethal injection, is supposed to look like," he said, and this wasn't it. "It's still very clear that they don't know what they're doing," he said. "They continue to make mistakes."[83]

These are the little things, a sprinkling of random mishaps that show just how delicate lethal injection is. Even the smallest mistakes are enough for an entire execution to go off the rails. But those mistakes pale in comparison to the things that routinely go wrong when executioners push the syringes of the drugs.

As we know, lethal injection uses bolus dosing, which (again) just means that executioners are injecting the entire amount of a drug at once. Bolus dosing is inherently tricky because it can cause a "blowout," which is what happens when a vein collapses from the pressure of a large volume of fluid being injected into the vein at once. "Whenever you are doing large amounts of bolus injections, you run the risk of IV disruption much more than otherwise," one doctor explains.[84]

The risk is especially high in the lethal injection setting for several reasons. The first is vein fragility. "The elderly have fragile skin and veins which may rupture on injection," one critical care journal states, and old age is not the only thing that makes the veins of death row prisoners fragile—years of drug use and poor general health are contributing factors too.[85] Weak, damaged veins are especially susceptible to collapsing from the pressure of a bolus injection of drugs because they're not strong in the first place. Turns out, the same factors that make a condemned prisoner's veins difficult to access also make them difficult to inject with a bolus dose of a drug.

The sheer size of the bolus dose being injected is another contributing factor. Again, massive amounts of drugs require massive amounts of volume to administer them. This means that the pressure being exerted on the vein in a lethal injection is especially high, creating a treacherous combination: strong pressure on weak veins. It's a recipe for disaster, but not before adding one last ingredient—operator error.

As we'll see in chapter 5, the people pushing the syringes in a lethal injection are nonmedical prison guards. They are not medical professionals trained on how to push a syringe so as not to blow the vein, and they're not pushing the syringes bedside, as in the clinical setting. They're in another room—an anteroom next to the execution chamber, with a hole in the wall so that a long tube can carry the drugs from one room to another. This setup requires around seventy-two inches (five feet) of tubing and that creates problems of its own. Leaks, kinks, clogs, problems with extension sets and connectors—lethal injection has seen it all. Long tubing is just another opportunity for a myriad of things to go wrong.

The fact that executioners are pushing the drugs from another room is treacherous not only because it necessitates the use of long tubing to deliver the drugs, but also because the distance makes it exceedingly difficult for executioners to know if they're pushing the plunger on the syringes too hard, which would inject the drugs too rapidly, causing a blowout. In the clinical setting, practitioners are trained to pay especially close attention to "tactile feedback" when pushing a syringe—subtle resistance that tells them to slow down so they don't blow the vein.[86] In the lethal injection setting, executioners say that they also push the syringes "by feel," but even if they had that sort of professional training, they don't have the sort of tactile feedback needed to do it.[87] Clayton Lockett's execution is a prime example. By the time one of the executioners said, "It's tough to push the plunger right now," Lockett had a bulge the size of a golf ball in his thigh.[88] Pushing the syringes from another room mutes any feedback that executioners would otherwise get by buffering it with five feet of line. Executioners are essentially pushing these drugs in the blind.

As a testament to just how hard this part of the process is, it merits mention that for a time, states experimented with a lethal injection "machine," a device that purported to push the plunger on the syringes just right. "Texas has done more than forty lethal injections, and about eighty percent of these executions have had one problem or another," the man who invented the device, Fred Leuchter, explained.[89] What happened to the lethal injection "machine" is a story all its own told in chapter 7, but to whet the appetite, it suffices to say that Leuchter's work ended when he was criminally charged with fraud.[90]

One last point merits mention here, and it goes to the poor conditions under which executioners are working in the anteroom. Sometimes these rooms are lit by a small lamp or red light. Other times executioners use flashlights to see what they are doing. Although there is a window between the anteroom and execution chamber, the window is heavily tinted or covered by blinds to prevent anyone from seeing the executioners who are pushing the drugs, so it isn't providing executioners with much light.

To appreciate the point, consider again the doctor-executioner who was using half the amount of sodium thiopental called for in Missouri's protocol because more than that wouldn't mix well in a fifty-milliliter syringe.[91] But why not just use more than one syringe? Lawyers asked that question, and here was his answer: "The people who do the injections are nonmedical and they're in the dark so they have a small flashlight [so] that they're able to quickly identify the syringes, make the appropriate connections and injections, disconnect, clamp the tube . . . Changing the number of syringes or the order of syringes was an unnecessary risk."[92] The task of pushing the drugs involves a number of subtasks, and those are opportunities for things to go wrong too.

That brings us back to infiltration—when a drug is injected into a prisoner's tissue rather than vein. Drugs might infiltrate if the catheter is not properly sited in the vein in the first place, or if an injection causes the vein to collapse. We've now talked about both. But infiltration can also occur if executioners push too hard on the syringes when they are injecting the drugs, causing the catheter to pop out of the vein and spill its contents into the surrounding tissue.

Sometimes when a catheter dislodges, the problem is obvious. A classic example is Texas's botched execution of Raymond Landry in 1988. There, executioners pushed the syringes so hard that the catheter dramatically popped out of Landry's vein and sprayed drugs across the room.

Other times, the problem is obvious only to the prisoner being executed. An example is Texas's execution of Joseph Cannon in 1998. Cannon's catheter popped out as soon as executioners started pushing the drugs, but they didn't know it until Cannon told them. After resetting the line, executioners allowed Cannon to give a second final statement so that his last words would not be "It's come undone."[93]

Yet other times, the problem is not obvious to anyone—at least not until it's too late. Even in the clinical setting, where the infiltration rate from "catheter slippage" is a whopping 10 to 30 percent, trained practitioners often miss early signs that an IV has become dislodged.[94] Turns out, the body has a number of cavities where fluid can pool undetected, at least for a time. One of these cavities happens to be the go-to spot for setting a catheter in lethal injection: the "antecubital fossa." The antecubital fossa is in the crook of the arm, on the front side of the elbow, and the fact that it offers a sizable cavity where a drug might easily infiltrate undetected makes it a particularly inopportune spot for lethal injection (anyone who knows basic anatomy would know this—the word "fossa" literally means cavity or space).

In the clinical setting, the risk of infiltration is managed with careful monitoring.[95] Lethal injection takes the opposite approach.

MONITORING THE EXECUTION

States monitor executions by lethal injection from two locations. One is the executioner's anteroom—the room adjacent to the execution chamber where executioners are pushing the drugs. Often (but not always), one of the executioners in the anteroom is assigned the task of monitoring the execution for signs of trouble through a window between the two rooms. This is a challenge.

Courts have repeatedly found the conditions of the anteroom grossly inadequate for monitoring an execution happening in the next room. In Missouri, for example, a court found that there was "little or no monitoring" from the anteroom because executioners couldn't see the prisoner's face, and "there are blinds on the window which are partially closed and obstruct the view."[96] In Tennessee, a court concluded that monitoring from the anteroom was inadequate because the executioner assigned to that task was "also charged with handing, in the proper order and in rapid fashion, eleven numbered syringes to the executioner who injects them into the IV line, and with receiving back from him, in turn, empty syringes."[97] And in California, a court found that "the lighting is too dim, and the execution team members are too far away, to permit effective observation of any unusual or unexpected movements" from the anteroom, concluding that "overcrowding, obstructed sight lines, and poor lighting . . . make accurate observations of the inmate during an execution extremely problematic."[98] If effective monitoring is going to happen, it's not going to come from another room. We'll need to go to the execution chamber for that.

States monitor an execution from inside the execution chamber in two ways. One is known as a "conscious check." A member of the execution team (typically a doctor, but not always) applies some sort of stimuli—pinching the prisoner, brushing their eyelashes, rubbing their sternum, or maybe just calling their name. If the prisoner responds, they are still conscious. If they don't, they are declared "unconscious" and the execution proceeds.

The problem with a conscious check, of course, is that it can only tell whether a prisoner is unconscious. It cannot tell whether a prisoner is unconscious at a depth where they are insensate to pain. On this point, what a doctor said in chapter 3 bears repeating here: "A patient asleep might not awaken to calling their name, or the stroke of the eyelashes or a pinch to the finger, but would certainly awaken to a blowtorch applied to the skin."[99] Lethal injection is the blowtorch in this scenario. Conscious checks are checking the wrong thing.

This is not to say that conscious checks have no value whatsoever. Conscious checks at least tell us whether a prisoner is still conscious (in which case they are most definitely *not* insensate). And conscious checks at least make executioners pause after the injecting the first drug, which gives the drug time to take effect that it otherwise would not have. Thus, while conscious checks don't do what observers think they do—they don't ensure that the prisoner is insensate to pain—they do two other pretty important things, which makes the fact that states don't have to do them at all especially lamentable.

In *Baze v. Rees*, the Supreme Court upheld what is known as the "rapid flow" method of lethal injection, greenlighting states to inject one drug immediately after the other.[100] As Justice Ginsburg noted in her *Baze* dissent, Kentucky had no excuse (and did not even try to offer one) for not at least pausing to see if prisoners were unconscious before injecting them with the excruciatingly painful second and third drugs.[101] A conscious check costs nothing and is easy enough to do. Even the most strident pro–death amicus brief in *Baze* argued that if the Court changed anything, "the only change required should be the addition of a conscious check."[102] But the Justices refused to do even that. Conscious checks could not make the "fine distinctions" that prisoners argued were necessary to ensure they were insensate to pain, the Justices reasoned, so states were not obligated to do them at all.[103]

The other monitoring that occurs inside the execution chamber is done by the warden. The warden is close to the prisoner, has an unobstructed view, and is specifically charged with monitoring the execution for mishaps. But wardens aren't medical professionals, which means that their ability to detect apparent problems is limited to problems that are apparent.

In the clinical setting, anesthesiologists look for subtle signs that an unconscious patient is still sensate. "The quick little motion at the ankle, small little movement of the fingers. . . . those are the areas of the body that the mind has the most control over," one anesthesiologist explains, so "they tend to be the ones that kind of express a certain regaining of consciousness early on." But recognizing such subtleties is "not something that you can teach to someone in a practice run through a prison ward," he goes on to say. "And it's not something that other physicians who are not anesthesiologists, who haven't seen a thousand or ten-thousand patients go to sleep, can necessarily just impart to a physician who practices in a different specialty."[104]

Now consider the answer that Kentucky's warden gave when asked how he'd determine whether an unconscious prisoner was still sensate: "I honestly don't know what you'd look for."[105] Wardens observing an execution know to look for one thing—visible signs of suffering. That's a problem not only because visible signs of suffering come too late, but also because once the paralytic takes effect, there won't be any.

States' use of a paralytic in lethal injection is more akin to *anti-monitoring*, and states engage in anti-monitoring in other ways as well. Tennessee's 2018 execution of Billy Ray Irick is a prime example. We met Irick briefly in chapter 2—he was the first prisoner executed after Tennessee's trial on midazolam.[106] All eyes were on Irick when the state was given the green light to execute, and, as we know, Irick turned purple and choked, coughed, and gasped for air as he died, straining against the restraints on the gurney. Not yet noted is that prison officials taped Irick's hands and fingers to the gurney, even though his wrists were already in tight restraints. "A trained observer knows that if a patient moves his fingers or hands, that is a clear indicator that they are not anesthetized," an anesthesiologist told the press, adding: "The taping of Mr. Irick's hands affirmatively prevented the warden from observing an important indicator that Mr. Irick was not anesthetized."[107] Why the state felt the need to tape Irick's hands it did not say, but perhaps Tennessee was taking its cues from Florida, which taped William Happ's hands when it conducted the nation's first execution with midazolam in 2013.[108]

Some say that concerns about monitoring are overblown. "This is an execution, not a surgery," Justice Scalia quipped during the oral arguments in *Baze*.[109] Monitoring mattered in the clinical context, Scalia argued, because there "you expect to bring the person back." In the execution context, you don't.

But this reflects a fundamental misunderstanding of the purpose of monitoring an execution. Monitoring matters not because states care about the prisoner waking up—they don't—but because they care (or at least should care) about whether the prisoner is actually asleep. It's the deep sleep of anesthesia that makes lethal injection even plausibly humane, and the only way to know whether a prisoner is ostensibly in that state is by monitoring.

Granted, monitoring only matters if executioners know what to do if something goes wrong, and all too often, they don't. Clayton Lockett's execution amply illustrated the point, but another memorable example is what one of Tennessee's executioners told interviewers in 2022. When asked what he would do if a prisoner showed signs of suffering, this executioner answered with depressing candor, "I wouldn't know." He added: "It ain't like I'm going to stop it unless the warden—unless the warden tells me to stop. . . . I'm not stopping once it starts. It's like a plane taking off. There's no stopping unless the warden tells me to stop."[110] Obviously, monitoring for mishaps doesn't matter when known mishaps would change nothing. But what an admission for the state to make.

"I don't know why they are so bad at this," one doctor said of the litany of errors that plague lethal injection.[111] We now know part of the answer: lethal injection is an exceedingly delicate, error-prone procedure. But an equally important part is who is doing it.

5

INEPT EXECUTIONERS

As we now know, lethal injection would pose challenges for even the most competent of medical professionals. But the people conducting executions by lethal injection are not the most competent of medical professionals. All too often, they are not competent—or medical professionals—at all.

People think (I did) that doctors are conducting executions by lethal injection. Not so. The typical lethal injection is conducted by minimally trained medical technicians and non-medical prison guards. Some are clearly unfit to carry out the state's most awesome exercise of sovereign power. Others are woefully unqualified. Still others are simply untrained. Putting all that together yields another piece of the lethal injection puzzle: inept executioners.

THE EXECUTIONERS WE KNOW

Some executioners we know because lethal injection litigation or investigative journalism has revealed their identity. Here is where we see who states consider qualified to carry out their most solemn task. What vetting do states do when selecting executioners? Consider who they choose.

For example, Missouri's chief executioner from 1995 to 2006 was Dr. Doe I—a.k.a. Dr. Alan Doerhoff. Doerhoff was responsible for fifty-four of Missouri's sixty-five executions between 1976 and 2006. He didn't push the syringes—prison guards did that—but he did most everything else. "Nobody will ever do as many [executions] as I have," he would later tell the press.[1]

We met Doerhoff in chapter 4—he was the doctor who was administering half the dose of sodium thiopental called for in the state's lethal injection protocol.[2] But that was not the most explosive revelation in his deposition testimony. When questioned about his mixing calculations, Doerhoff admitted, "I sometimes transpose numbers. . . . I am dyslexic," he explained, "so, it's not unusual for me to make mistakes."[3] (For the record, Doerhoff later stated that he was *not* dyslexic, he just sometimes mixed up numbers.)[4]

Missouri doubled down on the doctor, telling a federal court that it was "confident in Dr. Doe I's competence" and planned to continue to employ him to conduct executions by lethal injection.[5] But the court rejected its assurances in a 2006 ruling, writing:

> The Court . . . is gravely concerned that a physician who is solely responsible for correctly mixing the drugs which will be responsible for humanely ending the life of condemned inmates has a condition which causes him confusion with regard to numbers. As the Court has learned, the process of mixing the three different drugs and knowing the correct amount of the drugs to dissolve in the correct amount of solution involves precise measurements and the ability to use, decipher, and not confuse numbers.[6]

The court ruled that Missouri could not use the doctor "in any manner, at any level" in its executions by lethal injection. The state appealed, but wrote the appellate court after oral arguments to say that it would not be using Dr. Doe I in executions going forward.[7]

By then, investigative journalism had discovered the doctor's identity, and with it came another revelation: Doerhoff had been sued for medical malpractice over twenty times, and his hospital privileges had been revoked at two hospitals. Doerhoff had also been publicly reprimanded by the state medical board for hiding his malpractice suits from the hospitals where he practiced. All of this was known to the Missouri attorney general's office when it assured the court of Doerhoff's professional competence.[8]

The following year, Missouri's legislature passed a law stating that "a person may not . . . knowingly disclose the identity of a current or former member of an execution team," authorizing punitive damages for violations.[9] "It's not in a vacuum that the legislature acted to cover up and hide who's involved in executions," an ACLU lawyer observed, stating: "Their answer to the public finding out they had an incompetent doctor was making it impossible to find out who the doctor is."[10]

Upon his exit as Missouri's executioner, Doerhoff joined the staff of a local hair-removal business, and served as an executioner for the federal government and another state.[11] "The federal government chose to rely upon the only person in the country who has been explicitly barred by a federal court from participating in lethal injection executions," an amicus brief later wrote of the irony.[12] But Doerhoff took the continued work as a compliment, telling an interviewer that "federal and state authorities came to him because they were impressed with the fail-safe, three-drug system Missouri developed under his leadership."[13]

Missouri's experience brings us to Arizona, because Arizona was where Doerhoff went next to work as an executioner. Arizona knew what had happened in Missouri—it knew about the trial court's ruling and the malpractice suits behind it. But it hired Doerhoff anyway, and he conducted an execution for the state in 2007, just months after being barred from conducting executions in Missouri. When capital defense attorneys found out about it (there's a story as to how that happened), the prisoners next in line for execution sued.[14]

Arizona settled that suit in 2009, agreeing to a number of changes in its lethal injection protocol, including formal background and license checks of its executioners. But during the litigation, Arizona had said it was already conducting those checks, and discovery had revealed that Doerhoff wasn't the only executioner who had no business conducting executions. One of Arizona's three IV team executioners was Medical Team Member #3. Here is how a federal court described him:

Medical Team Member #3 did not attend medical school, was once a nurse, had his nursing license suspended, attended emergency medical technician training, and is not a licensed emergency medical technician. He now owns an appliance business in a state outside of Arizona. Following military service in Iraq, he has been treated by the Veteran's Administration for post-traumatic stress disorder. He has been arrested multiple times, including three times in ten days in Arizona for a DUI in 2007.[15]

In its settlement agreement, Arizona pledged to use only licensed medical personnel going forward, but the prisoners claimed that the state wasn't credible in this regard—the Department of Corrections (DOC) had said that it was already doing that, which turned out not to be true. But a federal court sided with the state in the skirmish. "Although plaintiffs may be skeptical about defendant's assurances," the court reasoned, "the record does not establish that defendants likely will fail to comply with the Arizona protocol in future medical team selections."[16] Let bygones be bygones.

Fast forward to 2011, when Arizona was back in federal court because the state had not made good on its promise. The DOC director admitted to conducting *five* executions with full knowledge that new Medical Team Member #4 did not hold a medical license of any kind.[17] The DOC also did not conduct a criminal history check on this team member. If it had, it would have learned that he had been charged with DUI in 2008, public intoxication in 2000, and writing a bad check before that. Medical Team Member #4 was a prison guard who had previously served as a medical corpsman in the military. He stated that his only screening was a phone call from the warden "asking whether he knew how to start an IV and whether he would have a problem doing it for an execution."[18] He was not asked any other questions, and at the time, he had not placed an IV in fifteen years. On paper, Arizona was dutifully screening its execution team members. But in reality, the state was doing nothing of the sort.

Lest one think Missouri and Arizona are exceptional in this regard, consider California. In 2006, a federal court struck down the state's lethal injection protocol, citing "inconsistent and unreliable screening of execution team members" as one of five reasons why.[19] Turns out, the execution team member responsible for the custody of lethal injection drugs had been disciplined for smuggling drugs into San Quentin before joining the execution team; two team members had been arrested for drunk driving; one suffered from depression and PTSD; and one had been out on a two-month medical leave from getting into a fight with a prisoner.[20] "Given that the state is taking a human life," the court stated, "the pervasive lack of professionalism . . . is deeply disturbing."[21]

And that's not all. The court also noted the "extremely troubling" disappearance of sodium thiopental that was ostensibly taken from the prison pharmacy for training purposes but never used and never returned. "These circumstances may warrant investigation by an appropriate law-enforcement agency," the court stated.[22] In California, the executioners were not just unfit—they were the chief suspects in a potential criminal investigation as well.

The federal government one-upped California when it hired a nurse for the Timothy McVeigh execution who had been charged with felony aggravated stalking and first-degree tampering with property, ultimately pleading no contest to the misdemeanor version of both charges. The nurse had left voice messages threatening a man who was seeing his estranged wife, saying "I'll burn your [expletive] house down and blow your [expletive] head off!" and also had smashed the windshield and headlights of the man's truck, ran over his mailbox, and smashed some windows of his home.[23] Federal officials knew of the convictions when it hired him—the nurse was on active probation and had to get permission from his probation officer to leave the state. "It seems bizarre to me that we would knowingly allow an offender, on active supervision, to participate in the execution process at any level," a probation supervisor had written while the department was considering the request.[24] But the permission was granted. In an internal memo, the administrator who confirmed the request for travel wrote: "It would be extremely problematic for [the nurse] and this department if the media got wind of this."[25]

And how did this nurse even get on the federal government's radar? He was recommended by Missouri's DOC. A nurse with his own serious criminal convictions was secretly conducting executions on behalf of the show-me state.

Lethal injection litigation in other states has likewise led to the revelation of executioners who are patently unfit for the job. In Maryland, for example, litigation revealed that one member of the state's execution team had been fired by a local police department and charged with poisoning several neighborhood dogs, while another execution team member had been suspended for spitting in prisoners' food.[26] In Tennessee, litigation revealed that a member of the execution team had pled guilty, twice, to possession of a controlled substance, and missed a scheduled execution because he was at an in-patient alcohol treatment program.[27] That was 2007. For a more recent example, we learned in 2021 that Tennessee's physician-executioner surrendered his surgery accreditation because of "too many malpractice suits"—at least ten by his estimation.[28] And for an even more recent example, try Alabama, which proudly announced that it was adding three medical technicians and a nurse to its execution team after its spate of botched executions in 2022, only to have lawyers tell a judge that they believe they have discovered the identity of one of these new team members—a person with multiple arrests for fraud and several civil judgments against them.[29]

These are just the executioners we *know*. But they are a chilling indication of the executioners we don't know. "Executioner jobs do not necessarily attract the best and brightest," one exposé on executioners observed.[30] But an even more telling comment came from the former head of Oklahoma's DOC in 2023. If Oklahoma continued to conduct executions, he told a legislative committee, "I'm guaranteeing you that you're going to have other botched executions." The prison staff charged with carrying out executions are "some of the lowest-paid state employees in government," he stated, adding: "It just takes one who doesn't do their job properly."[31] In executions, as elsewhere, you get what you pay for. No matter how good the state's protocol, it still has to be carried out by low-level DOC employees.

States assure us that executions by lethal injection are conducted with the utmost care and competence. But the few executioners we know demonstrate that this is nowhere near true. Exacerbating the problem is the fact that states can rely on a heavy layer of secrecy to cover the worst of their personnel choices. Most executioners are executioners we *don't* know, which means we need a different kind of information to figure out who they (generally) are.

THE EXECUTIONERS WE DON'T KNOW

For executioners whose identities have not been revealed, the most we can say about who they are comes from state lethal injection protocols. State protocols typically list the minimum qualifications for members of the execution team, so we at least know their baseline credentials. What can we say about executioners based on that?

State lethal injection protocols vary, but they are remarkably consistent in this respect: the only executioners required to have any credentials at all are members of the IV team, and placing a catheter is a task so distinctly medical that it is hard to imagine anyone without medical training doing it (although apparently this too has been tried).[32] As for the IV team, the required credentials are strikingly low, listing medical technicians—phlebotomists, emergency medical technicians, paramedics, and the like—as qualified IV team members, often coupling it with an experience requirement of one or two years.[33] Every other part of the execution is left to nonmedical prison personnel for whom there are no minimum qualifications at all.

It is worth pausing to appreciate the point. Prison guards are performing tasks that a pharmacist would do, mixing controlled-substance injectables and loading them into syringes. Prison guards are pushing the syringes, by feel, through five feet of tubing from an adjoining room. And a senior prison administrator—the warden—is monitoring the execution for medical mishaps like a ruptured vein or dislodged catheter. What could possibly go wrong?

To be fair, the protocol only sets the floor for the credentials of the execution team. Nothing prevents states from hiring a doctor to do all or part of this work, and we know that sometimes doctors do participate in executions by lethal injection. Doerhoff is a prime example. From time to time, we even see a state announce that it has an anesthesiologist on tap to supervise the execution and assist as necessary.

But every indication suggests that executioners of this caliber are exceedingly rare. By and large, doctors want nothing to do with lethal injection, and even when they participate, it is usually just to do a conscious check or set a central line when the IV team can't access a peripheral vein. They aren't playing a primary role, and we know this because decades of lethal injection litigation have given us a front-row seat as to who is: medical technicians and nonmedical prison personnel, with an occasional nurse here and there.

States tout the skill set that these positions bring to the table, and a prime example is Kentucky's stance in 2008's *Baze v. Rees*.[34] In *Baze*, Kentucky boasted at oral argument that "Kentucky uses what is probably literally the best qualified human being in the Commonwealth of Kentucky to place the IV line. It uses a phlebotomist who in her daily job works with the prison population. . . . This person places 30 needles a day."[35] Indeed, the Supreme Court in *Baze* lauded Kentucky's requirement that IV team members have "at least one year of professional experience as a certified medical assistant, phlebotomist, EMT, paramedic or military corpsman," calling it the state's "most significant" safeguard against a torturous death.[36]

Now consider the training and experience of this "most significant" safeguard. By way of training, a person can become a phlebotomist in as little as eight weeks, and most states do not require a certification test at the end.[37] You do the training, you're a phlebotomist, done and done. As for experience, the experience of a phlebotomist is limited by their scope of practice, and their scope of practice is drawing blood. "The job description is actually quite straightforward," one phlebotomist career guide website states. "A phlebotomist performs venipunctures and collects blood samples. That is the job in a nutshell."[38]

Presumably, this would make phlebotomists well qualified to draw a prisoner's blood. But it doesn't make them well qualified to set an IV line, which, as one doctor notes, is a "much more complex process with a much narrower margin of error."[39] In fact, setting an IV line is not something that phlebotomists are even *allowed* to do in the vast majority of states. Thirty-eight states require medical technicians to be licensed as an advanced emergency medical technician (A-EMT) or paramedic in order to set a peripheral IV.[40]

Granted, phlebotomists can get "IV-certified" to set catheters, usually in the hospital setting.[41] But as one court noted, the training involved for such certification (at least in the case at bar) involved one thirty-two-hour IV therapy course at a community college in which the executioner "was instructed on the insertion of IV catheters, but not in setting up IV lines."[42] That, and a four-hour refresher course five years later, was all the IV training that this particular member of the IV execution team had—but that was more than another member of the same IV team, who had only the four-hour training module.

Granted, EMTs and paramedics have more training under their belt and a broader scope of practice (although as noted, thirty-eight states would not allow even an EMT to set a catheter—a person has to be an advanced-EMT or paramedic for that).[43] A person can become an EMT by completing a six-to-twelve-month training program and passing an EMT certification exam,[44] and a person can become a paramedic by completing a six-month to two-year training program and passing a paramedic certification exam.[45] EMTs and paramedics do incredibly important work, saving lives every day. But they are trained for prehospital emergency medical care, and work under the confines of strict protocols established by physicians. In lethal injection, they are not acting under the direct or indirect supervision of a physician. They are acting as physician *substitutes*.

And the problem is not just training; it's also experience. IV insertion is a *practice-based* skill. A person cannot simply study their way into being good at it; they have to actually do it again and again. This isn't *practice makes perfect*. This is *practice makes minimally proficient,* which tells us two things.

First, IV team members should be setting IVs in the normal course of their work. "Just because a person is legally permitted by their licensure to do a medical procedure does not in any way mean that they are capable or competent," one doctor says, adding that when it comes to IV team executioners, "the important thing is that they do the procedure as part of their regular 'day job.'"[46] Even state experts agree, stating that IV team executioners "should be people who do this as a part of their daily job [because] they should be able to troubleshoot and that only comes with experience."[47] We don't know how often IV team members meet this qualification, but we know that setting an IV is not something that most EMTs and phlebotomists are even allowed to do, so it's definitely not within the ordinary course of their work.[48]

Second, the fact that setting an IV is a practice-based skill means that IV team members should have more than the paltry experience that state protocols require. To the extent that state protocols require experience at all, they tend to require a year of experience, maybe two. These are not seasoned professionals. Yet as we know, the conditions under which IV team members are operating are about as stressful as they get, the task of inserting an IV is about as challenging as it gets, and the margin for error is about as thin as it gets. Executioners need experience to handle the high-pressure, Herculean tasks that lethal injection asks of them, and that means there is one thing that IV team members should never be: new to the job.

States have defended their low standards by insisting that setting an IV isn't all that hard. It's a basic task, they say, and well within the skill set of your average medical technician. As one state expert put the point: "It all boils down to the skill level at getting a functioning IV in and you don't need a lot of fancy initials after your name to do that."[49]

But setting an IV for lethal injection is obviously not as easy as it's made out to be because medical technicians are routinely unable to do it. And it's certainly not a basic task for most phlebotomists and EMTs, whose positions don't even allow them to do it. One may not need a lot of fancy initials to set an IV, but the IV team members that states employ are a far cry from having fancy initials.

Time and again, IV team members fall shockingly short of the basic medical knowledge one would expect medical team members to have. For example, executioners have stated their intent to insert a catheter into the "saphenous vein in the arm" and "external carotid vein" in the neck, which would be fine except for the fact that neither of those vessels exist.[50] They have not understood that pushing a drug too fast could cause the IV to pop out or the vein to collapse.[51] And they have not known that anesthesia generally comes with a cessation of breathing, so if a prisoner is breathing, there's a good chance they are still sensate.[52] They have even (and inexplicably) inserted an IV into a prisoner's thumb.[53]

"It never occurred to me when we set this up that we'd have complete idiots administering the drugs," Jay Chapman later stated.[54] But these people aren't idiots. They're just in way over their head, performing tasks for which they are nowhere near qualified. The man who in chapter 4 thought lethal injection was great so long as executioners had some skill is the man who in chapter 5 concedes that they don't.[55]

Thus far, the discussion has proceeded as though setting a peripheral IV is the most complex medical task involved in lethal injection, and that may be true. But it also may not be true. If IV team executioners cannot set a peripheral line, they'll have to resort to a cutdown or central line, and no medical technician comes anywhere close to being qualified to do that.

To access a central vein, executioners will need the assistance of a doctor, but that is not something that just any doctor can do. Only a subset of doctors—surgeons, cardiologists, intensive care doctors, and the like—would have the skills to set a central line, and cutdowns are so rare in the clinical setting that they would only be within the skill set of a veteran physician.[56] As one state's expert conceded, placing an IV in the femoral vein is "not the sort of training I would expect a primary care physician to have."[57]

In the end, what states really need is an anesthesiologist. Those are the people with über-technical skills who could access the vein and then reliably bring someone to a state of anesthesia, where they then could die the death that Americans think they die now. But for reasons we'll see in chapter 7, states can't get those, so note what they do—they disaggregate the task instead.

Now the task is not getting the prisoner to a state of anesthesia. It is the more discrete task of inserting a catheter into a vein, and medical technicians can do that (probably). It is pushing the plunger on a syringe, and prison guards can do that (presumably). It is watching to see if something goes obviously wrong, and wardens can do that (maybe). *Voila.* States have provided an anesthetized death without a single person qualified to do it, and quite possibly without a single person qualified to insert an IV. Little wonder incompetence reigns.

TRAINING THAT ISN'T

Even if executioners are well qualified to conduct an execution by lethal injection, they may not be well prepared to do it. As we now know, lethal injection is different than what medical practitioners do in important, error-prone ways. To prepare for those differences, executioners have to *train.*

For the first thirty years of lethal injection, executioner training appears to have been more or less nonexistent. Consider, for example, California. When asked under oath what kind of training executioners received prior to an execution, one execution team member (who had participated in seven executions by lethal injection) replied: "Training? We don't have training, really."[58] Another member of the same execution team testified that "there isn't really much training," describing her job as "more a self-taught event."[59]

California was not alone. In the mid-2000s, Tennessee, Florida, and Arizona were also found to have woefully inadequate executioner training, and the problem was widely known to be more pervasive than that.[60] "Never in my wildest dreams did I foresee this procedure being carried out by untrained medical personnel," Jay Chapman stated at the time.[61]

Since then, states have boasted about the number of training sessions that their executioners have done, yet revelations of poorly trained executioners continue to come to light. After Clayton Lockett's botched execution in 2014, for example, the Oklahoma DOC promised to better train its executioners. But more mishaps occurred, and in 2016, a grand jury found that "most department employees profoundly misunderstood the protocol." Two years after Clayton Lockett's disastrous execution, executioners weren't any better prepared to conduct an execution than they were before. "This knowledge starts with training," the grand jury admonished. "Whoever takes part in executions in Oklahoma going forward must have an intimate knowledge of the policies and protocols surrounding an execution," it stated, adding: "This demands something more than repeated dry-runs and walk-throughs."[62]

Another example is Texas, the state that leads the nation in executions. In 2021, Texas inexplicably excluded the media from witnessing an execution. The ACLU claimed violations of state and federal law, issuing a statement stressing that "media access to executions is a critical form of public oversight as the government exerts its power to end a human life."[63] Texas officials pledged to investigate what went wrong, and shortly thereafter, issued a statement saying that despite "extensive training," staff had simply made a mistake.[64]

The ACLU was not satisfied, and requested records concerning the state's internal investigation under the Texas Public Information Act. The state denied the request, and a legal fight ensued. After what the ACLU called "six months of stonewalling," it finally received the records in 2022.

"These documents reveal a department woefully unprepared to carry out an execution due to confusion and lack of training," the ACLU stated after reviewing the records, noting that the documents themselves described staff as "not trained" and without "a clear understanding of [their] role."[65] One of these documents, for example, summarized an interview with an executioner who had participated in several executions. That document read: "To [one executioner's] knowledge, there are no written guidelines/protocols about the execution itself. He is aware of a document titled *Execution Procedure—April 2021*, however he stated he has not read it thoroughly."[66] "Multiple documents describe a picture of confusion," the ACLU stated of its review. "Taken together," it concluded, "these documents reveal a global lack of understanding about execution procedures generally."[67] No wonder Texas was so keen on keeping those documents under wrap.

Tennessee is yet another example. After revelations that the DOC was violating its own protocol, the governor commissioned an outside review of the state's lethal injection procedures, which issued its report in December 2022.[68] Executioners were required to review the protocol annually but there was no verification process to ensure that was happening, the report stated, and executioners were also required to attend a class on the protocol annually, but no executioner even mentioned that the class existed. Instructions for preparing the drugs were supposed to come from the pharmacy, the report went on to say, but executioners either didn't receive the instructions or didn't understand them, because their understanding contradicted the pharmacist's directions on the syringe size and window of time for using the drugs to be assured of their potency and sterility. One member of the execution team, the drug procurer, was given "zero guidance on how to carry out [his] tasks," the report stated, concluding more broadly that "while the [executioner] interviews were very insightful, they further showed the absence of adequate expertise, guidance, and counsel" surrounding Tennessee's lethal injection process."[69]

All three of these states are high-executing states. This is what lethal injection looks like in states that ostensibly know what they're doing. Imagine what it looks like in a state that does not.

Yet another way to assess the adequacy of training is to consider the multitude of things that executioners don't know. In lethal injection litigation, some executioners could not name a single drug in the state's lethal injection protocol.[70] Others could name the drugs, but had no idea what they did.[71] Still others could name the drugs, but thought they did one thing (put the person to sleep) when they did something else (produce paralysis).[72] Clayton Lockett's execution provides a prime example. "I wasn't briefed, nobody went over anything about what we could expect from this new drug," the paramedic told investigators.[73] What the doctor said was more telling yet: "I don't know what [the drugs] were. In fact I didn't really care to know what they were."[74]

That last part is important: executioners often don't *want* to know about the drugs they are injecting. "I don't want to know about it," one executioner stated when questioned about her knowledge of the drugs, adding: "I don't study. I just do the job."[75]

Maybe asking executioners to understand what they are doing is asking too much. An executioner in one state recalled that when explaining the job to a new recruit, "There was a surreal sense of, *I'm training this man to kill someone*."[76] Warden Trammell was bothered by the notion of training too. "The policy says you have on-the-job training," she told investigators after the Lockett execution, adding: "I mean, who does that? You know for—taking, killing a person."[77] We'll talk more about the trauma that executioners experience in chapter 8. For now, it suffices to say the trauma of training to kill someone may be its own reason why training isn't happening.

Even so, executioners who don't understand the lethal processes they are setting in motion also don't understand how those processes can go wrong. There are "known risks—accidents which, given enough of an opportunity, will occur—for which the executioners are completely unprepared," one federal court observed, adding: "In many cases, the executioners are not even aware that the risks exist."[78] Another federal court echoed the sentiment, observing that "team members almost uniformly have no knowledge of the nature or properties of the drugs that are used or the risks or potential problems associated with the procedure."[79] Executioners are walking a tightrope in the blind.

It is worth pausing to appreciate just how far these executioners are from the qualified medical professionals who are conducting lethal injection in our mind's eye. States leverage the medical model to create an aura of competence, credibility and careful oversight. But that narrative could not be further from the truth. "Rather than the clean, clinical procedures they mimic," one team of medical researchers writes, "lethal injections are furtive affairs, characterized by the slipshod efforts of poorly trained personnel."[80] This was true in the beginning, it was true twenty years ago, and it is no less true today.

6

THE DRUG SUPPLIER SAGA

In 2017, Arizona came up with a creative solution to the lethal injection drug shortage plaguing the state: BYOD. That's right—*Bring Your Own Drugs*. According to the new policy, prisoners could be executed with their own drugs if they wished; their lawyers just needed to bring them. "Arizona may have come up with the most original concept yet," *The Guardian* wrote, "an invitation for lawyers to help kill their own clients."[1] Lawyers for Arizona's prisoners were nonplussed. "It's not legal for me as a lawyer to go out and procure drugs for a client," one said.[2] It wasn't legal for any reason, but especially not when the reason was killing the client. Thus far, the state has had no takers.

BYOD is just one of a number of surreal spectacles that mark the saga of the search for lethal injection drugs. States can't get the drugs they need for lethal injection, and *It's all abolitionists' fault*. We'll be sorting out what is and isn't true on that score, but the real story lies in how little states care about the legality of their purchases or the quality of the drugs bought in the name of a humane death.

People think that the drugs that states use are regular (regulated) drugs. They aren't. This has a number of important implications, including some for ordinary folks like you and me. But that's the end of the story. Our journey starts at the beginning.

HOW THE LETHAL INJECTION DRUG SHORTAGE BEGAN

For the first thirty years of its existence, lethal injection used sodium thiopental as the all-important first drug in the three-drug protocol. Over time, the drug propofol replaced sodium thiopental in the practice of medicine, leading sodium thiopental manufacturers to exit the market, which in turn left the pharmaceutical company Hospira as the drug's sole domestic producer. In 2009, Hospira reported a shortage in the raw ingredients needed to produce sodium thiopental that first slowed, then halted its production.

But another development soon after would prove to be even more consequential. Hospira made sodium thiopental at its aging plant in North Carolina, and an FDA inspection in early 2010 revealed a number of deficiencies that would need to be remedied. Hospira decided that the better move was to relocate its operation to a production plant in Italy.

Italy, like other nations of Western Europe, is staunchly abolitionist on the death penalty, having seen for itself in World War II what power in the hands of bloodthirsty leaders could do. When Italy learned that Hospira would be making sodium thiopental on its soil, it refused to license Hospira's plant without a guarantee that the drugs produced there would not be used in executions. It also made not-so-veiled threats that Hospira could be held liable for its part in what Americans called the death penalty and Europeans called state-sponsored murder.

In January 2011, Hospira decided that the easiest way to satisfy Italian authorities was to stop producing sodium thiopental altogether—a decision that may or may not have had to do with the fact that the drug constituted less than 0.25 percent of Hospira's business.[3] "Hospira makes its products to enhance and save the lives of the patients we serve," the company stated in a press release, adding: "We cannot take the risk that we will be held liable by the Italian authorities if the product is diverted for use in capital punishment. Exposing our employees or facilities to liability is not a risk we are prepared to take."[4] With that, the sole domestic supplier of sodium thiopental exited the market for good.

By then, desperate states tired of waiting on Hospira's sodium thiopental had found a new supplier: Dream Pharma, a pharmaceutical distributor that turned out to be two desks and a filing cabinet in the back of a London driving school.[5] Lethal injection litigation in Arizona had revealed that the department of corrections (DOC) purchased its sodium thiopental from "England," and it wasn't hard to trace the shipment to Dream Pharma from there.[6]

The discovery led Great Britain to ban sodium thiopental exports to the United States. "The only trade we were doing on this drug was for capital punishment," a spokesperson stated, adding, "Our government is completely against capital punishment."[7] As Britain's business secretary told the press: "This country opposes the death penalty. We are clear that the state should never be complicit in judiciary executions through the use of British drugs in lethal injections."[8]

And so it came to be that by early 2011, two European governments had shut down two sources of sodium thiopental for US executions. Both moves were purely reactive, a response to revelations that businesses operating on their (abolitionist) soil were supplying executioners in the United States. But that gave rise to an idea: Why not impose a European Union export ban on drugs used in executions more broadly?

In December 2011, that is exactly what the EU did. It imposed strict export controls on drugs used for lethal injection, requiring authorities to halt export of a drug whenever they had "reasonable grounds" to believe it would be used in executions.[9] "I wish to underline that the European Union opposes the death penalty in all circumstances," the spokesperson who announced the policy stated.[10]

Ironically, those export controls had been there all along. Back in 2005, the EU instituted an export ban on all products used for capital punishment, citing its intent to be the "leading institutional actor and largest donor to the fight against the death penalty."[11] But the items listed in the European Union Torture Regulation were gallows, guillotines, gas chambers, and the like. Until 2011, it simply hadn't occurred to anyone to add therapeutic drugs to the list.

But doing so would be a game-changer. The EU's move halted not only the export of sodium thiopental to the United States, but also the export of any other drug reasonably at risk of being diverted for capital punishment. Consider, for example, propofol, the drug that replaced sodium thiopental in clinical practice (and yes, it's also the drug that was responsible for the death of Michael Jackson). Propofol is the anesthetic used in around 95 percent of American surgical procedures. It is used some fifty million times annually in the United States alone, and 90 percent of that supply comes from Europe.

Fast forward to 2012, when Missouri announced that it would use propofol in its next execution. The EU issued a statement saying that if Missouri did so, it would restrict the drug's importation to the United States. "If propofol was used in an execution, then the likelihood of sanctions or a ban exporting it from the European Union would become a reality," a pharmaceutical spokesperson stated, adding that the move "would lead to a shortage of the product that's used 50 million times a year in the U.S."[12] The medical community was outraged, issuing a public letter imploring Missouri not to use propofol in lethal injection and warning that doing so would "take the medical specialty of anesthesiology back 20 years."[13] Missouri blinked. The governor instructed the DOC to eliminate propofol from the state's lethal injection protocol, and no executing state has gone near the drug since.

This, then, is how the lethal injection drug shortage began—with a raw ingredient shortage and an inspection at an aging North Carolina plant, two developments that had nothing to do with death penalty abolitionists. Those developments led to European export controls on drugs used for lethal injection, and here we can say it *is* all abolitionists' fault, but those abolitionists have names. They are Italy, Great Britain, and the sovereign nations of Western Europe that joined to form the EU.

To the extent that the EU's part in the lethal injection drug shortage is recognized in the domestic death penalty discourse at all (and, by and large, it is not), it is viewed as an illegitimate power grab, an instance of European meddling into purely domestic affairs. A prime example is the indignation that Missouri's governor expressed at the prospect of EU export controls on propofol if the state used it in executions. "State and federal court systems, not European politicians, should decide death penalty policy," he stated.[14] Another example is an amicus brief filed with the Supreme Court in 2015's *Glossip v. Gross*. "We must not allow ourselves to be pressured and manipulated from Europe," the brief argued, characterizing the EU's export controls as "an assault on our sovereignty and our democracy."[15] By this view, the EU should mind its own business, and leave the American death penalty to those entrusted with its care: Americans.

Yet this reflects a fundamental misunderstanding of how international trade works. Sovereign nations can do as they please: that's us with the death penalty. But doing what a nation pleases can have consequences, because other sovereign nations can do as they please too. Included in that sovereignty is a nation's prerogative to withhold its products from other nations for any reason it wants, including disapproval of what those nations are doing with the products, or just disapproval of what those nations are doing generally. Nations do this all the time. As in, *we* do this all this time.[16] We just aren't used to it being done to us. Thus, those who lament EU export controls as an assault on our democracy need to explain why we are entitled to drugs for executions from countries that are fundamentally against executions—why our preferences should override theirs when it comes to *their* drugs.

The real problem is that we Americans are not used to being on the receiving end of what we've dishing out for decades. But in a world where over half of all nations have formally rejected the death penalty (two-thirds if one counts countries with a moratorium on executions), this is where we are, and where we'll be for the foreseeable future.[17] Apropos the point, in 2017, the EU spearheaded the Alliance for Torture-Free Trade, an alliance of fifty-seven countries whose goal is to "end the trade in goods used for capital punishment and torture" by adopting export restrictions on those goods.[18] It's the EU ban, but beyond the EU.

Yet, export controls were not the only headwind that states faced in the race to re-up their supply of lethal injection drugs. The other was Big Pharma.

ENTER BIG PHARMA

When the EU adopted its export ban, states first got by with a little help from their friends. Several states had stockpiled sodium thiopental, which they shared with other states like neighbors lending a cup of sugar. In 2011 alone, Georgia shared its supply of sodium thiopental with Kentucky; Tennessee shared its supply with Georgia and Arkansas; and Arkansas shared its supply with Oklahoma and Mississippi.[19] That same year, Arizona shared its supply with California, prompting a thank-you email from the California official who received the drugs. "You guys in Arizona are life savers," he wrote, apparently oblivious to the irony.[20]

In the name of lethal injection, drugs flowed back and forth across state lines with abandon, and, notably, without interstate licenses or the public oversight that comes with the formal procurement process. States shared and swapped drugs under the radar, so there was no mechanism to track (let alone regulate) these interstate drug transactions. The extent to which states are still sharing drugs today is anyone's guess, but we know from a Freedom of Information Act (FOIA) release that in 2015, Texas sent some of its pentobarbital to Virginia when Virginia realized that its drugs would expire before a scheduled execution date.[21] In sharing its drugs, Texas was just returning the favor—it had borrowed the same drug from Virginia in 2013.

But sharing drugs was a short-term solution. Drug stockpiles would eventually run dry, and states had no source on the horizon to re-up their supplies. States needed a new drug and the obvious choice was pentobarbital, the drug used in animal euthanasia. In 2011 alone, thirteen states adopted pentobarbital for lethal injection, using the drug in a slew of executions. And it was all made by the Danish pharmaceutical giant Lundbeck.

Lundbeck had the sole domestic production plant for injectable pentobarbital, so there was no question as to who had made the pentobarbital that states were using in lethal injection. The company issued a statement saying that "Lundbeck adamantly opposes the distressing misuse of our product in capital punishment,"[22] and a spokesperson spoke the words that would come to represent the view of pharmaceutical companies far and wide: "It's against everything we stand for."[23] Lundbeck then wrote to the governors and corrections departments in sixteen states, beseeching them not to use its drugs in executions. "We urge you to discontinue the use of [pentobarbital] in the execution of prisoners in your state because it contradicts everything we are in the business to do," the letter stated.[24]

These efforts had no effect, so in July 2011, Lundbeck solved the problem itself. "We have stated very clearly that we're in the business of improving people's lives, and using [pentobarbital] for capital punishment is against what we do," the company stated, announcing that it was abandoning its open market distribution system in favor of a tightly controlled closed distribution system with end-user agreements promising that Lundbeck's product would not be used in executions.[25]

Thus began a long and exhausting game of cat and mouse in which states tried to buy a drug for lethal injection, only to have its Big Pharma producer step in and choke off the supply. When Missouri stated its intent to use propofol in executions, for example, Fresenius Kabi, the German manufacturer of the drug, followed Lundbeck's lead and adopted a closed distribution system to prevent DOCs from accessing its drugs in the future. Today, more than two dozen pharmaceutical companies have adopted controlled distribution systems for the singular purpose of preventing executing states from purchasing their drugs.[26]

Especially noteworthy in this regard is the American pharmaceutical giant Pfizer, whose slogan is "Life is our life's work."[27] *That's* potentially awkward. In 2016, Pfizer joined other companies in adopting a closed distribution system to keep its products out of executioners' hands. "Pfizer makes its products to enhance and save the lives of the patients we serve," a company spokesperson stated. "Consistent with these values, Pfizer strongly objects to the use of its products as lethal injections for capital punishment."[28] The move marked a pivotal moment. "With Pfizer's announcement, all FDA-approved manufacturers of any potential execution drug have now blocked their sale for this purpose," said the London-based abolition group Reprieve.[29] The last available avenue for executing states to (legally) obtain Big Pharma's drugs had just closed.

That brings us to Reprieve. Reprieve is the sort of abolition group that critics are talking about when they say *It's all abolitionists' fault*. In fact, Reprieve may be *the* abolitionists in the *It's all their fault* refrain. If so, there's some truth to the claim. In 2010, Reprieve launched the Stop Lethal Injection Project (SLIP) in the wake of Dream Pharma's sale of sodium thiopental to executing states. Turns out, Dream Pharma's drugs were actually another company's drugs, and as soon as that company learned about the use of the drugs, it took steps to prevent its products from being diverted again. Drug companies weren't intentionally selling their wares to executing states, Reprieve found. They just weren't paying attention.

SLIP aimed to change that. The point was to draw attention to companies whose drugs were being used in lethal injection in hopes that the companies would do something about it. And they did. SLIP was spectacularly successful (or an unmitigated disaster, depending upon who you ask).

Critics say that Reprieve engaged in "intimidation and commercial harassment" by drawing attention to the source of the drugs used in lethal injection in an effort to get drug manufacturers to stop allowing their products to be used in this fashion.[30] And it's fair to say that Reprieve *did* pressure major pharmaceutical companies to control the downstream distribution of their products by shining a light on the way those products were used as a consequence of their open market distribution systems (although that's a far cry from intimidation and harassment).[31]

But it would be a mistake to infer from this tactic that these companies were once willing partners in the lethal injection enterprise. They were not. Executing states were just taking advantage of slack distribution systems to do what drug manufacturers were opposed to doing all along.

Consider, for example, the American pharmaceutical company Abbott Laboratories. Back in 2001—before anyone was paying attention—

Abbott wrote to state DOCs to say that its drugs were not to be used for lethal injection.[32] Abbott's motto is "A Promise for Life," and it's hard to imagine a more perverse use of "promise for life" drugs than using them to cause people to promptly die. The same could be said of Merck & Co., whose slogan is "Be Well." Or Teva: "Live Your Life." Or Allergan: "Our Pursuit: Life's Potential." Or Hospira: "Advancing Wellness." Any one of these could be fodder for a *Saturday Night Live* skit on the sheer absurdity of companies whose stated mission is to save lives selling their wares for executions. That's a public relations nightmare.

Cynics say that these companies don't really care about corporate core values; it's all about the bottom line. And that may (or may not) be true. But supplying drugs for lethal injection is downright terrible for business too. "A company in the business of healing people is putting its reputation at risk when it supplies drugs for executions," the manager of one state pension fund stated, adding: "The company is also risking association with botched executions, which opens it to legal and financial damage."[33] Tellingly, one major pharmaceutical company—Mylan—had $70 million divested when it couldn't guarantee investors that its products wouldn't end up in executioners' hands. (It can now.) "If clients find out we have shares in companies that supply that drug [for executions]," a spokesperson for the investment firm that divested the shares explained, "we have problems with our clients."[34]

In short, even Big Pharma's distribution controls are not in fact all abolitionists' fault. The fault lies in the fact that lethal injection requires a product whose producers are adamantly opposed to being used for executions. This is a problem inherent in the lethal injection enterprise. It is intrinsic to the project of using therapeutic drugs to kill.

And this stance is not limited to drugs. Back in 2006, Aspect Medical Systems learned that North Carolina had used one of its BIS monitors in an execution. The company promptly issued a statement objecting to such use and adopted a policy prohibiting sales to states absent a contractual provision promising that the monitor would not be used in executions.[35] Fast forward to 2023, when four medical supply manufacturers—makers of catheters, syringes, IV tubing, and the like—stated their (continued) opposition to the use of their products in lethal injection. If they learned that states were using their products for lethal injection, one spokesperson stated, "we would take whatever steps are required to ensure that the product is returned" and "pursue every option that we have to make sure it does not happen again."[36]

Even producers of nitrogen gas are telling states not to come their way. In 2019, the major gas manufacturer Airgas issued a statement saying that "Airgas has not and will not supply nitrogen gas or other inert gases to induce hypoxia for the purpose of human execution."[37] According to the company, "Supplying nitrogen for the purpose of human execution is not consistent with our company values." *Who knew*, the maker of gas for children's balloons and safety products like fire extinguishers doesn't want to be associated with state executions. Since then, two other major gas manufacturers have joined Airgas in putting contractual restrictions on the sale of their products.[38] States thinking that nitrogen gas is the answer to their drug supply problems may be in for a rough go.

WHAT ABOUT OTHER INTERNATIONAL SUPPLIERS?

When pharmaceutical companies started closing their drug distribution loopholes, executing states scrambled to get the drugs they needed through mid-level medical supply shops that stocked the drugs and were still willing to sell to state DOCs. But that too was a short-term solution. In due time, those supply shops would have to sign contractual agreements in order to re-up their supplies. States needed a supplier that was not bound by European export controls or corporate core values. What about other international suppliers?

This avenue had serious potential—there *were* suppliers abroad willing to sell their drugs with no questions asked about their intended usage. But there's always a hitch, and the hitch here takes us back to Dream Pharma. As we know, Dream Pharma was the catalyst for EU export controls on lethal injection drugs. But that's not the half of it—or rather, it *is* just the half of it, because Dream Pharma was also the catalyst for *import* controls on lethal injection drugs.

This leg of our journey starts back in 2010, when the Arizona DOC grew tired of waiting on Hospira's sodium thiopental and decided to take matters into its own hands. It found a supplier willing to sell the drug—Dream Pharma—and asked a pharmacist working with the state to take a look. "The Dream Pharma website leaves something to be desired," she wrote. "It makes me wonder whether Dream Pharma is reputable and where exactly the medication would be coming from."[39] The website had the pharmacist spooked. "There is a 'grey market' in the pharmaceutical industry," she stated, "and in this particular instance you need to be sure that the product is actually [sodium] thiopental and that it is going to work." Dream Pharma's drugs "might cause trouble you don't want in this particular situation," she warned, adding that it was "pretty likely" that the sodium thiopental for sale by Dream Pharma wasn't approved by the FDA.

The Arizona DOC made the purchase anyway, even as the DOC director notified others that "there may be an issue with FDA approval."[40] To grease the wheels, the director instructed Dream Pharma to make Phoenix the port of entry "to make sure that the people we spoke to here in Phoenix were the people who cleared [the shipment] because they're the ones who had all the communications from us."[41] The Arizona DOC also made what it called a "clerical error" when inputting the FDA product codes, marking the drugs as intended for "non-human" rather than human use.[42] The DOC later said this was a mistake on a drop-down menu, but as investigative journalism would later reveal, the two menu options were nowhere near each other, and the "clerical error" was made on three occasions in the fall of 2010.[43]

When the shipment arrived, the FDA inspected it "to ensure that the product was . . . actually what it was purported to be," and saw that it was not.[44] The drugs were for human use. Still, the agency gave itself a pass and used its "enforcement discretion" to look the other way.[45]

But the DEA saw things differently and took action to confiscate the drugs. The Arizona DOC did not have a permit from the DEA authorizing it to import controlled substances, so the shipment was "noncompliant" with the law.[46] This, too, the Arizona DOC knew on the front side when it went to import the drugs.[47]

Shortly thereafter, a group of condemned prisoners sued the FDA to force it to enforce the provisions of the Food, Drug, and Cosmetic Act (FDCA) at the border. As we know from chapter 2, the Supreme Court ruled back in the mid-1980s that the FDA's enforcement authority was discretionary, so the agency could do as it pleased.[48] But that case concerned drugs inside the country. The prisoners argued that border enforcement was different, and in 2012, a federal court agreed.

The FDCA had separate regulatory provisions for domestic and foreign drugs, the court noted, and by the FDCA's clear text, all drugs violating the import conditions "*shall* be refused admission."[49] As the court's opinion explained, "*No* drug may be legally imported unless it is both properly listed with the FDA and comes from a properly registered foreign drug establishment," and "Dream Pharma has neither registered with the FDA nor listed its [sodium thiopental] with the FDA."[50] Thus, while the FDA could use its enforcement discretion to forgo action for domestic violations of the FDCA, it could not ignore its mandatory duties to patrol drugs crossing the border. The court chastised the FDA for its "callous indifference" to the prospect of prisoners being injected with contaminated or otherwise substandard drugs, accentuating the point with the flourish "How utterly disappointing!"[51] *Ouch.*

In 2013, an appellate court unanimously affirmed the lower court's ruling. "The FDCA imposes mandatory duties upon the agency charged with its enforcement," the appeals court wrote, and "the FDA acted in derogation of those duties."[52] With that, the FDA was stuck, as in permanently stuck, enforcing the FDCA's import provisions at the border. Imports would have to be FDA-approved drugs coming from FDA-approved vendors, and those were requirements that grey market suppliers could not meet.

When combined with EU export controls, the 2013 ruling effectively shut down the international market for lethal injection drugs, and that should be all there is to say. But in 2015, the FDA intercepted shipments of sodium thiopental from India that were bound for the Texas and Arizona DOCs. A third shipment, bound for the Nebraska DOC, never got off the ground in India.[53] The sender of all three shipments was Harris Pharma. The FDA had previously warned states that importing sodium thiopental from Harris Pharma would violate the FDCA and that it was obliged to enforce the law, but Texas, Arizona, and Nebraska proceeded with the purchase anyway. Each state spent $25,000 ($26,700, including freight) for 1,000 vials of sodium thiopental, and Nebraska spent another $27,700 on pancuronium bromide along with it.[54]

Harris Pharma's sodium thiopental was an unapproved drug from an unapproved vendor and on top of that, it violated most every labeling requirement that the FDCA had. The labels had "no recommended dose and offer no instructions for reconstituting the powder inside the vials," the FDA wrote in a letter to Texas, and contained "no precautions, contraindications, or warnings, or other information required in prescribing information for health professionals."[55]

Texas demanded its drugs back and the FDA refused, so Texas sued the FDA over its "unjustified seizure."[56] The case went dormant in late 2017 and since then, the drugs have expired, rendering the litigation moot. But when it sued, Texas declared its intent "to continue importing [sodium thiopental] from the same foreign source, and with the same labeling, as the entry that the FDA is currently detaining."[57] Texas is all in on this foreign drug supplier, so let's talk about Harris Pharma.

Harris Pharma is just a guy named Chris Harris. Harris worked at a duty-free shop in one of India's international airports, then held a handful of jobs at various call centers, staying for around a year each.[58] After that, he began working with the Mumbai-based company Kayem Pharmaceuticals. Not *for* Kayem, but *with* it. Kayem's CEO said that the company wanted to get into e-commerce, and he was introduced to Harris online. Harris was good at sales, so they entered into a "commercial understanding."[59] That understanding soured when Harris sold Kayem's sodium thiopental to Nebraska in late 2010, and to South Dakota in early 2011, for use in lethal injection. (The DEA confiscated Nebraska's drugs, and South Dakota's drugs expired while mired in litigation, so neither shipment was actually used.) Harris and Kayem parted ways around the time of the South Dakota sale in 2011, and that's when Harris started Harris Pharma.

As Harris Pharma, Chris Harris reapproached Nebraska in late 2011 to propose another sale of sodium thiopental. But where did Harris get the drugs? Turns out, they were samples from the Swiss pharmaceutical company Naari. "The agreement with Mr. Harris was that he would use these vials for registration in Zambia," Naari's CEO stated, explaining, "Our intention was to get the product registered in Zambia and then begin selling it there, since sodium thiopental is used very widely as an anesthetic in the developing world."[60] Harris had taken Naari's samples and sold them to Nebraska. "Mr. Harris misappropriated our medicines and diverted them from their intended purpose and use," Naari stated. The Swiss company demanded its drugs back. Nebraska refused. A group of prisoners sued, and the drugs expired without ever being used.

That brings us to Harris Pharma's sale of sodium thiopental to three states in 2015. To be an FDA-approved vendor, a foreign establishment must have a manufacturing facility that the FDA can either inspect itself or partner with foreign authorities to inspect in order to ensure that the pharmaceuticals produced there meet quality control standards. That's a problem for Harris Pharma because the manufacturing facilities listed with the FDA and DEA aren't manufacturing facilities at all.

The facility listed with the FDA as the company's manufacturing plant is just a small rented office, one of sixty offices on the eighth floor of a large office complex in Kolkata, India. A laminated paper sign stuck on the door says "Harris Pharma—Manufacturer and Distribution," but Chris Harris has no pharmaceutical expertise and no employees, and the office space couldn't accommodate the laboratory equipment it would take to manufacture pharmaceuticals even if someone had the know-how to do it. The office complex manager says that Harris only comes in a couple of times a month, and that most of their communication is by email.[61] Whatever is happening in that office space, it is not the manufacture of pharmaceutical drugs.

Harris Pharma has a second business location, which is the address listed on the company's DEA form. But that address is an apartment in a residential neighborhood, a flat that Harris abandoned after being seven months behind on his rent. A neighbor reported that Harris had said that he "sold 'sexual feel drugs' on a website" and talked about working on a "big consignment" from the United States, boasting that "if he gets consignment, his life will be made."[62] The cell phone number that Harris gave his landlord has since been disabled, and the landlord has resigned to just swallow the loss on the rent.

Behold Harris Pharma, a storefront for a con man who takes other companies' drugs and sells them as his own. Harris Pharma is *exactly* the sort of shady supplier that the FDCA's import provisions were designed to keep from reaching domestic consumers. This guy is a poster child for the need to enforce the FDCA at the border.

Here is a good place to mention that if not for Texas's little border spat with the FDA and some top-notch investigative reporting, we wouldn't even know about Harris Pharma. As we will see, state secrecy laws protect against the disclosure of lethal injection drug sources, so we are left with states saying *Trust us, of course we're using a reputable supplier, how dare you suggest that we wouldn't.* And yet, Harris Pharma. And Dream Pharma before that. And another seedy supplier in India, Provizer Pharma, between those two. FOIA documents showed that in 2015, before turning to Harris Pharma, Texas tried to buy drugs from Provizer, but as *BuzzFeed News* reported, "Before the sale could happen, Provizer Pharma was raided by the Indian government, its facility shut down, its drugs seized, and five of its employees arrested."[63]

We know from lethal injection litigation that some states did next to nothing to investigate Harris Pharma before buying its drugs.[64] But that's better than Nebraska, which had bought drugs from Chris Harris twice before and knew exactly who it was dealing with when it bought his drugs in 2015—with no hesitation on the front side, one might add, and great indignation on the back side when its illegal purchase became $54,000 of taxpayer money down the drain.

It is no exaggeration to say that these states were caught in the act of smuggling illegal drugs across the border. That is literally what they were doing. We just aren't used to government officials (corrections department people, no less) being the ones doing it. People go to prison for this sort of thing. As in, *you and I* would go to prison for this sort of thing.

Policing commercial pharmaceuticals at the border is important because the border is the one place that the FDA can (mostly) control. Once those drugs get inside the border, the task becomes much harder, and that's especially true of drugs used for lethal injection because they are off-grid purchases and thus outside the formal supply chain from the start. Experience has shown just how porous the pharmaceutical supply chain can be when it comes to lethal injection drugs. Remember those drugs from Dream Pharma that Arizona shared with California in 2010? Litigation revealed that "substantial quantities" went missing from the California DOC's facilities.[65] We also know that some of Dream Pharma's sodium thiopental ended up behind the counter of a pharmacy in Georgia.[66] But whether those drugs came from the California DOC or the DOC in Georgia, which also had some of Dream Pharma's drugs, is impossible to say.

This is one reason why policy analysts care, *a lot*, about the FDA enforcing the border when drugs coming into the country are for lethal injection. "Once an illicit supply channel is established with a supplier, it is extremely challenging to control which drug products move through it and which customers they reach," one American Pharmacy Association paper reports, "particularly in a context where the FDA, DEA, and state boards of pharmacy are prevented from performing their usual regulatory duties because of secrecy."[67] Once illicit drugs cross the border, there's no telling where they will end up, and that means they could end up going to people like you and me. After all, states could never use all the sodium thiopental from their bulk purchases before it expired, even if they shared with other states. Harris Pharma's shipments contained one thousand vials *each*, and the entire country hasn't seen more than thirty executions per year for a decade. All those extra vials were either going to get destroyed or diverted to the black market, and one of those options would make serious money.

These sorts of risks are the reason why the FDCA's import provisions are a brick wall. Only FDA-approved drugs from FDA-approved vendors can come in; everything else "shall be refused admission."[68] Thus, a foreign supplier's drugs either meet the FDCA's requirements—in which case executing states *and everyone else* can buy them—or they don't, in which case no one can. Again, this isn't just about prisoners. It's also about you and me.

Because the FDCA is a brick wall, the only conceivable way that states could legally import Harris Pharma's drugs is if they weren't subject to the FDCA in the first place. But how nonsensical would it be to say that a drug—an actual pharmaceutical—isn't a drug subject to the FDCA?

In 2019, the Trump Administration's Department of Justice gave us our answer. DOJ's Office of Legal Counsel (OLC) wrote a memo to the attorney general opining that the FDA did not have jurisdiction over lethal injection drugs at the border (or anywhere else) because lethal injection drugs weren't drugs under the FDCA.[69] According to the OLC memo, an item may be a drug for some purposes but not for others: if it's a drug used for lethal injection, it's not a drug under the FDCA.[70]

The entirety of the OLC's argument turns on the meaning of the term "drug," which is defined in the FDCA. The FDCA states that an item is a drug if it is recognized as a drug by the *US Pharmacopoeia* (the official publication that lists all recognized medicinal drugs); if it is intended for use in the diagnosis, cure, treatment or prevention of disease; if it is intended to affect any function of the body; or if it is a component of one of those three qualifiers.[71]

Sodium thiopental is a pharmaceutical drug recognized in the *US Pharmacopoeia*.[72] It is an officially registered drug on the official registry of drugs—its Reference Standard Number is 1661002—and that's all it takes under the FDCA. Sure, common sense says that sodium thiopental is a drug, because it is literally a pharmaceutical drug. But we don't need common sense to settle this one. The plain text of the FDCA says that if it's a drug listed in the *US Pharmacopoeia*, then it's a drug under the FDCA.

The OLC memo ignores this definition entirely. It's as though this provision of the FDCA doesn't exist. Instead, we get twenty-six pages of jiujitsu moves about the purpose of a drug that are contorted in their own right but not even worth addressing because they just don't matter. Sodium thiopental is a drug under the FDCA by virtue of its *US Pharmacopoeia* listing, and that definition doesn't have a purpose requirement. If it's in the *US Pharmacopoeia*, it's a drug under the FDCA. That's it, we're done, the end.

It merits mention that in its suit against the FDA, not even Texas tried to argue that sodium thiopental was not a drug under the FDCA, and Texas has fought harder than anyone to get Harris Pharma's drugs. In its opening brief, Texas stated matter-of-factly that Harris Pharma's sodium thiopental "is a drug within the meaning of the [FDCA]."[73] The OLC's position was so untenable that it didn't even occur to Texas to take it.

How much does the OLC memo matter? The OLC has long maintained that its legal opinions are binding on other executive departments,[74] but to the extent that is true (the claim is hotly contested),[75] it would only be true to the extent that the OLC is acting under its statutory authority to render legal opinions "when requested" by department heads.[76] The FDA didn't request the OLC opinion here. The request came directly from Attorney General Bill Barr.

Multiple sources reported a "heated argument" between Barr and the then-head of the FDA over the importation of lethal injection drugs. Barr reportedly "wanted the FDA to allow drugs used for executions to enter the country without undergoing agency scrutiny" and the FDA refused to agree.[77] Aside from the fact that the FDA was under a *court order* to police the border, the agency knew as well as anyone the potential public health consequences of allowing those drugs into the country. In the end, the drugs expired, the litigation in Texas fizzled, and presidential administrations changed. Only the stain on the OLC's reputation for good legal work remains.

COMPOUNDING PHARMACIES

Compounding pharmacies became the supplier of choice (choice meaning necessity) for executing states when the FDA was court-ordered to police the border back in 2012, so at this point, states have used compounded drugs for over a decade. But over time, states' reliance on compounding pharmacies has grown as access to Big Pharma's drugs has dwindled, even as revelations of the problems with compounded drugs have continued to mount. In fact, the weight of those problems may be why executing states circled back to sketchy international suppliers like Harris Pharma in 2015.

Compounding pharmacies are pharmacies that prepare customized versions of FDA-approved drugs for those who cannot take medicines in their commercially manufactured form. For example, some people can't swallow pills, so they need their medicine in liquid form. Others may be allergic to some ingredient in a manufactured drug. Compounding pharmacies solve these sorts of problems, altering ingredients or mixing them in a different way to meet the specific needs of the person filling the prescription. That last part is important. Compounding pharmacies are like regular pharmacies—they are in the business of filling prescriptions. They just do it in a tailor-made way.

From the start, states viewed compounding pharmacies as a last resort for lethal injection drugs. Back in 2013, for example, one state attorney general described compounding pharmacies as "the only remaining option," even as he predicted that "there is no way a compounding pharmacy will pass the litigation muster."[78] The reason is that, as one pharmacy professor explains, there are "profound differences" between the pharmaceutical drugs manufactured by Big Pharma and the individually-mixed batches of drugs coming from mostly small, locally-owned compounding pharmacies.[79]

Part of the difference owes to their regulation. Because compounding pharmacies mix drugs to meet individual needs, their drugs are not subject to the FDA-approval process that governs manufactured drugs. FDA-approved drugs are subject to "good manufacturing practices"—GMPs—which set minimum standards for every aspect of the manufacturing process, from facility design, to the training of personnel, to the calibration and cleaning of equipment, to the testing done to ensure a drug's potency, purity, and quality. It's a whole thing. The FDA regularly inspects manufacturing facilities to ensure compliance with GMPs, and FDA-approved manufacturers are required to report any "adverse events" that may reflect upon the manufacturer's compliance with the GMP standards.

Compounding pharmacies are subject to none of that. They operate completely outside the FDA's regulatory framework. "Customers should be aware that compounded drugs are not FDA-approved," the FDA states on its website, explaining: "This means that the FDA does not verify the safety or effectiveness of compounded drugs. Consumers and health professionals rely on the drug approval process for verification of safety, effectiveness, and quality. Compounded drugs also lack an FDA finding of manufacturing quality before such drugs are marketed."[80] "In addition, and of particular concern," the FDA goes on to say, "poor compounding practices can result in serious drug quality problems, such as contamination or medications that do not possess the strength, quality, and purity they are supposed to have."[81]

This is not to suggest that compounding pharmacies are not regulated at all. They are. But their regulation is left to state boards of pharmacy and is notoriously lax.[82] A 2013 report issued by the US House of Representatives found that compounding pharmacies were "largely untracked, unregulated, and under-inspected by states across America."[83] "State boards of pharmacy generally do not know which pharmacies engage in compounding, do not know whether pharmacies ship compounded drugs across state lines, and do not know which pharmacies manufacture large quantities of compounded drugs," the report stated. According to the report, over twenty states did not keep historical records of inspections, which meant they weren't tracking which compounding pharmacies had repeatedly been cited for safety violations.[84]

The stark differences in regulatory frameworks has produced stark differences in the quality of the drugs produced. The failure rate for drugs produced by FDA-approved commercial manufacturers is less than two percent.[85] Random testing of compounded drugs over the last two decades has repeatedly put their failure rate at between 20 and 35 percent.[86]

That's the failure rate for compounded drugs *generally*. The risks are even greater when the drugs are sterile injectables as is the case with lethal injection. The creation of sterile drugs for IV administration is highly complex, and falls into a category that is literally called "high risk sterile compounding."[87]

Most compounding pharmacies lack the infrastructure for high risk sterile compounding. Their facilities, equipment, and air flow are not designed to prevent microbiological contaminants, and they lack the level of environmental monitoring that sterile compounding requires. As the FDA's website notes, the conditions of compounding pharmacies are vastly different from those of drug manufacturers subject to GMPs. Inspections of compounding pharmacies have found "toaster ovens used for sterilization, pet beds near sterile compounding areas, and operators handling sterile drug products with exposed skin, which sheds particles and bacteria."[88]

If compounding pharmacies were required to comply with GMPs for producing sterile injectable drugs, they would be required to adopt a number of environmental controls that would go a long way toward ensuring the quality of their sterile injectables. But they aren't, so the sterile injectables that they produce come with significantly greater risk of bacterial, fungal, and endotoxin contamination, as well as other flaws that affect the strength, quality, and stability of the drug from chemical degradation over time.[89] A tragic example is the fungal meningitis outbreak of 2012: a contaminated compounded injectable infected 750 people and killed 64, all patients who had received those injections as health care.

In the wake of the 2012 tragedy, Congress passed the 2013 Drug Quality and Security Act.[90] The DQSA established a federal regulatory scheme for compounding pharmacies, but its provisions only apply to "nontraditional" compounding pharmacies—pharmacies that are compounding on an industrial scale and thus are more like drug manufacturers than drug prescribers. The loophole that has long existed for local compounding pharmacies mixing individual prescriptions remains untouched.[91]

This is why the attorney general of one executing state thought there was "no way" that drugs compounded for lethal injection would pass constitutional muster. As lethal injection scholar Deborah Denno has noted, a faithful application of the Supreme Court's own precedent would have prohibited the use of compounded drugs in lethal injection long ago.[92] *Baze v. Rees* requires prisoners to show a "substantial risk of serious harm" to prove an Eighth Amendment violation.[93] That standard is plainly satisfied when executing states use compounded drugs. Compounded sterile injectable drugs are inherently high risk. They are literally "*high risk* sterile compounds," and that's not taking into account the lax regulation and high failure rate that pervade the compounding pharmacy industry generally.[94] But courts have not agreed, holding that the use of compounded drugs is not itself sufficient to prove a constitutional violation.[95]

All this is what we know about compounded drugs and sterile injectables generally. Now consider what happens when we add lethal injection to the mix. One wrinkle concerns the compounding process. The other concerns the pharmacies willing to do it.

First, the compounding process. The wrinkle here comes from the fact that although compounding pharmacies make the drugs, they don't make them from scratch. They start with premade active pharmaceutical ingredients (APIs). If compounding pharmacies were subject to federal regulation, they'd have to buy their APIs from FDA-approved suppliers. But they aren't, so they don't. State regulations typically provide that these pharmacies can use their "professional judgment" instead.

For some time now, the API for compounding pentobarbital has not been available on the domestic market, so pharmacy experts say that the pharmacies mixing pentobarbital for executions are almost certainly getting their APIs from the gray or black market.[96] An exception (sort of) is the compounded pentobarbital that the federal government used in its slew of executions in 2020. Turns out, the API for those executions came from a company called Absolute Standards, which does not make drugs for human consumption.[97] As two state legislators noted, Absolute Standards "is not a pharmaceutical corporation—it's a chemical company that makes solution for machines."[98] Upon being identified as an execution drug supplier, Absolute Standards pledged that going forward, it would mind its own business—making chemicals for calibrating machines.[99]

Hence we're back to where we started—there is no known domestic producer of pentobarbital API, so the APIs in compounded pentobarbital for lethal injection are almost certainly coming from grey or black market suppliers. "There are no guarantees that APIs purchased from the grey market are safe for use," one expert says, explaining that they "may be contaminated, super-potent or subpotent, non-sterile, or at risk of an unusually short shelf life."[100] This is why the American Veterinary Medical Association has taken a stand against compounded drugs using non-FDA approved APIs. "Veterinarians cannot guarantee the potency, purity, or safety of these unapproved bulk substances in a compounded product," the AVMA policy states, directing that unless medically necessary, compounded drugs using non-FDA-approved APIs should not be used on animals.[101] Here too, we're using drugs on prisoners that are not allowed for use on people's pets.

Now for the second wrinkle: the caliber of the compounding pharmacies willing to do the work. All three of the major trade groups representing the pharmacy industry have taken a stand against providing drugs for lethal injection.[102] As the press release of the American Pharmacists

Association—the leading voice of the pharmacy profession—explained, supplying drugs for lethal injection is "fundamentally contrary to the role of pharmacists as providers of health care."[103]

Included in these trade groups is the Alliance for Pharmacy Compounding (formerly the International Academy of Compounding Pharmacies). In fact, the APC was the first to issue a statement. It knows better than anyone that supplying drugs for lethal injection is just piling on to the public relations nightmare that has haunted the compounding pharmacy industry since the meningitis outbreak of 2012—especially given the risks associated with compounding quality sterile injectables and the botched executions that occur when contaminated drugs are used. As an example, the first execution using compounded pentobarbital was South Dakota's 2012 botched execution of Eric Robert, whose eyes stayed open during the entirety of his labored twenty-minute execution. Tests on the batch of compounded pentobarbital used in the execution revealed it was contaminated with a fungus.[104]

States have responded to the prospect of yet another industry taking a stand against selling its wares for lethal injection in two ways. One is deception. An example is Texas, which in 2011 was caught falsifying a prescription for compounded pentobarbital, listing the warden as the patient and the address as the Huntsville Unit Hospital, which had been closed since 1983. When the pharmacy figured out that the drug was for lethal injection, it canceled the order, and when prisoners got wind of what the state was doing, they sued.[105] "A federal civil complaint in Texas claims the defendants may have falsified prescriptions, lied to pharmacies and perhaps even broken the law," CNN reported in 2013, when the suit was filed. "But they're not drug runners," CNN noted. "They're officials from the Texas Department of Criminal Justice, responsible for executing death row inmates."[106]

Another example is Idaho. Idaho made the news in 2022 because it was trying to execute a prisoner in hospice care with late-stage bladder cancer, heart disease, and diabetes before he died on his own.[107] Unfortunately for the state, a public records request regarding lethal injection drug purchases that the state had been fighting for years was finally resolved by a court order to release the documents in late 2020. The court found that the Idaho DOC had withheld the documents in bad faith, awarding over $170,000 in attorney's fees to the plaintiff in the case and slapping a $1,000 personal fine on the DOC spokesperson.[108]

The court-ordered document release led to some impressive investigative journalism, which reported in 2022 that the Idaho DOC had used the Idaho Department of Health and Welfare to make a straw purchase of compounded pentobarbital from a pharmacy in Utah in late 2011.[109] A DHW spokesperson confirmed that it had indeed sent a "clinical pharmacist employee" to Salt Lake City for the drug transaction, which was paid for by "upward of $10,000 in cash."[110]

We'll see more straw purchases when we get to the latest development in the lethal injection drug saga—suits by Big Pharma for violating its distribution contracts—but here our focus is compounding pharmacies, and we have yet to discuss the other strategy that states have used to get around an industry that doesn't want to play: find low-caliber compounders who will.

State secrecy laws prevent a fully informed discussion of the compounding pharmacies that executing states use. Some may be great. But *every single one* of the handful of compounding pharmacies whose identities have been revealed tells us otherwise.

Consider, for example, the Apothecary Shoppe in Tulsa, Oklahoma. On at least three occasions in 2013 and 2014, Missouri DOC officials drove to Oklahoma with an envelope containing $11,000 in cash and returned with compounded pentobarbital for use in lethal injection.[111] The Apothecary Shoppe was not licensed to dispense or distribute controlled substances in Missouri (or Georgia or Louisiana, two other states that the Apothecary Shoppe had sent nondisclosure agreements to regarding the sale of drugs for lethal injection), and its interstate sale of a controlled substance without a prescription violated both state and federal laws.[112] When the Apothecary Shoppe's identity was revealed in 2014, a prisoner sued, and soon thereafter, the FDA and Oklahoma Board of

Pharmacy conducted an inspection of the premises, finding *1,892* regulatory violations.[113] The pharmacy's license was placed on probation, and it was fined $50,000. The company ultimately defaulted on loans and auctioned off its assets.

After the Apothecary Shoppe debacle, Missouri needed a new supplier of compounded pentobarbital and found one in 2014, using its newfound supply in seventeen executions.[114] Once again, investigative journalism revealed the source: Foundation Care, a compounding pharmacy in St. Louis with a history of regulatory run-ins with the FDA. In 2007, the FDA inspected Foundation Care in response to a physician's complaint that one of its drugs had caused a patient to become gravely ill. The inspection found that the pharmacy was not testing all of its drugs for sterility, and a lab sample showed that one of its drugs was contaminated with bacteria. The company first denied the contamination, saying it was dust, then said that it had purposely infected the vial as part of its own testing.[115]

Foundation Care was one of a number of "high risk" compounding pharmacies inspected by the FDA in the wake of the 2012 fungal meningitis outbreak. That inspection found poor environmental monitoring, inadequate cleaning of the clean room, shoddy glove and hand-washing practices, and a lack of routine testing for potency and purity.[116] Following its inspection, the FDA sent a letter to the Missouri Board of Pharmacy expressing concerns that Foundation Care's poor sterility practices "could lead to the contamination of drugs, potentially putting patients at risk."[117] It is not clear what, if anything, the state did in response, but in 2017, two Foundation Care employees—one of whom had been the head of pharmacy operations—accused the company of a number of violations of state law, and a former employee sued, claiming she was fired for criticizing the company's "serious operational violations."[118] Litigation revealed that Missouri knew about the complaints against Foundation Care when it contracted with the pharmacy to buy lethal injection drugs.[119] The pharmacy was ultimately sold to a corporate health care subsidiary, which promptly announced that Foundation Care would "never supply any pharmaceutical product to any state for the purpose of effectuating executions."[120]

Another example is Greenpark Compounding Pharmacy and Gifts, located in Houston, Texas. Greenpark admits selling compounded pentobarbital for a number of Texas executions in 2014 and 2015 (apparently, with some regret).[121] When the news broke, Greenpark was on probation with the Texas Board of Pharmacy for forging quality control documents and compounding the wrong drug for three children, one of whom required emergency care. It had also been cited for forty-eight safety violations over the prior eight years, including a citation for using improper procedures to prepare IV solutions.[122]

Greenpark stated that it no longer served as the state's lethal injection drug supplier, which is true—that dubious distinction goes to Rite-Away Pharmacy and Medical Supply, which in 2024 was revealed to be Texas's execution drug supplier from 2019 to 2023. Records showed that Rite-Away had been cited over a dozen times over the past decade for regulatory violations, with multiple inspections showing that it "repeatedly failed to maintain clean and sterile facilities."[123] The pharmacist who mixed the drug for executions stated that a prison official would hand-deliver the API powder for the job. "The powder came in a bag stamped with a photocopied label that [the pharmacist] guessed came from the original container," NPR reported, adding that the pharmacist thought that "the state purchased the larger stash from a 'chemical company.'" A bootleg label from a chemical company—sounds like Absolute Standards, but state secrecy statutes protect the source of even drug *ingredient* suppliers, so it is impossible to know for sure.

Yet another example is SureCare Specialty Pharmacy, located in El Paso, Texas. SureCare is the compounding pharmacy that was supplying Tennessee with drugs in 2022, when the governor stopped executions to conduct an independent review of the state's (non)compliance with its lethal injection protocol. Apparently, Tennessee first managed to buy *manufactured* drugs from SureCare, but soon after the sale was made, the manufacturer (Pfizer) was alerted of the violation of its distribution contract. "They want their drugs back bad," SureCare wrote to its contact at the Tennessee DOC.[124] It's not clear what happened to those drugs, but SureCare's access to controlled distribution products was restricted thereafter. The company then agreed to compound lethal injection drugs for the Tennessee DOC. Investigative journalism revealed that SureCare had previously been fined for failing to disclose an owner's misdemeanor charge to the state pharmacy board, and had been forced to recall some mislabeled compounded drugs.[125]

A final example is the Union Avenue Compounding Pharmacy in Tacoma, Washington, which sold Idaho compounded pentobarbital in 2012, the year after its straw purchase in Salt Lake City. Little wonder that Idaho fought so hard to keep its documents from reaching the public—they revealed that the Idaho DOC director and chief of prisons chartered a private plane to take them on a stealth trip to Washington with a suitcase full of $15,000 in cash, where they exchanged the money for drugs, allegedly in a nearby Walmart parking lot.[126] The owner of Union Avenue Compounding Pharmacy (who was also the pharmacist who made the sale) had her license placed on probation in 2017 for repeated inspection violations, including stocking expired drugs on shelves. She was one of just thirty-five of Washington's eleven thousand licensed pharmacists to have faced suspension in that two-year time frame.[127]

These are the suppliers we know, and they don't inspire confidence in the suppliers we don't know. Turns out, the kind of place that is open to selling death drugs for an envelope of cash is exactly as one might think. States say that their choices are limited—and *it's all abolitionists' fault*. This is the narrative used to justify state secrecy statutes, so we'll turn to it in earnest in chapter 9. Here our focus is not secrecy, but the choices that lurk behind it, and what little we know is enough to (once again) belie state claims that they are using reputable suppliers. They are not.

Sometimes the drugs themselves tell us that. In 2015, for example, Georgia had to halt an execution because the pentobarbital it planned to use was "cloudy."[128] The state said it would investigate and share its findings, then refused to do so, citing its secrecy statute. When a prisoner sued, the state disclosed what it had found: particles that looked like "clumps of cottage cheese floating in the solution," accompanied by a concession from the state's expert that the drug may have been improperly compounded.[129] We don't know whether Georgia still uses that pharmacy, or whether the pharmacy is also compounding sterile injectables for the public. But it's a good bet that Georgians would like to know.

One answer to the inherently high risk involved in compounding sterile injectables is to have them tested for purity and potency. But only four states require testing of compounded drugs in their lethal injection protocols, and even when testing is required, there is no guarantee that it is actually taking place.[130] This is why Tennessee's governor put executions on hold and commissioned an outside review of the state's lethal injection procedures: the DOC wasn't following the testing procedures set forth in its own protocol. Remember Tennessee's botched execution of Billy Ray Irick?[131] Turns out, the drugs used in that execution were beyond their expiration date and had not been tested for potency or endotoxins as required by the lethal injection protocol.[132] The state's outside review also found that the drugs for another execution were tested for potency *and failed*, but the prisoner chose to die by electrocution so they were never used.

Yet even aside from compliance snafus, testing drugs compounded for lethal injection is not the panacea it seems. For one thing, the testing is done by commercial testing facilities, and they *also* may not want to play. An example is the compounded pentobarbital that the federal government used in its rash of executions in 2020. The drugs in those executions were tested by DynaLabs, but it was done on the sly, as DynaLabs has a policy against testing compounded drugs for lethal injection. "We decided seven or eight years ago we were not going to test for compounds that were being used for putting anyone to death," one of the cofounders of the company stated.[133] He learned that his company had been used for testing lethal injection drugs from an investigative reporter, and initially thought the reporter was mistaken, until he confirmed through DOJ records that a batch of pentobarbital used in the federal government's executions had been tested at his lab. DynaLabs now states on its website that clients are required to sign a declaration stating that the drugs will not be used in executions.[134] "The identity of [testing] contractors remains a closely guarded secret," the journalist later reported, "even to some of the contractors themselves."[135]

In addition, these drug testing centers have quality control problems of their own. Neither the FDA nor state pharmacy boards have claimed full regulatory authority over testing centers, so they, too, appear to be falling through the regulatory cracks. It should come as no surprise, then, that a number of these labs have been cited by the FDA for deficiencies in their sterility and testing procedures, and that they likewise have a record of unreliable results.[136] As a case in point, the sterile injectables that infected over 750 people (and killed 64) with fungal meningitis in 2012 was tested by an outside lab, and passed.[137]

When it comes to compounded drugs, one last complication merits mention: their storage and expiration. Compounded pentobarbital doesn't last years like its manufactured version does. Once it has been compounded and put into a solution for IV injection, its expiration is a matter of days. If stored at room temperature, compounded pentobarbital expires in 24 hours. If refrigerated at a temperature between 2–8 degrees Celsius (35–46 degrees Fahrenheit), it expires in 72 hours. And if it is stored in a solid, frozen state at a temperature between −25 and −10 degrees Celsius (between −13 and 14 degrees Fahrenheit), it can last 45 days.[138] What are the chances that states are storing compounded pentobarbital in a manner that allows for its longest shelf-life, or that they're using the drug within a maximum of 45 days?

If you answered *slim to none*, you're in the right range. In 2022, prisoners in Texas sued the state for changing the expiration dates on its compounded pentobarbital. A review of the state's inventory records, including purchase and storage forms, revealed that the vials of compounded pentobarbital that the Texas Department of Criminal Justice (TDCJ) received in 2021 were more than 630 days old, and that the vials it received in 2019 were more than 1,300 days old.[139] The state had conducted dozens of executions with those drugs.

Texas responded that it had tested the vials and "extended" their expiration dates. Apparently, the state first made this move with drugs expiring in 2017, which perhaps explains why five of the thirteen prisoners that Texas executed in 2018 complained of burning sensations as they died, and a sixth writhed on the gurney.[140] A pharmacy professor reviewing the records pointed out that the TDCJ had conducted *potency* testing—which is fine for verifying that a drug contains the right amount of API, but does not test for degradation of the API as there isn't any when a drug is first compounded and potency testing is done. The TDCJ's test was "completely unscientific and incorrect," the professor stated, explaining that a stability study is required to extend the expiration date on a compounded drug.[141] "A stability study determines the proper expiration period," the professor stated, adding: "It is completely wrong to test the medication and to predict what the expiry is based on the current data without any stability study results."[142]

Reading the professor's report, one gets the sense that professionals in the field are aghast at state practices for handling the compounded drugs used in lethal injection. "This practice is completely unacceptable," the professor stated of the TDCJ's storage of the drug, which included testing samples and then putting the tested samples back with the stock.[143] Those samples are contaminated, the professor stated. That just isn't what one does. But it is with lethal injection.

That brings us to the suit that prisoners filed against Texas in 2022 for using expired drugs. The trial court held that the TDCJ's use of expired compounded pentobarbital was in violation of multiple state laws, but the Texas Court of Criminal Appeals ordered the judge to refrain from issuing an order staying the prisoners' executions on that basis.[144] A dissenting judge saw the ruling for what it was: "a Catch-22 in which death-row inmates have a civil remedy to pursue claims regarding the method of execution but may not stop the execution to raise them."[145] After the ruling, the state of Texas simply executed the plaintiffs one by one.

The other state that merits mention here is Arizona. Arizona paid $1.5 million in 2020 for 1,000 units of the API to make pentobarbital, shipped in "unmarked jars and boxes," and another $400,000 to turn the drug into a sterile injectable.[146] (The supplier of the API was later revealed to be Absolute Standards, the federal government's shadow supplier, which explains why the API arrived in unmarked jars and boxes—Absolute Standards doesn't make drugs for human consumption, so it wouldn't have had the FDA labels to slap on those jars and boxes.)[147] Thinking that its compounded pentobarbital would expire in ninety days, the state attorney general at the time, Mark Brnovich, requested expedited judicial review of pending executions, as the state had pledged in a prior settlement agreement not to use expired drugs. When prisoners pointed out that the expiration date of the compounded drugs was forty-five days, not ninety, the state admitted its mistake and asked for an even more compressed schedule. The court denied the request. "He has blown a million and a half dollars on a drug he can't legally use in Arizona," one of the prisoner's lawyers told the press.[148] Citizens of Arizona, this is how your tax dollars were spent.

Compounded lethal injection drugs turn out to be a *lot* of work for low-quality results. A 2020 study of Texas executions, for example, found that Texas's botch rate under its one-drug protocol using compounded pentobarbital was over three times as high as its botch rate using the old three-drug protocol.[149] So much for the one-drug protocol being more humane. Executing states would give anything to go back to the good old days of Big Pharma's reliable, long-lasting drugs. So that's what a number of them did—they went back to Big Pharma's drugs, just without letting Big Pharma know.

I'M GONNA SUE YOU!

The notion of using deception to buy drugs for lethal injection isn't new. States did it back in 2011 with compounding pharmacies. So why not do it with Big Pharma's (better) drugs?

The earliest known example of this is the Louisiana DOC in 2014, which turned to a local hospital for one of the drugs it needed for lethal injection, saying that the drug was "for a medical patient" and directing the drug to be sent to the DOC's medical unit.[150] "At no time was Memorial [Hospital] told the drug would be used for an execution," a hospital spokesperson stated when the ruse came to light, adding, "Had we known the real use, we never would have done it."[151] At the time, the incident appeared to be nothing more than a random lapse of ethical judgment that was an eyesore for the state. "State tricks hospital into giving it hard-to-find execution drugs," one headline read.[152]

But as time passed, it became increasingly clear that the move was not just a one-off. Over the past decade, a good half-dozen states have managed to buy drugs for lethal injection from companies that refuse to sell drugs for lethal injection, using pretense and deception to get around the contractual conditions on those sales.

Consider, for example, Ohio, which used its Department of Mental Health and Addiction to buy drugs from 2017 to 2019 because it knew that the manufacturers had end-user agreements on sales to prevent their products' use in lethal injection. "When you call them to see if they will sell to us, make sure you say we are the Department of Mental Health, do not mention anything about corrections in the phone call or what we use the drug for," one state official instructed in an email about the sale.[153]

For their part, drug manufacturers are done with the cat-and-mouse games that have plagued their relationships with executing states. Now they are suing.

First was McKesson, one of the nation's largest pharmaceutical distributors, which sued Arkansas in 2017 for "using deceit to illegally obtain pharmaceuticals" manufactured by Pfizer and distributed by McKesson.[154] McKesson had its own distribution controls in place—it stood to lose all its Pfizer business if it didn't—and the distributor claimed that the state "intentionally sought to circumvent McKesson's policies."[155] The DOC had purchased the drugs using the medical license of its medical director, McKesson stated, and had the drugs sent to a health-care facility to give the false impression that the drugs were ordered by a physician and would be used in the practice of medicine for a legitimate medical purpose.[156] Those sorts of shenanigans could cost the medical director his license, the Arkansas Medical Board confirmed.[157] Upon learning that a drug sold "under the auspices that it would be used for medical purposes" was instead to be used in an execution, McKesson contacted the DOC, which initially promised to return the drug but then repeatedly refused, ultimately saying that it would not do so unless the company supplied an alternative product for use in executions.[158] That's when McKesson sued.

The Arkansas DOC refused to say whose drugs it had, but Pfizer's tracking system flagged that a "restricted product" had been delivered to the Arkansas DOC, so that much was clear.[159] The state had two other manufacturers' drugs as well, but the manufacturers could only say that they had reason to believe that Arkansas had also "bypassed" their distribution controls and obtained their drugs "in violation of important contractual terms that the manufacturers relied on when selling these medicines."[160] These manufacturers filed an amicus brief in the case, stating that the state's deception in obtaining their products—and refusal to say whether it was even in possession of them—impeded their ability to enforce their contracts, or even know whether their contracts had been breached in the first place.[161] Astoundingly, Arkansas conceded that this was the point, writing in a separate suit over its secrecy provision the same year that secrecy was necessary so that manufacturers would not "interject themselves into litigation in an effort to halt the state's use of their drugs for capital punishment" and "implement even more distribution controls."[162]

The trial court issued a temporary restraining order preventing Arkansas from executing with the drugs it had bought from McKesson, finding that McKesson had shown both irreparable harm and a likelihood of success on the merits of the case.[163] But the Arkansas Supreme Court vacated the order, removed the judge from the case, and then lifted the temporary restraining order that the next judge entered, allowing the executions to go forward.[164] In April 2017, Arkansas executed four prisoners in eight days, and they did it with Pfizer's drugs. "Pharmaceutical companies are trying to circumvent the rule of law by using eleventh-hour litigation tactics to stall these lawful executions," the state's attorney general said when asked about the lawsuit.[165] It's not clear what "rule of law" the state AG thought was being circumvented, but we can safely say that it wasn't contract law because that dubious distinction goes to Arkansas—the state that purposely breached the terms of McKesson's distributor contract and then for good measure passed a secrecy statute in 2019 to cover its tracks in the future.

Suits against Nevada and Nebraska followed in 2018. The suit against Nevada came first, and was filed by the pharmaceutical mogul Alvogen. Alvogen's suit claimed that Nevada "intentionally defrauded Alvogen's distributor" into selling midazolam for lethal injection, demanding the return of its "illegally obtained property."[166] State officials knew that Alvogen had distribution controls in place to prevent its products' use in executions, the company alleged, yet they concealed the intended use of the drug and "implicitly made the false representation that they had a legitimate therapeutic rationale" for buying it—even going so far as to have drug shipped to a location over 200 miles from the state penitentiary "to further the implication that the midazolam was for a legitimate medical purpose."[167]

For Alvogen, the stakes were especially high. The company didn't want its drug used in an execution, but it *really* didn't want its drug used in a botched execution, and Alvogen knew all too well what midazolam could and could not do. "Midazolam is not approved for use [as the sole agent for the induction of anesthesia]," Alvogen stated, and executions using it "have led to widespread concern that prisoners have been exposed to cruel and unusual treatment."[168] The only thing worse than having a state misappropriate its drugs for an execution was having a state misappropriate its drugs for an execution *that was then botched*. Alvogen wanted nothing to with that sort of notoriety.

Once again, the trial court sided with the company, finding that Nevada had acted in "bad faith disregard for Alvogen's rights," using "subterfuge" to obtain Alvogen's midazolam for lethal injection in direct contravention of the distribution controls that it knew the company had in place to prevent such use.[169] In fact, the court noted, the purchasing pharmacy's first move when the state got caught was to ask the prison director whether he wanted to order more of the drug because they were about to be "cut off." The court further found that Alvogen had shown irreparable harm from the shady sale, including reputational damage, lost sales, and potential divestitures by investors, and issued an order prohibiting Nevada from using Alvogen's drugs in an upcoming execution. Nevada appealed, but the case soon became moot. The prisoner whose execution was pending committed suicide in 2019, and Nevada had no other executions pending before Alvogen's midazolam would expire. The parties settled the case in 2020, with Nevada agreeing to return the drugs (which had expired) in exchange for a refund.

That leaves the suit against Nebraska, which was filed in federal court by the German pharmaceutical company Fresenius Kabi.[170] "We made no sales to the Department of Correctional Services, nor have any of our authorized distributors," the company stated, alleging that its drugs "could only have been obtained by defendants in contradiction and contravention of the distribution contracts that the company has in place and therefore through improper or illegal means."[171] Fresenius Kabi alleged "grave harm to its reputation if products intended to help treat people are used to kill," and, like Alvogen, added to its list of harms the specter of a botched execution using its drugs.[172] Its paralytic required refrigeration between 36–46 degrees Fahrenheit, the company stated, but Nebraska's execution protocol called for the drug to be kept at "room temperature storage conditions."[173] The Nebraska DOC wasn't even storing Fresenius Kabi's misappropriated drug properly, so there was a good chance that the drug had degraded and would lead to a torturous death. Here again, Fresenius Kabi wanted nothing to do with that sort of sordid event.

Nebraska refused to say who manufactured its drugs, stating only that the drugs "were purchased lawfully and pursuant to the state of Nebraska's duty to carry out lawful capital sentences."[174] This time, the court sided with Nebraska, finding that the source of the drugs was secret, so the company's concerns were "speculative."[175] Fresenius Kabi appealed, pointing out that it was the only manufacturer that sold the drug in the 30-millileter vials that Nebraska possessed, and Nebraska countered that it was Fresenius Kabi's lawsuit that was drawing attention to its potential involvement, suggesting that any reputational injury the company suffered was its own fault.[176] The Eighth Circuit affirmed, and Nebraska used Fresenius Kabi's drugs in the nation's first ever execution with a four-drug protocol, which it botched.[177]

The most recent skirmish brings us back to Nevada, which in 2021 was once again called out for its illegal drug purchases, this time in a "cease and desist" letter from Hikma Pharmaceuticals. "Hikma has taken proactive action to prevent the sale and distribution of its products to NDOC [Nevada DOC]," the company stated. "Nonetheless, it appears that NDOC has ignored Hikma's repeated demands and, in knowing violation of Hikma's legal rights, express communications with NDOC and express policies and controls, NDOC surreptitiously obtained Hikma's [drug] for use in an execution."[178] Hikma wasn't messing around. "NDOC's purchase and intended use of Hikma's products for capital punishment is in violation of state and federal law, in knowing violation of Hikma's property and proprietary interests in its products, and these actions will cause significant damage to Hikma's business reputation and the interests of its investors," the company stated, demanding the return of its drug.[179]

Hikma was not new to Nevada's misconduct—it was one of two companies that had joined Alvogen's suit against Nevada in 2018. "This is not Hikma's first rodeo with NDOC on this issue," the "cease and desist" letter stated, adding that Nevada's DOC was "well aware of Hikma's long history of opposing the purchase and misuse of its life-saving products for capital punishment."[180] Nevada's repeated violation of Hikma's contractual rights "is nothing less than shocking, and embarrassing for the State of Nevada," the letter stated. In the end, Nevada's supply of Hikma's drugs expired before further action was taken.

One of the most curious features of these Big Pharma suits is the reaction of executing states: a mix of outrage at the fact that companies would sue to enforce their contracts and an obliviousness to the fact that *their* conduct is the reason for those suits in the first place. In the Nevada and Nebraska litigation, for example, a group of fifteen state attorneys general filed an amicus brief accusing the companies in those suits of "abusing the litigation process" by filing "frivolous claims."[181] "I will continue to fight for justice and support my colleagues against these meritless arguments in states like Nevada and Nebraska, where drug companies have asked courts to halt lawful executions," one state's attorney general told the press.[182] Another issued a similar statement, claiming that drug companies "stood between victims' families and justice" and that "no family should be deprived of their hard-won justice and closure because of the hypocritical actions of this drug peddler."[183]

Meanwhile, the fact that states are intentionally breaching contracts left and right appears to be entirely lost on these officials. Lethal injection litigation in Tennessee, for example, revealed that the state had bought midazolam for lethal injection from a manufacturer with distribution controls in place prohibiting the sale. When the company demanded its drugs back, the DOC refused because by its view, it purchased the drug legally. "And do you believe that purchasing midazolam in violation of distribution agreements is legal?" the DOC commissioner was asked under oath. His answer: "I'm assuming it's not illegal because it's—I felt like if it was illegal, I would not do it."[184] Only in the Twilight Zone of lethal injection is this sort of answer possible: *I assume it's legal, because I feel like if it wasn't, I wouldn't do it.*

This state of affairs is particularly ironic given that freedom of contract is a deeply embedded ideal in American culture and jurisprudence alike. "These are free market principles," the director of UK's Reprieve observes. "Right, left—that's something we can all get behind," she says.

"We all understand freedom of contract."[185] Indeed, the Constitution itself prohibits states from passing laws "impairing the obligation of contracts," although these breaches aren't laws or regulations, so the clause does not apply. Still, the typical contracts clause case—some challenge to a government law or regulation that impedes existing contracts[186]—is mere child's play compared to the government directly and intentionally breaching contracts between private parties. In two hundred years, we haven't seen anything like this. Nowhere else can one find the government surreptitiously breaching contracts between private parties operating in a free market. The founding fathers must be rolling over in their graves.

Yet even Big Pharma's suits are allegedly all abolitionists' fault. In their 2018 amicus brief, state attorney generals claimed that the suits were just another iteration of what Justice Alito famously referred to as "a guerilla war against the death penalty."[187] "If Alvogen is allowed to succeed," they argued in Nevada, "there is a substantial risk that pharmaceutical companies—prodded by anti-death penalty activists and defense attorneys—will flood the courts with similar last-minute filings every time a state attempts to see justice done."[188] The attorney for Nevada went one step further. "If third-party business interests can file these lawsuits," he told the court, "the death penalty is effectively dead."[189] *Translation: The only way we can keep executions going is by obtaining drugs by fraud in violation of private contracts. Sure, we took something without consent but it's the death penalty so we can do that.*

We've already talked about Big Pharma's authentic, and substantial, reasons for not wanting their drugs used in executions—no need to rehash that here. But it's worth noting the ridiculousness of the claim that abolitionists are the reason that major pharmaceutical companies are suing. There is no evidence whatsoever to support that claim, and abolitionists couldn't wield that kind of power over these drug manufacturing moguls if they tried. As one legislative white paper notes: "A company that has spent time and money putting restrictions in place to prevent its medicines from being diverted certainly does not want its contracts violated, nor its commercial interests undermined."[190]

This is why these drug manufacturing companies have actively opposed state secrecy statutes and filed briefs in support of litigation challenging their validity—they care, a lot, about their contract rights being respected. Pharmaceutical companies "have a keen and important interest in knowing whether any department of corrections ha[s] obtained their drugs despite and in contravention of their distribution controls and contracts," two German companies wrote in an amicus brief supporting a secrecy challenge in 2017, arguing that the state's efforts to deprive companies of that knowledge "imped[ed] their ability to preserve the integrity of their contracts."[191]

We'll spend an entire chapter talking about the reasons for state secrecy and its consequences, but for now, one can at least say this: executing states are using secrecy not to facilitate contracts with drug suppliers, but to surreptitiously break them. In fact, they are using secrecy to prevent companies from knowing whether their contracts have been broken in the first place. That's quite rich in light of Justice Alito's comment about "a guerilla war against the death penalty."[192] Guerilla warfare refers to unconventional fighting tactics like ambushes, sabotage, subterfuge—stealth moves that bypass the settled rules of engagement.[193] That doesn't describe the abolitionists in this story, but it does describe the actions of executing states.

Regardless of how future litigation over these breach-of-contract claims pan out, drug manufacturers are (largely) winning the day, and not just because the litigation itself often delays executions long enough for the drugs to expire. Big Pharma has a trump card to play, and companies are playing it.

THIS MATTERS TO YOU

We've already seen one way that the search for lethal injection drugs could affect ordinary people like me and you: illicit drugs crossing the border create an unregulated supply chain that could infiltrate back into the domestic drug supply.[194] But that's just the tip of the iceberg. The trump card that pharmaceutical companies are playing is a threat that if states continue to make straw purchases, they won't sell their medicine to executing states *at all*.

A prime example is Ohio. When Ohio was caught making straw purchases through its Department of Mental Health and Addiction, major pharmaceutical companies threatened to stop selling their drugs to any state agency that they suspected might divert those drugs from therapeutic use to executions, which would have kept critical medicines from veterans, youth, and patients receiving drug and alcohol addiction services. "If pharmaceutical companies discontinue supplying medications to the state of Ohio for these populations that are currently being served, it would put tens of thousands of our citizens at risk," the governor stated in 2019, putting executions on hold so the state could consider alternative execution methods that didn't require misappropriating companies' drugs.[195] Executions could only go forward if they could be done "without endangering other Ohioans," the governor said, pointing to "a real threat which we have to take into consideration . . . that the use of a particular drug . . . in a protocol might result in that particular drug company cutting off the State of Ohio."[196]

Hikma Pharmaceuticals, one of the companies that had issued the warning, stated that its admonition was not so much a threat as it was a reminder that wholly aside from its distribution controls, the EU had controls that prohibited the export of drugs that were reasonably likely to be diverted for use in lethal injection.[197] If Ohio didn't stop, it would shut *itself* out of the EU's drug trade. Other pharmaceutical companies have issued similar "reminders" to other executing states, and the message may be finally getting through.[198]

In the federal government's spate of executions in 2020, for example, a Bureau of Prisons memo to Attorney General Barr stated that pharmaceutical companies "would most likely take action against the Bureau of Prisons if they discovered the drugs were used for the purpose of execution, regardless of how we attained them." "Some have threatened to refuse to provide medications used for clinical treatment of inmates should they find out their drugs are being used for executions," the memo continued, stating, "Obviously, we do not want to put the clinical treatment of inmates under our care at risk."[199]

Then there are the public health risks of all the state practices that we've talked about, *combined.* In an amicus brief filed in the Supreme Court's 2019 lethal injection case *Bucklew v. Precythe*, a group of pharmacy and health policy experts—which included a former Commissioner of the FDA—wrote to the Supreme Court about the "serious public health risks" that states were creating in their search for lethal injection drugs. "Many states are undermining the drug control regime, seeking execution drugs through unauthorized channels, importing unapproved products or ingredients from overseas suppliers not subject to U.S. inspection or oversight, obtaining finished products from compounding pharmacies not regulated in that regard, and acting outside the bounds of federal law restrictions," the brief stated.[200] "Each of these facts is problematic individually from a health perspective," the experts explained. "Collectively, they could lead to a public health crisis." The brief implored the Supreme Court to tell executing states that they could not break the law in the name of enforcing it, stressing that "illicit supply channels create an undeniable risk that is broader than lethal injection."[201] *Dear Justices: Even if you don't care about prisoners, you should care about this.*

The Association for Accessible Medicines also filed an amicus brief in *Bucklew*, highlighting yet another way that state lethal injection drug practices place public health at risk: by diverting precious resources away from their medicinal uses.[202] All three of the drugs in the current three-drug lethal injection protocol are on the World Health Organization's "essential medicines" list, and all three are on the FDA's drug shortage list as well.[203] A 2017 study found that the stockpile of lethal injection drugs in just four states was enough to treat 11,257 patients, and in 2020, the COVID crisis led a group of health care professionals to write an open letter to state DOCs.[204] "As pharmacists, public health experts, and front-line ICU doctors serving patients at bedside, we write to inform you that many of the medicines your states are currently hold-ing for lethal injection are in short supply and desperately needed to treat patients suffering from COVID-19," the letter stated, explaining that sedatives and paralytics were already being rationed for patients in need of intubation and mechanical ventilation.[205] "We must prioritize saving the lives of patients over ending the lives of prisoners," the letter admon-ished, adding that "those who might be saved could include a colleague, a loved one, or even you." Notwithstanding the plea, state DOCs sat on their stockpiles.

As a final collateral consequence, consider the costs borne by you and me. The $100,000 here, $1.5 million there in taxpayer money for the drugs.[206] The hundreds of thousands of dollars in litigation expenses when states get sued. And the costs that pharmaceutical companies pass along to consumers to pay for those fancy product-tracking distribution systems to keep drugs out of executioners' hands. You didn't think Big Pharma was absorbing those costs, did you?

These sorts of consequences have some conservatives riled up. "You can't run around and say you are a fiscal conservative, or that you are pro-limited government and for the free market and then behave like this," a spokesperson of the group Conservatives Concerned about the Death Penalty says. "It's completely contradictory to every conservative value."[207] But if a state can't get the drugs it needs for lethal injection, what's it supposed to do?

WHAT'S A STATE TO DO?

Desperate times call for desperate measures, and the first desperate measure is to rush executions before the state's drug supply expires. For example, Arkansas scheduled eight executions on four days (*four double executions*) in a ten-day period in April 2017 because its supply of midazolam was about to expire.[208] All those executions didn't happen, but Arkansas did execute four prisoners in eight days in its "execu-tion blitzkrieg"—a macabre turn for a state that had not conducted an execution since 2005.[209] Kentucky, which had executed only three prisoners in thirty years, reportedly considered executing three *in one day* when it realized that its sodium thiopental was expiring in 2011.[210] And Tennessee asked its state supreme court to expedite eight executions in 2018 because its lethal injection drugs were expiring (five prisoners chose death by electrocution instead).[211] Other states have made similar moves. In fact, Nevada was asking for an expedited execution date in 2021 even as Hikma was telling the state to cease and desist from using its drugs.

But rushing executions is a short-term solution. Eventually, the drug supply will still run dry. What are states to do long-term?

One idea that has been floated over the years is for executing states to make their own lethal injection drugs. Missouri's attorney general said that the state "should establish its own laboratory to produce chemicals for use in executions" and Oklahoma's attorney general has suggested the same thing.[212] Now is a good time to remember that Missouri is the state that hired a doctor with over twenty malpractice suits to mix and measure its drugs, and Oklahoma is the state whose gross incompetence was chronicled in chapter 1. But aside from concerns about what the enterprise would look like in these states, there is a reason that executing states have not established their own lethal injection drug labs, and it comes down to the logistical and legal difficulties of doing so.

States aren't going to build a pharmaceutical manufacturing plant of their own, so what we're really talking about is a state-run compounding pharmacy that could mix drugs to order for lethal injection. For that, states would need equipment, ingredients, and a pharmacist willing to make the drugs. The set-up would be expensive (think facilities, equipment, environmental monitoring—all that a state would need to compound sterile injectables) but maybe not prohibitively so. At this point, it's only money, and states are already spending plenty. But where would states get the APIs?

Big Pharma produces APIs, but companies that are not willing to sell their products for lethal injection are not going to sell pieces of their products for lethal injection, and they're not going to allow their subsidiary companies to do so either. That means we're back where we started—gray-market and black-market suppliers, FDA import restrictions, and another never-ending search, this time for *pieces* of lethal injection drugs. States would also need to hire a pharmacist to compound the drugs, and the ethical implications (and optics) of working in a death drug lab would pose serious challenges of their own. And all that's aside from the fact that no corrections department can comply with the most basic of legal requirements for creating and dispensing compounded drugs: a valid prescription based on a legitimate medical need.[213]

It is unlikely that we'll see a death drug lab anytime soon—if it was doable, it'd already have been done. But the very fact that states have considered this possibility (and let's not forget BYOD) is a testament to just how desperate states are for lethal injection drugs.

States looking for lethal injection drugs are exhausted. Some hobble along, finding suppliers catch as catch can. Others are considering alternative ways to execute—some old, some new—that don't rely on unwilling, unsavory, or unlawful suppliers of lethal injection drugs. As the Oklahoma DOC director told the press when announcing its plan to use nitrogen gas, "I was calling all around the world, to the back streets of the Indian subcontinent," contacting "seedy individuals" in a "mad hunt" for lethal injection drugs.[214] It's hard to keep up with Chris Harris.

7

THE MEDICAL PROFESSION MANDATE

When New Jersey reinstated the death penalty in 1983, the state hadn't conducted an execution in twenty years, so no one knew how to conduct an execution by lethal injection. Doctors at the state prison refused to participate, citing medical ethics that required them to "support life, not end it," and that left prison officials thinking that they might have to conduct the executions themselves.[1] "That is not an easy task for an amateur," a reporter covering the quandary wrote.[2] Unsure of what else do to, officials called upon Fred Leuchter, an engineer who had worked with a number of states to refurbish their electric chairs, to build an apparatus that could take the place of doctors: a lethal injection *machine*.

The machine purported to mechanically inject prisoners with the right syringes, at the right time, and with just the right amount of pressure on the plungers. But after spending over $15,000 on the contraption, prison officials quietly set it aside. No one believed it would actually work, and someone still had to access the prisoner's veins. Besides, after the sale, Leuchter had gained notoriety for the Leuchter report, which purported to show that Auschwitz had no gas chambers and the Holocaust was a hoax. Leuchter's growing fame in neo-Nazi circles also had drawn attention to his credentials, revealing that he wasn't an engineer after all. All Leuchter had was a BA in history and a proclivity for making things up. Leuchter's misrepresentations led to criminal fraud charges, which he settled by serving two years of probation and pledging not to falsely represent himself as an engineer going forward. His reputation ruined, that was the end of Leuchter's lethal injection machine.

Today, Leuchter's lethal injection machine stands as a testament to the conundrum that states faced when they adopted a medicalized means of execution without the medical expertise to carry it out. As we know, states ultimately settled on medical technicians and prison personnel as their frontline executioners. But even those individuals were stand-ins for who states *really* wanted running the show: doctors.

Doctors are the experts of medicine. They have the most training and are best equipped to use the tools of medicine to competently conduct an execution. But doctors have a strong professional identity, and their ethos of life stands in sharp contrast to the executioner's pursuit of death. This has made doctors—or, more accurately, the community of doctors that comprises the medical profession—an unwilling partner in the execution enterprise.

This is not to suggest that doctors or other medical professionals have never been involved in executing criminals. They have. After all, the guillotine was named after French physician Joseph-Ignace Guillotin, who invented it. The electric chair was the suggestion of a dentist (for trivia buffs: that's the reason it was designed as a chair). And the gas chamber was developed by an Army medical corps officer. Aside from that, doctors have always been present to certify a prisoner's death once it has been declared by someone else.

But never before have doctors been an active participant in the execution itself. Whatever one might think of physician-assisted suicide, it's an entirely different ball of wax for doctors to be involved in inducing death against a person's will at the behest of the carceral state. For a profession pledged to life, it is hard to imagine a more taboo act.

But not all members of the medical profession agree. Dissenting voices have their reasons for supporting physician involvement in lethal injection—strong, practical reasons that highlight the medical profession's terrible predicament. This has muddied the waters of the profession's avowed noninvolvement, such that what organized medicine says and what doctors do may be two different things.

People tend to think that lethal injection has the endorsement of the medical community, a downstream effect of the (false) impression that it is a medical procedure performed by medical professionals. Nothing could be further from the truth. The medical profession has a mandate. Not everyone agrees with this mandate, but the medical profession's mandate is a critically important (and all too often overlooked) backstory that shapes what lethal injection looks like today. It is time we heard what the medical profession has to say.

ABOVE ALL, DO NO HARM

For over 2,500 years now, the practice of medicine has come with a simple and sacred command: *Above all, do no harm.* This is the short version of the fifth-century BC Hippocratic Oath. Medical students typically recite some version of the oath at "white coat" ceremonies signifying their entry into the profession and again at graduation. This solemn vow is considered to be the very foundation of the practice of medicine.

Why is the oath so important? The answer lies in the inherently invasive nature of the practice of medicine. As one doctor explains: "The public has granted us extraordinary and exclusive dispensation to administer drugs to people, even to the point of unconsciousness, to put needles and tubes into their bodies, to do what would otherwise be considered assault, because we do so on their behalf—to save their lives and provide them comfort."[3] We allow doctors to cut us open, knock us out, and explore every crevice of our bodies. To do that, we must have every confidence that doctors will use their power only for our good.

So foundational is the "do no harm" principle to the practice of medicine that it is widely viewed as intrinsic to (and thus inseparable from) the profession itself. "In truth, every move a doctor makes is woven with bioethical duty," one article states. "Anything short of this is just torture with a blade or a needle."[4] This is what the renowned physician-philosopher Leon Kass was getting at when he wrote, "A person can choose to be a physician, but [they] cannot choose what physicianship means."[5] The "do no harm" principle is baked into the professional identity of a physician. It is inherent in the meaning of what a doctor is and does.

This is why physician participation in lethal injection is so transgressive. Doctors have taken an oath to protect life, and using the healing arts to kill violates that oath in the most egregious of ways. "The prohibition against killing . . . stands as medicine's first and most abiding taboo," Kass explains, for "it is the dignity and mysterious power of human life itself . . . to which [the physician] has sworn devotion."[6] When a doctor participates in lethal injection, "the doctor is transformed from healer to executioner," another doctor writes. "It is the ultimate betrayal of trust."[7]

The Hippocratic Oath itself speaks directly to the point. The long version of the oath is famous for just one line—the promise to "never do harm to anyone"—but the next line reads: "*To please no one will I prescribe a deadly drug*, nor give advice which may cause his death."[8] That's right, the idea of lethal injection (or at the time, lethal *ingestion*) has been strictly forbidden for over 2,500 years by the very words of the Hippocratic Oath.

Now we can see why even physician-assisted suicide is controversial within the medical profession. But again, our concern is not the induction of death to further the personal autonomy of a terminally ill patient. It is the induction of death as court-ordered punishment to further the aims of the carceral state. "We don't kill people who want to live. We don't help others kill people who want to live," one doctor explains. "Once you cross the line as an agent/enabler of the state to cause death of someone not seeking to die, you are no longer a healer."[9]

All this is to say that the medical profession's opposition to physician participation in lethal injection is born of a strong sense of professional identity. As one bioethicist explains, it is "the proper, conditioned, professional reflex" to the invitation to do grave harm.[10] Asking doctors to help the state kill is like "asking a lifeguard to advise people on how to drown better," one doctor says.[11] It is asking someone to help do something that their occupation is devoted to prevent from happening at all.

TRANSCENDENT HARMS

Even when doctors don't participate, lethal injection imposes larger, transcendent harms upon the medical profession—an inevitable consequence of the fact that lethal injection cannot be divorced from its medical context. "Even without physician participation, the lethal injection process so closely mimics medical practice that the entire medical community is tied to the death chamber," one oft-cited author states.[12] Lethal injection is not the practice of medicine, but it uses the tools and techniques of the practice of medicine. It *repurposes* medicine, and thus implicates the medical profession whether doctors choose to be a part of it or not.

Within the medical literature, these transcendent harms are referred to as *corruption* and *exploitation*.[13] Lethal injection corrupts the medical profession, articles say, by undermining the foundation of trust upon which it is based and denigrating its moral stature. Executions are dirty business, and the medical profession is understandably fond of its white coats and all that they represent. As one medical journal puts the point: "The public may like executions, but no one likes executioners."[14]

Lethal injection also exploits the medical profession, articles say, by leveraging the profession's cultural cache to give legitimacy to a practice directly opposite of the values that it has vowed to protect. This is accomplished in at least three ways.

First, lethal injection falsely gives the impression of care and competence. "The state wishes the public to believe that lethal injection is subject to the same safety oversights as medical procedures," says Dr. Joel Zivot, a professor of anesthesiology and outspoken critic of lethal injection. But as Zivot explains: "This is a false claim. Lethal injection is not subject to anything within medical or pharmaceutical regulation."[15] The American Medical Association wrote about this in a 2018 amicus brief to the Supreme Court, accusing states of "intentionally mimicking a medical procedure, thereby deceiving . . . the public, which imagines safe oversight."[16]

Second, lethal injection gives the false impression that it has the backing of the medical profession. Lethal injection "deceptively places the physician's stamp of approval on an act that runs counter to the most basic values of the medical profession," one commentary claims.[17] The AMA's 2018 amicus brief wrote about this too, stating that lethal injection "falsely suggests to society that capital punishment can be carried out humanely, with the endorsement of the medical profession."[18]

Zivot thinks this is what states *really* get from physician involvement. Torturous drugs are going to cause torturous deaths no matter what, but he says having a doctor on board allows states to project the humanity of the medical profession onto a practice that does not deserve it. As Zivot puts the point, it allows states to say: *"Listen, we've got this, you know, we've got a doctor here. It's civilized, we're civilized people."*[19]

Third and perhaps most importantly, lethal injection makes state violence look like something else. Lethal injection is "the ultimate cleansing of human executions," one article says—an effort to make executions "akin to the painless 'putting to sleep' of our beloved pets, except under the guidance of enlightened and compassionate physicians rather than veterinarians."[20] Others echo the point, writing that lethal injection uses the imagery of healing to "sanitize executions" and whitewash the reality of what executions are.[21] That's a dangerous game, medical ethicists warn. "If the state wants to kill people, the state should take the responsibility for executions and not ask physicians to loan the halo effect of medicine," one article states.[22] Medicine should never be wielded as punishment, ethicists say, and punishment should never be so objectionable that it must hide under the cloak of medicine.

Here we see the scars of a profession clearly haunted by its role in the Nazi Holocaust. References to Nazi doctors pervade the medical literature on lethal injection and spill over into amicus briefs and opinion pieces, casting a long shadow over debates about lethal injection and physician participation in executions. Granted, comparisons to the Holocaust are perilous, as they risk trivializing the horrors of the past and/or overstating the dangers of the present. But the specter of Nazi doctors is an integral part of the medical community's conversation about lethal injection, and so it will be a part of our conversation too.

For the unfamiliar, Nazi Germany's T-4 program killed some 250,000 people labeled as "undesirables" by injecting them with phenol, using doctors to administer the injections.[23] Psychological trauma from killing by other, more violent means led the Nazis to look to the medical model, explains psychiatrist and cultural historian Robert Lifton in a widely acclaimed book on the topic.[24] The "medicalization of killing" is what allowed the killing to take place, Lifton writes, arguing that "the destruction of the boundary between healing and killing" was "at the heart of the Nazi enterprise."[25] As one Nazi doctor who he interviewed explained: "People felt this is not murder, it is a putting-to-sleep."[26] Doctors told themselves that these individuals were already condemned, so their work was euthanasia—"a good death."[27] As a matter of fact, "T-4" was just the code name for the project; its formal name was the "Nazi Euthanasia Program." If the state was going to euthanize people with phenol injections, doctors felt they were the ones to do it. This sentiment was captured in the T-4 program administrator's motto: "The syringe belongs in the hand of a physician."[28]

To be sure, there is an enormous difference between the genocidal mass murders of which the Nazi doctors were a part, and physician participation in executions that follow a lawful sentence of death. But there are striking similarities too. "The AMA is acutely aware of this stain on the medical profession," the AMA's 2018 amicus brief stated, referring to the Nazi doctors. "By refusing to participate in capital punishment, even when sanctioned by a free society," it went on to say, "physicians are making a statement—even if symbolically—that their role is not to serve the state as experts in killing, but to minister to their patients as healers."[29] What happened in the Holocaust was so unspeakably horrendous that doctors could never go near state killing again.

All this is the reason why many in the medical profession are against not only physician participation in lethal injection, but also lethal injection itself. "If the state wishes to execute individuals, that's the state's prerogative," says Zivot. "But I would ask them to stay away from everything that is mine, everything that is medicine," he says.[30] "Speaking as a physician, I just want to say: *Leave my stuff alone. Leave my profession out of it.*"[31]

A STRONG (BUT LARGELY UNENFORCEABLE) STAND

At this point, it should come as no surprise that the medical profession opposed lethal injection from the start. As a matter of fact, the medical profession opposed lethal injection almost ninety years *before* its start. In 1888, when a New York commission recommended the electric chair as an alternative to hanging, the commission considered—and *rejected*—the idea of lethal injection based in large part on "the almost unanimous protest of the medical profession."[32] Jay Chapman did no research, so he would not have seen that report, but he was well aware of the medical community's opposition to lethal injection because that was the reason he was involved in the first place—everyone else in the profession said no.

In the wake of Oklahoma's adoption of lethal injection, medical societies in other states mobilized to make their opposition known. Indeed, for a time, it appeared that the objections of the medical community would prevent lethal injection from gaining traction in other states. Doctors testified against lethal injection bills, and state medical societies took strong stands against them, resulting in a dozen states initially rejecting proposals to adopt lethal injection.[33] But the allure of a death that looked like sleep was too strong for states to resist, and the execution method eventually took the country by storm. At that point, the most that the medical profession could do was get the organizations that represented it to tell their members not to participate—and that is exactly what happened next.

The AMA—the "voice of American medicine"—was first, issuing a statement against physician participation in executions in 1980.[34] At the time, just four states had adopted lethal injection, and no state had actually used the new execution method (that didn't happen until 1982).

Today, that prohibition is codified as Rule 9.7.3 of the AMA Code of Medical Ethics: "An individual's opinion on capital punishment is the personal moral decision of the individual . . . [but] a physician must not participate in a legally authorized execution."[35]

The AMA's rule raises the question of what it means to "participate" in an execution, and the Code of Medical Ethics speaks to this too. Anything making lethal injection a reality in any way—from prescribing or preparing lethal injection drugs, to starting IV lines, to monitoring vital signs, to rendering technical advice, to supervising "lethal injection personnel"—is off-limits.[36] As one trade journal told its readers: "Don't advise, don't prescribe, don't inject."[37]

Over time, every national medical association in the country issued a statement prohibiting its members from participating in lethal injection, using the AMA's definition of what "participation" meant.[38] These include: the American Society of Anesthesiologists, the American Board of Anesthesiologists, the American College of Correctional Physicians, the American College of Physicians, the American Public Health Association, the American Nurses Association, the American Correctional Health Services Association, the American Psychiatric Association, the American Academy of Physician Assistants, the National Association of Emergency Medical Technicians, and the American Osteopathic Association. The World Medical Association and a host of state medical associations have issued statements as well.[39]

Of the various medical associations listed, two merit separate mention. One is the National Association of Emergency Medical Technicians (NAEMT). As we know, execution IV teams typically use medical technicians to insert the catheter for a lethal injection. In doing so, those technicians are violating the oath they *also* have taken to do no harm. "Regardless of the personal opinion of the EMT or paramedic on the appropriateness of capital punishment," NAEMT's position statement reads, "it is a breach of the foundational precepts of emergency medical services, and a violation of the EMT Oath, to participate in taking the life of any person."[40]

The other organization that merits mention is the American Society of Anesthesiologists (ASA). The ASA and its members have a special interest in lethal injection, because when we say that lethal injection mimics the practice of medicine, the medical professionals it is mimicking are *them*. This has made the ASA especially sensitive to calls from courts, commentators, and capital defense attorneys to come to the aid of states so that executions by lethal injection are at least performed in a competent manner. "Execution by lethal injection has resulted in the incorrect association of capital punishment with the practice of medicine, particularly anesthesiology," the ASA lamented in 2006.[41] In an open letter to members that same year, the president of the ASA issued his response:

> Lethal injection was not anesthesiology's idea. American society decided to have capital punishment as part of our legal system and to carry it out with lethal injection. The fact that problems are surfacing is not our dilemma. The legal system has painted itself into this corner and it is not our obligation to get it out.[42]

States adopted a medical means of execution without bothering to get the medical profession on board—and, more to the point, knowing that it was not. States made their bed. Now they could lie in it.

The American Board of Anesthesiologists (ABA) followed by incorporating the AMA's ethics rule into its own professional standing policy in 2010. "Anesthesiologists may not participate in capital punishment if they wish to be certified by the ABA," its announcement read, adding that "ABA certificates may be revoked if the ABA determines that a diplomate participates in an execution by lethal injection."[43] Board certification is generally required for hospital practice privileges, so revoking an anesthesiologist's certification would be a devastating sanction. The ABA wasn't playing. "Anesthesiologists are healers, not executioners," the board stated.[44] And with its threat to revoke the professional standing of anesthesiologists who violated their oath, the ABA would make sure they stayed that way.

The strident response of the medical profession to calls for physician participation in executions by lethal injection was ably captured in a physician's 2009 op-ed, which stated:

> Attention legislators, justices, and assorted members of the executive branch: We do not kill to fulfill the state's business. The Constitution says that you must not let prisoners suffer 'cruel and unusual punishment' and so you decide physicians would help you kill in a constitutional manner. That morally dubious thinking may be popular within your circles, but legal decisions aside, the white-coated set is simply not going to comply.[45]

As one medical journal article noted, the medical profession's response was "not simple reluctance, but down-right refusal to play the role of hand-maiden to the executioner."[46] States may have usurped medical tools and techniques, but they were not entitled to the expertise that went with them.

Yet aside from the ABA's threat to revoke board certification, these sorts of pronouncements were all bark and no bite. The most that medical professional organizations could do was revoke membership, but membership was purely voluntary, and had no effect on a physician's ability to practice. Most physicians weren't members in the first place.

If one wanted to suspend or revoke a physician's license for violating an ethics rule, the place to go was the state board of medicine, but these were hamstrung too. State medical boards are the chief regulators of the practice of medicine within each state. They are created by state medical practice acts, which give them statutory authority to award licenses to practice medicine within the state, publish guidelines for the ethical practice of medicine, and enforce those guidelines with disciplinary proceedings. Given that, state medical boards would appear to be the ideal place to enforce the ethical prohibition against participating in lethal injection.

But state medical boards haven't done so, and the reason they haven't is almost certainly because of what happened when one tried. In 2007, the North Carolina Medical Board announced that any physician who "facilitates [an] execution may be subject to disciplinary action by this board."[47] The state DOC sued, arguing that the board had overstepped its authority, and the state supreme court agreed. The high court reasoned that the state legislature had created the board in its medical practice act—the board was an arm of the state—and the state's lethal injection protocol allowed physician involvement.[48] As such, the board could not discipline doctors for participating in lethal injection—that would be tantamount to one arm of the state punishing what another arm of the state allowed. To this day, no doctor has ever been disciplined by a state medical board for participating in lethal injection, and given the fact that all state medical boards are an arm of the state, and every state but one (Kentucky) permits physician involvement in executions, it is likely that no doctor ever will be.

But just to hedge their bets, executing states across the country have since passed "shield" statutes to protect physicians who participate in lethal injection from disciplinary action by the state medical board. These statutes come in a variety of forms.[49] Some are "exemption" statutes stating that participation in executions is outside the practice of medicine and thus exempt from the medical board's authority. Others are "safe harbor" statutes protecting physicians from disciplinary action. Still others are "immunity" statutes precluding any and all liability, civil or criminal, for any act performed in good faith while participating in an execution, including acts that constitute gross incompetence. Whatever the flavor, these shield statutes are an astounding assault on the long-standing autonomy of the medical profession to enforce its professional standards and regulate its own members.

To appreciate the point, consider what it would look like if a similar rule applied to lawyers—an analogy not just for lawyers, but also any client they might represent (i.e., you). Lawyers are licensed by state bar associations and must be members in good standing to practice law in a state. State bar associations, like state medical boards, set professional standards for their members and can take disciplinary action when those standards are not met. Now imagine that a state legislature told its bar association: *We know you have your rules of professional conduct, but what we're doing is more important. So we're going to ask attorneys to break their ethical rules, and we are going to prevent you from doing a single thing about it.*

Lawyers take client confidences extremely seriously—it's one of the legal profession's most sacred rules—so let's say the law said this:

> *If your client is accused of [insert crime] and confesses to you, we ask that you disclose this to the state in some confidential way, even though it is a breach of your duty of loyalty to the client and completely antithetical to what representation means. True, clients won't trust you anymore, so the rule is damaging to the profession. And true, the state is capitalizing on that trust to serve its own purposes. But we will find a few attorneys who are willing to do this, and we will protect them from any professional consequences of such action by removing the act that violates your ethical rules from your jurisdiction entirely.*

If this is hard to imagine, it is because lawyers would never allow such a thing to happen. If only they were more protective of the other self-regulating profession—the one that saves lives.

None of this is to say that there are no consequences for doctors who participate in executions by lethal injection. If their identity is revealed—admittedly, a big *if*—they would suffer reputational harm and likely be ostracized by the larger medical community. That's not nothing.

But it is to say that sanctions are not enforcing the prohibition against participating in executions by lethal injection. What enforces the rule is the power of the precept itself—the profession's fidelity to the "do no harm" principle even in the absence of an effective enforcement mechanism. Yet this also means that there's nothing stopping doctors from participating if they want to—and they do. Or at least *a few* do, and all a state needs is one.

I DISSENT, IN THE NAME OF BENEFICENCE

Given that participation means participation in any way, doctors are def-initely participating in executions by lethal injection. Any time a doctor writes a prescription for lethal injection drugs, that doctor is participat-ing. We know from lethal injection litigation that doctors participate in other ways too: they conduct conscious checks, set central lines when the IV team cannot access a peripheral vein (which is common), and stand by as needed.

Maybe they do more than that. Maybe they're all in from the start. With secrecy statutes, it's hard to know the full extent of physician in-volvement, although doctors who have spoken publicly about their par-ticipation almost always go out of their way to say that they don't push the syringes that deliver the deadly drugs.[50] Prison personnel do that. Even these doctors appear to have a line they're not willing to cross.

What we do know is this: even if doctors are participating in execu-tions by lethal injection, their participation is limited. As lethal injection scholar Ty Alper, who has done extensive research on physician involve-ment in lethal injection, explains:

> You may have a doctor helping to mix the drug or helping to set the IV or overseeing the whole process, but you *don't* have a doctor monitoring anesthetic development or the maintenance of anesthesia throughout the execution. Instead, you have someone like the warden conducting something like a conscious check. . . . The warden goes in and shakes the inmate and that's supposed to determine whether he's under a suf-ficient level of anesthesia.[51]

When doctors participate in lethal injection, we tend to think they are doing the whole thing, or at least the most important things. Not so. "What I would want a doctor doing if I was laying on the table being executed is . . . making sure that I can't feel anything that's happening to me," Alper says, adding: "That's not happening in any state that I'm aware of."

The result is the worst of both worlds. Doctors are participating in executions, violating their ethical rules. But they aren't doing the things that we think comes with that participation.

Yet even the phenomenon of doctor participation may be smaller than the debate surrounding it would have us believe. Critics say that physician participation in lethal injection reflects "a dramatic failure of medical professionalism."[52] It's not clear that this is true. What we know suggests that we are likely talking about a dozen doctors (if that) in a sea of just over a million practicing physicians in the United States.

One data point is the work of Dr. Atul Gawande, a Harvard Medical School professor who conducted interviews with four physicians and a nurse who collectively participated in forty-five executions by lethal injection.[53] We'll be talking about this work shortly, but the point here is the small number of people conducting a large number of executions. Another data point is Alan Doerhoff—our malpractice-ridden doctor from chapter 5—who conducted executions not only for Missouri, but also two other states and the federal government. Some doctor-executioners *travel*. Yet another data point is the sheer paucity of executions nationally and their concentration in just a few states. The year 2023 was the nation's ninth consecutive year with less than thirty executions nationwide, and Texas and Florida conducted more than half of 2023's executions—fourteen of twenty-four—alone.[54]

These data points suggest that an exceedingly small number of doctors are participating in the lion's share of executions. These are the medical profession's dissenting voices, and they are joined by dissenting voices in the medical literature and larger public discourse who support their work.[55] Why do doctors participate in lethal injection, and why do some say it is the right thing for doctors to do?

One reason *not* part of the conversation but that merits mention anyway is money. A doctor willing to participate in executions is a precious commodity, and states will pay dearly for it. In 2022, investigative reporting in Oklahoma broke the news that whoever the state's doctor-executioner is, they are getting paid $15,000 in cash per execution—in theory, for less than an hour of "work"—and in light of the state's plan to expedite the executions of twenty-eight prisoners, that doctor stood to make $420,000 from the executions, and another $56,000 for attending training sessions over the course of two years.[56] That's upwards of a *half-million dollars* for a couple dozen cameo appearances. When Arizona's death chamber was up and running, it paid doctors even more—$18,000 in cash per execution.[57] No doctor yet has said that they're participating in executions for the money. But the fact that they can make a killing from state killing has to be worth something.

Now, for the reasons that doctors do give. Here, Gwande's interviews with four doctors and a nurse who participated in executions by lethal injection are enlightening. "None were zealots for the death penalty, and none had a simple explanation for why they did this work," Gawande reported. "The role, most said, had crept up on them."[58] To illustrate the point, Gawande paraphrased one doctor's account as follows: "The technicians would stick and stick and, after half an hour, give up. . . . Dr. A had placed numerous lines. Could he give it a try? OK, Dr. A. decided. Let me take a look. This was a turning point, though he didn't recognize it at the time. He was there to help, they had a problem, and so he would help. It did not occur to him to do otherwise."[59] Gawande explained that "just by being present, by having expertise, he had opened himself to being called on to do steadily more, to take responsibility for the execution himself."[60]

As another example, the doctor in Clayton Lockett's execution had been told that his role was just to declare unconsciousness and pronounce death. "I was hesitant to do anything," he told investigators, adding that at one point during the execution, he had said: "I don't know, you know, what my status is inside here. I'm not supposed to be doing anything except you know, deciding whether he was unconscious and then declaring him deceased."[61] The doctor had been told that he might have to insert an IV "in an emergent situation" but that was something he didn't think he would actually have to do.

But responsibility creep (like money) is an explanation for participation, not a defense. Perusing the medical literature, one finds a number of defenses, but the most common argument offered is also by far the strongest: because the skills of a physician are so desperately needed.

Some pain is avoidable, some not. Torturous drugs make torturous deaths a given, but the sort of grisly botched executions that Clayton Lockett and Ángel Díaz suffered because the drugs weren't even going into their veins was entirely avoidable. Of course, having a doctor on board doesn't mean that avoidable pain will be avoided. It didn't work out that way for Clayton Lockett. But errors conducting the exceedingly delicate procedure of lethal injection are a cause of torturous deaths all their own, and that cause can be virtually eliminated by ensuring that executions by lethal injection are at least conducted in a competent manner.

"So long as the state uses the tools of the physician to kill its citizens, those who wish to step in to ensure that executions are, at the very least, competently handled should have the option to do so," wrote one pair of doctors in a *New York Times* editorial, arguing, "No matter where you come out on capital punishment, no one should be sentenced to a botched execution."[62] Another dissenting voice lamented that while well intentioned, medical ethics rules "have mostly kept the amateurs and their ad hoc methods on the job."[63] Here, then, is the pitch for physician participation in lethal injection: prisoners will suffer *more* without it.

This is the principle of *beneficence*, and it comes from another ethical command that has been attributed to Hippocrates (and others): "To cure sometimes, to relieve often, and to comfort always."[64] Beneficence requires that when doctors cannot save life, they comfort in death instead.

Physicians who participate in executions say this is exactly what they are doing. "The way I see it, this is an end-of-life issue, just as with any other terminal disease. It just happens to involve a legal process instead of a medical process," explained one of the doctors that Gawande interviewed. A condemned prisoner "is no different from a patient dying of cancer," he said, "except his cancer is a court order."[65] Another interviewee stated, "We, as doctors, are not the ones deciding the fate of this individual."[66] The fate of condemned prisoners is sealed. That's what makes them *condemned.*

"Are you, as a doctor, going to let this person stab the inmate for half an hour because of his inexperience?" the nurse in Gawande's study asked, answering: "I wasn't. I had no qualms. If this is to be done correctly, if it is to be done at all, then I am the person to do it."[67] Similarly, a doctor who was interviewed for a documentary on physician participation in lethal injection explained: "The one thought I had over and over again was if it were me there or a family member, would I want somebody like me there? And the answer was yes."[68]

These dissenting voices highlight the dreadful choice that lethal injection forces the medical profession to make: stay true to its ancient oath and stand idly by while prisoners suffer protracted, excruciatingly painful deaths, or turn its back on the oath that defines it in order to provide a competent death. This is the so-called "Hippocratic Paradox"— physician participation is both necessary for a reliably competent execution *and* prohibited by medical ethics rules—and it is deeply destructive to the profession as a whole.[69] Both horns of the dilemma impose harms, and the choice that it forces upon the medical profession (and division it creates in doing so) is a harm unto itself.

For the medical profession, the choice is distressing but clear. "In return for possible reduction in pain," a report of the American College of Physicians states, the physician "becomes the handmaiden of the state as executioner."[70] Beneficence in executions is not free standing. Beneficence and maleficence are inextricably intertwined. As Gawande puts the point, "The hand of comfort that more gently places the IV, more carefully times the bolus of potassium, is also the hand of death."[71] The hand that kills gently, kills nevertheless.

Moreover, acquiescence to medicalized executions imposes harms of its own, physicians say, "prolonging the acceptability of a practice that tears at the fabric of standard medical norms."[72] Physician participation in lethal injection just stabilizes its use, doing well what doctors should not be doing at all. "The medicalization of execution I think does impact public perception," one doctor-executioner reflected. "Does that make us more comfortable with capital punishment?" he asked, then answered: "Probably."[73]

Should the medical profession bend to the reality of medicalized executions to at least provide a competent death? The answer is not for an outsider to say, but echoes of a past paradox are plainly present in today's debate. *If it is to be done at all, then I am the person to do it* is not so different from *The syringe belongs in the hands of a physician.*

THE LAW AND THE MEDICAL PROFESSION'S MANDATE

From the start, medical ethics have been an integral part of the legal wrangling over lethal injection. What would the law do with the medical profession's mandate? The answer came in two Supreme Court cases.

One is 2008's *Baze v. Reez*. In *Baze*, the prisoners argued that if Kentucky insisted upon retaining the three-drug protocol, it could at least do a better job of ensuring that executions were carried out in a competent manner. Kentucky had nonmedical prison personnel performing medical tasks for which they were not qualified, the prisoners argued, and they certainly weren't qualified to do what needed to be done for a nontorturous death by torturous drugs: reliably achieve a state of anesthesia.

Kentucky answered that the prisoners were trying to "transform the execution chamber into a surgical suite" (oblivious to the fact that its adoption of lethal injection already had).[74] Medical ethics didn't allow doctors to participate, the state argued, so requiring medical expertise would amount to prohibiting an execution by lethal injection altogether. The Supreme Court agreed. The call for medical professionals to conduct a medicalized execution, the *Baze* opinion would say, was "nothing more than an argument against the entire procedure."[75]

In a separate opinion devoted solely to the medical ethics issue, Justice Alito acknowledged that trained professionals could minimize the risk of pain. "But the ethics rules of medical professionals—for reasons

THE MEDICAL PROFESSION MANDATE

that I certainly do not question here—prohibit their participation in executions," he wrote.[76] Lethal injection "must not be blocked by procedural requirements that cannot practicably be satisfied," Justice Alito admonished, apparently unaware of the fact that ethics rules prohibited medical technicians from participating too.[77] Medical personnel were already violating their ethical rules. They were just setting the IV and then leaving the room.

In *Baze*, the Supreme Court held that the law would not require what medicine did not allow, ending once and for all the notion that prisoners were entitled to executions by more than prison guards and medical technicians. Faced with the fact that medical expertise was both necessary for a reliably competent execution *and* prohibited by medical ethics rules, the Court ruled that the standard for a reliably competent execution would give way.

The Justices could have said to executing states: *You knew that the medical profession was not a willing partner in the execution enterprise due to ethical precommitments that go to the heart of the profession itself, and yet you adopted this method of execution anyway. Your failure to think through the execution method that you yourselves chose does not mean that you can execute prisoners in a thoroughly amateur fashion.*

But the Justices didn't say that. Instead they said: *We know that expertise would make lethal injection less risky, but expertise is not available because of medical ethics rules, so lethal injection need not be less risky.*

What a boon for executing states. Under *Baze*, states are able to have their cake and eat it too, doing everything they can to give executions the look and feel of a medical act without having to provide the medical expertise that we assume comes with it. As Ty Alper's work has shown, states have managed to make medical ethics rules work for them, turning the prohibition on physician involvement into a powerful argument to lower the legal standard of competency and expertise—even as doctors are in fact participating.[78]

Forced to choose between ethics and expertise, *Baze* told states they didn't need expertise. But states knew better, and their solution to the impasse was to go the other way, telling doctors they didn't need to worry about medical ethics rules. That's the reason for the shield laws: states need doctors no matter what the Justices say.

In 2019, medical ethics once again came to the fore in *Bucklew v. Precythe*. The Supreme Court in *Glossip v. Gross* had held that prisoners challenging an execution method must provide the state with an alternative way to execute them, and in *Bucklew*, the trial court had ruled that the prisoner failed to meet that morbid burden.[79] That's where medical ethics came into play: the doctor who testified for the prisoner told the court that he could critique the state's method, but he could not speak to the feasibility of an alternative method of execution. "As a medical doctor, I am ethically prevented from prescribing or proscribing a method of executing a person," he stated. "I am bound by these ethics, and am prohibited from assessing whether a different form of execution would be feasible."[80]

The AMA submitted an amicus brief in *Bucklew* to express outrage at lethal injection once again inviting doctors to violate their medical ethics—this time, at the behest of prisoners trying to vindicate their constitutional rights. Lethal injection "attempts to medicalize [an execution] in a self-deceiving effort to mitigate its barbarity," the AMA wrote. The brief left no doubt as to where the AMA stood. "Society wants to delude itself into a belief that capital punishment no longer represents a weighted moral choice, but is now somehow scientific—nearly antiseptic," the AMA stated, adding: "The medical profession, whose 'essential quality' is an interest in humanity and which reveres human life, should have no part in this charade."[81]

Bucklew raised the question of whether the prisoner would get the same break as the state did in *Baze*. Would the Justices say, as they did in *Baze*, that the law would not require what medical ethics would not allow?

The answer was no. Bucklew was required to show that his alternative execution method came with a lower risk of pain, the Supreme Court ruled, and this he failed to do.[82] The *Bucklew* opinion read as though medical ethics had no implications whatsoever in the case, but the Court's silence spoke volumes. In *Baze*, medical ethics mattered. In *Bucklew*, they didn't. The only consistency in the cases was a ruling that cut against the prisoners and in favor of the state.

WHAT LETHAL INJECTION LOOKS LIKE TODAY

Despite the Supreme Court's best efforts to free lethal injection from the ethical constraints that bind it, the fact that lethal injection is inextricably tied to medicine means that it is also inextricably tied to the medical profession's mandate. "Medicine has dismantled the death penalty," Deborah Denno wrote of lethal injection in 2007, and it continues to have a stunning impact on what lethal injection looks like today.[83]

Start with executioners. In 2022, Nevada announced that it didn't have any, and thus could not go forward with its next execution even if it could get past the legal hurdles to do so and its fight over Hikma's drugs. The state had a doctor and two emergency medical technicians tapped for the execution (another doctor had been "excluded" upon learning "additional information").[84] But when a judge asked the DOC to provide information about these executioners' credentials—information the court would review and redact as needed to protect their anonymity—all three backed out. "NDOC no longer has an attending physician or EMTs willing to participate in the execution," a spokesperson stated.[85]

States like Nevada may eventually find a doctor to participate in executions by lethal injection, but there's no question that the ethical prohibition against doing so (and the reputational risks of violating it) makes this quest more difficult. States are looking for people at the margins of the profession—doctors willing to eschew an oath that the vast majority of the profession finds inviolable. As we know from Missouri and Tennessee's malpractice-ridden doctors, these doctors may be marginal in other ways as well. High profile botched executions only exacerbate the problem, making physician participation in executions what one observer calls a "medical pariah issue" that is "shaming away" those who otherwise may have been willing to participate.[86]

Next consider the dearth of technical advice supporting state lethal injection protocols. If states don't have a physician at an execution, that impacts the execution. If states don't have a physician helping them design their lethal injection protocols, that impacts *every* execution.

Medical ethics govern not only the practice of medicine, but also the medical science behind it. "The expertise of doctors and biomedical researchers was developed by individuals, institutions, and science dedicated to saving and improving human lives," one team of researchers writes. "Appropriating that knowledge to kill is an appalling betrayal of the core values of medical research."[87] This is why the prohibition against physician participation in executions includes giving states technical advice. In fact, the long form of the ancient Hippocratic Oath is explicit on this point, stating: "I will not give a lethal drug to anyone if I am asked, *nor will I advise such a plan*."[88]

We have seen the impact of this prohibition. This is how we ended up with Jay Chapman designing the nation's first lethal injection protocol. And this is why the drug used in Clayton Lockett's execution came from an attorney surfing the web. Even the short-term success of a fraud like Fred Leuchter was only possible because of the Grand Canyon-sized void in expert advice on lethal injection.

"Identifying qualified medical personnel willing and able to provide advice to the state regarding lethal injection options continues to be challenging and time-consuming," one state attorney general has conceded.[89] As Deborah Denno explains: "It's not like you have a scientific expert sitting there and saying 'these are the drugs you should use and in this amount.' To the contrary, I think one of the reasons we see these constant problems . . . is these people, either they're getting no advice whatsoever or the advice they're getting is very bad and it's all under the table."[90]

A striking example is the (professional) demise of anesthesiologist Mark Dershwitz as the go-to expert for lethal injection litigation in executing states. Dershwitz testified for twenty-two states in lethal injection litigation over the course of a decade, but he was widely suspected to be doing more than just testifying, and that suspicion was confirmed in 2014, when he was caught advising Ohio on its lethal injection protocol.[91] Dershwitz denied it, but emails told a different story, and he found himself at risk of losing his board certification with the ABA. An announcement from Dershwitz followed shortly thereafter: "As requested by the ABA, I do not discuss lethal injection in any venue."[92]

The upside of Dershwitz's exit was that a number of his opinions in court (and presumably out of court too) had proven to be flat-out wrong. All those claims by a state expert that didn't pan out in chapter 2—those were claims that Dershwitz had made.[93] But when Dershwitz stepped down, states turned to Dr. Roswell Evans, and his claims turned out to be no better. The story of lethal injection is a story of states stuck with bum advice or none at all, and the reason for that is medical ethics.

Now add the shortage of lethal injection drugs to the mix. One can only imagine how desperate states must be for expert advice as they face the ever-present need to come up with new drug protocols in response to an ever-shrinking market for lethal injection drugs. Here, the lack of medical expertise is a double whammy. It results in ill-conceived execution protocols that are then implemented by executioners who are ill-prepared to deal with their consequences. As bioethicist Arthur Caplan puts the point, executions by lethal injection are conducted by "a hodgepodge of prison execution workers whose medical knowledge is iffy, and when you take away their traditional supply of drugs, they are out to sea in a tiny rowboat, not sure what to do."[94]

States cannot change the ethical foundation of the practice of medicine. They cannot resolve the inherent tension between the medical profession's ethos of life and the executioner's pursuit of death. As was true of drug suppliers, this is a problem endemic to the lethal injection enterprise. It is a problem that no state can fully mitigate or fix.

8

THE PRISON PROBLEM

Executions are a prison practice, and prisons are notoriously tight-lipped about what they do and how they do it. We are entering into what Justice Kennedy once called "the hidden world of punishment."[1] In this world, prison authorities reign as the resident experts in discipline and security. There's just one thing not on the list: lethal injection.

Prison administrators don't know how to kill with drugs any more than your average person on the street. We have seen glimpses of how this dearth of expertise plays out in practice, passing glances at ineptitude while exploring other topics. But we have not yet turned our focus to the internal workings of the government agency responsible for conducting these executions. As we will see, corrections departments pile on to the lethal injection mess with their own mistakes and maladministration, exacerbating problems we already know about and adding a problem that most people don't: the corrections department itself.

Revelations of this problem are relatively new, and the reason is information—as in, for the longest time, we didn't have any. "While some scientists use microscopes or telescopes or particle accelerators," one expert explains, "the study of lethal injection relies on attorneys and judges to bring forth the raw data."[2] Just unearthing that data has taken decades—the first evidentiary hearing on lethal injection was not until *fifteen years* after states started using it.[3]

But over time, the view of lethal injection that has emerged is unlike anything anyone would have imagined in the early years of its existence. "The more data states reveal about their lethal injection procedures, the more those states demonstrate their ignorance and incompetence," writes lethal injection scholar Deborah Denno.[4] "The more information that states reveal," she observes, "the more we realize that they don't know what they are doing."[5]

Yet the fact that it has taken decades to get a behind-the-scenes view of lethal injection has only served to calcify the conventional narrative that states are careful and competent, making it all the more difficult to challenge. Settled conceptions are a tough nut to crack. So it's time to get cracking.

DELEGATING DEATH

One of the earliest pieces of legal scholarship on lethal injection had a title that began "*When Legislatures Delegate Death*,"[6] and it perfectly captured what state legislatures did: they delegated death to corrections departments. Most lethal injection statutes just say "execution by lethal injection" or "execution by substances in a lethal quantity sufficient to cause death."[7] By and large, state legislatures only knew enough to say something to the effect of *We want lethal injection*. So that's what they said.

For the record, saying more than that is not an impossible feat for a legislative body. As lethal injection scholar Ty Alper's work has shown, most state legislatures have passed animal euthanasia statutes that contain a host of specifics for inducing a humane death by drugs when it comes to our family pets.[8] They just haven't done the same for humans.

In time, vague lethal injection statutes would prove useful for departments of corrections (DOCs) as they scrambled to find substitute drugs, and there is some evidence that legislatures intentionally left the details blank so that lethal injection protocols could be revised as new drugs became available.[9] But the scant legislative history of these hopelessly vague statutes suggests that they were also a product of plain inattention. Vague statutes allowed legislatures to reap the political benefits of lethal injection, signaling support for the death penalty and a commitment to humane executions without bearing the costs of having to figure out what that actually meant. If the devil is in the details, these provisions were downright saintly.

But whatever their genesis, these generic statutes led to the whole-sale delegation of all things lethal injection to state DOCs. Every iota of lethal injection decision-making—from the number of drugs in the protocol, to the drug choices and their amounts, to what happens, when, and by whom—is left to prison administrators to figure out for themselves, with no guidance from state legislatures on the front side and no standards by which to judge their decisions on the back side. To say that lethal injection is grossly underregulated by state legislatures is itself a gross understatement. In the vast majority of states, lethal injection is not regulated by the legislature *at all*.

In any other universe, this sort of unbridled discretion on matters of life and death by administrators with no expertise at least would have triggered heightened scrutiny of state lethal injection protocols. But the Supreme Court went with deference instead. According to the plurality in *Baze v. Rees*, deference was proper because close judicial scrutiny "would substantially intrude on the role of state legislatures in implementing their execution procedures."[10] This might have made sense if state legislatures actually *had* a role in implementing their execution procedures. But they don't.

This was not some point of minutiae that the plurality in *Baze* just happened to miss. Justice Stevens wrote a concurrence in the case stating that "the drugs were selected by unelected Department of Corrections officials with no specialized medical knowledge and without the benefit of expert assistance or guidance. As such, their drug selections are not entitled to the kind of deference afforded legislative decisions."[11] As lethal injection scholar Eric Berger observes, the plurality in *Baze* "deferred to a state that had largely abdicated responsibility," attributing the legislature's democratic pedigree to what was in reality a political process failure.[12]

The question du jour in legal circles is whether these generic lethal injection statutes violate the "non-delegation doctrine." In theory, the non-delegation doctrine limits what legislatures can constitutionally delegate, requiring some sort of guidance when delegating to agencies so they do not run amok with legislative power.[13] This doctrine would seem to pose a problem for generic lethal injection statutes. After all, what is the guidance for implementing lethal injection when all the statute says is *we want lethal injection?*

In 2012, the Arkansas Supreme Court agreed, striking down the state's lethal injection statute on non-delegation grounds. "A statute that, in effect, reposes an absolute, unregulated, and undefined discretion in an administrative agency . . . is an unlawful delegation of legislative powers," the court stated.[14] It then went on to say: "It is evident to this court that the legislature has abdicated its responsibility and passed to the executive branch, in this case the ADC [Arkansas Department of Corrections], the unfettered discretion to determine all protocol and procedures, most notably the chemicals to be used, for a state execution."[15] The high court required the legislature to actually legislate, and the legislature then chose the one-drug protocol.

Granted, Arkansas is the only state in the Union to have invalidated a lethal injection statute on non-delegation grounds, and plenty of prisoners have made the claim. But the principles that drive the doctrine are undeniably powerful here. Lethal injection requires delicate policy choices at every turn: How much pain is acceptable? What kinds of risks are acceptable when it comes to the drugs and their quality? How much expertise for conducting the execution is enough? And what about expertise when writing the protocols themselves? There are no innocuous decisions when a state is determining how to kill its citizens. Every choice has massive moral and constitutional dimensions that ought not to be left to nameless agency employees who were not chosen to speak for the people on such sensitive issues.

In this regard, a dissent from Justice Gorsuch in a 2019 federal non-delegation case comes to mind. The case concerned agency decision-making regarding the federal sex offender registry, and Gorsuch's dissent noted the perils of unfettered discretion by non-elected agency employees in this arena. "Those affected are some of the least popular among us," the dissent read. "But if a single executive branch official can write laws restricting the liberty of this group of persons, what does that mean for the next?"[16] Condemned prisoners subject to lethal injection are the "next." They are literally the least popular among us, and every concern about consequential choices being left to the unfettered discretion of nonelected agency employees who may have little regard for the cohort of people subject to them applies tenfold here.

All this is just the delegation side of the equation. We haven't yet turned our attention to those on the receiving end of the delegation. The entire premise of the modern administrative state is institutional competency and agency expertise, and when it comes to lethal injection, prison personnel don't have it. To fully appreciate the point, however, requires a closer look at corrections departments.

EXPERTISE, ANYONE?

Those who have watched testimony in lethal injection trials have been struck by how little corrections department officials know about their own lethal injection protocols. Deborah Denno, who testified in the *Baze v. Rees* trial in Kentucky, later wrote about the oddity of listening to the testimony of prison officials who were on the one hand articulate and professional, and on the other, palpably ignorant of the procedure they were in charge of administering.[17] Those officials were the "victims of legislatures' statewide romance with lethal injection—the details of which are left to the imagination of ill-informed prison personnel," Denno wrote, adding: "This process does not seem fair to those on the lowest level of the political hierarchy, much less to the inmates who bear the brunt of such an irresponsible degree of delegation."[18]

A decade later, in 2018, award-winning journalist Liliana Segura reported on a lethal injection trial in Tennessee, describing the warden as "alarmingly ill-informed, unfamiliar with various details of the protocol and unable to answer what, if anything, he would do if problems arose."[19] When asked if he knew the difference between sodium thiopental and midazolam, his answer was no. "For all the blame heaped on activists and capital defense attorneys," Segura wrote, "the trial would reveal the recklessness and repeated mistakes shown by the state."[20]

This is not to fault prison officials for lacking expertise. These people are not medical professionals. As Eric Berger, who has both litigated lethal injection as a practicing attorney and written about it as a scholar, reflects:

> I did not come away with the impression that the responsible state offi-
> cials were vicious people who enjoyed inflicting pain. Nor did I think that
> they had made the decision to ignore the Constitution and get away with
> what they could. Rather, I think the state had given some employees a
> difficult task for which they were mostly poorly qualified.[21]

They were "out of their depth," Berger writes, "tasked with an extremely difficult job without the training or resources to even know where to begin."[22]

What do prison administrators do when they have been given a job but don't know how to do it? They do what anyone might do: they give it to someone else. Oklahoma's DOC gave the task of creating the nation's first lethal injection protocol to the state medical examiner, Jay Chapman. Missouri's DOC gave the task to a malpractice-ridden doctor, who stated under oath: "[The DOC director] has no background in medicine. . . . he's totally dependent on me advising him what could and should and will be done."[23] And New Jersey's DOC (along with the DOCs in several other states) gave the task to Holocaust denier Fred Leuchter. Even after Leuchter's fake credentials came to light and wardens shunned him in public, they continued to ask him for advice on the sly, so desperate were they for someone, *anyone*, who could tell them how to conduct an execution by lethal injection.[24]

The latest trend is to give the task to lawyers. We saw this in Clayton Lockett's execution, where the state's protocol gave the warden "sole discretion" to decide what drugs to use in an execution, but the decision was made by two lawyers.[25] The same was true in Tennessee. The warden's ignorance of his own execution procedures "was galling," Segura reported. "But it was not entirely surprising" as the warden "had largely delegated his duties to his general counsel."[26]

The problem with lawyers deciding what drugs to use is threefold. First and most obviously, lawyers don't know any more about what drugs to use than prison personnel do, and we know from Lockett's execution what they do to figure it out: they surf the web.[27] Second, and less obviously, having lawyers involved in the decision-making process protects the process from disclosure under the attorney-client privilege and attorney work product doctrine, hermetically sealing it from scrutiny, even pursuant to court-ordered discovery. Some say this is the very point.[28] Third and finally, delegating protocol choices to lawyers not only hides decision-making, but also skews it. Lawyers are litigators. They are advocates searching for the best way to protect their clients. Maybe this coincides with a humane execution, maybe it doesn't. But they are not neutral truth-seekers searching for the most humane way to conduct executions.

We have now seen the delegation problem, and we have seen the lack of expertise on the receiving end of the delegation. All that's left is to see the results.

PROTOCOL PROBLEMS

A lethal injection protocol is the instruction manual. It's the document that says how the state will conduct an execution by lethal injection. Poorly drafted protocols lead to poorly performed executions, and this is especially a problem when executioners are unqualified and/or untrained, as they don't have their own wealth of knowledge to fall back on or fill in the blanks. Protocols that make no sense or simply skip over important parts of the execution are asking executioners to access a skill set that they don't have. Imagine executioners who don't know what they're doing trying to navigate a lethal injection on their own.

Deborah Denno's pioneering work collecting state lethal injection protocols offers a shocking view of what these protocols looked like twenty-five years after lethal injection was first adopted.[29] Consider

Kentucky, the state in 2008's *Baze v. Rees*. In 2001, Kentucky's DOC denied an open records act request for its lethal injection protocol, stating that releasing the protocol would pose "a threat to security."[30] Denno asked an assistant to call the DOC, and when he did, he was told that there *wasn't* a protocol on how executions by lethal injection were conducted. "The protocol would be dictated by each case as it comes up," a DOC employee told him.[31] This ad-hoc approach "screamed out an absence of care and planning," Denno noted of the exchange.[32]

Texas is another example. In 2004, the Texas Department of Criminal Justice (TDCJ) refused to disclose its lethal injection protocol upon request by a local paper, stating in a letter from its general counsel:

> Information about execution procedures is held in the strictest of confidence, is generally not reduced to writing, and is known only to a few people within the Department. That confidentiality is maintained to ensure that security procedures established for executions are not compromised. Thus, to the extent we have written policies and procedures responsive to your request, that information has been found to be confidential and not available to the public.[33]

But lethal injection litigation in Louisiana revealed a trip by the Louisiana DOC's lawyer to the Texas TDCJ to learn about lethal injection. The lawyer stated under oath that the Texas warden had said that he "didn't really have so much of a policy about it, as he did just sort of—they did whatever worked at the time."[34]

Missouri is yet another example. We've talked about Missouri's malpractice-ridden doctor improvising the amount of sodium thiopental used in executions because the drug wouldn't mix well.[35] Not yet noted is the role that the state's protocol played. When asked under oath if any part of the execution procedure was written down, the doctor answered, "I've never seen it." "There's no guide that you follow as you're doing it?" an astounded lawyer for the prisoners asked next. The doctor's answer: "Absolutely not."[36]

Reflecting on the case, the federal judge who presided over the litigation later shared that going into it, he had made certain assumptions. Those were:

> First, that the state of Missouri had a written execution protocol; second, that it had been subjected to due diligence before implementation; third, that this protocol was approved by either the legislative and/or executive (Department of Corrections) branches of the Missouri government, and fourth, that trained medical personnel implemented it properly and consistently.[37]

"Those assumptions did not withstand the rigors of discovery and examination," the judge wrote. "None of these assumptions proved to be true."[38]

A similar story could be told of other states. Louisiana, for example, did not have a written protocol for the first nine years that it used lethal injection, executing seven prisoners with a protocol that prison personnel explained was passed along by "word of mouth."[39] How is it possible that the instruction manual for how to kill people by a complicated quasi-medical procedure was being handed down orally from one generation of executioners to the next like a family recipe?

Astoundingly, in Arizona, that may still be true. Under new leadership, the Arizona DOC announced in 2023 that it did not have "the necessary institutional knowledge and expertise to conduct an execution."[40] The new DOC director was unable to find any written operating procedures for conducting an execution by lethal injection, and had resorted to asking staff members how it was done. Lawyers for the state informed a court in subsequent litigation: "Thus far, [the DOC director] has received only 'anecdotal accounts from staff members,' which have given him 'serious concerns about the qualification and competency of the compounding pharmacist and the process used to compound the current supply of lethal injection drugs.'"[41] "While the Director continues to gather important information about the Department's recent practices and assess its present ability to carry out an execution," the lawyers stated, "one thing is clear: the state is in no position to conduct an execution."

"I don't think it's a secret that we inherited one of the worst, most incompetent and most ill-funded Department of Corrections in the country," the new Arizona attorney general stated. "And I don't think that it takes a leap to suggest that we should understand whether they are capable of carrying out the death penalty before we do it."[42] The new AG, who is not personally opposed to the death penalty, stated that she was not confident that Arizona could carry out executions in a lawful manner—"if it could perform one at all."[43] Now is a good time to note that in 2020, the Arizona DOC spent $1.5 million on drugs, even as it was being held in contempt of court for failing to provide minimally adequate health care for its prison population (which resulted in a fine of another $1.4 million).[44] What a difference leadership makes.

Thus far, we've talked about unwritten protocols, but written protocols can be problematic too. Today's protocols are often too vague to give executioners meaningful guidance, and a prime example is the protocol used in the federal government's 2020 executions. "There is no explicit instruction regarding the implementation of the protocol from the day prior to the execution to the declaration of death," an expert reviewing the protocol noted, listing seven implementation questions (some with multiple subquestions) that were simply not addressed by the protocol at all.[45] But that's better than Missouri's lethal injection protocol, which is just two pages long.[46] *Two.* Imagine the executioners discussed in chapter 5 trying to implement that.

Lack of guidance isn't the only problem with vague protocols. Another is that they hide discretion, making it nearly impossible for prisoners to identify and challenge the choices that executioners make (which may be the point). "Ambiguity and discretion provide executioners with a kind of blank check that brings lingering, fraught deaths into the fold of acceptable executions," death penalty scholar Austin Sarat writes, noting that "almost anything that happens during an execution can now be said to fit within the terms of state protocols."[47] It's hard to say that a state violated its protocol when the protocol doesn't say enough to know whether it has been violated.

Then there are the protocols that are specific, but make no sense. Tennessee's protocol in 2007, for example, simply cut and pasted "lethal injection" over its prior references to "electrocution," resulting in a manual that told executioners to shave the prisoner's head and have a fire extinguisher handy.[48] As another example, North Carolina's lethal injection protocol in 2004, which was used in eighteen executions, called for half the dose of the anesthetic to be administered at the start of the execution process, and the other half to be administered at the end, after injecting the drug that triggers cardiac arrest.[49] For a time, Oklahoma did the same thing. "It is nonsensical to administer any drug, and especially an anesthetic drug, to a dead person," a doctor reviewing the protocol stated, adding that the DOC "cannot possibly understand the function of the drugs if it believes this order of drug administration is appropriate."[50]

IMPLEMENTATION SNAFUS

Executions are staged events. As one warden says, "Like it or not, you are putting on a show."[51] When all goes as planned, executions by lethal injection communicate a sense of competence and control. But as we know from chapter 4, executions by lethal injection often don't go as planned. They are marred by a litany of implementation snafus, revealing ineptitude and carelessness at virtually every turn.

But we've already seen ineptitude and carelessness in implementation snafus, you say. And this is true—no need to rehash those examples here. Instead, we'll consider three examples that show us something that others don't.

First is California. The federal court judge who invalidated California's lethal injection protocol in 2006 later wrote about the evolution of his views, confiding that going into the litigation, his "immediate reaction . . . was extremely skeptical."[52] The judge denied a stay of execution for the first prisoner who raised a lethal injection claim, and did the same for the second. By the time the third prisoner filed a claim, the judge wrote, "an issue that I had dismissed as a desperate, transparent ploy to postpone an inevitable execution had begun to seem serious and substantial."[53] He decided to take a closer look.

By the time he was finished, the judge had conducted an extensive fact-finding process that included five days of formal hearings, consideration of "a mountain of documents," and a field trip to the state's execution chamber. "The record in this case is replete with evidence that in actual practice [California's lethal injection protocol] does not function as intended," the court stated, naming five "critical deficiencies" that rendered the state's lethal injection protocol constitutionally inadequate:

Inconsistent and unreliable screening of execution team members.

A lack of meaningful training, supervision, and oversight of the execution team.

Inconsistent and unreliable record-keeping.

Improper mixing, preparation, and administration of sodium thiopental by the execution team.

Inadequate lighting, overcrowded conditions, and poorly designed facilities in which the execution team must work.

Those were the just the italicized subject headings in the court's written opinion. After each one were astonishing accounts of carelessness and incompetence.[54] "I cringed when I read news accounts suggesting that I was considering whether lethal injection is unconstitutional because a condemned inmate might suffer 'some' pain," the judge later stated.[55] Concerns about lethal injection are not about *some* pain. They're about torturous pain that a civilized society would never condone if the true nature of the problem were known.

Our second example is Tennessee. As we know from other chapters, Tennessee's governor put executions on hold in 2022 to conduct an outside review of the state's failure to comply with its lethal injection protocol. The saga started when a prisoner's attorney made a routine request to see the test results for the compounded drugs that the state would be using in an upcoming execution. That set off a series of internal texts revealing that the requisite testing had not been done, which led to a last-minute reprieve from the governor, citing a "technical oversight" in the execution preparation process.[56] But it quickly became apparent that the problem was bigger than just a technical oversight in one execution. Hence the outside review.

In late 2022, the review reported its findings.[57] The state had not complied with its lethal injection protocol since 2018, the report stated, documenting violations of the protocol in all seven executions conducted during that time. The drugs were not properly tested in any of those executions, the report stated, because the drug procurer never gave the pharmacy a copy of the protocol, which contained the testing requirements. And the drug procurer never gave the pharmacy a copy of the protocol, the report went on to say, because nothing in the protocol instructed him to do so. In fact, the protocol did not address the drug procurer's position or duties at all. His work was completely "off the books" and he had no medical training, so he didn't have a sense of what was needed on his own. "The fact of the matter is not one TDOC employee made it their duty to understand the current Protocol's testing requirements and ensure compliance with same," the report blasted.[58]

The state's lethal injection protocol also contained no specifications for storing and preparing compounded lethal injection drugs. "[Compounded drugs] have a very short shelf life," the report stated, "and this information is seemingly essential to ensuring an execution is carried out only with viable [drugs]." The drug procurer's understanding was that the drugs should be "a little freezing."[59] But the drugs have strict storage guidelines requiring storage at between −10 and −25 degrees Celsius, and the review found that on several occasions, the logs indicated that the drugs were not being stored at the proper temperature, while on other occasions, the log entries did not list temperature readings at all.

The protocol also did not tell executioners how far in advance to remove the drugs from storage and prepare them in a syringe. The pharmacy's handling instructions likewise did not say, so there was no guidance whatsoever on this critically important step of the process.[60]

Worse yet, the outside review found that two members of the execution team *knew* that the drugs had not been tested in accordance with the lethal injection protocol and yet were ready to go forward with the next execution anyway.[61] What started as a series of inadvertent mistakes had ripened into knowing violations of the lethal injection protocol. "There may be factual inaccuracies or misstatements in some of [the state's] filings," attorneys for Tennessee notified the court in a pending challenge to the state's lethal injection protocol.[62]

At least the governor of Tennessee is showing a commitment to remedying the problems. "It's a very important issue that has to be done correctly," he told the press. "And we will take time to fix the protocol and to make certain that we don't move forward until everything is in place."[63] A top priority, the governor stated, was changing the DOC's leadership, which the report had blamed for its "tunnel-vision, result-oriented lens."[64] Shortly thereafter, the state announced the appointment of a new head of the Tennessee DOC. He was the former deputy director of the Arizona DOC, the same person who oversaw Arizona's three botched executions in 2022, and presumably its purchase of $1.5 million in drugs to do it.[65] Maybe he has a growth mindset.

Alabama offers prisoners the option of dying by nitrogen gas, so our third example looks at the administrative side of that protocol option. When Alabama adopted nitrogen gas as an execution method in 2018, it gave prisoners an election form to record their choice. Then the state began seeking death warrants for those who had not chosen death by nitrogen gas (which was not yet operational). One was Alan Miller. Miller said he chose nitrogen gas—he asked for the form and turned it in. The state said it had no record of that, and moved forward with his execution date, so Miller sued. The trial court found "consistent, credible, and uncontroverted direct evidence" that Miller had submitted the election form as directed; the Alabama DOC just lost it.[66] As the appellate court wrote: "Prison officials at Holman [Prison] chose not to keep a log or list of those inmates who submitted an election form choosing nitrogen hypoxia. They lost or misplaced the election form submitted by another inmate at Holman . . . and a prison guard did not turn in the form of a third inmate."[67] Alabama's position was that Miller had "alleged, at most, that ADOC [the Alabama DOC] was insufficiently careful with handling his method-of-execution form."[68] But according to the state, "the guarantee of due process has never been understood to mean that the state must guarantee due care on the part of its officials." There's a claim we don't see every day—due process doesn't require due care when the state takes a life.

In separate legal proceedings over the exact same form, Alabama showed that it didn't even know what its system for distributing the form was, resulting in sanctions against a lawyer in the state AG's office for repeatedly making false claims about it to the court. "The court finds that the improper conduct here was reckless, particularly given that this is a case involving the death penalty," the court stated, imposing a $1,500 fine to "be borne personally" by the attorney and issuing a formal reprimand of the AG's office.[69] Alabama can't get either the forms or the facts right in the simplest administrative endeavor. But gassing prisoners to death will probably work out just fine.

OKLAHOMA'S DATE WITH A GRAND JURY

When it comes to incompetence, nothing compares to Oklahoma. After its botched execution of Clayton Lockett in 2014, Oklahoma's next date with death was the execution of Charles Warner in January 2015. Warner was the other prisoner scheduled to die on Lockett's execution date—he was the prisoner whose execution was stayed when Lockett's execution went haywire. Warner was also the original named plaintiff in *Glossip v. Gross*, the Supreme Court's 2015 lethal injection case. That case came to the Supreme Court as *Warner v. Gross*, but while the Justices were deciding whether to decide it, Warner's execution date came and the Court denied him a stay. Oklahoma executed Warner in short order, so when the Justices did decide to hear the case seven days later, its name rolled over to the next prisoner in line, Richard Glossip.

Warner's execution was problematic in its own right. "It feels like acid," he said on the gurney, and his last words were "My body is on fire."[70] Something had gone wrong in Warner's nearly twenty-minute execution, but it would be months before anyone would know what.

Next in line for execution was Richard Glossip, who had just lost his case at the Supreme Court. Glossip's execution was set for September 2015, but forty-five minutes after it was scheduled to start, the governor issued a stay, stating in a press release that "last minute questions were raised today about Oklahoma's execution protocol and the chemicals used for lethal injection."[71] *Huh, wonder what that was all about.* It didn't take long for the media to find out. Glossip had been on the verge of being executed with the wrong drug—and his near miss was the fate that had met Warner.

The Oklahoman discovered the mistake when it looked closely at Warner's autopsy report, which had recently been released by the state medical examiner.[72] Oklahoma's lethal injection protocol called for potassium chloride as the third drug in the three-drug protocol, and that's what the execution logs said was injected. But Warner's autopsy report said otherwise. It said that although Warner's body showed up with three emptied syringes labeled as potassium chloride, the twelve vials used to fill those syringes actually contained potassium acetate, and that's what was actually injected.

The third drug in the three-drug protocol was already going to be torturous, so as a practical matter, the mistake didn't make much difference. But Oklahoma didn't have the authority to inject prisoners with just any drug. Its legal authority was limited to the drugs listed in the protocol, and potassium acetate wasn't one of them.

Turns out, the Oklahoma DOC's own inventory records showed that the wrong drug had been received for the Warner execution. Vials of potassium acetate were photographed upon receipt by the DOC and logged on an inventory form. But no one noticed the mistake at the time, and no one told the public when it was discovered the day of Glossip's scheduled execution. "We cannot trust Oklahoma to get it right or to tell the truth," Glossip's attorney told the press.[73] A grand jury was convened to investigate how the DOC procured the wrong drug for an execution not once, but twice.

In 2016, the grand jury issued its report. Its findings were explosive, detailing failures at virtually every step of the execution process by virtually every person involved. "Department of Corrections staff, and others participating in the execution process, failed to perform their duties with the precision and attention to detail that the exercise of state authority in such cases demands," the report stated, followed by a detailed account of all that had gone wrong.[74] It was a long list.

The problem began when the DOC director violated the protocol by asking the DOC general counsel to obtain the drugs rather than the H-unit section chief who was assigned the task under the protocol. This created confusion over whose responsibility it was to verify that the proper drugs had been received, and that left the DOC vulnerable to what happened next: the pharmacist, selected based on the fact that he was willing to do the work, ordered the wrong drugs.

The DOC had placed the order over the phone, and the pharmacist inadvertently ordered potassium acetate rather than potassium chloride for Warner's execution, then selected a "reorder" function to re-up the supply for Glossip.

From there, the failures snowballed. As the grand jury reported, the DOC's general counsel "failed to inventory the execution drugs as mandated by state purchasing requirements."[75] A DOC staff member "failed to inspect the execution drugs while transporting them into the Oklahoma State Penitentiary." The warden "failed to notify anyone in the [DOC] that the wrong drug had been received." The H-unit section chief "failed to observe that the [DOC] had received the wrong execution drugs." And the executioners who were part of the IV team "failed to observe that the [DOC] had received the wrong execution drugs."

No one had noticed the anomaly in Warner's execution, and no one noticed it in Glossip's pending execution—except Warden Anita Trammell, who didn't say anything because she figured "that must be a generic" and she wasn't responsible for ordering the drugs.[76] Turns out, Trammell was also the one who had mindlessly logged the potassium acetate as potassium chloride on the inventory form for Warner's execution.[77] In this way, her sins were twofold—not noticing the discrepancy in one case, and not telling what she noticed in another. "Although the department and the state would have suffered embarrassment and criticism had Warden A told someone the wrong drug had been received for the Warner execution," the grand jury's report stated, "it is inexcusable for a senior administrator with 30 years as a department employee to testify that 'there are just some things you ask questions about, and there's some things you don't.'"[78]

Part of the problem, the grand jury concluded, was the DOC's obsession with secrecy. "The paranoia of identifying participants clouded the department's judgement and caused administrators to blatantly violate their own policies," the report stated. It then listed how:

> There was no written order for the drugs and the pharmacist did not receive a hardcopy of the protocol until after ordering the drugs. . . . Cash was used to pay for the drugs. No formal invoice was obtained for the drugs. The inspector general did not include the drug names on the chain of custody form. The drugs bypassed security in an unmarked box with no inventory included when entering the prison.[79]

If the DOC had adhered to *any* of its own record-keeping requirements, it likely would have noticed that it had the wrong drug. But it didn't.

And that wasn't the worst of it. The state's most egregious behavior occurred when the IV team leader—a doctor—noticed that he was filling the syringes for Glossip's execution with the wrong drug and promptly informed DOC officials. The grand jury found that the governor's general counsel "advocated [that] the Department proceed with the Glossip execution using potassium acetate," even though the lawyer knew it was not authorized by the lethal injection protocol.[80]

"The governor's general counsel stated potassium chloride and potassium acetate were basically one in the same drug, advising the deputy attorney general . . . to 'Google it,'" the report stated.[81] (The deputy attorney general said that she did so and found that the two drugs were not the same.)[82] The general counsel also "argued heavily against publicly disclosing that the wrong drug was used" in Warner's execution, stating that issuing a stay for Glossip "would look bad for the state of Oklahoma because potassium acetate had already been used in Warner's execution."[83]

The grand jury was appalled. "It is unacceptable for the governor's general counsel to so flippantly and recklessly disregard the written protocol and the rights of Richard Glossip," its report stated.[84] Ordering the wrong drug was one thing. Forging ahead with an execution *knowing* it was the wrong drug, and trying to hide the mistake was quite another.

By the time the dust had settled, the DOC director had "retired" and the warden and governor's general counsel had resigned.[85] The state's attorney general issued a statement acknowledging that "a number of individuals responsible for carrying out the execution process were careless, cavalier, and in some circumstances dismissive of established procedures that were intended to guard against the very mistakes that occurred."[86] Still, the attorney general (and the governor too) expressed confidence in the DOC's ability to competently conduct executions going forward.[87] Some people are optimistic that way.

Fast forward to October 2021. After a six-year hiatus, the state was ready to resume executions again, announcing that "extensive validations and redundancies have been implemented since the last execution in order to ensure that the process works as intended."[88] Oklahoma then proceeded to execute John Grant, who, as we know from chapter 2, convulsed and vomited on the gurney as he died.[89] After Grant's execution and two others, evidence came to light that the DOC had *again* injected prisoners with the wrong drug. The state's lethal injection protocol called for vecuronium bromide as the second drug in the three-drug protocol. The "shadow board" system that executioners used for syringes showed that *rocuronium* bromide was used instead.[90]

In the ensuing litigation, the DOC director testified that this was a "transcription error" on the shadow board—the drugs were accurate, the shadow board was not.[91] Thus, while it was true that executioners conducted three executions with drug labels telling them that they were using the wrong drug and *failed to notice* in any of them, the labels themselves were wrong, so in the end, the drugs were right.

EXPLAINING INEPTITUDE: THEY'RE DEAD, AREN'T THEY?

How do we explain such shocking displays of ineptitude? What we're seeing goes well beyond a lack of medical expertise. Alabama couldn't even get a form right. Oklahoma couldn't get the label right on a shadow board whose sole purpose was to properly identify the drugs. Now is a good time to remember what the former head of Oklahoma's DOC told a legislative committee in 2023: the prison staff charged with carrying out these executions are "some of the lowest-paid state employees in government."[92] You get what you pay for.

Even so, something else is also at work, and to see what that is, we need to ask a different question. Instead of asking, *Why are we seeing such incompetence?* we might have a better understanding if we asked, *What are a prison's institutional objectives when it comes to an execution?* Institutional culture informs institutional behavior, and corrections departments have priorities that are internal to their organizational structure and thus baked into the lethal injection enterprise as a matter of institutional design. What might we learn by turning our gaze away from state actors, and towards the institutional context in which they operate?

In the execution context, prisons get their marching orders not only from the legislature, but also from the court or governor that issues the death warrant. DOCs execute condemned prisoners only when they receive a death warrant telling them to do so. Once a death warrant has been issued, their job is to carry it out. It is not a job they relish. But it is a job that must be done, and they are the ones to do it.

This second source of agency directives introduces a competing priority for prison personnel: conducting executions on schedule. This agency mandate is pressing and concrete, particularly when compared to the more nebulous objective of a humane execution. As Deborah Denno has observed, many of the decisions regarding lethal injection reflect prison officials' "desperate attempts to adhere to their execution schedules."[93] When a death warrant has been issued, prison officials become singularly focused on one objective: getting death done.

A 2006 Human Rights Watch report on lethal injection has a title that begins *So Long as They Die*.[94] The more one knows about lethal injection, the more one sees how on-point that title truly is. But there's no need to take HRW's word for it. Prison officials say so themselves.

One example comes from lethal injection litigation in California in 2006—the litigation that inspired an essay on the experience by the presiding judge.[95] When asked what makes for a "successful execution," the warden answered that a successful execution was an execution in which "the inmate ends up dead at the end of the process." When asked if it included anything else, he stated, "I'm thinking not."[96]

It is tempting to dismiss the comment as sarcasm, except other wardens have made similar remarks when they thought they were talking in discrete company. Remember the Louisiana DOC lawyer who testified about a trip to Texas to learn about lethal injection? She also relayed what the warden said about his approach to lethal injection. She stated that the warden told her team: "The only thing that mattered was that the guy ended up dead and that he wasn't worried too much about the amount of medicine. He had certainly used the same types of medicine, but that he wasn't totally concerned about the amounts or what it may or may not do. They ended up dead, and that's all he was worried about."[97]

"The rest of our conversation tracked the same thing," the Louisiana lawyer stated. "He was not terribly concerned about policy, procedure, or who did what, when, where. Just so the right result happened." The "right result" wasn't a humane execution. It was just an execution where the prisoner ended up dead.

This same view is apparent in what executioners say in the aftermath of a botched execution. The execution of Clayton Lockett is a prime example. "We don't know why everybody's calling it a botched execution," one executioner told investigators. "It was a successful execution. He's dead." Another executioner confided: "I don't want to sound cold or anything—I mean the guy died. I mean we carried out an execution. Did it take a little long? Well, longer than the other ones, but it's a—I mean, it was all, you know, a new process. . . . Yeah, they had a problem with the vein. Yeah. It happens all the time. It's still—we still had an execution."[98]

Others involved in Lockett's execution took a similar view. "I mean . . . it's not the best one we've ever done," the paramedic conceded. Still, she stated, "I don't term that execution as a botched execution because the end result was that he was to be dead. That was his sentence, to be dead, and he was before he left that room."[99] This was Warden Trammell's view too. "Should it have taken that long? No. Was there mistakes made? Yes," she told investigators, "but it was the ultimate goal was to execute the offender," and that's what executioners did. Even the official who led the state's (non)independent review refused to say that the execution was botched. "How you describe this execution is how you describe it," he said. "At the end of the day, the drugs we used to execute inmate Lockett for the crimes he committed worked."[100]

You and I might think that an execution that goes epically wrong and results in grotesque suffering is a botched execution. But the comments of those tasked with conducting executions by lethal injection reveal a fundamentally different conception of what a successful execution looks like. It's just an execution where the prisoner ends up dead.

But talk is cheap. Actions speak louder than words, so if we really want to know where prison priorities lie, all we need to do is recall a few of the choices we have seen prison personnel make. Time and again, we have seen corrections department officials cut corners, bend rules, and break the law just to get death done.

A prime example is their willingness to buy lethal injection drugs from pretty much anyone willing to sell them. Compounding companies with over 1800 regulatory violations? No problem. Drug distributors operating in the back of a London driving school? Why not. Scam artists who misappropriate other companies' drugs, set up fake manufacturing shops, and leave without paying their rent? Sounds great. We'll litigate *for years* for access to that.

The untold story of lethal injection is at its core a story about states caring more about getting death done than making good on the promise of a humane execution. It is a running tally of maladministration and mishaps backed by a demonstrated disregard for how condemned prisoners die at the hands of the state. A capital defense attorney in one lethal injection trial referred to the state's administration of lethal injection as "a timeline of indifference."[101] But the attorney could have been talking about most any state. And she could have been talking about most any time. We are now forty-five years into the lethal injection era, and she could have been talking about the *entire* time.

This is not to say that prison officials don't care about torturous deaths. They do—presumably because they don't *want* to cause unnecessary suffering, but also because visibly botched executions can severely disrupt their organizational goals. Botched executions can cause public outcry, and that brings bad publicity and political controversy to DOCs. Botched executions are also traumatizing for executioners, and prison officials care about the psychological toll on their employees. A poignant example is a 2018 op-ed penned by the former commissioner of the Tennessee DOC. Pointing to botched executions using midazolam in seven states, the op-ed expressed concern that Tennessee's new protocol created the risk of "unnecessary and damaging trauma" to prison staff. "The current plan to conduct executions in Tennessee using risky drugs from unreliable sources places a heavy burden on our corrections professionals," the former commissioner wrote, without a single word about the inmates whose torturous deaths she took as a given.[102] Prison administrators have a number of priorities in the execution context, but what a prisoner experiences takes a backseat to them all.

There is a psychological component to the indifference we are seeing too, and a 2022 report by National Public Radio shed light on what is driving it.[103] NPR interviewed twenty-six people who participated in more than two hundred executions across seventeen states, reporting just how deeply destructive their execution work was. Executioners experienced alcoholism, drug addiction, insomnia, hair loss, night terrors, and the urge to commit suicide, among other afflictions.

"People think that it would be so easy to go up and execute someone who had committed such heinous acts," one warden stated. "But the truth is killing a human being is hard."[104] "You have to transform yourself into that person who will take a life," an executioner explains, adding: "You can't tell me I can take the life of people and go home and be normal."[105] The family member of another executioner, who was described as "withdrawn and unrecognizable at home," stated: "Nobody stops to think, somebody has to carry it out. Somebody has to be the one."[106] As one executioner put the point: "Every single one of the death certificates says state-assisted homicide. And the state was me."[107]

"In an execution," one former DOC director explains, "the condemned prisoner is a known human being who is totally defenseless when brought into the death chamber. Staff members know that he has been secured safely for many years before his execution and poses no threat to them."[108] This makes the task of executing them especially traumatic. "You're working with a prisoner for 10 years, you've interacted with them every single day, and you can feel they've changed," a retired corrections officer says. "All of a sudden they flip the switch, and now it's like: 'OK, we're going ahead and killing them.' There has to be an underlying effect from that, without a doubt."[109]

The sheer trauma that executioners experience from killing at the state's behest is the reason why in 2024, Oklahoma's attorney general and

DOC director asked the Oklahoma Court of Criminal Appeals to slow the state's pace of executions from once every sixty days to once every ninety days. "This pace . . . protects our team's mental health and allows time for them to process and recover between the scheduled executions," they stated.[110] The court granted the motion, but not without dissent on the bench. One judge stated during oral arguments that executioners needed to "suck it up." The DOC needed to "man up" and stop with the "sympathy stuff," he said, telling the DOC director: "If you can't do the job, you should step aside and let somebody do it who can."[111]

What do executioners do to survive such self-destructive work? Social psychology has an answer: they emotionally detach, turning inner conflict into indifference with the help of a variety of psychosocial mechanisms.[112] As one prison official explains: "We do these things that personally you would normally never be involved in, because they're sanctioned by the government, and then we start walking through them in a mechanical fashion. We become detached. We lose our humanity."[113]

So powerful is this need to detach that a group of former corrections officers—most of whom had firsthand experience as executioners— submitted an amicus brief in 2019's *Bucklew v. Precythe*. "Executions take a steep toll on the people who oversee and perform them," the brief began.[114] "The more fortunate cope by distancing themselves from their humanity," it continued, while "others fail to manage the trauma." But botched executions "make it impossible for them to dissociate from the horror of their task," the brief stated matter-of-factly.

Those who have managed to fully detach emotionally from their task display a stunning callousness. "There's nothing to it," one executioner says, adding: "It's not different to me executing somebody and goin' to the refrigerator and getting a beer out of it. . . . It's just a procedure, and they happen to be part of it. . . . I go there to do a job, and I do it and leave."[115] Executions may have bothered this executioner at first, but over time, he just got used to it.

Here again, this is not to suggest that botched executions don't matter, even to those who are detached. As another executioner explains: "If something goes wrong, your ass is gonna swing. . . . Mess up an execution, or you don't get the man dead like you should get him dead, there'll be hell to pay."[116] This executioner was not indifferent to a botched execution. His concern just didn't include the prisoner on the receiving end of it.

One takeaway from this discussion is the need to candidly acknowledge the deeply destructive nature of what we are asking executioners to do. "There is a part of the warden that dies with his prisoner," one warden explained, and the same is likely true of every prison staff member involved.[117] This recognition leads to another: asking executioners to care may well be asking too much. When the job is taking someone's life— not asking for death in a courtroom, or imposing it as a judge, or even issuing a death warrant, but doing the actual killing—the innate need for self-protection may well dictate that executioners *not* be mindful of how a prisoner dies at the hands of the state. And that, in turn, suggests that abject indifference may, like other problems we've discussed, be endemic to the execution enterprise. If it happens because it is necessary, then it necessarily happens.

RESISTANCE TO CHANGE

Prison officials are accustomed to operating with little legislative or judicial oversight. As Justice Brennan observed back in 1981, "Courts have been especially deferential to prison authorities in the adoption and execution of policies and practices."[118] Over time, this deference has led to another distinct feature of a prison's institutional culture: fierce independence and notorious resistance to change.[119]

Back in the mid-2000s, states' stubborn resistance to change drew the attention of courts and commentators alike as lethal injection litigation started bringing problematic state practices into the limelight. In litigation hot spots across the country, it was apparent that the problems with lethal injection were longstanding and that DOCs had little interest in solving them on their own. "Corrections agencies continue to display a remarkable lack of due diligence with regard to ascertaining the most 'humane' way to kill their prisoners," sentencing scholar Doug Berman observed in 2006, listing a number of changes that DOCs could have made to improve their execution processes, but didn't.[120]

Nearly two decades later, Berman's observation is still true. DOCs today are not revising their protocols to make them better. They are revising their protocols to make them *different*, mostly in response to drug shortages. To the extent DOCs are forced to make improvements at all, they are making superficial, cosmetic changes—token revisions that make it look like they are taking steps to prevent further botched executions while maintaining the status quo.

Consider, for example, Oklahoma. Oklahoma's revised protocol after the botched execution of Clayton Lockett called for the person monitoring the execution to have medical training. From a distance, this looked like a meaningful reform. But the protocol also named the "H-unit section chief" as the person doing the monitoring. "So does he have medical training?" a corrections department official was asked under oath. "The H-unit section chief has informal training as to what to look for in a line that may or may not fail," the official answered. "When the IV team comes in, he'll receive training from them."[121] Turns out, "medical training" wasn't medical training as you and I understand the term. It was nothing more than an IV team member briefing a nonmedical prison employee, something that IV team members were already doing.

In the wake of Richard Glossip's near miss of being executed with the wrong drug, a bipartisan review commission was formed to examine all aspects of Oklahoma's death penalty, including its execution procedures. In 2017, the commission issued its report, unanimously recommending that the state refrain from executions "until significant reforms have been accomplished."[122] In 2022, when the state resumed executions, the cochairs of the commission wrote an op-ed to say that "after five years, virtually none of our recommendations have been adopted."[123]

Another example is Alabama. In the wake of its string of botched executions in 2022, the governor put executions on pause for a "top-to-bottom review" of the DOC's execution procedures.[124] Ignoring calls for an independent review, the governor tapped the DOC to conduct a review *of itself*. Shortly thereafter, the DOC reported that all was well—executioners just needed more time for IV access and more straps to secure prisoners on the gurney.[125] "No one buys this sham of a review," one reporter stated. "And the reason we don't buy it is because we all have functioning brains."[126]

The prisoner next in line for execution in Alabama—James Barber—sued, seeking discovery as to what went wrong in 2022's executions and (more importantly for his purposes) what the state had done to remedy those deficiencies. Alabama's response was to set a short execution date, then argue that there was no time for more than cursory discovery.[127] Indeed, the state argued that its three-hour-long execution of Joe Nathan James—the longest execution in United States history—was "successful" because at the end, James was dead.[128]

The Supreme Court allowed the execution to proceed, prompting a stinging dissent by Justice Sotomayor. Alabama "has conducted a secret, internal review with no published report or finding," she wrote, adding: "The state has not only failed to account for what went wrong, but also actively obstructed Barber's attempts to find out what happened."[129] This was not justice, Sotomayor argued, writing that "the Eighth Amendment demands more than the state's word that this time will be different." But apparently it didn't. She was the dissent.

JUDICIAL ABDICATION

For those wondering how states can get away with all we've seen chronicled in the pages of this book, the answer is that the Supreme Court has completely abdicated its responsibility to enforce the Eighth Amendment. The Court has refused to constrain executing states in any way, instead erecting a set of impenetrable barriers to Eighth Amendment protection in execution challenges. Lower courts are expected to toe the line, and they do, upholding even manifestly torturous drug protocols and egregiously careless state practices.

Thus far, we have considered the Supreme Court's lethal injection cases in the context of other discussions. Here, we briefly turn our focus to the decisions themselves to see the edifice of non-protection that the Justices have built. Much might be said about the Supreme Court's decisions in this area, and legal scholars have dissected the rulings more thoroughly than is possible here. But even a cursory review is enough to make the point that under current doctrine, Eighth Amendment protection is an illusion.

The Supreme Court has decided three cases on the merits of a lethal injection challenge: *Baze v. Rees* in 2008, *Glossip v. Gross* in 2015, and *Bucklew v. Precythe* in 2019. In *Baze*, the Court announced that prisoners challenging lethal injection must show "a substantial risk of serious pain" to make out a constitutional violation.[130] In *Glossip*, the Court explained that "substantial risk" actually meant "sure or very likely," and added a requirement that prisoners challenging their execution method provide states with an alternative way to kill them.[131] And in *Bucklew*, the Court told prisoners that they had to give *a lot* of details when they provided the alternative means of execution, way more than they knew, and also they had to show that the state "superadded" pain.[132]

It is worth pausing for a moment to tease out the two points from *Bucklew*, not only because this is where the law stands now, but also because they show just how insurmountable the hurdles are for constitutional protection in this arena. In *Bucklew*, the prisoner complied with *Glossip*'s morbid "alternative method" requirement by naming nitrogen gas as the alternative means of execution. Faulting Bucklew for presenting a "bare-bones proposal," the Court stated:

> He has presented no evidence on essential questions like how nitrogen case should be administered (using a gas chamber, a tent, a hood, a mask, or some other delivery device); in what concentration (pure nitrogen or some mixture of gases); how quickly and for how long it should be introduced; or how the state might ensure the safety of the execution team, including protecting them against the risk of gas leaks.[133]

Just so we're clear about what happened here, the Supreme Court required Bucklew—the prisoner sitting in his cell on death row—to provide the state with details of how to conduct an execution by nitrogen gas that he played no part in creating. And not just any details, but crazy details. Like what concentration the gas should be. And what safety measures to employ for the people *who are killing him*.

The other holding in *Bucklew*—that the prisoner must show that the state is "superadding pain"—is every bit as outrageous. Now it is no longer enough to show that torturous pain is "sure or very likely" (already an impossibly high standard). Now prisoners have to show that the state is doing something extra to make it that way. In short, they must show "the deliberate infliction of pain for the sake of pain."[134] Short of states intentionally *trying* to torture prisoners—which nobody does anymore, and even if they did, who would admit it?—a majority of the Supreme Court has concluded that the Eighth Amendment simply has nothing to say about how prisoners are executed.

This is why people paying attention called *Bucklew* "bloodthirsty" and "medieval."[135] But the dearth of people paying attention was (and is) a problem of its own. "While the ruling in *Bucklew* is certainly callous and cruel," *The Intercept* wrote, "it is also a reminder of how little most Americans have paid attention to what states have been doing in their name."[136] *Let this book change that.*

One suspects that the Justices in *Bucklew* are just fine with the public not paying attention to what they've done to the Eighth Amendment. After all, it's awfully hard to announce that the American people aren't protected against torturous punishments by their government—that an execution can be as torturous as the state wants so long as the state isn't sadistically adding pain and a prisoner can't adequately devise their own death.

A striking example of the point comes from oral arguments in *Bucklew*. "So are you saying that even if the method imposes gruesome, brutal pain, you can still go forward?" Justice Kavanaugh asked the state's lawyer. The lawyer hemmed and hawed. Justice Kavanaugh asked again. "So

you're saying that even if the method imposes gruesome, brutal pain . . ."
And again the lawyer squirmed. "Is that a yes?" Justice Kavanaugh persisted. "Yes, it is, Your Honor," the lawyer finally conceded, "And that is
the holding of *Glossip*."[137] It took asking the question three times to get
a "yes" out of the state's lawyer, and even then the answer was, *Yes but
we're not asking for that—you already did it when you said that a showing
of torture alone wasn't enough, that prisoners also had to provide the state
with an alternative way to kill them.* Under current doctrine, torture *is*
constitutionally permissible. It's just a position so morally bankrupt that
even a lawyer for the state had a hard time saying it out loud.

This is why states can do whatever they want, and it brings us back to
resistance to change. The nub of the problem is that states can't make Big
Pharma sell them drugs. They can't make doctors participate. And they
can't make scientists tell them how to best kill. Lethal injection doesn't
work without the support of a number of independent actors, and states
unequivocally do not have it. In theory, the Eighth Amendment would
force states to face this reality and find another way to conduct executions, but the Supreme Court has eviscerated Eighth Amendment protection, so we are stuck with tortured doctrine and torturous deaths.

"America is terrible at killing people legally," observed *Politico Magazine* in 2014,[138] before a decade of events would attest to this truth. Unable to fix the real problems with lethal injection, states nibble around
the edges and follow the advice that beauty experts have been giving for
years: if you can't fix a flaw, *hide it.*

9

THE SECRECY SOLUTION

In 2017, Arkansas conducted two executions just hours apart—the nation's first back-to-back executions since 2000. The second execution was temporarily delayed by a claim that the first prisoner's death was "torturous and inhumane"—a claim that the state called "utterly baseless."[1] According to the claim, IV team executioners had tried for forty-five minutes to place a catheter in the prisoner's neck. A court allowed the second execution to proceed, but an autopsy later revealed a curious detail on the first prisoner's corpse: "tan colored makeup" covering five puncture wounds on his neck and collarbone area.[2] Someone was trying to cover their tracks.

In the world of cosmetics, that makeup is called "concealer"—a fitting name for the larger phenomenon that covers all things lethal injection: secrecy. Secrecy is the reason Americans *think* they know about lethal injection, but don't. The story of lethal injection is a story about secrets, and here you will see how those secrets are kept.

THE STATE SECRECY TWO-STEP

States use secrecy to hide the problems with lethal injection in what one might call "the state secrecy two-step," and here's how this dance around the facts goes: first, states do everything possible to cover up botched executions and other embarrassing finds, then they do everything possible to ensure there will be no embarrassing finds in the future. Commentary by death penalty scholar Austin Sarat in 2022 sums up the first step nicely. "Botched executions are a repeated feature of the death penalty system in the United States," he wrote. "But from listening to the after-the-fact accounts of state officials, you would never know. They seem to have developed a shared understanding for reassuring the public that there was nothing to see or worry about, even when an execution goes wrong."[3]

We caught our first glimpse of this move in chapter 1, when Oklahoma officials stated that Clayton Lockett "remained unconscious" throughout his execution, so he could not have been in pain—even as he was talking and trying to get up off the gurney.[4] But several other egregiously botched executions that we have discussed feature this sort of whitewashing as well.

In Florida, for example, officials insisted that nothing went wrong in the grotesquely botched execution of Ángel Díaz, who had chemical burns nearly a foot long on each arm.[5] The warden who oversaw the execution said that Díaz showed no signs of distress, even as witnesses said he was grimacing in pain and gasping for breath for a good twenty-five minutes of his execution. According to the warden, Díaz was not writhing on the gurney as witnesses said, but was "merely stretching to see a clock in the death chamber."[6] *I know I'm in the midst of being executed, but I wonder what time it is.*

In Arizona, officials insisted that the nearly two-hour long execution of Joseph Wood—the man who gasped for breath over 640 times and was injected with fifteen doses of the two-drug protocol—was not botched because he was "comatose and never in pain."[7] Wood was effectively "brain dead,"[8] officials stated, but a Stanford professor of neurology shot back: "If you are taking breaths, you are not brain dead. Period. That is not compatible with brain death, at all. In fact, it is not compatible with any form of death."[9] At the state's press conference, a reporter asked: "How is a two-hour execution *not* botched?"[10] He didn't get an answer. The official walked away as he was asking the question.

And in Ohio, officials stated that "the process worked very well" on the backside of the twenty-six-minute long execution of Dennis McGuire, the man who gasped and choked in the longest execution in Ohio's history—an execution so horribly botched that a prison official reportedly mouthed "I'm sorry" to McGuire's family members.[11] "The

Department remains confident . . . that the inmate was completely unconscious and felt no pain," a DOC spokesperson told the press. Meanwhile, an execution witness wrote an op-ed titled: "I Witnessed Ohio's Execution of Dennis McGuire. What I Saw Was Inhumane."[12]

Three other examples of the phenomenon merit more than a brief mention, and Alabama's botched execution of Joe Nathan James in 2022 is at the top of the list. This is the execution that opened the book—this is where our journey began. The three-hour execution that set a record as the longest in United States history has always deserved more than an opening paragraph, but more than that had to wait until our turn to secrecy because what the James execution best shows is all that we don't know.

What transpired in the three hours that executioners were trying to set James's IV? Alabama is not saying, but here's what we do know. We know that when the curtain was finally opened three hours later, James was motionless and nonresponsive, lying on the gurney with his eyes closed. He remained unresponsive when the death warrant was read and when he was asked if he had any final words, he said nothing—not even "No." Something was wrong, but no one knew what. James had planned his final words; they included an apology to the victim's family, which had advocated to spare his life.[13] James had become a devout Muslim in his twenty-three years on death row, and had planned to pray the *shahada* at his execution as well.[14] Alabama officials denied sedating James before the curtain was opened. Knocking him out before his execution would have been a massive violation of the state's protocol, although one suspects that this is exactly what Alabama did. James had several puncture wounds not in the vicinity of a vein, and if those were from intended intramuscular injections (as opposed to sheer incompetence), the only reason for such an injection would have been sedating James.[15] When asked point blank if James was even conscious, a DOC spokesperson stated: "I cannot confirm that."[16] *Why not?* We don't know.

Although James was unresponsive throughout the entirety of his execution, reporters stated that when the drugs were injected, "James blinked and his eyes fluttered briefly."[17] Alabama uses a three-drug midazolam protocol, and if James had been drugged to oblivion but was still sensate to the excruciating pain of the second and third drugs, that eye-fluttering would have been all he could do to express torturous pain. The timing of the eye-fluttering suggests this is what was happening, but without knowing the events that made James unresponsive in the first place, even that much is just an educated guess.

This was the reason for conducting an independent autopsy—to get answers that the state wasn't providing. An investigative journalist was present and wrote about the "carnage" that "told a radically different tale than the narrative offered by the Alabama Department of Corrections, even to the naked eye." A corpse couldn't lie. "Something terrible had been done to James while he was strapped to a gurney behind closed doors," wrote Pulitzer Prize finalist Elizabeth Bruenig. "What observers do see looks vaguely surgical," she wrote. "What they don't looks like a war crime."[18] One of the doctors who attended the autopsy noted that James's "hands and wrists had been burst by needles in every place one can bend or flex." Whoever was doing the puncturing, he wrote, "was unqualified for the task in a most dramatic way."[19]

This is what we know, and it makes Alabama's claim that "nothing out of the ordinary" happened a demonstrably false representation (that's being polite). When pressed, the Alabama DOC commissioner stated that he could not "overemphasize this process," saying: "We have protocols and we're very deliberate in our process, and making sure everything goes according to plan."[20] But that was no answer for the bruises on James's knuckles and wrists, or the puncture wounds in his musculature nowhere near the vicinity of a known vein, or the deep, jagged incision that pathologists suspect was a cutdown, which is not authorized under Alabama's protocol. Nor was it an explanation of how or why James showed up for his execution already out cold. Whatever happened in that three-hour window, it was definitely not part of the "process" because the process is stated in the protocol, and the protocol didn't allow any of those things. "It appears that the state thought no one would catch it at what it was doing, and in most cases it would be correct," Bruenig reflected, adding, "that alone is haunting."[21]

How can it be that we just don't know what happened in the longest execution in US history? Alabama knows. It's just not telling. The *Montgomery Advertiser* submitted a public records request for records related to the execution, but the DOC denied the request, writing that the information requested was "protected and confidential, security sensitive information that does not reasonably need to be viewed by the public and would be detrimental to the public's best interest."[22] How the information was "security sensitive" and why sharing it would be "detrimental to the public's best interest" the state did not say.

Meanwhile, the family of Joe Nathan James has sued the state of Alabama, with the prestigious law firm Arnold & Porter representing it pro bono. Aside from being subjected to a torturous execution, the suit claims that James was deprived of his last act of autonomy—his final words. "We're seeking compensation for his family because that's the available remedy, but really, our goal in filing this lawsuit and working on behalf of Mr. James' family is to invite some transparency, to shed some light for Alabama," an attorney on the case stated.[23]

Whatever Alabama is hiding, it must be quite something. Back in 2018 when it tried and failed to execute Doyle Lee Hamm, litigation over that botched execution resulted in a court order to unseal the requested records.[24] "The public needs to know how the state administers its laws," the court wrote, adding that "without such knowledge, the public cannot form an educated opinion on this very important topic."[25] Shortly thereafter, Alabama entered into a confidential settlement that allowed it to keep its records to itself. In return for secrecy, the state agreed not to reexecute Hamm, but instead let him die on his own (which he did). The state that loves its pound of flesh apparently loves secrecy more.

Our second example brings us back to Oklahoma. Oklahoma's first execution since 2015 (when it executed Charles Warner with the wrong drug) was its execution of John Grant in 2022. We met Grant back in chapter 2—he is the prisoner who vomited on the gurney and suffered from flash pulmonary edema as he died.[26] Here, we revisit Grant's execution to detail the facts and see the spin that the state put on them.

Witnesses were consistent. "Almost immediately after the first drug was administered, Grant began convulsing, so much so that his entire upper back repeatedly lifted off the gurney," one media witness reported.[27] "As the convulsions continued, Grant then began to vomit," he wrote. "Multiple times over the course of the next few minutes, medical staff entered the death chamber to wipe away and remove vomit from the still-breathing Grant."[28] An Associated Press reporter corroborated the account. "He began convulsing about two dozen times—full-body convulsions," the AP reporter stated, adding: "Then he began to vomit, which covered his face, then began to run down his neck and the side of his face."[29] The AP reporter stated that he had witnessed fourteen executions and had never seen a prisoner vomit, and he consulted with a retired AP reporter who had witnessed hundreds of executions over the years and could only remember one prisoner vomiting.[30]

But according to Oklahoma officials, Grant was executed "without complication."[31] Witness accounts of Grant vomiting were "embellished," the DOC director claimed, stating that the convulsions were "dry heaves" and the vomit was "regurgitation."[32] "I will agree that inmate Grant's regurgitation was not pleasant to watch," the director stated, "But I do not believe that it was inhumane."[33] Oklahoma's position was that Grant was unconscious while he was "regurgitating," so he couldn't feel a thing.[34] The state did not explain why, if that was true, Grant was not declared unconscious during this time. A media witness tweeted his response: "As a witness to the execution who was in the room, I'll say this: repeated convulsions and extensive vomiting for nearly 15 minutes would not seem to be 'without complication.'"[35]

Our third example is Arkansas's botched execution of Kenneth Williams in 2017. Williams was the fourth and final prisoner executed in Arkansas' eleven-day rush to execute prisoners before its midazolam expired. Media witnesses reported that a couple of minutes after being injected with midazolam, Williams began "coughing, convulsing, lurching, jerking, with sound that was audible even with the microphone turned off."[36] Witnesses heard a "moan or a groan" as this was happening, and reported that "Williams' body jerked 15 times in quick succession—lurching violently against the leather restraint across his chest."[37] Even after the lurches subsided, witnesses stated that Williams was gasping with labored breaths. "It was clear that he was in trouble," one reporter said. "It was clear he was striving for breath."[38] The reporter had witnessed ten executions, and had never seen one like this.

But Arkansas officials maintained that the execution had gone off without a hitch. One even called it "flawless."[39] A DOC spokesperson stated that what media witnesses reported as convulsing was just an "involuntary muscular reaction to the midazolam."[40] Williams's lawyer was outraged, calling the execution "horrifying" and accusing the state of "trying to whitewash the reality of what happened." The state's account was "sanitized almost to the point of being unrecognizable," he stated, calling for an independent investigation into what went wrong.[41] But the governor dismissed the suggestion, saying it was unnecessary as "there was not any indication of pain."[42]

Panning out to this phenomenon more broadly, the federal government's 2020 execution spree featured accounts so blatantly inconsistent with what media witnesses saw that the accounts themselves became news. "Executioners Sanitized Accounts of Deaths in Federal Cases," an Associated Press headline blared, reporting: "The sworn accounts by executioners, which government filings cited as evidence that lethal injections were going smoothly, raise questions about whether officials misled courts." Execution witnesses reported seeing violent chest heaves, but according to executioners, those were merely snores from "a deep, comfortable sleep." As reported by the AP, "all employed the same sleep metaphors."[43]

For every example here, there are many more that never made the pages of this book.[44] But the point is not the examples; it's the pattern. When an execution goes obviously awry—when witnesses report seeing prisoners heave, writhe, moan, lurch against the restraints, clench their fists and jaws, and flutter their eyes ever so slightly as they die—state officials simply deny it. They stridently claim that these unmistakable signs of suffering did not happen. Then states cite those accounts in court, and feed them to the public, to defend and perpetuate the myth of a humane execution by lethal injection.

One state senator summed up the situation with refreshing (if not depressing) candor, stating:

> Lethal injection, I believe, is sold to the public as humane. . . . It is as if we are selling the idea that this is just putting your pet to sleep, [but] that's not what it is. And then in order to perpetuate that lie, we have to lie and lie and lie and lie and lie again. This is a terrible position to put our public servants in.[45]

It's also pretty terrible for the public on the receiving end of those lies, and for the prisoners suffering torturous deaths. By my count, that was five lies to perpetuate the first one, which sounds about right.

Tracking this phenomenon puts in sharp relief Alabama's official response to its first execution by nitrogen gas. (They are calling it "nitrogen hypoxia" because they don't want to use the word "gas," but while we're on the topic of whitewashing—make no mistake, this is gassing someone to death.) As we know from chapter 2, the execution of Kenny Smith lasted twenty-two minutes, and he thrashed about for a good four of them, then struggled to breathe for several more. Yet, as we also know from chapter 2, Alabama touted the execution as "textbook" and announced it a smashing success.[46] Indeed, Alabama's DOC commissioner stated that "nothing was out of the ordinary from what we were expecting."[47] But that of course was not true, because what Alabama was expecting—what it told courts to expect in legal filings—was "unconsciousness in seconds."[48]

For a sense of perspective, consider what the victim's son, who attended Smith's execution, said about it: "We were told by some people that worked [in the prison] that he'd take two or three breaths and he'd be out and gone. That ain't what happened. After about two or three breaths, that's when the struggling started. . . . With all that struggling and jerking and trying to get off that table, more or less, it's just something I don't ever want to see again."[49] Turns out, watching someone get tortured to death is a grotesque experience, even for those who think the person deserves to die.

When the son returned to his hotel, he saw a press conference about the execution in the lobby. "We just sat there and listened, and about half of what he said had really happened. They played it up pretty good. Wasn't expecting that," he stated. People expect government officials to tell the truth about the state's ultimate exercise of sovereign power. Time and again, they don't.

But whitewashing the facts is not the only thing states do to hide torturous deaths from the public. They have brazenly closed the blinds in the midst of an execution to keep witnesses from seeing what is happening.[50] They've altered execution logs.[51] And when the heat is *really* on, they have followed their flat denials with "independent reviews," which predictably come back saying that the prisoner did not suffer and (with the exception of a tweak here and there) the process worked as it should. States even prevent media witnesses from bringing writing materials into the viewing room. "The point, of course, is to control the narrative," journalist Liliana Segura writes of the no-pen-and-paper policy, and this is true.[52] But the same could be said of these other moves too.

What is striking is just how strident officials are in denying there is even a problem, and how committed they are to defending the execution at all costs. *The prisoner didn't suffer, the execution wasn't botched*—as if just saying something could make it so. States have mastered step one of the state secrecy two-step. Now let's look at step two.

THE SECRECY TWO-STEP: STEP TWO

Secrecy after the fact of a botched execution is akin to a call for cleanup on aisle five. The better move for executing states is to avoid the need for cleanup in the first place. Hence, step two of the state secrecy two-step: after doing everything possible to cover apparent problems, next do everything possible to prevent problems from becoming apparent.

Consider first the execution itself. States do a number of things to prevent problems with an execution from becoming apparent in the first place, and their use of a paralytic is at the top of the list. Lethal injection is just poisoning people to death, and if that sounds jarring, it's a testament to the work that the paralytic does. The paralytic is the reason why even the most torturous drug combinations produce an ostensibly "humane" execution. When states use a paralytic, every bit of the execution is secretized so there is nothing but peaceful slumber for execution witnesses to see.

A 2021 lawsuit filed by the Nevada Press Association sought to bar the state's use of a paralytic in lethal injection for this very reason. "By creating a chemical curtain . . . for the sole purpose of obscuring the prisoner's reaction to the drug[s]," the NPA argued, the state "inevitably burdens" the public's right to know whether the state is torturing prisoners to death.[53] "We should know what the state is doing in our name," it stated. It's hard to argue with that.

States also prevent execution problems from becoming apparent by limiting what witnesses can see and hear. In all but a handful of states, for example, the viewing curtain is not opened until after the prisoner's IV has been placed.[54] That leaves one of the most problematic parts of the execution—establishing IV access—entirely outside of public view. When states set the IV behind closed doors, they are conducting a key part of the execution in secret: the only person who could tell us what happened during that process is dead. Little wonder that states routinely puncture prisoners a dozen times or more to get IV access. No one is watching. The state has free rein.

Can you imagine Alabama trying to set an IV on Joe Nathan James for three hours with people watching? Sure, we'd know what happened. But it likely wouldn't have happened at all. Witnesses would have gone nuts, and if the sheer outrage of what was happening in real time didn't force the state to stop, a court almost certainly would have. It is hard to imagine a judge allowing executioners to continue to puncture a prisoner for three hours. As Megan McCracken, a lawyer who has worked on lethal injection cases through UC Berkeley's death penalty clinic, told the press: "It is only because of the total lack of transparency surrounding executions in Alabama that the DOC was able to spend such a long time on failed IV access attempts."[55] Whatever the constitutional prohibition on a "lingering death" means, three hours surely meets the definition.[56]

The very possibility of this sort of egregious state conduct is the reason why the 2021 lawsuit by the NPA also challenged the state's policy of raising the blinds in the execution chamber only after establishing the prisoner's IV. As the executive director of the NPA told the press, "The people of Nevada have a right to know if the state performs its executions humanely, and the press has a First Amendment right and responsibility to report it."[57] Notably, the NPA cited the need to "counterbalance the official narrative offered by the government" as one of the reasons why witnessing executions in their entirety was important, claiming that the state's restricted viewing policy was "designed to limit what reporters can see and to prevent them from reporting if something goes wrong."[58]

Most states also turn off the sound in the execution chamber after the prisoner delivers their last words. *Why.* Seriously, why do that? There is no reason to turn off the sound of an execution other than to make sure witnesses don't hear it. In doing so, states make it harder for media witnesses—who are serving as the public's eyes and ears—to know what is happening during an execution and to determine whether what executioners say is true. In the slew of federal executions in 2020, for example, executioners described the sounds coming from prisoners as "snores."[59] That didn't make sense in light of the violent chest heaves that media witnesses were seeing, but the sound was turned off, so their ability to counter the government's narrative was limited. This appears to be the point. If not, what is?

A little digging around produced two data points for consideration. One is Oklahoma, which did not have a no-sound policy until the botched execution of Clayton Lockett in 2014. The state rewrote its protocol in the aftermath of that execution, and one change was for executioners to turn off the mic after a prisoner's last words.[60] The state's response to an execution where the prisoner's utterances undermined the (false) narrative that he was unconscious was to simply remove the ability to hear those utterances in the future.

The other data point is Arizona, which had a long-standing no-sound policy in place at the time of its nearly two-hour-long execution of Joseph Wood in 2014. Witnesses in Arizona view executions through a soundproof window, but because Wood's execution took so long, the sound was periodically turned on for brief updates. "The gasping and gulping sounded like a freight train," a witness to the execution stated.[61]

After the execution, the press sued, arguing that the no-sound policy burdened its First Amendment right to observe executions in their entirety, and in 2019, a federal court agreed.[62] Arizona had defended the policy in part by saying it could lead to the identification of executioners by their voice—a claim that the court rejected, noting that witnesses could already hear executioners' voices before the mic was cut off. But more noteworthy here was the state's other justification: "allowing witnesses to hear the sounds of the entire execution process could increase the risk of litigation."[63]

That's right, Arizona said that it turned off the sound because what witnesses might hear could get it sued. "Arizona does not have a legitimate penological interest in hampering efforts to ensure the constitutionality of its executions," the court stated. With that, it ruled that Arizona had to leave the sound on during executions, stating that "allowing witnesses to hear the sounds of the entire execution process will ensure informed and accurate media coverage of the event, which in turn will help the public determine whether executions in Arizona are being carried out in a humane and lawful manner."[64] This is the litigation we should see in every no-sound state.

Last but not least in the category of limiting access to information on the front side of an execution is excluding some media outlets from being execution witnesses *at all*. State lethal injection protocols generally allow the DOC to select a certain number of media witnesses for an execution (the number varies from state to state), but the protocols don't say how those selections are to be made. This means that DOCs have unfettered discretion to select—and exclude—whoever they want, and they use it.

For example, the Arizona DOC denied the *Arizona Republic*'s request to serve as a media witness in all three of the executions that the state carried out (and botched) in 2022.[65] The *Arizona Republic* is Arizona's leading newspaper—it has the largest circulation in the state—and a representative from the paper had attended every one of Arizona's executions going back at least twenty years. But the *Arizona Republic* reported on the state's nearly two-hour-long execution of Joseph Wood in 2014, and its reporting was part of the reason for the national outrage at what happened. The paper also reported on Arizona's attempt to illegally import execution drugs from Harris Pharma in 2015.[66]

When the Arizona DOC declined the *Arizona Republic*'s request for media access to the first of the state's three executions in 2022, the paper's executive editor contacted the governor's office for an explanation. He spoke with then-governor Ducey's chief of staff, who "just scoffed," the executive editor said. The chief of staff told him that "if the *Republic* did not print 'false information,' the news organization might be treated differently."[67] Ah, a claim of "fake news" (*because I don't like it*) and an admission of viewpoint discrimination to go with it—a First Amendment lawyer's dream.[68]

In Missouri, as another example, the reporter who broke the story on the DOC's use of a compounding pharmacy with over 1800 regulatory violations applied to be a media witness 17 times, and 17 times the DOC passed him by, offering no explanation for its repeated refusal to seat him as a witness. The ACLU finally sued on his behalf, and Missouri settled in 2018, agreeing that going forward, media organizations would choose the media witnesses for executions, rather than the DOC.[69]

It's not clear whether Texas's failure to seat any media witnesses at all in a 2021 execution is part of what free press organizations view as a "troubling trend" of hostility toward members of the press covering state executions.[70] Texas said it was just a mistake. And Alabama's ridiculous clothing inspections of two veteran female reporters at the three-hour-long James execution in 2022 (one of whom was told her skirt was too short, although she had worn it to witness several prior executions) was likely more about slowing down the arrival of the press than maintaining the propriety of proper dress for an execution.[71] After all, the reporter ended up borrowing fishing waders from a photographer and attaching their suspenders under her skirt to hold them up. That and a pair of tennis shoes were deemed just fine.

Whatever those incidents were about, one can at least say this: as the problems with lethal injection have mounted, states have increasingly turned to secrecy and obfuscation, and as they have done so, members of the media have increasingly called them out on this move. That, in turn, has led to aggression toward the media itself, which has manifested in subtle and not-so-subtle ways. "We are very concerned about the state's apparent retaliation against media organizations critically reporting on government activities," a Freedom of the Press Foundation spokesperson stated about Arizona's treatment of the *Arizona Republic*.[72] Given the spate of attacks on the press in recent years, they should be.

Thus far, we have talked about step two of the secrecy two-step in the context of executions. But the phenomenon is much bigger than that. Most of step two happens well before the prisoner ever enters the execution chamber. That's where secrecy statutes come into play.

SECRECY STATUTES

States do all sorts of things to hide the behind-the-scenes maneuvers necessary to make lethal injection work. For example, consider again the testimony of the Louisiana DOC lawyer about her team's trip to Texas— the same trip where the Texas warden said he didn't really have a process and only cared that the prisoner ended up dead. *But why go all the way to Texas to hear that?* The reason, the lawyer stated, was that when she reached out by phone for advice about lethal injection, the warden stated that "he didn't say these things on the phone that he would rather say in person." In fact, when her entourage met with the warden in Texas, he "asked if any of us had tape recorders, if any of us were wired" before discussing lethal injection.[73]

We have glimpses of the steps that states take to protect their processes from scrutiny, but by and large, the best indication of these efforts is their success. Outside the litigation context—which has slowly chipped away at the wall of secrecy that states have built—there is a complete blackout of information about state lethal injection processes. We know next to nothing about how most protocols were chosen, or a myriad of other choices that DOCs make—decisions that any other government entity would have to document and present for public inspection.

Secrecy statutes do the same thing as these opaque secrecy measures; they just take a different approach. Secrecy statutes are formal, visible, *codified* efforts to hide what is happening behind the scenes so that it never becomes public. They are just a statutory version of the state secrecy two-step, codifying step two.

Lethal injection secrecy statutes grew organically from the clandestine nature of the drug transactions themselves. Having no prescription for a prescription-only drug from a prescription-only provider meant sales under the table, and that meant payments in cash, drug buys in off-site locations, no receipts, no acquisition forms or processes, and coded references to drug suppliers in any record, with the preference being no record at all. The idea was to leave no paper trail, and it was largely successful—but for the fact of state freedom of information acts (FOIAs).

State FOIAs require disclosure upon request of records regarding government transactions, and buying drugs is a government transaction, so whatever records states had were still subject to FOIA disclosure, and even limited disclosures could be plenty damning. Hence the need for secrecy statutes—statutes that put the equivalent of a Harry

Potter cloak of invisibility over all procurements concerning lethal injection in executing states.

Today, virtually every state that is actively conducting executions has a secrecy statute. Most of these statutes prohibit even courts from peeking behind the veil of secrecy to see what the state is doing, effectively removing DOCs from judicial oversight altogether. Still others provide for civil or criminal liability for unauthorized disclosures. One state, Georgia, has even declared information about lethal injection a "confidential state secret" (whatever that means).[74]

Two things are clear from the timing of these statutes. One is that they are often a direct response to states losing FOIA lawsuits. Consider, for example, Indiana. Litigation in Indiana resulted in a 2016 court order requiring the state to release records regarding its efforts to obtain lethal injection drugs under the state's Access to Public Records Act. But the state legislature had a better idea: it would pass a secrecy statute instead and simply make it retroactive. On the last day of its 2017 legislative session, that is exactly what the state did. At 2 a.m., the legislature passed a general spending bill that had a secrecy provision tucked away in the fine print of its 175 pages. State officials then tried to tell the court that the new legislation nullified its ruling. The court was not impressed. "The General Assembly may not change the result of [this] litigation," it ruled. "While other requests may be precluded by the statute, blocking [the public records] request after this Court has already ordered the Department to produce the documents violates . . . Indiana's Constitution."[75] The court then awarded $538,000 in attorney's fees for the state's bad faith noncompliance, which was affirmed by the Indiana Supreme Court in 2021.[76]

Other states have likewise passed secrecy statutes in direct response to losing FOIA litigation. In 2019, for example, Arkansas passed a secrecy statute that effectively negated a court's FOIA ruling from the year before. Arkansas' new statute prohibits disclosure of the identity of pharmaceutical manufacturers whose drugs are used for lethal injection, and makes recklessly disclosing their identity a *felony* punishable by up to six years in prison and a $10,000 fine.[77] *We're not only going to breach manufacturers' contracts, we're going to make a felon out of anyone who dares to get in our way.*

Idaho is another example. After a protracted three-year battle, the state lost its fight to keep its lethal injection drug transactions secret in a 2020 court ruling that was affirmed on appeal in 2021.[78] Like Indiana, the state was ordered to pay attorney's fees for its bad-faith noncompliance with its open records statute. In 2022, Idaho passed a secrecy statute to exempt itself from FOIA obligations going forward.

The other thing clear from the timing of these statutes is that they are often a direct response to embarrassments for executing states. It is no accident that Missouri passed its secrecy statute just after its chief executioner was found to be a malpractice-ridden doctor. Or that Idaho passed its secrecy statute in the wake of revelations about clandestine, out-of-state drug purchases with bundles of cash. Or that Georgia passed its secrecy statute after it was discovered that the state's lethal injection drugs came from a distributor operating out of the back of a London driving school. Or that Ohio passed its secrecy statute in the aftermath of the botched execution of Dennis McGuire.

"After Flawed Executions, States Resort to Secrecy," a 2007 headline in the *New York Times* read.[79] In 2015, *Slate Magazine*'s article "The Capital Punishment Cover-Up"[80] showed that nothing had changed in the intervening eight years. As Dahlia Lithwick wrote for *Slate*: "Amid the recent rash of high-profile screw-ups in executions, new cover-up measures have been passed in more than two dozen states, allowing departments of corrections to increasingly refuse to disclose where their execution drugs come from, how and if they were tested, and whether corrections officers are qualified to administer them correctly."[81] Scandals are only scandals if people know about them. Secrecy statutes make sure that people don't.

Secrecy statutes complicate the story of broad delegation of legislative power told in chapter 8. State legislatures delegate on the front side, then provide cover for DOC decisions on the back side. In this way, state legislatures are more than unthinking pass-the-buck delegators. They are complicit in all the dirt that secrecy sweeps under the rug.

THE REASONS FOR STATE SECRECY STATUTES

States say secrecy statutes are a necessary evil. Death penalty laws are on the books, they say, and the government's job is to enforce them. "Our goal is to allow the Department of Corrections to implement the laws . . . that the people of Arkansas overwhelmingly support," the state legislator who sponsored Arkansas's secrecy bill stated.[82] The Arkansas governor expressed a similar view, explaining: "The will of the people . . . will be stymied if you don't have the capacity to acquire those drugs, and confidentiality is an important part of that."[83]

Secrecy statutes are necessary, the argument goes, because drug suppliers will be subject to harassment and threats of violence—perhaps even violence itself—if their identities are known. "As we have said repeatedly, disclosing the identity of the pharmacy will result in the harassment of the business and will raise serious safety concerns for the business and its employees," a spokesperson for the Texas Department of Criminal Justice (TDCJ) stated in 2017.[84] "The entire reason for Oklahoma's confidentiality statute is to protect those who provide lethal injection drugs to the state from threats, coercion and intimidation," Oklahoma's attorney general stated when the validity of its secrecy statute was litigated in 2014.[85] Florida's 2022 secrecy statute was likewise touted as a way to protect drug suppliers from "potential harassment, intimidation or harm" from anti–death penalty activists.[86]

By this view, secrecy is not the problem. Secrecy is the solution. Secrecy is necessary to thwart abolitionist attempts to obstruct the death penalty and subvert majority will. It is a rational response to the "guerilla war against the death penalty" that Justice Alito pointed to in *Glossip v. Gross*.[87] In short, *it's all abolitionists' fault.*

So is it?

States are right when they say that without secret sales, there won't be sales at all. States that don't have a secrecy statute are generally not executing, and the reason is that they can't get the drugs.[88] But why states need secrecy to make these drug purchases matters. As Justice Scalia famously wrote: "There are laws against threats and intimidation, [but] harsh criticism, short of unlawful action, is a price our people have traditionally been willing to pay for self-governance."[89]

The question, then, is what is driving the need for secrecy. Is it threats and intimidation? Or just harsh criticism, the price we pay for self-governance?

Texas is the only state with a well-developed record on this issue, and the only state whose judiciary has found evidence sufficient to substantiate the state's claim of a threat of violence. The issue came up in FOIA litigation when the state claimed that it was entitled to a statutory exemption for disclosures posing "a substantial threat of physical harm." The trial court and court of appeals rejected the claim in 2017, but the Texas Supreme Court reversed, finding that an email sent by a college professor in *Oklahoma* to a compounding pharmacy in *Oklahoma* was a threat of violence that justified secrecy in *Texas*.[90]

The email was sent to the Apothecary Shoppe, just after it was outed for supplying drugs for lethal injection. In the email, the professor suggested that the Apothecary Shoppe ought to beef up its security, writing: "As the folks at the federal building can tell you, it only takes one fanatic with a truckload of fertilizer to make a real dent in business as usual."[91] The professor signed his name to the email, and was apparently befuddled when the FBI showed up at his door to investigate. That prompted the professor to send a follow-up email—this time to the lawyer for the prisoners in the Texas FOIA suit. The professor explained that he was not trying to threaten the pharmacy, writing: "Even if one fanatic (a term nobody ever uses to describe himself, note) . . . chose to go on the attack, I felt, and thought I had made it clear, that they would be reckless not to consider this possibility and to take appropriate action."[92]

Tellingly, the FBI knew nothing about an alleged threat to the Apothecary Shoppe until a reporter called to ask about it. At the time, the Associated Press was making calls to determine whether the email had been reported to federal, state, or local law enforcement authorities in Texas or Oklahoma.[93] It had not. The Apothecary Shoppe must have sent the email to its contact at the Oklahoma DOC, who then sent it to Texas to use in its litigation, as law enforcement was not involved at all.

Curiously, a compounding pharmacy *in Texas* was identified as a supplier of lethal injection drugs during the pendency of the Texas FOIA litigation, and a "small group of protesters" gathered in front of the shop.[94] Police were called but it was a peaceful protest and the protesters were well within their rights. "There were no problems at the location whatsoever," the sheriff's office told the AP.[95] Perhaps now is a good time to point out that anti–death penalty activists don't even think condemned murderers deserve to die, so it's a good bet that they aren't into harming pharmacists to make the point.

So there you have it. This is the entirety of the record of threats of violence, across all states and all identified suppliers. As the American Bar Association noted in a 2015 report: "Such claims have not been verified in any state seeking to shield information concerning execution drug suppliers from the public, either through prosecution, litigation, or other publicly available evidence."[96]

Secrecy statutes aren't about protecting drug suppliers from threats of violence. If they were, the best evidence of threats wouldn't be some college professor's email. If they were, someone, somewhere, would have felt threatened enough to notify the authorities. If they were, evidence of threats would have mounted as journalists have unveiled these pharmacies' identities. None of that is happening.

What *is* happening when a compounding pharmacy is identified as a lethal injection drug supplier is a torrent of criticism and bad publicity— what one article describes as "always non-violent, but always unnerving."[97] The "unnerving" part is important. Just because these pharmacies aren't receiving threats of violence or being subjected to the sort of intimidation and harassment that is legally actionable doesn't mean they are impervious to negative attention. Hate mail, angry calls, excoriating blog posts, protests—these are all part of what is sometimes called the "name and shame" game, and *no one* wants to be publicly shamed, least of all little mom-and-pop businesses.

The business side of the ledger is important too. There simply isn't enough death to be in the death drugs supply business full time. The pharmacies that are supplying lethal injection drugs are in the death drug business on the side, which means they still need to mind the bottom line. Bad publicity is bad for business, and the spotlight may lead to a public airing of dirt (sometimes literally) that small businesses would rather their customers not see. No compounding pharmacy wants reports of its poor sterility practices and regulatory violations in the papers and on the internet. No business wants attention drawn to the fact that it is operating outside the expressed norms of its industry. That's the sort of bad publicity that can drive customers away for good.

This, then, is what secrecy statutes are really about: protecting drug suppliers from public scorn and the financial repercussions that come with it. As a lower court in the Texas FOIA litigation wrote: "There are myriad reasons why a private business or professional involved in the [lethal injection drug supply] process would not want that fact known publicly—potentially adverse marketplace effects, unwanted publicity, critical written or oral communications from members of the public, or protests, to name but a few of the unpleasantries that can accompany one's association with such a controversial public issue."[98] Secrecy statutes protect drug suppliers from these sorts of "unpleasantries," removing impediments that may keep drug suppliers from supplying drugs at all.

State officials have said so themselves. For example, a spokesperson for the Arkansas DOC explained that a secrecy statute was necessary because "sellers were concerned about adverse publicity and the loss of business if they were identified as suppliers of drugs used for executions."[99] Similarly, the sponsor of North Carolina's secrecy bill stated, "I think the drug maker, if that business is disclosed, they worry about all the demonstrators that will appear at their door. So what we're trying to do is protect them."[100] The attorney for Indiana stated that the state's secrecy statute was to protect suppliers from "public shaming, public protests, hate mail and lawsuits."[101] And in Oklahoma, the state attorney general defended the state's secrecy statute with the claim that "participants have a privacy interest in not being subjected to public scrutiny based on their involvement in an event that engenders so much controversy."[102]

To be clear, participants do not have a "privacy interest" in evading public scrutiny when engaging in controversial transactions with the government. That's completely made up. State FOIAs are a testament to the importance of transparency in government transactions, and not a single one of them contains an exception for transactions that are controversial. In fact, the very point of FOIA—that the government should be accountable to the people it represents—cuts the other way. When the government is engaging in controversial transactions, those transactions should get more public scrutiny, not less.

Secrecy statutes do the opposite. They shield the government's drug deals from public criticism, and that's not just their effect. That is also their intent. To borrow from a federal judge on this point, secrecy statutes are "motivated by an interest in suppressing lawful protest."[103] They are designed to *hide* the deal so the government can *do* the deal.

It is worth pausing to appreciate how utterly exceptional secrecy statutes are in this regard. It is hard to think of another context where the government tells us that it can only do a transaction if it suppresses lawful protest. And it's hard to think of another context where the response to public criticism is to simply conceal the transaction altogether.

A useful comparison is the abortion context. Back when abortion was one of our constitutional rights, the rule was that those who provided abortion services were not entitled to keep their identity secret, even in the face of true threats. In the abortion context, we said to providers: *Abortion may be a constitutional right, but we're not going to protect your identity. We're going to allow all sorts of laws designed to name and shame you, and if you don't like it, then you should stop providing abortions.* We said public shaming was a legitimate response to a practice that some considered morally objectionable; it was public criticism of a controversial practice, and it fed our democratic discourse. And we could say the *exact same thing* about the suppliers of lethal injection drugs. But we don't.

This brings us back to Justice Alito's comment about abolitionists waging "a guerilla war against the death penalty."[104] What Justice Alito calls "guerilla warfare" is known in most legal circles as the exercise of free speech, with dramatically different democratic implications. Justice Alito views abolitionists as thwarting majority will on the death penalty, but public dissent is one of the hallmarks of our democratic discourse, and the entire point of secrecy statutes is to stifle public dissent. That's the purpose, that's the effect. For executing states, the real problem with picketing and other forms of public dissent is *not* that it's stealth warfare taking place in the shadows. The problem is that it is taking place in the light for all to see. But that's not guerilla warfare. That's just free speech that Justice Alito doesn't like.

Thus far, we've talked about secrecy statutes as if their sole purpose is to protect willing suppliers of lethal injection drugs. But that is not the only reason why states are passing these statutes. States are also passing secrecy statutes to prevent *un*willing suppliers from finding out about the surreptitious sales of their drugs.

Astoundingly, the sponsor of South Carolina's secrecy statute admitted this was true. "You've got a law and can't carry it out because of some corporate policy," he said in his pitch for state secrecy in 2023.[105] No need for surmising, we know what South Carolina's secrecy statute is about: enabling the state to get around "some corporate policy" preventing drug sales for lethal injection. All that trickery and bad faith that we saw in chapter 6—South Carolina's statute was passed for the very purpose of enabling that.

This is why drug manufacturers are united in their opposition to state secrecy statutes. They have lobbied against their passage in state legislatures. They have filed briefs against their validity in state and federal courts. And they have sued to get their misappropriated drugs back, challenging state secrecy as an illegitimate means of preventing them from enforcing their own contracts. As we saw in chapter 6, pharmaceutical companies have claimed "a keen and important interest" in knowing whether DOCs are intentionally circumventing their distribution controls.[106] Having gone to the trouble of establishing those controls, these companies want and expect their contracts to be respected.

So when states say that their secrecy statutes are to protect drug suppliers, it's important to ask which suppliers they mean. To the extent that state secrecy statutes are about protecting suppliers at all, they are about protecting outliers in the compounding pharmacy industry. But those same statutes are also *un*protecting major drug manufacturers by thwarting their ability to enforce their own contracts. Indeed, in South Carolina (one suspects elsewhere too), *un*protecting drug manufacturers is the very point.

Lawyers for condemned prisoners say that states are passing these statutes for another reason as well: to hide state malfeasance and stave off legal challenges. It's not happenstance, they say, that states started passing these statutes when their desperation for drugs led them to shady suppliers and law-breaking. "The premise that these participants must be shielded for their safety has no factual basis," one attorney says. "It is manufactured to avoid accountability."[107] Lethal injection expert Deborah Denno agrees, stating: "My own research indicates that in modern times, death-penalty states' aversion to transparency is far more rooted in the desire to conceal inconsistencies and incompetence."[108] Shockingly, Oklahoma DOC officials have all but said so themselves, telling a grand jury in 2015 that secrecy was used "to make purchases more difficult to track and therefore harder to legally challenge."[109]

Whether or not states are passing secrecy statutes for the purpose of hiding improper and/or illegal conduct, it is at least the case that secrecy statutes *allow* such conduct to be hidden, giving states virtual impunity when exercising their greatest power. We know what states have done behind the veil of secrecy. We've seen violations of state and federal laws, intentionally breached contracts, clandestine drug deals with an assortment of sketchy suppliers, patently problematic executioners, and a myriad of other choices that no state official could defend.

In the end, it is easier for states to defend secrecy than the unsavory, illegal, and price-gouging deals that secrecy is hiding. States blame abolitionists for the need for secrecy, but one suspects that they are quietly thanking their lucky stars for a legitimate reason to hide their illegitimate choices. Secrecy is a saving grace for executing states.

THE COST OF SECRECY

We have already seen some of the costs of secrecy. Costs to pharmaceutical companies duped into participating in executions against their will. Costs to the integrity of the domestic drug supply chain. Costs to taxpayers and to the rule of law. And costs to the condemned prisoners who bear the brunt of the state's indefensible choices. Here, we'll step back to consider what remains: the larger institutional costs of secrecy covering lethal injection.

First is what secrecy does to judicial oversight. Courts are our constitutional guardians. When all else fails, we count on courts to stand against government overreaching. That is an impossible task when courts don't know what DOCs are doing. Some secrecy statutes purport to remove all things lethal injection from the purview of the judiciary. Others don't go that far, but *any* information kept from courts imperils their ability to make an informed ruling in the case.

An illustrative example comes from 2015's *Glossip v. Gross*.[110] Oklahoma told the Supreme Court in the *Glossip* litigation that it turned to midazolam because it couldn't buy pentobarbital. No compounding pharmacy would sell the drug, the state claimed, submitting a heavily redacted letter to prove the point. But the letter looked familiar, and some sleuthing by investigative journalists revealed why: it was from a compounding pharmacy *in Texas*, demanding that the *Texas Department of Criminal Justice* return its drugs.[111] Oklahoma had blacked out the word "Texas" and submitted another state's letter as its own—an "inadvertent mistake," the state attorney general said when the story broke.[112]

In the end, not even the state's blatant misrepresentation mattered to the majority in *Glossip*. But it should have—or at least it *could* have. Absent top-notch investigative reporting, no one would have known that the state was misrepresenting the facts before the United States Supreme Court. Secrecy allows state actors to make misrepresentations with impunity. If no one knows what the DOC is doing, the DOC can pretty much do whatever it wants.

Another example comes from the 2022 legislative hearings on Idaho's secrecy bill (now law). Testifying against the bill was a retired federal judge who had presided over a challenge to Idaho's lethal injection protocol back in 2011, which, as we now know, was when the Idaho DOC made a straw purchase of lethal injection drugs in Salt Lake City using a clinical pharmacist from the Department of Health and Welfare.[113] Turns out, that drug deal happened the very day that the judge was holding a hearing on the state's lethal injection protocol. State officials withheld that information, the judge told legislators, "even though they were well aware that I was concerned about the hasty manner in which the state was going about this execution."[114] The judge couldn't say whether the information would have changed his ruling, but stated that "it certainly would have been something I would have looked at carefully." At the very least, the state's shady purchasing practices were a relevant consideration in the case he was deciding. He should have known.

Next is what secrecy costs us in democratic accountability. People cannot hold their government accountable for what they don't know, and secrecy makes sure that people know as little as possible. To the extent that the American public is operating under a vast misimpression about lethal injection, we can thank state secrecy for that. Secrecy prevents public scrutiny—that's the very point—and it does so for the purpose of stifling public debate. That's what makes it so pernicious. "Secrecy not only prevents the public from having robust, informed, and honest discussion about the death penalty," a Death Penalty Information Center report on lethal injection secrecy explains, "it also makes public oversight impossible."[115]

This recognition provides an important reality check on the Supreme Court's admonition that courts should stay out of regulating the death penalty and let the people resolve such debates themselves.[116] That's hard to do when the public doesn't even know what it is purportedly approving. And it doesn't work to say that people support the death penalty so everything else is fair game. One might very well support the death penalty but not support torturing people to death, or spending $1.5 million of taxpayer money on a couple of botched executions, or having government officials lie, cheat, and steal in their name. "They don't want you to know this," one ACLU lawyer stated, "because they don't want the public to understand how outrageous their entire execution process is, including the taxpayer money."[117] Lies matter. Law-breaking matters. Gross incompetence and malfeasance matter. As the judge who testified against Idaho's secrecy bill told legislators, "It's the details that matter."[118] The point of state secrecy is to make sure you don't have any.

The cost to democratic accountability is especially high in the death penalty context, as the state is at its most powerful moment. "Our government should not have anything to hide when it comes to the most serious thing that the government does, which is kill a human being," the lawyer in one state's FOIA litigation told the press.[119] Whatever one might think of the death penalty as a general proposition, Americans should know how the ultimate penalty is being carried out in their name. This is no time to hide what the state is doing. We should be demanding more scrutiny of the choices states make, not settling for less.

A separate but related harm is the cost that secrecy imposes on our free press. "One of the primary purposes of a free and independent press is to perform a watchdog function over government activities," a lawyer in one media suit says.[120] The press has clearly served that role here. Indeed, the press is a good part of the reason we know anything about lethal injection at all. Time and again, state officials make bald claims about the people, products, and processes involved in lethal injection—*and people believe them*—only to have investigative journalists later show that those claims weren't true. Now is a good time to remember that it was the media that exposed Missouri's use of a malpractice-ridden doctor, and unearthed the ugly truth about Harris Pharma, and revealed the troubled compounding pharmacies supplying lethal injection drugs to various states. To the journalists who provided much of the fodder for this book, I salute you.

Secrecy statutes burden the press' ability to perform this critically important function, not only by making information about lethal injection exponentially harder to get, but also by making it unlawful (criminal, even) to then share it. As a case in point, the *Columbia Journalism Review* wrote about the hard questions that journalists faced in the wake of Missouri's secrecy statute, which provided for civil penalties (including punitive damages) for the disclosure of the identity of any current or former member of an execution team, which was defined broadly to include suppliers of lethal injection drugs.[121] When investigative journalists pieced together that the Apothecary Shoppe in Oklahoma was supplying Missouri executioners, the paper "had to grapple with the possibility of opening itself up to penalties if it went ahead" with the story.[122] One paper decided not to publish the name of the pharmacy. Another paper went the other way, and the information made its way to the public, and now, to the readers of this book. "We are a journalistic outlet and our focus is on what the public has a right to know," the reporter who wrote the story stated.[123] But if the paper had followed the law, the truth would never have been known.

Finally, secrecy imposes costs on the integrity of state institutions by incentivizing DOCs to act on their worst impulses. If state officials want to make illegal drug purchases or buy drugs from the sketchiest of suppliers, these are the laws that allow them to do that. And secrecy statutes play an important role in resistance to change as well. If states can't fix a problem, they hide it, and if they can hide a problem, they are much less interested in fixing it. "Until death-penalty states are willing to focus more on solutions than secrecy, lethal injection as a method of execution will remain mired in an endless cycle of difficulty and disorder," Deborah Denno wrote in 2015.[124] Secrecy statutes create the worst possible combination: insiders who can't get lethal injection right, and outsiders who aren't privy to what's wrong.

ARE STATE SECRECY STATUTES CONSTITUTIONAL?

The larger institutional costs of state secrecy statutes—the damage they do to the ability of courts to do their job, and the press to do its job, and the people in a democracy to do their job—raises the question of whether these statutes are constitutional. Can states simply exempt their legislation from judicial review? Can they put content restrictions on the press? And can they keep information relevant to whether an execution will be torturous from the prisoners who will be subject to it?

Courts are still sorting this out, but the trend has been for lower courts to find a constitutional violation of some sort, only to have the highest courts at the state and federal levels reverse, rejecting the notion that secrecy statutes pose a constitutional problem of any kind. For an extended analysis, legal scholarship is the place to look.[125] Here, the aim is to set forth the basic nature of the claims so readers can at least understand the stakes.

First, the First Amendment claims, because they go to the heart of a functioning democracy. Press organizations have mainly taken aim at provisions in secrecy statutes that penalize the disclosure of information. Such provisions are an impermissible "content-based restriction on speech," they say, "a gag order on potentially adverse reports that could inform the public debate over capital punishment."[126] "These laws are unconstitutional, even immoral," one legal journalist argues, "because they seek to hide from the American people material information about the means and manner of some of the most controversial aspects of capital punishment."[127]

Can you think of another context where the press has revealed lawbreaking and malfeasance by the government, and then the government passed a law prohibiting further reporting on that very issue, and courts said this was okay? Me either. It's one thing for a state to say, *We aren't going to disclose who our executioners or drug suppliers are.* It's another thing entirely for the state to say, *And if you figure it out on your own, we're going to make you civilly and perhaps criminally liable if you tell anyone. Heck, we'll even make you a convicted felon in one state.* We don't have to talk about the chilling effect on the press (although we could). The chill is in the text itself, which tells the press there is something they can't write about, however unseemly and unlawful it may be. That seems to me an unconstitutional restraint on the First Amendment freedom of the press. But in the weird world of lethal injection, where every other value must give way to make the system work, higher courts have not agreed.

Next is the assault on the judiciary, because its role in our constitutional democracy is every bit as critically important. Here again, it's one thing for a state to say, *We aren't going to disclose who our executioners or drug suppliers are.* It's another thing entirely for a state to say, *And not even a court can see what we're doing. We're taking our stinky, unlawful practices entirely outside the realm of judicial review.* How is that not a violation of separation of powers? It just can't be the case that the legislature can pass a law that says courts considering whether the state's conduct is unconstitutional can't know what the conduct is. But in the weird world of lethal injection, it *is* the case, apparently, because higher courts have let these provisions stand.

These claims are often couched as due process or "access to court" claims—claims that by placing the information outside even the court's purview, they deny prisoners their due process right of judicial review. An example is what the trial court said in Lockett's challenge to the state secrecy statute. "I do not think this is even a close call," the court stated. "To say that no one, not even the court, has access to that information, I think that does deny them access to court."[128] *Of course it does. And it was meant to.*

One federal appellate court did strike down a state secrecy statute on this ground in 2014, stating: "We, and the public, cannot meaningfully evaluate [an] execution protocol cloaked in secrecy."[129] The Supreme Court summarily vacated the ruling.[130] No reason, just did it. The prisoner—Joseph Wood—was executed by Arizona the next day. The execution took an hour and fifty-seven minutes. At the time, it was the longest execution in US history.

Since then, appellate courts have fallen into line and upheld these provisions, but even here, federal judges have written separately to express dismay. "We cannot fulfill our constitutional role of determining whether a state's method of execution violates the Eighth Amendment's prohibition against cruel and unusual punishment," one judge lamented,[131] while another stated: "I am equally concerned about this Court's ability to meaningfully discharge its constitutional duty to assess the risks associated with [this] execution against relevant Eighth Amendment standards."[132] Yet another wrote that "if a skilled lawyer were instructing the state on how best to avoid *any* meaningful review of the constitutionality of its execution procedures, he would be hard pressed to improve on the unconscionable regime that the state has adopted."[133] It is both the case that appellate courts have rejected these claims *and* the case that jurists at all levels have recognized their merit.

Finally, consider the Eighth Amendment "cruel and unusual punishments" clause. Prisoners challenging their execution under the Eighth Amendment can't just throw out accusations, nor will educated guesses do. As the Supreme Court has admonished, "Speculation cannot substitute for evidence that the use of the drug is 'sure or very likely to cause serious illness and needless suffering.'"[134] Showing that a state's lethal injection protocol is "sure or very likely" to cause needless pain and suffering is an astronomically high evidentiary standard. The point here is that prisoners are subject to this astronomically high standard *and also* denied access to the information needed to meet it.

A number of jurists have recognized the constitutional catch-22 that secrecy statutes create, and the abject unfairness of denying prisoners access to the information they need to prove their Eighth Amendment claims, and then dismissing those claims because the prisoners didn't prove them. But the point is perhaps best captured by one federal court's opinion, which stated:

The necessary is also the withheld: *you must give us that which you cannot have to give.* In order to challenge the use of a drug that will be used to execute them, inmates must explain why use of that drug presents a risk of substantial harm. But the inmates are not allowed to know from where the drug came, how specifically it was manufactured, or who was involved in the creation of the drug. . . .

A proponent of Kafkaesque absurdity might be proud of such a byzantine method for pursuing the protection of a constitutional right, even if the drafters of the United States Constitution might not. A right bereft of an effective, meaningful means to protect that right is arguably nothing more than an illusion to appease a society that conveniently and comfortingly seeks to tell itself that it kills with fairness.[135]

Alas, the court concluded, the law left no room but to dismiss the claim, so that is what it did.

Why are higher courts not finding some kind of constitutional violation in this patently unfair state of affairs? The cases offer a hodgepodge of reasons. The court in Lockett's case, for example, said that he couldn't show "actual prejudice"—that is, he couldn't show the difference that having the information would make.[136] But how is one to show the difference that information would make when they don't even know what that information is?

A concurrence in the same case offered another reason. According to that judge, Lockett's challenge to the secrecy statute was "frivolous and a complete waste of time." The judge explained:

The plaintiffs have no more right to the information they requested than if they were being executed in the electric chair, they would have no right to know whether OG & E or PSO were providing the electricity; if they were being hanged, they would have no right to know whether it be by cotton or nylon rope; or if they were being executed by firing squad, they would have no right to know whether it be by Winchester or Remington ammunition.[137]

This concurring judge might have thought about the fact that who provides the bullets makes no difference in an execution by firing squad, and the same is true of who provides the rope in a hanging or the electricity in an electrocution. But if one of these suppliers had, say, a 25–30 percent failure rate that caused torturous deaths, we'd have an actual comparison on our hands.

Other courts have relied on long-standing doctrine that prisoners do not have a right to "discover grievances."[138] Prisoners are not entitled to a fishing expedition, courts say, and this is what prisoners are doing. But as Eric Berger notes, the prisoners who make these claims are not fishing.[139] They know their claims. They just don't have access to the evidence to prove them. "Perhaps the state's secrecy masks a 'substantial risk of serious harm,' but it does not create one," one federal appellate court reasoned.[140] And this was a result the court thought was okay.

The irony of this state of affairs is that states looking to shut down lethal injection challenges by making them impossible to prove have inadvertently given prisoners yet another thing to litigate. And states seeking to avoid criticism by secretizing their troubled processes have instead given critics even more to criticize. Secrecy was designed to hide all that is wrong with lethal injection. Instead, it has shown all that is wrong with the executing state.

In 2018, cultural historian Colin Dickie wrote: "The work of American torture has always been twofold: not just the violence itself, but the complex legal and rhetorical strategies that obfuscate it away to maintain a myth of America as a civilized place without cruel and unusual punishment."[141] He wasn't writing about lethal injection. But the fact that modern executions weren't a part of his essay (or the book he was reviewing) is just a testament to how utterly effective the obfuscation of lethal injection is.

"At its core, this is not a death-penalty story," one reporter says, "It's a story about government secrecy."[142] In the end, the story of lethal injection is a story about both. It is a story about all the ways that states have proven themselves unworthy of the astounding power to kill, and all the ways they have tried to cover that up.

"I'm not saying no state should ever carry out an execution," one policy analyst says. "I'm saying if you're untrustworthy, you should not carry out an execution."[143]

I don't trust these people.

Do you?

EPILOGUE

This book was based on research—copious amounts of it—and the research speaks for itself. But that research has changed me in unexpected ways, and it is only fitting to end by sharing an insight that was not part of this project, but that I learned along the way. I have been writing about the death penalty for almost two decades, and have always viewed condemned prisoners as people who did horrible, unspeakable things (probably), but still deserved the protection of the law. Arguably, even more so. But I confess that I have kept my distance from the humanity of the faceless convicted capital murderers I have been studying all these years.

This project has offered (insisted upon, even) a front-row seat to who these people are. Many, too many to count, found redemption on death row, and prayed to their Lord and Savior, Yahweh or Allah, as they died, some after starting prison ministries. As Saul became Paul, so it is for many on death row.[1] Others were just deeply broken people, desperate to go back to their younger selves and warn them to stop before it was tragically too late. Over and over, this was a theme in the last statements I read. A few went out defiantly, but very few. For the vast majority of these prisoners, it was evident that the person who committed that terrible crime just wasn't there anymore.

This sense was ably conveyed in the post-execution statement of the lawyer for Dustin Lee Honken, one of the prisoners in the federal government's 2020 execution spree. "There was no reason for the government to kill him, in haste or at all," the lawyer stated. "In any case, they failed. The Dustin Honken they wanted to kill is long gone."[2]

Prison guards said the same of Brian Dorsey in 2024. More than seventy correctional officers signed a letter to Missouri's governor asking that Dorsey's death sentence be commuted to life without parole. Then one of them wrote an op-ed to make the plea public. "We Corrections Officers Know Brian Dorsey Has Changed. Gov. Parson, Don't Execute Him," the title read.[3] "Dorsey has been under a death sentence in Missouri for seventeen years, and there is no dispute that he committed murder," the veteran corrections officer wrote, then stated: "Yet, far from being the 'worst of the worst,' Dorsey exemplifies the growth, transformation and redemption that are possible when someone is committed to turning their life around after making a terrible mistake. . . . There isn't a nicer guy than Brian. . . . We know that he was convicted of murder, but that is not the Brian Dorsey we know."

Brian Dorsey was housed in the 'honor dorm' of the prison. He served as the prison barber for over a decade, cutting the hair of not only his fellow prisoners, but also the warden and prison staff. Imagine what that looked like, the warden trusting a condemned murderer with a pair of scissors at his neck. "Mr. Dorsey is an excellent barber and a kind and respectful man," the corrections officer insisted. "I do not hesitate to say that executing Brian Dorsey would be a pointless cruelty."

Yet once a death warrant is issued, the machinery of death is nearly impossible to halt. The governor declined to intervene, and the prison guards who had come to know and respect Brian Dorsey were then forced to kill him. The op-ed had warned that "taking Dorsey's life would be especially traumatizing for many current and former [prison] staff members, myself included, who have come to respect and care for this exemplary inmate." Surely Brian Dorsey was not the only casualty that day.

As I was putting the finishing touches on this book to send it into production, I felt a deep sorrow, and frankly, shame, knowing that this extraordinary exemplar of redemption was about to be killed by the prison staff who had come to know and respect him. Over seventy prison guards could not save Dorsey, though they tried mightily and were joined by a host of others, including family members of the victims and five of the jurors who sentenced him to death.

Nothing can stop the gears of the machinery of death from grinding. The only way to prevent such senseless acts of cruelty is to retire the machine altogether.

I see this now in a way I didn't before. Before, I saw the law—a long list of broken promises of fairness and procedural protections. I thought of this project as just another broken promise to add to that long list. Now I see humanity in full flower, and I cannot *unsee* it.

This is what studying executions does: it forces us to pay attention to who these people are at the *end*. Not who they were in their worst moment, but who they have become—and who others are capable of becoming. In our mind's eye, we tend to freeze these people in a single moment in time. I myself have done so. But time works changes, and studying executions has been a potent reminder that humans have the greatest capacity to change of all.

A sense of urgency comes with this insight. Today, there are over 2,300 people on death row—all subject to the very state actors you have read about in this book. As you read this, dozens upon dozens of prisoners are scheduled to die at the hands of the state. Each with a story. Most with regret. All more than their worst moment.

The death penalty is not a given. It is a choice, and choices are subject to change. But that would require actually thinking about state killing, and the point of lethal injection is to make it so we don't. This work must be mighty important, because states have gone to extraordinary lengths to maintain the façade of an execution that looks like something else.

In the name of lethal injection, states have broken state and federal laws. They have deliberately breached private contracts and misled sellers with straw purchases. They have asked medical professionals to violate the ethics of their profession. And they have put people like you and me at risk of being cut-off from the medicines we need. Through it all, states have sacrificed not only their professed commitment to humane executions, but also important values—government transparency, regulatory compliance, freedom of contract, respect for the rule of law, and the utmost care in the most solemn of duties. Every principle we profess to hold dear must bend a knee to the lie of lethal injection.

There are countless reasons to oppose the death penalty, but the one that lethal injection brings to the fore is a recognition that the state at its most powerful moment is also the state at its worst. The story of lethal injection shows time and again that the state has no business being in the business of killing. How ironic that the execution method adopted to save the death penalty has become the latest reason to get rid of it.

Acknowledgments

Acknowledgments are personal, and this one will be more so than most. I begin by saying that I was called to write this book. The story of that call is better told in person than here, and I hope that this acknowledgment will open doors for me to share an amazing testimony. Here, it suffices to cite the passage where it all began, Psalm 45:1: "My heart is overflowing with a good theme; I recite my composition concerning the king; my tongue is the pen of a ready writer." There is a grace on this book, and I will forever be grateful to have had this special walk to research and write it. I'm not saying I got it right. But I simply cannot write an acknowledgment without first acknowledging the Lord I serve. *Produce your cause, saith the Lord, bring forth your strong reasons . . . Make it plain, so he may run who reads it.* This I have endeavored to do.

Now, for the rest. It took me a good five years to research and write this book, and then another for it to find the right home. I thank my agent, Laura Yorke, who never gave up on me, and later shared that she didn't take my book because she thought some big trade press would buy it; she took it because she thought it was important and wanted to help usher it into the world. I thank my dear friend Katie Meighan, who gave me a month-long writing retreat in Rome to finish the book that included meals, a beautiful view, and two lovely dogs. I thank the community of friends and colleagues who supported me along the way, in particular Scott Sundby, who encouraged me from day one; Michael Meltsner, who gave great advice at key points along the way; Carol Steiker, who championed this project, made connections for me, and read numerous drafts of my proposal; Jordan Steiker, who likewise championed this project and also invited me to University of Texas to workshop a chapter of the book; Eric Berger, who was my resident lethal injection expert, and who diligently (and so helpfully) read a draft of this book; Deborah Denno, who encouraged me to take on this project, answered questions along the way, and whose pathbreaking work informed so much of my own; Brandon Garrett, who gave me great advice many times over; Austin Sarat, who supported this project from the start and whose work I relied on in many places in this book; Alex Klein, who read several chapters and sent helpful comments and updates along the way; and Will Berry and Meghan Ryan, who cheered me on and always included me in their own programming. Countless others in the death penalty scholarly community supported this work—as did countless scholars in the constitutional law space, where I spent much of my time before taking on this project. A special thanks to the several scientists and doctors who answered questions along the way, in particular, Pam Knapp, who answered random questions about science more times than I can count. Special thanks also to Cynthia Jones, my angel on an airplane; Dale Baich, whose connections as a lethal injection litigator landed me some important documents that I otherwise would not have had; Mike Farrell, who supported me in numerous ways and gave me a platform with Death Penalty Focus; Lauren Bell, who offered great advice as a lay reader when I was stuck; and Jake McMahon, my *Stanford Law Review* editor from years earlier who graciously gave me comments on early drafts of the chapters of this book. While I'm at it, thank you Sarah Jakes Roberts, Stephanie Ike, Steven Curtis Chapman, and Jeremy Camp—each of you sustained me in an important way on this journey.

My own faculty was nothing short of amazing. My dean Wendy Perdue's support through writing grants and research assistance sustained the work that made this project possible. My dear friend and colleague Jim Gibson read every chapter (some several times), as well as the final draft, and offered amazing comments each time. Danielle Stokes and Danielle Wingfield were my go-to prayer warriors on this book—both were so important. John Douglass (repeatedly) helped me hone the introduction. Tracy Cauthorn helped me build what became an electronic library of lethal injection sources to manage all the material; Dave Johnson used his network to help me build my platform; and Rebecca Crootoff roped in her doctor husband to lend a hand. Thanks, Doug! The entire faculty at Richmond Law read chapters, came to talks, and sent thoughtful emails after pondering my work.

On the research side, I could not have done this without the fantastic support of the Richmond Law Library, particularly Joyce Janto, who took the lead on hard to find sources. Also, my research assistants: I had a team of two to three per year, for just over five years. Special thanks to Bailey Ellicott and Joanie Fasulo, who brought this project home, giving me their all to get this across the finish line. Special thanks also to my readers and researchers over the years: Ken Anderson, Tova Cohn, Liz Diehr, Kaitlyn Dobbins, Athena Dufour, Lauren Earley, Karena Eidum, Amelia Gilmer, Elisabetta Grande, Rachel Gropper, MaryAnn Grover, Renee Hayes, Dan Hogan, Kaitlin Hopingardner, Rachel Hott, Win Jordan, Zack MacDonald, Sara Morrison, Robin Nagel, Ashley Nelson, Emily Powell, Benedict Roemer, JEB Stuart, Snapper Tams, Alyssa Thompson, Holly Wilson, and Caitlin Yuhas.

A special note of thanks to NYU Press, in particular my editor, Clara Platter. Clara was an amazing partner in the publication process, and I credit her wise counsel to scrap my conclusion and write an epilogue instead. I also had a talented production team, with special thanks to Valerie Zaborski and Jenny Rossberg for working tirelessly to bring this book to its potential and then tell the world about it. Sarah Russo and the entire team at Page One Media, I'm so thankful for you too!

Finally, my family: my husband, John, who supported me in a myriad of ways (too many to list here, but coffee, comments, confidence, and carving out time for writing are high on the list); my daughter Julia, whose sage advice helped set my direction at key moments in the text; my daughter Jessica, who turns out to be a talented editor; and my sister Mandy, who read chapters and gave me feedback *for years*, and then read the entire book again to help make this accessible to a lay audience. It does in fact take a village!

Notes

INTRODUCTION

1 *Alabama's Execution of Joe Nathan James, Jr: What We Know, Don't Know about 3-Hour Delay*, MONTGOMERY ADVERTISER (Aug. 17, 2022).

2 Jay Reeves, *Alabama Pausing Executions after 3rd Failed Lethal Injection*, ASSOC. PRESS (Nov. 21, 2022). The state was ready to resume executions just three months later. Kim Chandler, *Alabama Governor Says State Will Resume Executions*, ASSOC. PRESS (Feb. 24, 2023).

3 Marty Schladen and Randy Ludlow, *Dewine Again Delays Columbus Man's Execution after Admitting State Can't Get Lethal Injection Drugs*, COLUM. DISP. (July 31, 2019); Andrew Welsh-Huggins, *Governor: Ohio Having Difficulty Finding Execution Drugs*, ASSOC. PRESS, (July 31, 2019).

4 David R. Dow and Jeffrey R. Newberry, *Conceptual and Scientific Defects in the Supreme Court's "Method of Execution" Jurisprudence*, 92 YALE J. BIOL. MED. 793 (2019) (of the 364 executions from 2009-2019, 358 were conducted by lethal injection).

5 Noah Caldwell, Ailsa Chang, and Jolie Myers, *Gasping for Air: Autopsies Reveal Troubling Effects of Lethal Injection*, NAT'L PUB. RADIO (Sept. 21, 2020).

6 In re: Ohio Execution Protocol Litigation (Henness) at *63, 2019 WL 244488 (S.D. Ohio, Jan. 14, 2019) (concluding that lethal injection protocol causes "a sense of drowning and the attendant panic and terror, much as would occur with the torture tactic known as waterboarding").

7 Garry Wills, *The Dramaturgy of Death*, N.Y. REV. OF BOOKS (June 21, 2001). For an in-depth discussion of the point, see Leigh B. Bienen, *Anomalies: Ritual and Language in Lethal Injection Regulations*, 35 FORDHAM URB. L.J. 857 (2008).

8 *See* DAVID GARLAND, PECULIAR INSTITUTION: AMERICA'S DEATH PENALTY IN AN AGE OF ABOLITION (2012). In this regard, it is no accident that the death penalty is reserved exclusively for the underclass and inflicted disproportionately upon Black and Brown bodies. The status of those who receive the death penalty, as opposed to those who are eligible for it, is an important part of the death penalty story—it's just not the part of the story that I tell.

1. THE EXECUTION OF CLAYTON LOCKETT

1 Michelle Charles, *Top 10 Stories of 2014—No. 4: Fallout from Botched Execution Brings Death Penalty Challenges*, STILLWATER NEWS PRESS (Dec. 27, 2014).

2 Morgan Whitaker et al., *Oklahoma Governor Orders "Independent Review" of Execution*, MSNBC (May 1, 2014).

3 Andrew Cohen, *After Oklahoma's Botched Execution, Here Comes the Cover-Up*, THE WEEK (Jan. 8, 2015); Ziva Branstetter & Barbara Hoberock, *Investigation into Botched Execution to Be Headed by Former DOC Worker*, TULSA WORLD (May 3, 2014).

4 For a time, portions of the transcript were publicly available, and even now, one can find parts of it on file in Warner v. Gross, No. CIV-14–0665-F, 2014 WL 7671680 (W.D. Okla. Dec. 22, 2014). Special thanks to Jen Moreno and the Berkeley Eighth Amendment Project for sharing the full transcripts so I could fill in the gaps. All quotes or assertions not marked with an endnote come from those transcripts, which are on file with author.

5 *Oklahoma Court Rules Lethal Injection Drug Secrecy Law Unconstitutional*, OKLA. NEWS 4 (March 26, 2014) (quoting judge's ruling from bench). For the written ruling, see Lockett v. Evans, No. CV2014330, 2014 WL 6809140 (Okl. Dist. Apr. 1, 2014) (finding that state secrecy statute "is an unconstitutional denial or barrier to Plaintiffs' right to access the Courts").

6 Lockett v. Evans, 329 P.3d 755, 756–57 (Okla. Crim. App. 2014) (discussing procedural history of case).

7 Lockett v. Evans, 356 P.3d 58, 61 (Okla. 2014).

8 Exec. Order 2014–08 of Gov. Mary Fallin (Apr. 22, 2014).

9 Barbera Hoberock, *State Rep. Christian Won't Drop Efforts to Impeach Five Oklahoma Supreme Court Justices*, TULSA WORLD (Apr. 25, 2014).

10 Erik Eckholm, *Execution Case Roils Oklahoma Courts*, N.Y. TIMES (Apr. 22, 2014).

11 Andrew Cohen, *Oklahoma Just Neutered Its State Supreme Court*, THE WEEK (Apr. 29, 2014).

12 Chapter 2 provides an introduction to the three-drug protocol, and chapter 3 provides a deep dive into the drugs that the various lethal injection protocols use.

13 Transcript of District Court's Ruling before the Hon. Stephen P. Friot at 61, Warner v. Gross, No. CIV-14–0665-F, 2014 WL 7671680 (W.D. Okla. Dec. 22, 2014) (quoting protocol).

14 *See* Cary Aspinwall & Ziva Branstetter, *Execution of Clayton Lockett Described as "a Bloody Mess," Court Filing Shows*, TULSA WORLD (Dec. 14, 2014) (emails from the Attorney General's office "repeatedly insisted DOC was solely responsible for the protocol").

15 Appellants' Opening Brief at 58–59, Warner v. Gross, 776 F.3d 721 (10th Cir. Jan. 12, 2015).

16 Transcript of District Court's Ruling, *supra* note 13, at 59.

17 Okla. Dep't Pub. Safety, "The Execution of Clayton D. Lockett," at 22 (2014) [hereinafter "Okla. Dep't Pub. Safety Report"]. The full report is available at dpic-cdn.org.

18 Transcript of Testimony of Eric Katz, M.D., at 564, Warner v. Gross, No. CIV-14–0665-F, 2014 WL 7671680 (W.D. Okla. Dec. 22, 2014).

19 *Id.* at 565.

20 Sw. Inst. Forensic Sci., Case No. IFS-14–07742-CC, Autopsy Report–Lockett, Clayton Derrell, at 2 (2014) [hereinafter "Official Autopsy Report"] ("There is a needle mark of the left wrist. Three needle marks are present of the left antecubital fossa. Two needle marks are present of the left upper arm.").

21 Aspinwall & Branstetter, *supra* note 14.

22 Lockett's family sued Oklahoma following its horribly botched execution and named Dr. Johnny Zellmer as the physician involved in the execution. Ziva Branstetter, *Lawsuit Names McAlester ER Physician as Execution Doctor*, TULSA WORLD (Oct. 14, 2014). Ironically, Zellmer is affiliated with the "Caring Hands" Healthcare Center. *See* OUR PROVIDERS, CARING HANDS HEALTHCARE CENTERS, chhcok.com ("Southeastern Oklahoma's most trusted providers all in one place").

23 Transcript of Testimony of Eric Katz, M.D., *supra* note 18, at 561, 563.

24 *Id.* at 563–64.

25 Toxicology found midazolam in the tissue near Lockett's femoral IV site, indicating that the IV had infiltrated early in the execution—when the midazolam was still being administered. Okla. Dep't Pub. Safety Report, *supra* note 17, at 13.

26 Transcript of Testimony of Lisbeth Exon, at 355–57, Warner v. Gross, No. CIV-14–0665-F, 2014 WL 7671680 (W.D. Okla. Dec. 22, 2014).

27 Transcript of District Court's Ruling, *supra* note 13, at 53.

28 Transcript of Testimony of Lisbeth Exon, *supra* note 26, at 356.

29 Official Autopsy Report, *supra* note 20, at 3.

30 Transcript of Testimony of Lisbeth Exon, *supra* note 26, at 356.

31 Transcript of District Court's Ruling, *supra* note 13, at 54.

32 *Inmate Clayton Lockett Finally Dies of Heart Attack 40 Minutes After Botched Execution Is Stopped*, NEWSWEEK (Apr. 30, 2014).

33 Official Autopsy Report, *supra* note 20, at 5, 11; United Forensic Serv., P.C., P14–0514, Indep. Autopsy Examination of Clayton Lockett, at 1 (2014) [hereinafter "Independent Autopsy Report"].

34 Shawn McGinnis, *Vein on Oklahoma Inmate "Exploded" During Botched Execution: Report*, KTLA-5 (Apr. 29, 2014).

35 Official Autopsy Report, *supra* note 20, at 11.

36 Independent Autopsy Report, *supra* note 33, at 1. This autopsy specifically noted "the unlikelihood that antemortem dehydration played a role in a failed or ineffective lethal injection procedure." *Id.*

37 Okla. Dep't Pub. Safety Report, *supra* note 17, at 15, 25.

38 *Id.*

39 Transcript of District Court's Ruling, *supra* note 13, at 33.

40 *See* Transcript of Testimony of Eric Katz, M.D., *supra* note 18, at 571.

41 Greg Botelho & Dana Ford, *Oklahoma Stops Execution after Botching Drug Delivery; Inmate Dies*, CNN (Oct. 9, 2014), www.cnn.com.

42 Transcript of Testimony of Eric Katz, M.D., *supra* note 18, at 588.

43 Transcript of Testimony of David Lubarsky, M.D., at 216, *Warner v. Gross*, No. CIV-14–0665-F, 2014 WL 7671680 (W.D. Okla. Dec. 22, 2014).

44 Transcript of Testimony of Lisbeth Exon, *supra* note 26, at 358.

45 Transcript of District Court's Ruling, *supra* note 13, at 55.

46 Okla. Dep't Pub. Safety Report, *supra* note 17, at 14.

2. FAUX SCIENCE

1 Nathalie Baptiste, *"This Isn't Science": We Have No Idea How Much Pain Inmates Feel during Execution*, MOTHER JONES (May 15, 2017) (quoting biologist Teresa Zimmers).

2 Gregg v. Georgia, 428 U.S. 153 (1976).

3 William J. Wiseman Jr., *Confessions of a Former Legislator*, CHRISTIAN CENTURY (June 20, 2001). Separate and apart from this, a state senator sought the advice of Dr. Stanley Deutsch, who was then head of the Oklahoma medical school's anesthesiology department. Deutsch sent a letter with recommendations, but it was dated after introduction of the lethal injection bill and two days prior to passage in the senate, so it is unlikely to have affected Oklahoma's legislative process, which was already underway based on Chapman's proposal. *See* Deborah W. Denno, *The Lethal Injection Quandary: How Medicine Has Dismantled the Death Penalty*, 76 FORDHAM L. REV. 49, 67–68 (2007) (relaying involvement of Deutsch and concluding, "By all accounts, then, Chapman was the major, if not the primary, creator of lethal injection.").

4 Denno, *supra* note 3, at 66 (quoting Jay Chapman). *See also* Mike Ward, *Death Penalty's Drug Cocktail Rooted in Texas: Other States Adopted Method Chosen with Little Scientific Basis*, AUSTIN AMERICAN-STATESMAN (May 28, 2006) (Jay Chapman "had no pharmacological training, just an opinion and a willingness to help").

5 HUMAN RIGHTS WATCH, SO LONG AS THEY DIE: LETHAL INJECTIONS IN THE UNITED STATES 15 (2006) (quoting Jay Chapman).

6 Macrina Cooper-White, *Here's the Scary Truth about Science & the Death Penalty*, HUFFINGTON POST (Mar. 13, 2014) (quoting Debby Denno).

7 Ty Alper, *What Do Lawyers Know about Lethal Injection?*, 1 HARV. L. & POL'Y REV. (online) (March 3, 2008).

8 Baze v. Rees, No. 04-CI-01094, 2005 WL 5797977, at *2 (Ky. Cir. Ct., July 8, 2005). *See also id.* ("In developing a lethal injection protocol, [the Kentucky DOC] did not conduct any independent scientific or medical studies or consult any medical professionals concerning the drugs and the dosage amounts to be injected . . . Kentucky appears to be no different from any other state.").

9 Brief for the Fordham University School of Law, Louis Stein Center for Law and Ethics as Amicus Curiae in Support of Petitioners at 15, Baze v. Rees, 553 U.S. 35 (2008).

10 Josh Sanburn, *Lethal Injection's Fatal Flaws*, TIME (May 15, 2014) (quoting Jay Chapman).

11 Ziva Branstetter, *"Father of Lethal Injection" Talks about History, His Legacy to Oklahoma*, TULSA WORLD (Feb. 18, 2019) (quoting Jay Chapman).

12 Brief for Petitioners at 8, Baze v. Rees, 535 U.S. 35 (2008) (quoting former Kentucky Warden Phil Parker).

13 HUMAN RIGHTS WATCH, *supra* note 5, at 9 (quoting Donald Courts, pharmacy director of Louisiana State Penitentiary).

14 Allison J. Nathan & Douglas A. Berman, *Baze-d and Confused: What's the Deal with Lethal Injection?*, 156 U. PA. L. REV. 312, 315 (2008); *see also* Berkeley Death Penalty Clinic, *Baze v. Rees Q&A*, at 13 ("The adoption of lethal injection protocols throughout the United States can best be described as a cascade of misinformation whereby authorities in one jurisdiction copied, sometimes verbatim, the procedures of another."), www.law.berkeley.edu.

15 Teresa A. Zimmers et al., *Author's Reply, Inadequate Anesthesia in Lethal Injection for Execution*, 366 LANCET 1074, 1075 (2005).

16 Associated Press, *Execution Drugs Don't Work, Study Says*, NBC NEWS (Apr. 24, 2007) (quoting biologist Teresa Zimmers).

17 David Biello, *Reasonable Doubt*, 297 SCI. AM. 20, 21 (2007).

18 HUMAN RIGHTS WATCH, *supra* note 5, at 51 (discussing Texas policy change in 1989); Noah Caldwell et al., *Gasping for Air: Autopsies Reveal Troubling Effects of Lethal Injection*, NAT'L PUB. RADIO (Sept. 21, 2020).

19 Leonidas G. Koniaris et al., *Inadequate Anaesthesia in Lethal Injection for Execution*, 365 LANCET 1412 (2005) [hereinafter "*Inadequate Anaesthesia*"]; Leonidas G. Koniaris et al., *Lethal Injection for Execution: Chemical Asphyxiation?*, 4 PLOS MED. 646 (2007) [hereinafter "*Chemical Asphyxiation?*"].

20 *Inadequate Anesthesia, supra* note 19.

21 *Id.* at 1412–13.

22 *Id.* at 1413.

23 *Id.* at 1414.

24 Caldwell et al., *supra* note 18 (quoting forensic pathologist Derrick Pounder). *See also* Jonathan I. Groner et al., *Correspondence: Inadequate Anaesthesia in Lethal Injection for Execution*, 366 LANCET 1073, 1073 (2005) (noting that most samples in the Koniaris study were collected twelve or more hours after death, and that because thiopental is a rapidly diffusing agent that would redistribute into fat and muscle even after death, the concentrations found would not be indicative of the amount of thiopental in their system at the time of death); Mark Dershwitz & Thomas K. Henthorn, *The Pharmacokinetics and Pharmacodynamics of Thiopental as used in Lethal Injection*, 35 FORDHAM URB. L.J. 931, 951 (2008)

("Thiopental undergoes postmortem redistribution. This means that the blood concentration of thiopental continues to decrease even after the inmate's death and the cessation of circulation.").

25 Teresa A. Zimmers et al., *supra* note 15 (plotting times from prisoners' death to autopsy on graph, showing that concentrations in blood did not fall with increased time between execution and blood sample collection). *See also* Teresa A. Zimmers & Leonidas G. Koniaris, *Peer-Reviewed Studies Identifying Problems in the Design and Implementation of Lethal Injection for Execution*, 35 FORDHAM URB. L.J. 919, 924–25 (2008) (noting that all claims that the study was flawed "were refuted definitively in a point-by-point, peer-reviewed response by the original authors"); *id.* at 925 ("[Sodium] thiopental resembles many other drugs that distribute rapidly from blood into tissues during life, then re-distribute from tissues to blood after death. This suggests that post-mortem serum thiopental levels might actually under-estimate levels in life. . . . To date, the *Lancet* paper has withstood three years of scrutiny in the scientific literature without having a single claim disproved or even substantively challenged.").

26 *See Chemical Asphyxiation?*, *supra* note 19. They also studied execution logs in North Carolina, but only the California portion of the study is relevant here.

27 Morales v. Hickman, 415 F. Supp. 2d. 1037, 1043–44 (N. D. Cal. 2006) (quoting Dr. Mark Dershwitz).

28 *Chemical Asphyxiation?*, *supra* note 19, at 649. California has conducted thirteen executions in the modern death penalty era; two were by lethal gas.

29 *See* David Waisel, *Physician Participation in Capital Punishment*, 82 MAYO CLIN. PROC. 1073, 1073–74 (2007) ("In the absence of a hands-on assessment of anesthetic depth, sustained apnea becomes a reasonable surrogate for adequate delivery of the massive doses of sodium thiopental. Sustained apnea guarantees a sufficient depth of anesthesia. In contrast, spontaneous ventilation after sodium thiopental indicates that the desired dose of sodium thiopental was not delivered. Spontaneous ventilation does not indicate awareness, but it also does not confirm anesthesia."). *See also* American Society of Anesthesiologists, *Statement on Continuum of Depth of Sedation: Definition of General Anesthesia and Levels of Sedation/Analgesia* (Oct. 23, 2019), www.asahq.org ("General Anesthesia is a drug-induced loss of consciousness during which patients are not arousable, even by painful stimulation. The ability to independently maintain ventilatory function is often impaired."); Emery N. Brown, *General Anesthesia, Sleep, and Coma*, 363 N. ENGL. J. MED. 2638, 2639–40 (2010) ("The return of spontaneous respirations is typically one of the first clinical signs observed once peripheral neuromuscular blockade is decreased. This marks the patient's return from a functional state that approximates brainstem death.").

30 Dershwitz & Henthorn, *supra* note 24, at 948 ("The potassium chloride should cause cessation of cardiac electrical activity within two minutes of injection.").

One of these six prisoners was a seventy-six-year-old man with a long history of heart disease who had suffered a heart attack five months before he was executed. When asked why he did not promptly die from the overdose of potassium chloride, the warden told reporters, "This guy's heart has been beating for 76 years, and it took a while for it to stop." *See* Morales v. Tilton, 415 F.Supp. at 1046 n15.

31 *See* Dershwitz & Henthorn, *supra* note 24, at 948 ("There have been several executions in California in which a second dose of potassium chloride was given, as mandated by the protocol, because cessation of electrical activity on the ECG did not occur after the first dose. One possible explanation is that the potassium chloride was not injected through a working intravenous catheter. Another more plausible explanation is that the potassium chloride did not circulate to the heart from the site of the intravenous injection."); *Chemical Asphyxiation?*, *supra* note 19, at 649 (same); *see also* Zimmers & Koniaris, *supra* note 25, at 928 ("Thus in cases where thiopental and potassium chloride are insufficient to cause death, death is likely effected by paralysis and asphyxiation.").

32 *See* Morales v. Tilton, 465 F. Supp.2d 972, 980 (N.D. Cal. 2006).

33 Denno, *supra* note 3, at 75 (quoting Jay Chapman).

34 Adam Liptak, *States Hesitate to Lead Change on Executions*, N.Y. TIMES (Jan. 3, 2008).

35 Michael Norman, *Why New Jersey Is Leaning into Executions by Lethal Injection*, N.Y. TIMES at B-6 (May 18, 1983) (quoting state senator Dr. Thomas H. Paterniti).

36 Patrick Malone, *Death Row and the Medical Model*, HASTINGS CTR. REPORT 5 (Oct. 1979) (quoting state senator Les Houston).

37 JONATHAN R. SORENSEN & ROCKY LEANN PILGRIM, LETHAL INJECTION: CAPITAL PUNISHMENT IN TEXAS DURING THE MODERN ERA 10 (2006) (quoting Reverend Clyde Johnston).

38 Liliana Segura, *"Our Most Cruel Experiment Yet": Chilling Testimony in a Tennessee Trial Exposes Lethal Injection as Court-Sanctioned Torture*, THE INTERCEPT (Aug. 5, 2018) (quoting state representative Chris Newton), theintercept.com. For a more recent example, see Craig Shoup and Kirsten Fiscus, *Tennessee Lawmaker Apologizes after Suggesting "Hanging by Tree" as Method of Execution*, THE TENNESSEAN (March 2, 2023) (quoting state representative Paul Sherrell, who suggested "hanging by tree" as an alternative execution method).

39 *See* Garrett v. Estelle, 556 F.2d. 1274 (1977), *rev'd* 556 F.2d 1274 (1977), *cert. denied* 438 U.S. 915 (1978).

40 SORENSEN & PILGRIM, *supra* note 37, at 9 (quoting state senator Bill Braecklein).

41 Branstetter, *supra* note 11 ("Before the vote, [Oklahoma state representative Bill] Wiseman reportedly gave each lawmaker two photos of an inmate who had died in the electric chair.").

42 Abdur'Rahman v. Bredesen, 181 S.W.3d 292 (2005).

43 Baze v. Rees, 535 U.S. 35 (2008).

44 *Id.* at 72–73 (Stevens, J., concurring).

45 *Id.* at 50.

46 *Id.* at 58. Conspicuously absent in *Baze* was any mention of the FDA drug approval process, an entire regulatory framework built on the proposition that veterinary science provides an appropriate guide for drug practices in humans.

47 Segura, *supra* note 38.

48 Associated Press, *Florida Executes Woman's Killer*, HERALD-TRIB. (Oct. 15, 2013) (reporting that the first execution using midazolam caused "more body movements after losing unconsciousness" than when the state used other drugs).

49 Tasneem Nashrulla, *What 13 States Aren't Telling You about How They Execute Prisoners*, BUZZFEED (June 16, 2014).

50 Declaration of Mark Dershwitz, M.D., Ph.D., Cooey v. Strickland, 2009 WL 6686345 (S.D. Ohio Nov. 30, 2009); Ben Crair, *Exclusive Emails Show Ohio's Doubts about Lethal Injection*, NEW REPUBLIC (Aug. 17, 2017) (quoting Dr. Mark Dershwitz).

51 Crair, *supra* note 50 (quoting Dr. Mark Heath).

52 *Id.* (quoting Dr. Mark Dershwitz).

53 In re Ohio Execution Protocol Litig., 994 F. Supp. 2d 906, 913 (S.D. Ohio 2014).

54 Devi Nampiaparampil & Hormis Thaliath, *Lethal Injection Execution of Ohio Child Killer "Too Easy," Victim's Family Says*, NEWSWEEK (July 26, 2017).

55 Lawrence Hummer, *I Witnessed Ohio's Execution of Dennis McGuire. What I Saw Was Inhumane*, THE GUARDIAN (Jan. 22, 2014).

56 Associated Press, *Family Sues in Protracted Ohio Execution*, N.Y. TIMES (Jan. 25, 2014); Liliana Segura, *Ohio's Governor Stopped an Execution over Fears It Would Feel Like Waterboarding*, THE INTERCEPT (Feb. 7, 2019) theintercept.com ("According to the suit, one prison official 'mouthed "I'm sorry"' to his relatives in the execution chamber.").

57 Crair, *supra* note 50.

58 Michael Kiefer, *Reporter Describes Arizona Execution: 2 Hours, 640 Gasps*, ARIZ. REPUBLIC (Jul. 26, 2014).

59 Glossip v. Gross, 576 U.S. 863 (2015).

60 Deposition of Dr. Roswell Lee Evans, Abdur'Rahman v. Parker, 558 S.W.3d 606 (Jun. 27, 2018).

61 *Lethal Injections: Last Week Tonight with John Oliver* (May 6, 2019). *See also* Segura, *supra* note 38 ("When it comes to the case law on lethal injection, *Glossip* is a major part of the problem. Like other decisions that have enshrined junk science into law, the ruling gave legal legitimacy to the findings of a pharmacist who had been widely discredited even before Supreme Court justices heard oral arguments.").

62 Transcript of Direct and Cross Examination of Dr. Roswell Lee Evans at 648, Warner v. Gross, No. CIV-14–0665-F, 2014 WL 7671680 (W.D. Okla. Dec. 22, 2014).

63 *Id.* at 639–40, 647–48.

64 The majority in *Glossip* responded to the claim that Evans's theory was "entirely unsupported" by stating matter-of-factly that "it was supported by Dr. Evans' expertise and decades of experience. And it would be unusual for an expert testifying on the stand to punctuate each sentence with citation to a medical journal." *Glossip*, 576 U.S. at 892 n.8. For the record, Evans had no expertise or experience, and punctuated *no* sentence with citation to a medical journal.

65 Radley Balko, *Key Expert in Supreme Court Death Penalty Case Facing Serious Questions about Credibility*, WASH. POST (Apr. 28, 2015).

66 Annie Waldman, *Key Expert in Supreme Court Lethal Injection Case Did His Research on Drugs.com*, PROPUBLICA (Apr. 28, 2015).

67 Transcript of Direct and Cross Examination of Dr. Larry Sasich at 336, Warner v. Gross, No. CIV-14–0665-F, 2014 WL 7671680 (W.D. Okla. Dec. 22, 2014).

68 Transcript of Oral Argument at 7, Glossip v. Gross, 576 U.S. 863 (2015).

69 *Id.* at 26–27, 40.

70 *Id.* at 46–47.

71 Joint Appendix 1, at 327, Glossip v. Gross, 576 U.S. 863 (2015) ("This is essentially an extrapolation from a toxic effect. We really are not talking about a clinical effect. We're talking about inducing a toxic reaction.") (Testimony of Dr. Roswell Evans).

72 AMERICAN SOCIETY OF HEALTH SYSTEM PHARMACISTS, AHFS DRUG INFORMATION® (2017) at 2749 ("Because distribution of midazolam may be altered in geriatric patients . . . the manufacturer recommends that dosage of the drug be selected carefully in this age group. . . . In addition, rare fatalities (possibly associated with cardiorespiratory depression) have been reported in geriatric and/or high-risk surgical patients receiving IV or IM midazolam (often in combination with other CNS [central nervous system] depressants).").

Evans correctly reported midazolam's TD_{LO} as .04-.07 mg/kg. Of note, he also *in*correctly reported it as 40–70 mg/kg, a three-decimal mistake that the district court brushed aside, stating that there was "no need to dwell on the fact that he misplaced a decimal point in one of his observations about the possible lethal effect of midazolam." Court's Ruling on Plaintiff's Motion for Preliminary Injunction at 39–40, Warner v. Gross, No. CIV-14–0665-F, 2014 WL 7671680 (W.D. Okla. Dec. 22, 2014). Evans made a number of other mistakes as well, but the district court (and then appellate court) held that none of them "seriously undercut" his credibility. Warner v. Gross, 776 F.3d. 721, 734, 735 (2015).

73 B. Schläppi, *Safety Aspects of Midazolam*, 16 BR. J. CLIN. PHARMACOLOGY 37–38S (1983) (reporting midazolam's LD_{50} as 75 mg/kg in rats and 50 mg/kg in mice when IV administration).

74 *PubChem: Midazolam*, National Library of Medicine, National Institutes of Health, pubchem.ncbi.nlm.nih.gov (noting that studies "have demonstrated minimal toxicity for midazolam, as for other benzodiazepines"). *See also* Martin Schulz et al., *Therapeutic and Toxic Blood Concentrations of Nearly 1,000 Drugs and Other Xenobiotics*, CRITICAL CARE 16: R136 (2012) (table of 1,000 drugs, along with therapeutic dosages, and where available, toxic concentrations and elimination half-lives, and listing no toxic concentration for midazolam). In re: Ohio Execution Protocol Litigation (Henness), at *49, 2019 WL 244488 (S.D. Ohio, Jan. 14, 2019) [hereinafter "Henness"] ("Dr. Antognini's opinion that midazolam is itself a lethal drug is belied by the sole study he cites for that assertion, which found that a high dosage of midazolam *when combined with an opioid* posed a high risk of hypoxemia and apnea.") (citing P. L. Bailey et al., *Frequent Hypoxemia and Apnea after Sedation with Midazolam and Fentanyl*, ANESTHESIOLOGY 73:826–30 (1990) ("Midazolam alone produced no significant respiratory effects.").

75 *Benzodiazepines: Range of Toxicity*, at www.jodrugs.com. *See also id.* (noting that "ingestion of up to 2000 mg of diazepam has resulted in only minor toxicity"). *See generally* George M. Brenner & Craig W. Stevens, *Sedative Hypnotic and Anxiolytic Drugs*, in PHARMACOLOGY 207 (4th ed. 2013) ("Because the benzodiazepines have fewer adverse reactions and drug interactions and are safer in cases of overdose, they have largely replaced the barbiturates and other older drugs."); S. John Mihic et al., *Hypnotics and Sedatives, in* GOODMAN & GILMAN'S THE PHARMACOLOGICAL BASIS OF THERAPEUTICS 339 (Laurence L. Brunton et al. eds., 13th ed. 2018) ("Mainly because of their remarkably low capacity to produce fatal CNS depression, the benzodiazepines displaced the barbiturates as sedative-hypnotic agents.").

76 *Glossip*, 576 U.S. at 888 ("But it was *petitioners'* burden to establish that midazolam's ceiling occurred at a dosage below the massive 500-milligram dose employed in the Oklahoma protocol and at a point at which the drug failed to render the recipient insensate to pain. They did not meet that burden.") (emphasis in original).

77 Brief of Sixteen Professors of Pharmacology as Amici Curiae in Support of Neither Party at 20, Glossip v. Gross, 576 U.S. 863 (2015) ("The fact that midazolam does not ever achieve general anesthesia is consistent with, and explains, the clinical uses of the drug. In fact, it is widely recognized in the scientific and medical community that midazolam alone cannot be used to maintain adequate anesthesia for surgery.").

78 *Glossip*, 576 U.S. at 885–86.

79 *Id.* at 888.

80 Eric Berger, *Gross Error*, 91 WASH. L. REV. 929, 1004 (2016).

81 Abdur'Rahman v. Parker, No. 18-183-III (Chancery Ct. for Davidson County, TN, July 26, 2018); Segura, *supra* note 38 (reporting on and quoting testimony at trial).

82 Expert Report of Dr. David J. Greenblatt, M.D., in *Henness, supra* note 74, at 7 (noting publication record that includes 786 peer-reviewed articles, 174 book chapters, 103 editorial responses to other works, and 12 authored or coauthored books, and listing them at the end of his report). *Id.* at 8–9 (noting a total citation count of 67,339, and ranking as one of the 1300 most cited scientists, across all scientific fields, of all time). Henness, *supra* note 74, at *27 (recognizing Greenblatt as "arguably the preeminent scholar on the pharmacological effects of benzodiazepines, including midazolam").

83 Segura, *supra* note 38 (quoting Greenblatt's testimony in Tennessee case).

84 *Id.*

85 *Id.* (quoting Judge Ellen Hobbs Lyle).

86 Dave Boucher et al., *Tennessee Executes Billy Ray Irick, First Lethal Injection in States Since 2009*, THE TENNESSEAN (Aug. 9, 2018).

87 *Henness, supra* note 74, at *10.

88 *Id.* at *71.

89 *Id.* (quoting *Glossip*, 576 U.S. at 978) (Sotomayor, J., dissenting).

90 In re Ohio Execution Protocol Litigation, 937 F.3d 759, 762 (6th Cir. 2019). *See also id.* ("neither pulmonary edema nor the symptoms associated with it qualify as the type of serious pain prohibited by the Eighth Amendment."). The Supreme Court denied certiorari, but the claim was so outrageous that it drew a separate statement from Justice Sotomayor. Henness v. DeWine, 141 S. Ct. 7 (2020) (mem) (Statement of Justice Sotomayor respecting the denial of certiorari) (criticizing lower court's reasoning and concluding, "The Sixth Circuit erred in enshrining hanging as a permanent measure of constitutionally tolerable suffering.").

91 Segura, *supra* note 56.

92 Glossip v. Chandler, at *16, 2022 WL 1997194 (W.D. Okla., June 6, 2022).

93 *See* chapter 1, text accompanying note 45.

94 Liliana Segura & Jordan Smith, *Oklahoma Attorney General Asks Court to Overturn Richard Glossip's Conviction*, THE INTERCEPT (Apr. 6, 2023), theintercept.com; Byrnn Gingras, *Before His 9th Scheduled Execution, Now on Hold, Richard Glossip Said He Hoped His Fate "Can Never Happen to Anybody Else Again,"* CNN (May 25, 2023) www.cnn.com ("'There has never been an execution in the history of this country where the state and the defense agreed that the defendant was not afforded a fair trial. . . . Oklahoma cannot become the first.'") (quoting state Rep. Kevin McDugle and noting that McDugle and the attorney general are republicans). In January 2024, the Supreme Court granted certiorari in the case—this time, to consider whether Glossip should be subject to execution at all. Glossip v. Oklahoma, 144 S.Ct. 691 (2024).

The *Glossip* case has caused some conservatives to rethink their support for the death penalty altogether. Adam Kemp, *The Oklahoma Case Pushing State Republicans to Rethink the Death Penalty*, PBS NEWSHOUR (May 30, 2023).

95 Colleen Wilson, *Autopsy Report for Death Row Inmate John Grant Shows Fluid in Lungs, Aspiration on Vomit*, KOKH-TV (Feb. 7, 2022), okcfox.com.

96 *Id.*

97 *Lethal Injection Is Not Humane*, 4 PLOS MED. 603, 604 (2007).

98 Cary Aspinwall & Ziva Branstetter, *Execution of Clayton Lockett Described as a "Bloody Mess," a Court Filing Shows*, TULSA WORLD (Dec. 14, 2014).

99 William Wan & Mark Berman, *States to Try New Ways of Executing Prisoners. Their Latest Ideas? Opioids*, WASH. POST (Dec. 9, 2017).

100 Heckler v. Chaney, 470 U.S. 821 (1985). For a discussion of the litigation, *see* Michele Stolls, Heckler v. Chaney: *Judicial and Administrative Regulation of Capital Punishment by Lethal Injection*, 11 AM. J.L. & MED. 251, 253–55 (1985).

101 Chaney v. Heckler, 718 F.2d. 1174, 1190 (D.C. Cir. 1983).

102 *See* Heckler, 470 U.S. at 835.

103 Glossip, 576 U.S. at 881.

104 Cooey v. Strickland, 604 F.3d 939, 948 (6th Cir. 2010) (Martin, J., dissenting).

105 For a sampling of the literature, see, e.g., Seema K. Shah, *Experimental Execution*, 90 WASH. L. REV. 147 (2015) (arguing that "by trying novel drugs, drug combinations, and dosages to see if they will work, states are conducting a type of biomedical research" and thus they should be bound to a similar "ethical and regulatory framework."); Paul Litton, *On the Argument That Execution Protocol Reform Is Biomedical Research*, 90 WASH. L. REV. 87 (2015) (disagreeing with Shah's arguments); Brief of the Advocates of Human Rights as Amicus Curiae in Support of Petitioners, Glossip v. Gross, 576 U.S. 863 (2015) (arguing that lethal injection violates human rights treaties by impermissibly experimenting on human subjects).

106 New State Ice Co. v. Liebmann, 285 U.S. 262, 311 (1932) (J. Brandeis, dissenting) ("It is one of the happy incidents of the federal system that a single courageous state may, if its citizens choose, serve as a laboratory; and try novel social and economic experiments without risk to the rest of the country."); *see also* Am. L. Inst., *Who Decides? States as Laboratories of Constitutional Experimentation* (Dec. 22, 2021), www.ali.org.

107 Maurice Chammah et al., *After Lethal Injection*, MARSHALL PROJECT (June 1, 2015) (quoting state representative Mike Ritze).

108 *Id.* (quoting Christine Pappas, one of the report's coauthors).

109 Eli Hager, *Why Oklahoma Plans to Execute People with Nitrogen*, MARSHALL PROJECT (Mar. 15, 2018), www.themarshallproject.org (quoting state representative Mike Christian).

110 Austin Sarat, *Alabama Is Confused about Its Own Ability to Carry Out Executions*, SLATE (Jul. 5, 2023); slate.com (quoting state representative Mike Christian).

111 Hager, *supra* note 109.

112 One author's last name is Pappas. In the report, it is spelled Papas. Deborah W. Denno, Six *U.S. Execution Methods and the Disastrous Quest for Humaneness*, in

COMPANION ON CAPITAL PUNISHMENT AND SOCIETY 17 (Fleury-Steiner & Sarat, eds. 2024) (forthcoming) (on file with author).

113 Scott Christianson, *How Oklahoma Came to Embrace the Gas Chamber*, NEW YORKER (June 24, 2015); Josh Sanburn, *The Dawn of a New Form of Capital Punishment*, TIME (Apr. 17, 2015).

114 Wan & Berman, *supra* note 99.

115 Opposition to Application for a Stay of Execution Pending Petition for Writ of Certiorari and Brief in Opposition, at 22, Smith v. Hamm, No. 23A688 (S.Ct. 2024).

116 *Id.* at 15.

117 Nicholas Bogel-Burroughs and Abbie VanSickle, *Alabama Executes Kenneth Smith by Nitrogen Hypoxia*, N.Y. TIMES (Jan. 25, 2024). *See also* Nicholas Bogel-Burroughs, *A Select Few Witnessed Alabama's Nitrogen Execution. This Is What They Saw.*, N.Y. TIMES (Feb. 1, 2024) (reporting accounts of media witnesses, including their own trauma from witnessing the execution).

118 Jeff Hood, *I Witnessed Alabama Execute a Man Using Nitrogen Gas. It Was Horrific and Cruel*, USA TODAY (Feb. 19, 2024).

119 *Id.*

120 Bogel-Burroughs and VanSickle, *supra* note 117.

3. TORTUROUS DRUGS

1 State v. Mata, 275 Neb. 1 (2008); Dawson v. State, 274 Ga. 327 (2001). Both cases were decided under their respective state constitutions. In addition, in 2022, a South Carolina trial court found death by electrocution unconstitutional under its state constitution, but the state supreme court reversed. *See* Owens v. Stirling, No. 2022-001280 (S.C. July 31, 2024).

2 Rick Rojas, *Why This Inmate Chose the Electric Chair Over Lethal Injection*, N.Y. TIMES (Feb. 19, 2020) ("'When everything works perfectly, it's about 14 minutes of pain and horror,' said [one capital defender]. 'Then, they look at electrocution, and how long does it take?'").

3 Sometimes states use vecuronium bromide or rocuronium bromide rather than pancuronium bromide. All three are paralytics and functionally equivalent for the purposes of lethal injection.

4 Declaration of Mark J. S. Heath, M.D., Cooey v. Strickland (S.D. Ohio, Feb. 14, 2008). *See also* Expert Report of Dr. David Lubarsky, M.D., In re: Ohio Execution Protocol Litigation (Henness) (S.D. Ohio, Oct. 27, 2018) (describing the paralytic's effect as "a sensation akin to being buried alive"); HUMAN RIGHTS WATCH, SO LONG AS THEY DIE: LETHAL INJECTIONS IN THE UNITED STATES 2 (2006) ("If the prisoner is not sufficiently anesthetized before being injected with pancuronium bromide, he will feel himself suffocating but be unable to draw a breath—a torturous experience, as anyone knows who has been trapped underwater for even a few seconds.").

5 Expert Declaration of Gail A. Van Norman, M.D., at 34, Roane v. Barr (D. D.C., Nov. 1, 2019).

6 Mark J. Heath et al., *Revisiting Physician Involvement in Capital Punishment: Medical and Nonmedical Aspects of Lethal Injection*, 83 MAYO CLIN. PROC. 115 (2008).

7 David Kroll, *The Drugs Used in Execution by Lethal Injection*, FORBES (May 1, 2014) (quoting Peter A. Lipson, M.D.).

8 Transcript of Mark Heath, M.D., at 130, Baze v. Rees (Circuit Ct. Ky., April 20, 2005).

9 Brief of Anesthesia Awareness Campaign, Inc. as Amicus Curiae in Support of Neither Party, at 8–9, in Baze v. Rees, 553 U.S. 35 (2008) (discussing anesthesia awareness and practice advisories issued by the American Society of Anesthesiologists, American Association of Nurse Anesthetists, and Joint Commission on Accreditation of Healthcare Organizations). For the most recent information about the incidence of anesthesia awareness, see www.anesthe-siaawareness.com.

10 *Id.* at 5–6.

11 Ty Alper, *Anesthetizing the Public Conscience: Lethal Injection and Animal Euthanasia*, 35 FORDHAM URB. L.J. 817, 844 (2008) (providing in-depth analysis of state animal euthanasia laws and concluding: "In sum, there are only eight states whose euthanasia laws would even arguably allow the use of a procedure like the one used in human lethal injections.").

12 Baze v. Rees, 553 U.S. at 102 (Thomas, J., concurring) ("The evil the Eighth Amendment targets is intentional infliction of gratuitous pain."); Bucklew v. Precythe, 587 U.S. 119, 133 (quoting Justice Thomas's concurring opinion in *Baze*); *id.* at 134 ("The question in dispute is whether the State's chosen method of execution cruelly superadds pain to the death sentence."). For a discussion of these cases, see chapter 8, text accompanying notes 130–37.

13 Baze v. Rees, 553 U.S. 35 (2008).

14 *Id.* at 57–58.

15 Mark Dershwitz & Thomas K. Henthorn, *The Pharmacokinetics and Phamacodynamics of Thiopental As Used in Lethal Injection*, FORDHAM URB. L.J. 931, 946 (2008) ("The potassium chloride should cause cessation of cardiac electrical activity within two minutes of injection."). *See also* Baze v. Rees, 553 U.S. at 73 (Stevens, J., concurring) ("Nor is there any necessity for pancuronium bromide to be included in the cocktail to inhibit respiration when it is immedi-ately followed by potassium chloride, which causes death quickly by stopping the inmate's heart.").

16 Transcript of Oral Argument at 33, Baze v. Rees, 553 U.S. 35 (2008).

17 *Id.* at 43. To his credit, Justice Stevens concluded that the state's dignity interest was "woefully inadequate," writing: "Whatever minimal interest there may be in ensuring that a condemned inmate dies a dignified death, and that witnesses to the execution are not made uncomfortable by an incorrect belief (which could easily be corrected) that the inmate is in pain is vastly outweighed by the risk that the inmate is actually experiencing excruciating pain that no one can detect." *Baze v. Rees*, 553 U.S. at 73 (Stevens, J., concurring). But Justice Stevens then voted to uphold Kentucky's protocol, so all the hand-wringing was for naught.

18 Denise Grady, *Doctors See Way to Cut Suffering in Executions*, N.Y. TIMES (June 23, 2006) (quoting state expert stating that barbiturates could cause "significant involuntary jerking" that could be "disturbing to witnesses," then adding an addendum stating that the article "misstated an effect of a fatal overdose of a barbiturate drug, sodium thiopental. The drug does not cause involuntary jerking movements before death even when used alone.").

19 William Wan & Mark Berman, S*tates to Try New Ways of Executing Prisoners. Their Latest Idea? Opioids*, WASH. POST (Dec. 9, 2017).

20 Glossip v. Gross, 576 U.S. 863, 877 (2015).

21 *See* chapter 2, text accompanying notes 77–78.

22 *See* chapter 2, text accompanying notes 54–58.

23 Liliana Segura, *Will the Supreme Court Look behind the Curtain of Lethal Injection?*, THE INTERCEPT (Apr. 30, 2015).

24 *Glossip*, 576 U.S. at 977 (Sotomayor, J., dissenting).

25 Wan & Berman, *supra* note 19 (quoting Dr. Mark Heath, professor of anesthesiology at Columbia University). Even the states' go-to expert, Dr. Mark Dershwitz, testified that an injection of potassium chloride "would make a conscious person scream in agony." *Id.*

26 Harbison v. Little, 511 F. Supp. 2d 872, 883 (M. D. Tn. 2007) (quoting Dr. David Lubarsky); Petition for a Writ of Certiorari, at 7 n.9, Howell v. Florida (S. Ct., Feb. 25, 2014) (quoting Dr. David Lubarsky).

27 Gavin Lee, *A Painless Cocktail? The Lethal Injection Controversy, in* THE DEATH PENALTY TODAY at 106 (Robert Bohm ed., 2008).

28 *Baze*, 553 U.S. at 53.

29 Within the field of anesthesiology, the different levels of sedation are sometimes referred to as gradations of *depressed* consciousness, while anesthesia is referred to as the *loss* of consciousness altogether—i.e., unconsciousness. Hence the confusion. *See, e.g.*, the Joint Commission, *Sedation and Anesthesia— Understanding the Assessment Requirements*, available at www.jointcommission. org. For clarity, I refer to unconsciousness by its ordinary understanding, and quote medical professionals only when the context is clear that they are using the term in this way as well.

30 In re Ohio Execution Protocol Litigation (Henness), at *36, 2019 WL 244488 (S.D. Ohio, Jan. 14, 2019) (quoting Dr. David Lubarsky) [hereinafter "Henness"].

31 American Society of Anesthesiologists, *Statement on Continuum of Depth of Sedation: Definition of General Anesthesia and Levels of Sedation/Analgesia* (Oct. 23, 2019), www.asahq.org.

32 *Id.*

33 *Henness, supra* note 30, at *22 (quoting Dr. Matthew Exline, director of the medical intensive care unit at The Ohio State University Medical Center). *See also id.* at *25 ("ICU practitioners are admonished, as a scientific principle, to assume that all unconscious patients are capable of feeling pain when exposed to noxious or painful stimuli such as the injection of potassium chloride or the development of pulmonary edema.") (quoting Exline report).

34 *Bucklew*, 587 U.S. at 132 ("The Eighth Amendment does not guarantee a prisoner a painless death."); *see also Glossip*, 576 U.S. at 869 ("The Constitution does not require the avoidance of all risk of pain."); *Baze*, 553 U.S. at 47 ("It is clear, then, that the Constitution does not demand the avoidance of all risk of pain in carrying out executions."). Countless courts have now parroted the point. *See, e.g.*, In re Ohio Execution Protocol Litigation, 946 F.3d 287, 290 (2019) ("'The Eighth Amendment does not guarantee a prisoner a painless death,' so it is immaterial whether the inmate will experience *some* pain.").

35 Nolan Clay, *Executions in Oklahoma Remain on Hold until Judge Rules on Constitutionality of Method*, THE OKLAHOMAN (March 7, 2022) (quoting Oklahoma Solicitor General Mithun Mansinghani).

36 Henness, *supra* note 30, at *47 ("distinguishing between 'induction of anesthesia,' which is 'a process,' whereas 'general anesthesia is a state of being of the patient'") (quoting Dr. Craig W. Stevens); *see also id.* at *22 ("The induction of anesthesia has nothing to do with being insensate.") (quoting Dr. David Lubarsky).

37 The notion that surgeons never cut skin during the induction phase goes back to 1936, when Dr. Arthur Guedel first identified four stages of anesthesia, writing that even in the second stage, "operative procedure or preparation of the surgical field at this time is dangerous. . . . The anesthetist may need to rely entirely upon whether or not there has been sufficient time for anesthesia to have reached the third stage. When in doubt, he must wait much longer than he thinks necessary before permitting surgery." Arthur E. Guedel, M.D., *Anesthesia: A Teaching Outline—Stages of Anesthesia*, 15 ANESTHESIA AND ANALGESIA (Jan.–Feb. 1936). As others have noted, Guedel's first and second stages are what is known today as the induction phase, and the maintenance phase, when surgeons may cut skin, is Guedel's stage 3. *See, e.g.*, Brian S. Freeman, M.D., *Stages and Signs of General Anesthesia*, *in* Brian S. Freeman & Jeffrey S. Berger, ANESTHESIOLOGY CORE REV. (McGraw Hill 2024); Bidal A. Siddiqui & Peggy Y. Kim, *Anesthesia Stages*, STATPEARLS (Jan. 2023), www.ncbi.nlm.nih.gov.

38 As just one example, consider the amicus brief submitted by a group of pharmacology professors in Glossip v. Gross, 576 U.S. 863 (2015). The brief stated that "midazolam does not ever achieve general anesthesia," noting that "it is widely recognized in the scientific and medical community that midazolam alone cannot be used to maintain adequate anesthesia for surgery," but also referred to midazolam as being "incapable of inducing unconsciousness" and stated that "even an excessive dose of midazolam will not result in unconsciousness." Brief of Sixteen Professors of Pharmacology as Amici Curiae in Support of Neither Party, Glossip v. Gross at 8, 20 (2015). The professors were not denying midazolam's ability to put a person to sleep—clearly it can, just not at a depth that equates to anesthesia. But their use of the term "unconscious" as synonymous with insensate is the very sort of thing that has allowed executing states to misconstrue the studies and attribute qualities to these drugs that they clearly do not have.

39 The court in 2019's Ohio lethal injection litigation caught this move. *See* Henness, *supra* note 30, at *40 ("Dr. Antognini fails to acknowledge the difference between 'unconsciousness,' which he does not define but which is a state of sedation that can be interrupted by noxious stimuli, and 'anesthesia,' a state during which a person is not arousable by painful stimuli. Dr. Lubarsky cited several studies that illustrate Dr. Antognini's failure to recognize the difference between these two medical terms."); *id.* at *26 ("Dr. Exline next turned to the assertion by Defendants' experts that patients who are 'unconscious' are unable to feel pain. He took issue with the 'loose' use of the term 'unconscious.'"); *id.* at *47 ("Further, Dr. Stevens argued that 'Dr. Buffington continues to confuse the states of sedation and general anesthesia.'"); *id.* at *48 (noting that "not one of the studies Dr. Antognini cited used the term 'unconsciousness' to mean 'insensation' or 'unconsciousness sufficient to protect the inmate from the severe pain and suffering associated with the drugs in Ohio's lethal injection protocol.'") (quoting Dr. Stevens).

40 *Baze*, 553 U.S. at 53 ("It is uncontested that, failing a proper dose of sodium thiopental that would render the prisoner unconscious, there is a substantial, constitutionally unacceptable risk of suffocation from the administration of pancuronium bromide, and pain from the injection of potassium chloride."). *See also* Liliana Segura, *Ohio's Governor Stopped an Execution Over Fears It Would Feel Like Waterboarding,* THE INTERCEPT, Feb. 7, 2019, theintercept.com (noting that the Supreme Court has "conflated insensateness and unconsciousness, two concepts whose distinctions are hugely consequential. This error has been replicated by the lower courts, while execution after execution has shown that unconsciousness cannot protect people from the torturous effects of lethal injection.").

41 Deborah W. Denno, *Back to the Future with Execution Methods, in* THE EIGHTH AMENDMENT AND ITS FUTURE IN A NEW AGE OF PUNISHMENT 212, 218–19 (Meghan J. Ryan & William W. Berry III eds., 2020). For helpful charts comparing the various lethal injection protocols in different states, see *id.* at 219–22.

42 *PubChem: Thiopental,* NATIONAL LIBRARY OF MEDICINE, NATIONAL INSTITUTES OF HEALTH, pubchem.ncbi.nlm.nih.gov.

43 Teresa A. Zimmers et al., *Lethal Injection for Execution: Chemical Asphyxiation?,* 4 PLOS MED. 1, 6 (Apr. 2007).

44 Affidavit of Mark Dershwitz, M.D., PhD, at 5, Emmett v. Johnson (E.D. Va., Aug. 27, 2007) ("By the time all 2 grams of the thiopental sodium solution are injected, it is my further opinion, to a reasonable degree of medical certainty, that over 99.99999% of the population would be unconscious."); *id.* at 3–4 ("Even in persons of greater size or with inherent drug tolerance . . . the listed probabilities would not be altered in any meaningful way.").

45 *See* chapter 2, text accompanying note 28.

46 Zimmers et al., *supra* note 43, at 6.

47 *Id.*

48 *Id.*

49 *Id.* at 2. This portion of the study's results are discussed more extensively in Teresa A. Zimmers & Leonidas G. Koniaris, *Peer-Reviewed Studies Identifying Problems in the Design and Implementation of Lethal Injection for Execution*, 35 FORDHAM URB. L.J. 919, 926 (2008).

50 Zimmers & Koniaris, *supra* note 49, at 927 (when scaled to body weight, "the equivalent dose range in jurisdictions using 2 grams thiopental would be 6.6 to 30 mg/kg.").

51 Zimmers et al., *supra* note 43, at 3.

52 Zimmers & Koniaris, *supra* note 49, at 927.

53 Leonidas Koniaris et al., *Inadequate Anesthesia in Lethal Injection for Execution*, 365 THE LANCET 1412, 1412 (2005) ("A person anticipating execution would be fearful, anxious, and hyperadrenergic, and would need a higher dose of thiopental than would a premedicated surgical patient.").

54 Zimmers et al., *supra* note 43, at 4 (reporting that when scaled to body weight, the 5g dose of sodium thiopental equated to a range of 17–75 mg/kg).

55 HUMAN RIGHTS WATCH, *supra* note 4, at 17 (quoting Louisiana State Penitentiary pharmacy director).

56 State v. Rivera, No. 04CR065940, 2008 WL 2784679, at 1 (Ohio Ct. Com. Pl. June 10, 2008).

57 *PubChem: Pentobarbital*, NATIONAL LIBRARY OF MEDICINE—NATIONAL INSTITUTES OF HEALTH, pubchem.ncbi.nlm.nih.gov. Pentobarbital is not used, or FDA approved, for the induction of anesthesia, so determining its peak effect—which as a barbiturate could conceivably include sedation to the point of anesthesia—is a challenge. Most discussions of pentobarbital's peak effect are in the pediatric context, where peak effect is noted as deep sedation; thus, the time it takes to move from deep sedation to anesthesia, assuming the drug would get there at all, would be even longer. *See, e.g.*, Steven M. Green & Baruch Krauss, *Procedural Sedation and Analgesia*, in PEDIATRIC EMERGENCY MEDICINE 1119–37 (Jill M. Baren et al. eds. 2008) ("When carefully titrated IV, sedation is evident within 5 minutes"); OXFORD TEXTBOOK OF PAEDIATRIC PAIN (Patrick J. McGrath & Bonnie J. Stevens et al. eds., 2013) ("Onset of action after IV administration is rapid, resulting in moderate-deep sedation within 3 to 5 minutes");

Richard F. Kaplan & Charles J. Cote, *Sedation for Diagnostic and Therapeutic Procedures Outside the Operating Room, in* A PRACTICE OF ANESTHESIA FOR INFANTS AND CHILDREN (4th ed. 2009) ("Sedation starts in 3 to 5 minutes and peaks in 10 minutes"); Donna M. Moro-Sutherland et al., *Comparison of Intravenous Midazolam with Pentobarbital for Sedation for Head Computed Tomography Imaging,* 7–12 ACAD. EMERGENCY MEDICINE 1370 (2000) (pediatric study showing average induction time of pentobarbital at six minutes).

58 Death Penalty Information Center [hereinafter "DPIC"], *State-by-State Execution Protocols,* deathpenaltyinfo.org. Those eight states are Arizona, Georgia, Idaho, Missouri, South Carolina, South Dakota, Texas, and Utah.

59 For a helpful discussion of the point, and a graph showing how many executions were conducted under each protocol from 2008–19, see Eric Berger, *Evolving Standards of Lethal Injection, in* THE EIGHTH AMENDMENT AND ITS FUTURE IN A NEW AGE OF PUNISHMENT, *supra* note 41, at 234–53; *id.* at 252 (graph).

60 The United States has conducted over 1500 executions since 1976. Texas alone has conducted over 500 of those. DPIC, *Executions by State and Region since 1976,* deathpenaltyinfo.org.

61 Grady, *supra* note 18. *See also* Elizabeth Cohen, *Lethal Injection Creator: Maybe it's Time to Change Formula,* CNN, www.cnn.com (when asked why he included a paralytic, Chapman answered, "It's a good question. If I were doing it now, I would probably eliminate it.").

62 HUMAN RIGHTS WATCH, *supra* note 4, at 23 (quoting Dr. Mark Dershwitz); Grady, *supra* note 18 (quoting Dr. Mark Dershwitz as saying that death by the one-drug protocol could take as long as 45 minutes and would cause "significant involuntary jerking").

63 Talia Roitberg Harmon et al., *Examination of Decision Making and Botched Lethal Injection Executions in Texas,* 64 AM. BEHAV. SCIENTIST 1, 8–9 (2020).

64 *See* chapter 6, text accompanying notes 19–21 (states sharing execution drugs); 111–12 (Missouri buying execution drugs from a pharmacy in Oklahoma); 124–125 (Tennessee buying execution drugs from a pharmacy in Texas); 126–27 (Idaho buying execution drugs from pharmacies in Utah and Washington).

65 Baze v. Rees, 553 U.S. 35 (2008); Glossip v. Gross, 576 U.S. 863 (2015); Bucklew v. Precythe, 587 U.S. 119 (2019). For a discussion of these cases, *see* chapter 8, text accompanying notes 130–37.

66 Associated Press, *Florida Executes Woman's Killer,* SARASOTA HERALD-TRIBUNE (Oct 15, 2013).

67 *See* chapter 2, text accompanying notes 54–58.

68 DPIC, *supra* note 58. States currently using midazolam in the three-drug protocol are Oklahoma, Ohio, Mississippi, Alabama, and Arkansas. Two other states—Virginia and Florida—have used midazolam in the three-drug protocol, but no longer do. Virginia abolished the death penalty in 2021, and Florida has since moved to using etomidate, discussed at text accompanying *infra* notes 129–30.

69 *See* chapter 2, text accompanying note 47.

70 Amnesty International, *Lethal Injection: The Medical Technology of Execution*, at 10 (Jan. 1998).

71 *See* Kroll, *supra* note 7; Transcript of Preliminary Injunction Hearing, at 223, Warner v. Gross (N.D. Okla. Dec. 23, 2014) (testimony of Dr. David Lubarsky) ("Midazolam is indicated for things that don't have a great deal of noxious stimuli, painful stimuli, like colonoscopies. But even then, they usually combine midazolam with some narcotic because midazolam is usually insufficient.").

72 *See* Label: Midazolam Injection USP; Midazolam Sodium Chloride Injection for Intravenous Use, www.accessdata.fda.gov [hereinafter "FDA-approved Midazolam Label"]. In lethal injection litigation, state experts have claimed that a megadose of midazolam will work faster, but studies of the drug show that larger doses don't yield a faster response and as at least one court has noted, the state expert making the claim "did not provide, nor could he identify any article that supports his view, and he acknowledged that the FDA's package insert for midazolam does not back up his opinion on this point." Henness, *supra* note 30, at *55. *See also* F. H. Sarnquist et al., *A Bioassay for a Water-Soluble Benzodiazepine against Sodium Thiopental*, 52 ANESTHESIA 149–53 (1980) ("The onset time of sleep was 1.7 minutes, and did not differ among the low, medium, and high midazolam doses"); J. A. S. Gamble et al., *Evaluation of Midazolam as an Intravenous Induction Agent*, 36 ANESTHESIA 868–73 (1981) ("Although it may be counter-intuitive, larger drug doses do not lead to faster time of effect."); J. W. Mandema et al., *Pharmacokinetic-Pharmacodynamic Modelling of the EEG Effects of Midazolam in Individual Rats: Influence of Rate and Route of Administration*, 103 J. PHARMACOLOGY 663–68 (1991) (reporting that maximal (peak) sedative effect occurs between ten and twenty minutes after IV administration); J. W. Mandema et al., *Pharmacokinetic-Pharmacodynamic Modelling of the Central Nervous System Effects of Midazolam and Its Main Metabolite Alpha-Hydroxymixazolam in Healthy Volunteers*, 51 CLINICAL PHARMACOLOGY & THERAPEUTICS, 715–28 (1992) (reporting that peak depression of central nervous system did not occur until between seven and fifteen minutes after administration).

73 *Henness, supra* note 30, at *45 (quoting Dr. Craig W. Stevens).

74 Fernanda Santos, *Executed Arizona Inmate Got 15 Times Standard Dose, Lawyers Say*, N.Y. TIMES (Aug. 1, 2014) (quoting Dr. Joel Zivot).

75 Expert Report of Craig W. Stevens, Ph.D, at 5, Glossip v. Gross (Sept. 10, 2015).

76 George M. Brenner & Craig W. Stevens, *Sedative Hypnotic and Anxiolytic Drugs*, *in* BRENNER AND STEVENS' PHARMACOLOGY 192 (4th ed. 2013).

77 S. John Mihic et al., *Hypnotics and Sedatives*, *in* GOODMAN & GILMAN'S THE PHARMACOLOGICAL BASIS OF THERAPEUTICS 339, 341 (Laurence L. Brunton et al. eds., 13th ed. 2018); Kroll, *supra* note 7 (referring to Goodman & Gilmann text as "the holy book of the pharmacology discipline").

78 Ronald D. Miller et al., MILLER'S ANESTHESIA 837 (8th ed. 2015); *Henness*, *supra* note 30, at *26 ("Miller's is a text acknowledged to be the authoritative text in anesthesiology by every expert witness who was asked.").

79 J. G. Reves et al., *Midazolam: Pharmacology and its Uses*, 62 ANESTHESIOLOGY 310, 318 (1985). Even the veterinary science literature recognizes the point. In animal euthanasia, midazolam is sometimes given as a pre-euthanasia drug to calm animals that are aggressive or fearful. A leading treatise on animal euthanasia states that in high doses, this can cause "a sleep-like state," but "sedated animals can become aroused by strong stimulation such as a painful procedure." Louisa Tasker, *Methods for the Euthanasia of Dogs and Cats: Comparison and Recommendations*, WORLD SOCIETY FOR THE PROTECTION OF ANIMALS 13 (2008).

80 Expert Report of Dr. David J. Greenblatt, M.D., In re: Ohio Execution Protocol Litigation (Henness) (S.D. Ohio, Oct. 27, 2018) at 18; *see also id.* ("As a matter of scientific certainty, midazolam simply cannot make a person insensate by way of suppressing consciousness to a deep enough level."). Dr. Roswell Evans—the state's sole expert when midazolam was litigated in 2015—subsequently conceded that Greenblatt's description of the science surrounding midazolam was "accurate." *See* Petition for Writ of Certiorari, Zagorski v. Parker, at 16 (Oct. 9, 2018) (quoting from trial court record where Evans agreed with Greenblatt and other experts that "midazolam was not capable of bringing inmates to a surgical plane of anesthesia").

81 Expert Report of Dr. David J. Greenblatt, M.D., *supra* note 80, at 32.

82 *Id.* at 36.

83 *See, e.g.*, A. E. Ibrahim et al., *Bispectral Index Monitoring during Sedation with Sevoflurane, Midazolam, and Propofol*, 95 ANESTHESIOLOGY, 1151–59 (2001) (reporting that the mean BIS for patients administered midazolam did not drop below 65). Three additional studies—all relied on by Oklahoma's experts in the 2022 litigation over midazolam—are discussed at *infra* text accompanying notes 108–11.

84 Expert Report of Dr. David J. Greenblatt, M.D., *supra* note 80, at 22. Greenblatt went on to say:

> For example, studies conducted by Bührer and Stanski (attached to this report) used the EEG as an objective window on the brain to measure the depth of sedation. . . . My group collaborated with Bührer and Stanski on those studies because they sent some of their blood samples to our lab to be analyzed. Bührer and Stanski reached two principle findings in their studies. First, they demonstrated that when there is an increase in dose of midazolam beyond a certain level, there will not be an associated or parallel increase in the depth of sedation. When they went from 7.5 mg to 15 mg, there was a measurable increase in sedation on the EEG. But when they increased from 15 mg to 25 mg, there was no further increase in sedation.

Id. at 23 (discussing M. Bührer et al., *Electroencephalographic Effects of Benzodiazepines. II. Pharmacodynamic Modeling of the Electroencephalographic Effects of Midazolam and Diazepam*, 48 CLINICAL PHARMACOLOGY AND THERAPEUTICS 555–67 (1990); M. Bührer et al., *Electroencephalographic Effects of Benzodiazepines. I. Choosing an Electroencephalographic Parameter to Measure the Effect of Midazolam on the Central Nervous System*, 48 CLINICAL PHARMACOLOGY AND THERAPEUTICS 544–54 (1990)). *See also* Expert Report of Craig W. Stevens, PhD, *supra* note 75, at 12 ("The estimated brain concentrations for midazolam under the Oklahoma lethal injection protocol are about *20 to 25 times higher than the concentration of midazolam that produces a ceiling effect.* . . . A 20 mg IV dose of midazolam would be expected to reach the threshold concentration of midazolam to produce a ceiling effect."); *id.* at 13 ("It is misguided and without any pharmacological or scientific reasoning to think that giving greater doses of midazolam can produce the effects that can be obtained using thiopental or pentobarbital.").

85 *Henness, supra* note 30, at *46 (quoting Dr. Craig Stevens).

86 Noah Caldwell et al., *Gasping for Air: Autopsies Reveal Troubling Effects of Lethal Injection*, NAT'L PUB. RADIO (Sept. 21, 2020) (quoting Dr. David Lubarsky); Transcript of Preliminary Injunction Hearing, *supra* note 71, at 151 (testimony of Dr. David Lubarsky) ("In the original landmark review article published in 1985 by Reves et al., it was very clear that they stated that the drug was—had failed when it was used as both an induction and maintenance agent in terms of blunting the effect of surgery.").

87 Dr. Lubarsky is now Vice Chancellor of Human Health Sciences and Chief Executive Officer of the U.C. Davis Health System. He was named one of 2022's "100 Most Influential People in Health Care." health.ucdavis.edu.

88 Transcript of Preliminary Injunction Hearing, *supra* note 71, at 200, 203, 223 (testimony of Dr. David Lubarsky).

89 Petition for Writ of Certiorari, Howell v. Florida, at *5–6, 2014 WL 78719 (Feb. 25, 2014) (quoting testimony of Dr. David Lubarsky).

90 *Id.* (quoting Dr. Roswell Evans, who, when asked, "Now, you would never use midazolam alone as an anesthetic in a major surgery, would you?" answered: "No. That's not common practice."); Testimony of Dr. Joseph Antognini, Glossip v. Chandler, 2022 WL 1997194 (W.D. Okla., June 6, 2022) [hereinafter "Glossip v. Chandler (2022)"], at 10 (explaining that midazolam isn't used as the sole anesthetic for surgery because it would take "a very large dose to be able to achieve that" but conceding the absence of any study supporting that assertion).
In the 2022 Oklahoma litigation over midazolam, the court quoted one of the state's experts—Dr. Ervin Yen—as stating that although he has never used midazolam to get a patient to a BIS score lower than 70, that's because "he wouldn't want to do that, because 'there's a chance that the patient could stop breathing, be obstructed.'" Glossip v. Chandler (2022), *supra*, at *13. But as the

ASA chart produced in the court's own opinion (and also here in this chapter) states, "spontaneous ventilation" is "frequently inadequate" when a patient is under general anesthesia, and "intervention is often required" to clear their airway. *Id.* at *12. So the notion that midazolam *could* achieve anesthesia, but a doctor wouldn't want to use it that way because it would stop breathing, is nonsensical—*that's* what anesthesia does.

91 Liliana Segura, *"Our Most Cruel Experiment Yet": Chilling Testimony in a Tennessee Trial Exposes Lethal Injection as Court-Sanctioned Torture*, THE INTERCEPT (Aug. 5, 2018) (quoting Dr. Craig Stevens), theintercept.com. *See generally* Vuyk et al., *Intravenous Anesthetics, in* MILLER'S ANESTHESIA, *supra* note 78, at 842 ("Benzodiazepines lack analgesic properties and must be used with other anesthetic drugs to provide sufficient analgesia.").

92 FDA-approved Midazolam Label, *supra* note 72. *See also* Mary A. Gutierrez et al., *Paradoxical Reactions to Benzodiazepines: When to Expect the Unexpected*, AM. J. OF NURSING 34–39 (July 2001).

93 Michael A. Frölich et al., *Effect of Sedation on Pain Perception*, 118 ANESTHESIOLOGY 611–62 (2013).

94 *Bucklew*, 587 U.S. at 137 (holding that "a punishment is unconstitutionally cruel [when it] 'superadds' pain well beyond what's needed to effectuate a death sentence."). *Bucklew* is discussed in chapter 8, text accompanying notes 132–37.

95 Carissa Mancuso et al., *Paradoxical Reactions to Benzodiazepines: Literature Review and Treatment Options*, 24 PHARMACOTHERAPY 1177, 1185 (2004).

96 Carol Paton, *Benzodiazepines and Disinhibition: A Review*, 26 PSYCH. BULL. 460, 460 (2002); D. L. Gardner & R. W. Cowdrey, *Alprazolam-Induced Dyscontrol in Borderline Personality Disorder*, 142 AM. J. OF PSYCHIATRY 98–100 (1985).

97 FDA-approved Midazolam Label, *supra* note 72.

98 Brief of Sixteen Professors of Pharmacology, *supra* note 38.

99 *Glossip*, 576 U.S. at 888. *See* chapter 2, text accompanying note 78.

100 Brief of Sixteen Professors of Pharmacology, *supra* note 38, at 20.

101 Brief of Fifteen Professors of Pharmacology as Amici Curiae In Support of Certiorari, Otte v. Erdos, 2017 WL 3142305 (2017), at 12-13.

102 *Id.* at 7.

103 *See* chapter 2, text accompanying notes 68-70.

104 Transcript of Oral Arguments, at 34–36, Glossip v. Gross, No. 14–7955 (Apr. 29, 2015).

105 *Id.*

106 *Id.*

107 Glossip v. Chandler (2022), *supra* note 90. This case was first discussed in chapter 2, text accompanying notes 92–94.

108 Glossip v. Chandler (2022), *supra* note 90, at *13 ("Midazolam has been demonstrated to be capable of inducing a BIS score well below 60 and in some cases below 40.").

109 Wakako Miyake et al., *Electroencephalographic Response Following Midazolam-Induced General Anesthesia: Relationship to Plasma and Effect-Site Midazolam Concentrations*, J. ANESTHESIOLOGY 386, 390 (Mar. 13, 2010). *See* Expert Report of Joseph F. Antognini, M.D., Glossip v. Chandler (2022), *supra* note 90, at 13–14 (discussing Miyake study).

All three of Oklahoma's experts denied that midazolam had a ceiling effect. *See* Expert Report of Antognini, Glossip v. Chandler (2022), *supra* note 90, at 26 (opining that midazolam's ceiling effect is "fraught with uncertainty"); Declaration of Daniel E. Buffington, Glossip v. Chandler (2022), *supra* note 90, at 15 (opining that "a purported midazolam 'ceiling effect' is purely a speculative concept"); Expert Report of Irvin Yen, Glossip v. Chandler (2022), *supra* note 90, at 7 ("It is possible that midazolam has a ceiling effect. But I am not aware of any scientific study showing at what dose, or what level of unconsciousness, that ceiling effect (if any) occurs. Personally, I have never witnessed a ceiling effect during my many uses of midazolam.").

It is worth noting that the studies these experts cited to say that midazolam doesn't have a ceiling effect also don't say what these experts say they say. The Hall study explicitly states of its findings: "At least in practical terms, there appears to be a ceiling to the anesthetic efficacy of midazolam." The Inagaki study states: "Benzodiazepine receptors will become saturated at a sufficient level of serum midazolam concentration. The present results indicate clearly that the midazolam action to potentiate the anesthetic action of halothane has a saturable nature." And the Melvin study, which does contain the line "No ceiling effect appears with larger doses of midazolam," says this in the context of "patients anesthetized with halothane." It's a study about midazolam's multiplier effect with an actual anesthetic, which is not in play here. *See* Richard I. Hall et al., *The Anesthetic Efficacy of Midazolam in the Enflurane-Anesthetized Dog*, 68 ANESTHESIOLOGY 862, 865 (1988); Yoshimi Inagaki et al., *Anesthetic Interaction between Midazolam and Halothane in Humans*, 76 ANESTHESIOLOGY ANALG. 613, 616 (1993); M. A. Melvin et al., *Induction of Anesthesia with Midazolam Decreases Halothane MAC in Man*, 53 ANESTHESIOLOGY (1980).

110 Jin Liu & Singh H. White, *Electroencephalogram Bispectral Analysis Predicts the Depth of Midazolam-Induced Sedation*, ANESTHESIOLOGY 64 (Jan. 1996). *See* Declaration of Daniel E. Buffington, *supra* note 109, at 13 (discussing Liu study).

111 R. Bulach et al., *Double-Blind Randomized Controlled Trial to Determine Extent of Amnesia with Midazolam Given Immediately before General Anesthesia*, 94 BR. J. OF ANESTHESIOLOGY 300 (March 2005) (finding average BIS score of 71, and values as low as 66). *See* Declaration of Daniel E. Buffington, *supra* note 109, at 13 (discussing Bulach study).

Of note, Buffington cites the Bulach study for the proposition that "standard doses of midazolam can already achieve mild, moderate, or deep anesthesia, and general anesthesia when dosed accordingly." But patients in the Bulach study received propofol to achieve general anesthesia, not midazolam. Tellingly, even the study's author, Dr. Richard Bulach, told the press that he disagrees with Buffington's interpretation of the results of his study. *See* Lauren Gill & Daniel Moritz-Rabson, *This Pharmacist Said Prisoners Won't Feel Pain During Lethal Injection. Then Some Shook and Gasped for Air*, PROPUBLICA (April 29, 2023), www.propublica.org.

112 *See* Gill & Moritz-Rabson, *supra* note 111 (exposé on Daniel Buffington, noting more broadly the "small pool of experts" willing to defend midazolam in the three-drug protocol); Annie Waldman, *Key Expert in Supreme Court Lethal Injection Case Did His Research on Drugs.Com*, PROPUBLICA (Apr. 28, 2015), www.propublica.org (exposé on Roswell Evans and Mark Dershwitz, quoting law professor Deborah Denno as saying, "The Departments of Corrections are pretty desperate to find experts who can support their point of view. States have had a lot of trouble finding experts to come forward, and when they do come forward, they are not qualified."); Isaac Arnsdorf, *Inside Trump and Barr's Last-Minute Killing Spree*, PROPUBLICA (Dec. 23, 2020) www.propublica.org (discussing Dr. Joseph Antognini). *See also* Henness, *supra* note 30, at *62 (describing Antognini is "an outlier in the field of anesthesiology"); *id.* at *38 (quoting another expert as stating that "Dr. Antognini's opinion is not generally accepted in the medical community and the only person holding it is Dr. Antognini himself."); *id.* at *48 (quoting different expert as stating that, as to Dr. Antognini's opinion that midazolam has analgesic properties, he is "iconoclastic in that belief. In other words, he is an outlier, perhaps even an extreme outlier, because everything I have read, *Miller's Anesthesia* book and all the classic and well-known authoritative texts do not say that midazolam has any analgesic action.").

The court in 2022's *Glossip* case found particularly credible the testimony of Dr. Ervin Yen, calling him "a fresh face in this case, and a credible one at that." Glossip v. Chandler (2022), *supra* note 90, at *5. Dr. Yen is a practicing anesthesiologist, and presumably a very good one, but his report and testimony were based solely on his experience using midazolam, and, notably, that experience had nothing to do with massive doses of the drug, so it is little wonder that he had no knowledge of midazolam's ceiling effect or maximum effect on a BIS monitor. *See, e.g.*, Expert Report of Irvin Yen, *supra* note 109, at 5 ("My experience has always been that the more midazolam I give a patient, the lower the BIS reading goes."); *id.* at 7 ("It is possible that midazolam has a ceiling effect. But I am not aware of any scientific study showing at what dose, or what level of unconsciousness, that ceiling effect (if any) occurs. Personally, I have never witnessed a ceiling effect during my many uses of midazolam."). In addition, Dr. Yen is a former Republican state senator, and although the court rebuffed any insinuation of bias on this basis, the death penalty is a highly politized issue in Oklahoma and Republicans are its most staunch supporters. See Chapter 1. Having taught evidence for over two decades, I strenu-ously disagree that this is somehow an illegitimate basis for impeachment on bias.

113 Glossip v. Chandler (2022), *supra* note 90, at *4, 10–11.

114 *Id.* at *10 n.21.

115 Reves, *supra* note 79, at 317 (emphasis added).

116 *See supra* notes 29-33 and accompanying text.

117 Midazolam (Pfizer label): labeling.pfizer.com (emphasis added). The state and its experts quoted this very language. *See, e.g.,* Declaration of Daniel E. Buffington, *supra* note 109, at 6 (quoting language that says "before administration of other anesthetic agents" but then ignoring it); Defendant's Motion for Summary Judgment at 7, Glossip v. Chandler (2022), *supra* note 90 (same). Notably, there is no engagement whatsoever with the obvious questions that arise from the state's claims: If midazolam could achieve anesthesia on its own, why would the instructions say "before administration of other anesthetic agents"? And why would it not be approved by the FDA as the sole anesthetic in surgical procedures?

118 *Henness, supra* note 30, at *27 (quoting Dr. David Greenblatt).

119 *Id.*

120 AMERICAN SOCIETY OF HEALTH SYSTEM PHARMACISTS, AHFS DRUG INFORMATION® (2017). *See* www.ashp.org ("The AHFS Drug Information® Database is the most comprehensive evidence-based source of drug information complete with therapeutic guidelines and off-label uses. . . . [It is] the only remaining original federal compendium whose authority for establishing accepted medical uses includes the broadest scope of drugs and indications."). It is also outrageously expensive, so only professionals in the field—or academics with excellent library support—would even have access to this material. Shout out to the Richmond Law library for making it happen.

121 *Id.* at 2,744 (emphasis added). The AHFS DI® goes on to say: "For induction of general anesthesia, midazolam should be administered prior to other anesthetic agents. When midazolam is administered prior to other IV agents for induction of anesthesia, the initial dose of each of these agents may be substantially reduced, in some instances to as low as 25% of the usual initial dose of the individual agents." *Id.* at 2,746.

122 Defendant's Motion for Summary Judgment, *supra* note 117, at 23. *See also* Expert Report of Antognini, *supra* note 109, at 27 ("How 'painful' is drug-induced diaphragm paralysis and apnea, such as that caused by the second drug in the Oklahoma protocol? . . . Obviously, the distress was not so much that any volunteer would not have done the study again."); *id.* at 25 ("In my opinion, deep coma-like unconsciousness (as produced by high anesthetic doses) is not needed to ensure lethal injection does not pose a risk of severe pain.").

123 Segura, *supra* note 91; Butler Snow, *Tennessee Lethal Injection Protocol Investigation Report and Findings* 8 (Dec. 13, 2022); Melissa Brown and Josh Keefe, *Who Executes Tennessee's Death Row Inmates?* THE TENNESSEAN (May 25, 2022).

124 *Henness, supra* note 30, at *12–14 ("On balance, the accounts given are sufficiently consistent with one another and with prior lay descriptions of midazolam-initiated executions to be accepted as factual, yet different enough to belie any sense of repetition from one to the other.").

125 *Id.* at *28 (quoting Dr. David Greenblatt and discussing studies); Expert Report of Dr. David J. Greenblatt, M.D., *supra* note 80, at 21–22. For the studies, see, e.g., David J. Greenblatt et al., *Rapid Recovery from Massive Diazepam Overdose*, 17 J. OF AM. MED. ASS'N 240 (Oct. 20, 1978); David J. Greenblatt et al., *Acute Overdosage with Benzodiazepine Derivatives*, 21(4) CLINICAL PHARMACOLOGY AND THERAPEUTICS 497–514 (Apr. 1977); M. Divoll, *Benzodiazepine Overdosage: Plasma Concentrations and Clinical Outcomes*, 73 PSYCHOPHARMACOLOGY 381–83 (1981); M. Divoll, *Pharmacokinetic Study of Lorazepam Overdosage*, 137 AM. J. PSYCHIATRY 11 (Nov. 1980). Fun fact: these are the studies that establish midazolam's incredibly low toxicity. *See* chapter 2, text accompanying note 72-75 (discussing midazolam's toxicity).

126 *Henness, supra* note 30, at *28 (quoting Dr. David Greenblatt); Expert Report of Dr. David J. Greenblatt, M.D., *supra* note 80, at 22 ("With extremely large doses of benzodiazepines alone, the patients were sleepy and sedated, but they remained sensate, and they did not have problems with their breathing or respirations. . . . When the patients mixed diazepines with other drugs, the situation became more problematic.").

127 *Henness, supra* note 30, at *49.

128 Brenner & Stevens, *supra* note 76, at 214. *See also* Expert Report of Dr. David J. Greenblatt, M.D., *supra* note 80, at 29 ("But, to be blunt, that basic argument is not real, actual science."); *id.* at 33 ("Misinterpreting or misrepresenting the science as the state does will not make [the science] any less scientifically valid or accurate. And repeating on numerous occasions that misinterpretation or misrepresentation of the science, as the state does, will not make that inaccuracy any more correct.").

129 FDA-approved Midazolam Label, *supra* note 72 ("Duration of anesthesia is dose dependent but relatively brief, usually three to five minutes."); Kathryn Harkup, *Untried and Unethical: Why Nevada's New Lethal Injection Crosses a Line*, THE GUARDIAN (Nov. 14, 2017).

130 DPIC, *Behind the Curtain: Secrecy and the Death Penalty in the United States* at 56 (Nov. 20, 2018) (discussing signs of distress in etomidate executions), deathpenaltyinfo.org.

131 JoAnne Young, *Questions Surround What Happened in 14 Minutes Witnesses Were Blocked from Seeing Nebraska Execution*, LINCOLN J. STAR (Sept. 7, 2018).

132 *Id.*

133 *Id.*

134 *Id.*

135 Caldwell et al., *supra* note 86.

136 Segura, *supra* note 91.

137 Caldwell et al., *supra* note 86.

138 *Id.*; Henness, *supra* note 30, at *63 ("All medical witnesses to describe pulmonary edema agreed it was painful, both physically and emotionally, inducing a sense of drowning and the attendant panic and terror, much as would occur with the torture tactic known as waterboarding.").

139 Rachel Weiner, *Ricky Gray Executed in Virginia*, WASH. POST (Jan. 18, 2017); Rachel Weiner, *Ricky Gray's Execution Took More than 30 Minutes. His Attorneys Want to Know Why.* WASH. POST (Jan. 19, 2017).

140 Ed Pilkington, *Virginia Set to Execute Man Using "Potentially Torturous" Drug Cocktail*, THE GUARDIAN (July 5, 2017).

141 Frank Green, *Pathologist Says Ricky Gray's Autopsy Suggests Problems with Virginia's Execution Procedure*, RICHMOND TIMES DISPATCH (July 7, 2017).

142 *See* chapter 2, text accompanying note 81.

143 Caldwell et al., *supra* note 86.

144 *See* chapter 2, text accompanying note 83.

145 *See* Expert Declaration of Gail A. Van Norman, M.D., at 32, 36, Roane v. Barr (D.C. Cir. Nov. 1, 2019). The caustic nature of the solution also explains why prisoners executed with the one-drug protocol often claim that the injection burns.

146 Caldwell et al., *supra* note 86 (quoting Dr. Philippe Camus).

147 Expert Declaration of Gail A. Van Norman, M.D., *supra* note 145, at 50.

148 *Id.* at 35.

149 *Id.* at 31.

150 Roane v. Barr, 471 F.Supp.3d 209, 219 (2020); *see also id.* at 218 ("The scientific evidence before the court overwhelmingly indicates that the 2019 protocol is very likely to cause plaintiffs extreme pain and needless suffering in their executions.").

151 Barr v. Lee, 591 U.S. 979 (2020). *See id.* at 986 (Sotomayor, J., dissenting) ("The Court forever deprives respondents of their ability to press a constitutional challenge to their lethal injections, and prevents lower courts from reviewing that challenge.").

152 Michael Tarm, *Lawyers: Autopsy Suggests Inmate Suffered during Execution*, ASSOC. PRESS (Aug. 21, 2020).

153 For the autopsy, see dpic-cdn.org.

154 *Barr*, 591 U.S. at 981.

155 Caldwell et al., *supra* note 86.

156 *See* Expert Report of Antognini, *supra* note 109, at 23–24.

157 Caldwell et al., *supra* note 86 ("The froth was a clue: it meant that the inmates were still alive and trying to breathe as their lungs filled with fluid, because froth could form only if air was still passing through the lungs. It also meant that the pulmonary edema was being caused by the first drug given during a lethal injection, since the second drug, a paralytic, stops the inmate's breathing altogether."); Henness, *supra* note 30, at *16 (finding that the first drug, midazolam, must be causing the pulmonary edema because "once fully effective, rocuronium bromide 'would prevent the development of frothy fluid in the lungs and airways because as a neuromuscular blocking agent it paralyzes the muscles of respiration which would stop the flow of air necessary for production of froth.'") (quoting Dr. Mark Edgar, citing 44 (3) JOURNAL OF CLINICAL INVESTIGATION 458–64 (1965)).

158 *See, e.g.*, Expert Report of Antognini, *supra* note 109, at 20 ("Furthermore, midazolam, as administered according to the Oklahoma protocol, will produce unconsciousness well before the full 500 mg dose is administered. . . . the inmate will have received sufficient midazolam to become unconscious. Pulmonary edema, even if it occurs immediately ante-mortem, would not be sensed by the inmate who has received midazolam.").

159 Henness, *supra* note 30, at *29 (quoting Dr. David Greenblatt); *see also* Expert Report of Dr. David J. Greenblatt, M.D., *supra* note 80, at 45–46.

160 Henness, *supra* note 30, at *30.

161 Expert Report of Dr. David J. Greenblatt, M.D., *supra* note 80, at 24–26. Here is the key passage:

> The Bührer and Stanski studies also showed that as the size of the dose of midazolam increased, the time to peak sedative effect also increased. The higher the dose, the greater the delay. The reason for that can be found in the formulation of the drug and its intravenous preparation, which is formulated in acid to keep it in solution. Recall that midazolam is a benzodiazepine with an accessory ring called in imidazole ring. When the drug is in acid, the ring is open. And the drug actually undergoes a conformational change of its structure when the ring is open. The ring-open form is pharmacologically inactive. The drug solution must be buffered by the blood back to the normal pH 7.4 for that ring to close and for the drug to become active and be able to reach and affect the brain. . . . In my 1989 study, a 9 mg dose did not reach peak sedative effect for 15 minutes. The 500 mg dose of midazolam . . . is approximately 50 times larger than the 9mg dose for which peak sedative effect took 15 minutes.

162 Expert Declaration of Gail A. Van Norman, M.D., *supra* note 145, at 36 (citing studies showing that acute pulmonary edema from pentobarbital occurs "virtually immediately, well within the time frame before peak drug effects on the brain have occurred").

163 Austin Sarat et al., *The Fate of Lethal Injection: Decomposition of the Paradigm and Its Consequences*, 11 BR. J. AM. LEG. STUDIES 1, 20–21 (2022) ("In 83 lethal injections, the inmate spoke or made noise after the injection began, utterances that ranged from screams, to sobs, to slurred sentences. Commonly, inmates exhibit unusual breathing patterns, body movement, and dramatic changes in skin color. Seventy-three included coughing, snorting, and other sudden respirations.").

164 Michael Tarm, *Executioners Sanitized Accounts of Deaths in Federal Cases*, ASSOC. PRESS (Feb. 17, 2021) (quoting Dr. Kendall Von Crowns, chief medical examiner, Tarrant County, Texas).

165 *Id.* (emphasis added). *See also id.* ("All the journalist reports said the movements happened within minutes of injections.").

166 Segura, *supra* note 91 (quoting Dr. Mark Heath).

167 For examples, see *id.*

168 Henness, *supra* note 30, at 26 ("The neuroscience literature [] demonstrates that even outwardly unresponsive patients can manifest changes in their brain wave activity, via electroencephalogram (EEG) when exposed to painful stimuli, demonstrating continued sensation.") (quoting Dr. Matthew Exline). Roane v. Barr, 471 F.Supp.3d 209, 219 (2020) ("Dr. Van Norman specifically states that barbiturates like pentobarbital render patients 'unresponsive' but still conscious and capable of experiencing the severe pain associated with flash pulmonary edema. While Dr. Antognini disputes these findings, he does not undermine them.").

169 *Henness, supra* note 30, at *30–31 (quoting Dr. David Greenblatt). As an example, media witnesses reported that in the federal government's 2020 execution of Wesley Purkey, Purkey was "blinking repeatedly as the pentobarbital was injected" but otherwise showed no "obvious signs that he was in pain." Tarm, *supra* note 164. But Purkey's autopsy showed that he suffered from fulminate pulmonary edema as he died.

170 Defendant's Post-Trial Summary of Expert Testimony and Proposed Findings of Fact from Fact Witness Testimony, Glossip v. Chandler (2022), *supra* note 90.

171 Dave Boucher & Adam Tamburin, *Tennessee Execution: Billy Ray Irick Tortured to Death, Expert Says in New Filing,* THE TENNESSEAN (Sept. 7, 2018).

172 Glossip v. Chandler (2022), *supra* note 90, at *6 n.17.

173 Stephen Cooper, *On Slicing and Sticking Condemned Men in Alabama,* MONTGOMERY ADVERTISER (Oct. 31, 2022) (quoting Dr. Joel Zivot).

174 Emmett v. Johnson, 532 F.3d 291, 311 (2008) (Gregory, J., dissenting).

4. AN EXCEEDINGLY DELICATE, ERROR-PRONE PROCEDURE

1 Willie Francis survived Louisiana's first attempt to execute him by electrocution in 1946. Whether the state could try again was the question in *Louisiana ex rel. Francis v. Resweber,* 329 U.S. 459 (1947). The answer was yes.

2 Broom v. Shoop, 963 F.3d 500, 504 (6th Cir. 2020). *See also* Fred Barbash, *After 18 Botched IV Attempts on a Screaming, Bleeding Inmate, Ohio Gets Another Chance To Execute Him,* WASH. POST (Mar. 17, 2016) ("And in the course of that time period, they jabbed, poked and stuck the man at least 18 times, twisting and turning catheters this way and that. They made holes in his arms, legs and elbows, his wrists, the backs of his hands and his ankles, inserting catheter needles repeatedly into 'already swollen and bruised sites,' according to court documents. His veins bulged. One of them 'blew.' They took breaks, leaving the man on the gurney, and then came back to try again. The medical team, according to court documents, 'would withdraw the catheter partway and then reinsert it at a different angle, a procedure known as 'fishing.''").

3 Ed Pilkington, *"Surreal Spectacle": US Botched 35% of Execution Attempts This Year*, THE GUARDIAN (Dec. 16, 2022) ("As 2022 draws to a close, a new grim distinction can be attached to it: in America it was the year of the botched execution.").

4 *See* AUSTIN SARAT, GRUESOME SPECTACLES: BOTCHED EXECUTIONS AND AMERICA'S DEATH PENALTY 5 (2014) (around 3 percent of all executions were botched between 1890–2010); AUSTIN SARAT, LETHAL INJECTION AND THE FALSE PROMISE OF HUMANE EXECUTION 67 (between 2010 and 2020, the botch rate for lethal injection was just over 8 percent). *See also* Khaleda Rahman, *Lethal Injections Are to Blame for Over 100 Botched Executions in America*, NEWSWEEK (Dec. 8, 2022) (discussing Sarat's work showing that the overall botch rate for lethal injection is 7.12 percent, but from 2010 to 2020 it is 8.4 percent).

5 Morales v. Tilton, 465 F.Supp.2d 974, 979 n.8 (N.D. Cal. 2006).

6 Thiopental Sodium package insert, Lake Forest, IL: Hospira, Inc., 2011, dailymed. nlm.nih.gov. As stated in the instructions, each 500 mg dose of sodium thiopental requires 20 ml of diluent to achieve the proper 2.5 percent concentration. For the math, 500mg/20ml = 25 mg/ml = 2.5 percent.

7 Joint Appendix, at 747, Baze v. Rees, 553 U.S. 35 (2008).

8 South Dakota's botched execution of Eric Robert in 2012 is a prime example. *See South Dakota Carries Out Execution Using Contaminated Compounded Drugs*, DEATH PENALTY NEWS (Oct. 17, 2012), deathpenaltynews.blogspot.com ("Mr. Robert reportedly took 20 minutes to die and opened his eyes during the process, after which they remained open until the end. A certificate of analysis of the pentobarbital which was used in the execution found that it was contaminated with a fungus.").

9 Thiopental Sodium package insert, *supra* note 6.

10 Abdur'Rahman v. Bredesen, No. M2003–01767–COA–R3–CV, 2004 WL 2246227, at *4 (Tenn. Ct. App. Oct.6, 2004) ("The three-drug lethal injection protocol in the Department's Execution Manual calls for the intravenous injection of three drugs in the following order . . . . The first syringe contains five grams of sodium [thiopental] mixed in a solution with 50 cc of sterile water."). *See also* Affidavit of Dr. David A. Lubarsky, M.D., Harbison v. Little, 511 F.Supp.2d 872 (M.D. Tenn., June 15, 2007) ("The description of the drugs involved highlights the type of confusion and error in the mixing and administration of drugs which can lead to inadequate anesthesia. For instance, the Warden's response indicates that 5 grams (5000 mg) of sodium [] thiopental is administered in a 50 cc, or 50 ml, solution. The concentration of the thiopental therefore is 100 mg/ml. Thiopental, however, is never mixed in that fashion, and the physician's order is for 5 grams in a 25mg/ml solution (which is the standard mixing concentration)."). For the math, 5 grams in a 50 ml solution = 5000mg/50ml = 100 mg/ml = 10%.

11 Harbison v. Little, 511 F.Supp.2d 872, 897 n.20 (M.D. Tenn. 2007).

12 Taylor v. Crawford, 2006 WL 1779035, at *3 (W.D. Mo. 2006).

13 *Id.* at *3.

14 *Id.* at *4–5.

15 *Id.* at *5, 7. For the math, 2.5 grams in a 50 ml solution = 2500 mg/50ml = 50 mg/ml = 5% solution.

16 *Id.* at *8.

17 *Morales,* 465 F. Supp.2d at 980.

18 Harbison v. Little, 511 F.Supp.2d at 898; *id.* at 903 ("The new protocol presents a substantial risk of unnecessary pain; that risk was known to Commissioner Little, and yet disregarded.").

19 *Id.* at 876, 897.

20 Baze v. Rees, 553 U.S. 35 (2008).

21 *Id.* at 37.

22 Harbison v. Little, 571 F.3d 531, 538 (6th Cir. 2009).

23 Butler Snow LLP, *Tenn. Lethal Injection Protocol Investigation: Report and Findings* 8–9, 14 (Dec. 13, 2022), ewscripps.brightspotcdn.com.

24 *Id.* at 14.

25 *Id.* at 37–38.

26 David Waisel, *Physician Participation in Capital Punishment,* 82 MAYO CLINIC PROC. 1073, 1074 (2007).

27 JON SORENSEN & ROCKY LEANN PILGRIM, LETHAL INJECTION: CAPITAL PUNISHMENT IN TEXAS DURING THE MODERN ERA 15 (2006).

28 STEPHEN TROMBLEY, THE EXECUTION PROTOCOL: INSIDE AMERICA'S CAPITAL PUNISHMENT INDUSTRY 75 (2002).

29 *See* Mark Dershwitz & Thomas K. Henthorn, *The Pharmacokinetics and Pharmacodynamics of Thiopental As Used in Lethal Injection,* FORDHAM URB. L.J. 931, 946 (2008) ("The largest commercially available syringes used in medicine are 60 ml. The above [three-drug] protocol therefore requires eleven syringes."). *See also* Taylor v. Crawford, 487 F.3d 1072, 1082 n.4 (8th Cir. 2007) ("Specifically, [Missouri's lethal injection] procedure requires 15 syringes—the first 4 syringes contain a total quantity of 5 grams of thiopental, the next syringe contains only saline solution, then 60 milligrams of pancuronium bromide, then saline solution, then two syringes containing a total of 240 milliequivalents of potassium chloride, and the tenth syringe contains saline solution. Four additional syringes, each containing an extra 1.25 gram dose of thiopental, are prepared in case additional anesthetic is required, and one additional syringe of extra saline solution is prepared."). Missouri now uses a one-drug protocol with six syringes. Katie Moore, *Where Does Missouri Get the Drugs It Uses to Execute Prisoners? The Supplier Is a Secret,* KANSAS CITY STAR, Jan. 5, 2024 ("syringes one, two, four and five are filled with five grams each of pentobarbital. Syringes three and six contain saline. Syringes one and two are injected, followed by saline. If the person has not died, syringes four, five and six are used.").

30 *About Colour Blindness*, www.colourblindawareness.org (reporting that color blindness or color vision deficiency (CVD) affects approximately 1 in 12 men—8 percent).

31 Glossip v. Chandler, 2022 WL 1997194, at *7–8 (W.D. Okla. 2022).

32 For a sampling, *see* SARAT, GRUESOME SPECTACLES, *supra* note 4; Michael Radelet, *Examples of Post-Furman Botched Executions*, DEATH PENALTY INFO. CTR (listing sixty of the most well-known botched executions), deathpenaltyinfo.org.

33 Florida Corrections Comm'n, *Supplemental Report—Methods of Execution Used by States* 10 (1997).

34 *See* Expert Declaration of Gail A. Van Norman, M.D., at 37, Roane v. Barr (Nov. 1, 2019), www.fcc.state.fl.us.

35 But also, I'm sure they are genuinely interested in you. *See IV Therapy Tips & Tricks for Nurses*, NURSEBUFF.COM, www.nursebuff.com ("Try to establish a rapport with your patient to make them feel more relaxed. This can help make the veins easier to access. . . . The moment you spot the right vein, start asking the patient random questions like '*What do you do for a living?*' or '*How many kids do you have?*' as a distraction. Insert the IV as the patient answers your questions.") (emphasis in original).

36 *How Not to Blow a Vein: 20 Useful Tips For Nurses*, NURSEBUFF.COM (Jan. 28, 2018), www.nursebuff.com ("Geriatric patients, for example, normally have weak vein walls due to age-related degeneration of connective tissues.").

37 *See* Atul Gawande et al., *Perspective Roundtable: Physicians and Execution*, 358 N. ENGL. J. MED. 448, 449 (2008); *On Lethal Injections and the Death Penalty*, HASTINGS CENTER, at 2 (1982).

38 Liliana Segura, *Cruel and Unusual: A Second Failed Execution in Ohio*, THE INTERCEPT (Nov. 19, 2017).

39 Yes, he actually said that. Jake Bittle, *The Cruel and Unusual Punishment of Doyle Lee Hamm*, THE NATION (Mar. 2, 2018).

40 Liliana Segura, *Another Failed Execution: The Torture of Doyle Lee Ham*, THE INTERCEPT (Mar. 3, 2018), theintercept.com. For one journalist's reaction, *see* Roger Cohen, *Death Penalty Madness in Alabama*, N.Y. TIMES (Feb. 27, 2018) ("That might just qualify, against stiff competition from the highest office in the land, as the dumbest statement of 2018.").

41 Jimmy Jenkins, *Behind the Black Curtain: Republic Reporter Describes "Surreal" Frank Atwood Execution*, ARIZ. REPUBLIC (Jun. 8, 2022).

42 *Id.*

43 @JimmyJenkins, X (Twitter), June 8, 2022, 2:21 p.m., x.com.

44 Jenkins, *supra* note 41.

45 Elizabeth Cohen, *Lethal Injection Creator: Maybe It's Time to Change Formula*, CNN (Apr. 30, 2007), www.cnn.com (quoting Jay Chapman).

46 Melvin Wingersky, *Report of the Royal Commission on Capital Punishment (1949–1953): A Review*, 44 J. CRIM. L. CRIMINOL. POLICE SCI. 695, 714 (1954).

47 In February 2024, Idaho abandoned the execution of Thomas Creech after eight attempts to access his veins using vein finders, hot compresses, and blood-pressure cuffs over the course of nearly an hour. Creech suffers from Type 2 diabetes, hypertension, and edema, and has spent 50 years on death row, making him one of the country's oldest death row prisoners. Austin Sarat, *Another Botched Lethal Injection, Another Official Refusal to Accept Responsibility for Failure in the Execution Process*, VERDICT (March 1, 2024), verdict.justia.com.

48 *See* chapter 1, text preceding note 19.

49 For visuals, see *How to Suture: Ligation and Closure of Bleeding Tissue*, YOUTUBE (Apr. 2, 2020), www.youtube.com; *Chemical Cauterization: Understand Wound Care*, YOUTUBE (Nov. 18, 2022), www.youtube.com.

50 *See* Joel Zivot, *Lethal Injections Are Crueler than Most People Imagine. I've Seen the Evidence Firsthand*, SLATE (Nov. 30, 2022), slate.com. Alabama said that no cutdown occurred, but did not explain the reason for the incision and has fought valiantly against attempts to conduct a limited (and veiled) deposition of the IV team members to determine what happened—thus far successfully.

51 Joseph Wood's execution was discussed in chapter 2, text accompanying note 58.

52 *Clarence Dixon Execution Updates*, ARIZ. REPUBLIC (May 11, 2022).

53 The procedure starts the same as the normal catheterization process—a catheter (which, again, is just a small, thin tube) is inserted into the vein by a needle, which is then removed, leaving the catheter in place. Then a long guide wire is threaded through the catheter, where the needle once was, and deep into the vein. Then the original catheter is removed and a second, longer catheter is fitted over the wire; then the wire is removed, leaving the longer catheter in place. For a visual, *see Femoral Central Line*, YOUTUBE (Mar. 21, 2013), www.youtube.com.

54 Christopher A. Troianos, M.D. et al., *Guidelines for Performing Ultrasound Guided Vascular Cannulation: Recommendations of the American Society of Echocardiography and the Society of Cardiovascular Anesthesiologists* 1291 J. AM. SOC. ECHOCARDIOGR. 1292 (2011); *see also* Expert Declaration of Gail A. Van Norman, M.D., *supra* note 34, at 37 ("Central venous access catheters (CV lines) are, in the words of one author 'relatively dangerous, problem-prone devices'. . . . The overall rate of vascular complications during placement ranges as high as almost 1 in 5. All complications are significantly affected by the experience of the person placing the line.").

55 Troianos, *supra* note 54, at 1292. *See also* Avani R. Patel et al., *Central Line Catheters and Associated Complications: A Review*, 11 CUREUS 4717 (May 22, 2019) (reporting a complication rate of 10 percent for experienced practitioners and 19 percent for inexperienced practitioners).

56 *American Society of Anesthesiologists Task Force on Central Venous Access, Practice Guidelines for Central Venous Access* 541 (Mar. 2012).

57 Troianos, *supra* note 54, at 1292.

58 *Id.* at 1293–94 ("The operator must have an understanding of probe orientation, image display, the physics of ultrasound, and mechanics of image generation. . . . The technique also requires the acquisition of the necessary hand-eye coordination to direct probe and needle manipulation. . . . This skill set must then be paired with manual dexterity to perform the three-dimensional (3D) task of placing a catheter into the target vessel while using and interpreting 2D images."); *id.* (noting that using ultrasound to place a central line in the femoral vein is particularly tricky because "the left side of the screen displaces structures toward the patient's right side. . . . Therefore, screen left and right will not follow standard conventions but rather vary with site and needle insertion orientation.").

59 Expert Declaration of Gail A. Van Norman, M.D., *supra* note 34, at 38; *id.* ("To summarize, placement of a central line for venous access during judicial lethal injection is common, is fraught with potential mechanical complications, and requires personnel experienced and adept in their placement.").

60 Michael Kiefer & Dale Baich, *Poorly Executed: IVs and Ironies*, ARIZ. MIRROR (Apr. 26, 2023).

61 Brief for Respondent at 22, Baze v. Rees, 553 U.S. 35 (2008).

62 Cohen, *supra* note 45.

63 Radelet, *supra* note 32.

64 Ben Crair, *Photos from a Botched Lethal Injection*, NEW REPUBLIC (May 29, 2014).

65 *Id.*

66 *Id.*

67 *Id.*

68 *Id.*

69 For a visual, see Chris Kitching, *Killer's Skin Rips and He "Chokes for Air" in "Worst Botched Execution Ever,"* DAILY MIRROR (Oct. 20, 2019).

70 *Id.*

71 Crair, *supra* note 64.

72 Mike Cason, *Judge Questions Alabama about Problematic Lethal Injections*, AL.COM (Oct. 13, 2022), www.al.com. The state of Alabama did not have an answer to the question.

Here is a good place to note that in the clinical setting, the standard practice is to stop after two attempts to access a vein. *See* INFUSION THERAPY STANDARDS OF PRACTICE at S97 (8th ed. 2021) (standard 34). Shout out to John Lain for regularly donating blood and asking about the number of sticks allowed for a venipuncture on his most recent visit.

73 Lee Hedgepeth, *"Unending Torture": Following Rule Change, Alabama Governor to Decide How Long State Can Attempt Executions*, CBS42.COM (Jan. 13, 2023) www.cbs42.com.

74 Stephen Cooper, *On Slicing and Sticking Condemned Men in Alabama*, MONTGOMERY ADVERTISER (Oct. 31, 2022).

75 Frank Green, *After Delay in Ricky Gray Execution, Department of Corrections Changes Execution Protocol*, RICHMOND TIMES-DISPATCH (March 15, 2017).

76 *Id.*

77 Radelet, *supra* note 32 (quoting final statement of Bennie Demps).

78 Kiefer & Baich, *supra* note 60; *see also* Lopez v. Brewer, 680 F.3d 1084, 1093 (2012) (Pregerson, J., dissenting from denial of rehearing en banc) (discussing coded communications with attorney).

79 Matt Ford, *An Oklahoma Execution Done Wrong*, THE ATLANTIC (Oct. 8, 2015). *See also* chapter 8, text accompanying note 72.

80 Jeremiah Hassel, *Anthony Sanchez's "Botched" Death Row Execution as "Hand Turned Blue" and Nurses "Panicked,"* MIRROR US (Sep. 30, 2023).

81 *Id.*

82 *Id.*

83 *Id.*

84 *Harbison*, 511 F.Supp.2d at 889 (quoting testimony of Dr. David Lubarsky).

85 Caroline Lake & Christina L. Beecroft, *Extravasation Injuries and Accidental Intra-Arterial Injection*, 10 CONTINUING EDUCATION IN ANESTHESIA CRITICAL CARE & PAIN 109, 109 (Aug. 2010).

86 Declaration of Mark Heath, M.D., at 11–12, Cooey v. Strickland, No. 2:04-cv-1156, 2008 WL 8004052 (S.D. Ohio 2010). *See also* Lake & Beecroft, *supra* note 85, at 109 ("Anesthetists become familiar with the anticipated resistance to injection, and an alteration in the perceived pressure required to inject should raise the suspicion of cannula misplacement.").

87 *Baze*, 553 U.S. at 122 (Ginsburg, J., dissenting) ("Kentucky's protocol does not specify the rate at which sodium thiopental should be injected. The executioner, who does not have any medical training, pushes the drug 'by feel' through five feet of tubing.").

88 *See* chapter 1, text accompanying note 31.

89 TROMBLEY, *supra* note 28, at 73.

90 *See* chapter 7, text following note 2.

91 *See supra* text accompanying note 14.

92 *Taylor*, 2006 WL 1779035, at *5.

93 HUMAN RIGHTS WATCH, SO LONG AS THEY DIE: LETHAL INJECTIONS IN THE UNITED STATES 49 (2006) (discussing Joseph Cannon execution).

94 Lake & Beecroft, *supra* note 85, at 109.

95 *See id. See also* Affidavit of Mark Heath, M.D., at 5, Rhoades v. Reinke, 830 F.Supp.2d 1046 (D. Idaho 2011) ("The signs of an infiltrated IV are often very subtle, and can easily be missed by an inexperienced practitioner. Indeed, even a highly experienced practitioner may initially fail to detect an infiltrated IV, although the likelihood of this error occurring is reduced by accrued practice experience.").

96 *Taylor*, 2006 WL 1779035, at *8.

97 *Harbison*, 511 F.Supp.2d at 892; *id.* (noting that with everything else that the executioner was doing, "it is difficult to imagine what level of monitoring actually occurs.").

98 *Morales*, 465 F.Supp.2d at 980–81.

99 *See* chapter 3, text accompanying note 30.

100 *Baze*, 553 U.S. at 60.

101 *Id.* at 121 (Ginsberg, J., dissenting) ("These checks provide a degree of assurance—missing from Kentucky's protocol—that the first drug has been properly administered. They are simple and essentially costless to employ, yet work to lower the risk that the inmate will be subjected to the agony of conscious suffocation caused by pancuronium bromide and the searing pain caused by potassium chloride. The record contains no explanation why Kentucky does not take any of these elementary measures.").

102 Brief of Amicus Curiae of the Criminal Justice Legal Foundation in Support of Respondents, at 27, Baze v. Rees (Dec. 7, 2007).

103 *Baze*, 553 U.S. at 60.

104 Transcript of Direct & Cross Examination of Dr. David Lubarsky, Warner v. Gross, at 29, No. 5:14-cv-00665-F (N.D. Okla. Dec. 23, 2014).

105 Brief for Petitioner, at 18, Baze v. Rees, 553 U.S. 35 (2008) (No. 07-5439).

106 *See* chapter 2, text accompanying note 86.

107 Dave Boucher & Adam Tamburin, *Tennessee Execution: Billy Ray Irick Tortured to Death, Expert Says in New Filing*, THE TENNESSEAN (Sept. 7, 2018) (quoting Dr. David Lubarsky).

108 *Behind the Curtain: Secrecy and the Death Penalty in the United States*, DEATH PENALTY INFO. CTR. at 55 (Nov. 20, 2018). Florida officials later stated that taping was necessary to ensure that prisoners did not flash gang signs or make obscene gestures during their executions, but there was no evidence that this was happening, and the state's rationale was even more suspect when after Happ's problematic execution, Florida started "tenting" the sheet over prisoners, rather than lying the sheet flat across their body, preventing witnesses from seeing body movements. *Id.*

109 Transcript of Oral Argument at 16, Baze v. Rees, 553 U.S. 35 (2008).

110 Melissa Brown & Josh Keefe, *Who Executes Tennessee's Death Row Inmates? Court Records Provide a Rare Glimpse—in Their Own Words*, THE TENNESSEAN, May 25, 2022.

111 Jimmy Jenkins et al., *In Murray Hooper Execution, Arizona Struggles with Lethal Injection for 3rd Time*, ARIZ. REPUBLIC (Nov. 16, 2022).

5. INEPT EXECUTIONERS

1 John E. Dannenberg, *Executioner Banned in Missouri but Available for Hire Elsewhere*, PRISON LEGAL NEWS (May 15, 2009); www.prisonlegalnews.org.

2 *See* chapter 4, text accompanying notes 13–14.

3 Taylor v. Crawford, No. 05-4173-CV-C-FJG, 2006 WL 1779035 (W.D. Mo. 2006), at *5.

4 Dannenberg, *supra* note 1.

5 Taylor v. Crawford, 487 F.3d 1072, 1077 (8th Cir. 2007).

6 *Taylor*, 2006 WL 1779035, at *7.

7 *Taylor*, 487 F.3d at 1077 n.3 ("In a post-oral argument submission, the State informed our court that it was no longer its intention to utilize the services of Dr. Doe I.").

8 Jeremy Kohler, *Lake Hospital's Letters Deal Crucial Blow to Credibility of Execution Doctor*, ST. LOUIS POST-DISPATCH (Jan. 20, 2008). For more about Doerhoff's misadventures, *see id.*; John E. Dannenberg, *Missouri Execution Nurse, Doctor Have Questionable Histories*, PRISON LEGAL NEWS (July 15, 2008), www.lakeexpo.com.

9 Mo. Rev. Stat. §546.720 (2007).

10 Deron Lee, *The First Amendment vs. Death Penalty Secrecy Laws*, COLUMBIA JOURNALISM REV. (Mar. 7, 2014) www.cjr.org (quoting Anthony Rothert, legal director of the Missouri ACLU); Katie Moore, *Where Does Missouri Get the Drugs It Uses to Execute Prisoners? The Supplier Is a Secret*, KANSAS CITY STAR (June 12, 2024) (also quoting Rothert).

11 Kohler, *supra* note 8.

12 Brief for Amici Curiae Michael Morales, Michael Taylor, Vernon Evans Jr., and John Gary Hardwick Jr., in Support of Petitioners at 16, Baze v. Rees, 553 U.S. 35 (2008).

13 *AP Interview: Doctor behind Executions Speaks Out*, NEWSCHANNEL10.COM (Aug. 15, 2008), www.newschannel10.com.

14 For the story of how Doerhoff's involvement in Arizona's execution was discovered, *see* Michael Kiefer and Dale Baich, *Poorly Executed: How Arizona Has Failed at Carrying Out the Death Penalty*, ARIZ. MIRROR (Apr. 24, 2023).

15 Dickens v. Brewer, No. CV07–1770–PHX–NVW, 2009 WL 1904294 *16 n.6 (D. Ariz. 2009).

16 *Id.* at *23.

17 West v. Brewer, No. CV–11–1409–PHX–NVW, 2011 WL 6724628 *6 (D. Ariz. 2011).

18 *Id.* at *7.

19 Morales v. Tilton, 465 F.Supp.2d 972, 979 (N.D. Cal. 2006).

20 *Id.*; Elizabeth Weil, *The Needle and the Damage Done*, N.Y. TIMES (Feb. 11, 2007).

21 *Morales*, 465 F.Supp.2d at 980.

22 *Id.* at 979 n.9.

23 Jeremy Kohler, *Execution Nurse Had Criminal Past*, ST. LOUIS POST-DISPATCH (Jan. 12, 2008) at A1.

24 *Id.*

25 *Id.*

26 Stephanie Mencimer, *State Executioners: Untrained, Incompetent, and "Complete Idiots,"* MOTHER JONES (May 7, 2014).

27 Harbison v. Little, 511 F.Supp.2d 872, 887–88 (M.D. Tenn. 2007). The warden also testified that he did not conduct background checks on his executioners. *Id.* at n.14.

28 Melissa Brown & Josh Keefe, *Who Executes Tennessee's Death Row Inmates? Court Records Provide a Rare Glimpse—and in Their Own Words*, THE TENNESSEAN (Mar. 25, 2022).

29 Elizabeth Bruenig, *Alabama Wants to Kill Jimi Barber*, THE ATLANTIC (Jul. 17, 2023).

30 Stephanie Mencimer, *Autopsy Shows Just How Royally Oklahoma Screwed Up Clayton Lockett's Execution*, MOTHER JONES (Jun. 13, 2014).

31 Austin Sarat, *A State with One of the Highest Execution Rates Considers a Moratorium*, SLATE (Oct. 12, 2023), slate.com.

32 For state protocols, *see State-By-State Execution Protocols*, DEATH PENALTY INFO. CTR., deathpenaltyinfo.org. For an example of nonmedical prison personnel attempting to place a catheter, see Jürgen Martschukat, *"No Improvement Over Electrocution or Even a Bullet"—Lethal Injection and the Meaning of Speed and Reliability in the Modern Execution Process, in* THE ROAD TO ABOLITION? THE FUTURE OF CAPITAL PUNISHMENT IN THE UNITED STATES 252, 265 (Charles J. Ogletree, Jr., and Austin Sarat, eds. 2009) ("On top of that, an obviously medically inexperienced prison employee, who had volunteered to handle the needle, had difficulties in finding Charles Brooks's veins, and the blood splattering on the sheet indicated barbarity and a highly unprofessional handling of the execution."); Jim Edwards, *New Jersey's Long Waltz with Death*, N.J. L.J. (Nov. 25, 2002) ("In Virginia, prisons were using corrections officers to insert needles, [an insider] added.").

33 *See State-By-State Execution Protocols*, *supra* note 32.

34 Baze v. Rees, 553 U.S. 35 (2008).

35 Oral Argument *27–28, Baze v. Rees, 553 U.S. 35 (2008).

36 *Baze*, 553 U.S. at 55.

37 Jocelyn Blore, *Becoming a Phlebotomist: Accredited Programs, Certification and Salary*, MEDICAL TECHNOLOGY SCHOOLS (Dec. 12, 2023), www.medicaltechnologyschools.com ("Education programs can take from as little as eight weeks to less than a year to finish depending upon the school type, and program students enroll in. . . . Certification is required in only a few states, so it is possible to be working as a phlebotomist in less than a year, particularly when a student enrolls in one of the quicker-paced programs.").

38 *Plebotomy Training and Career Guide: What Does a Phlebotomist Do Anyway?*, phlebotomytraining.careers/.

39 Declaration of Mark Heath, M.D., at 8(i), Cooey v. Strickland, No. 04CV01156, 2009 WL 6686344 (S.D. Ohio Dec. 2, 2009).

40 Nat'l Ass'n of State EMS Officials, *National EMS Scope of Practice Model 2019: Including Change Notices 1.0 and 2.0 (Report No. DOT HS 813, 151)*, NAT'L HIGHWAY TRAFFIC SAFETY ADMIN. (Aug. 2021), at 4, 28, www.ems.gov/.

41 *See Plebotomy Training and Career Guide*, *supra* note 38 ("In some less common instances, a phlebotomist needs to insert a catheter into an artery or pull arterial blood, though this is usually done in a hospital setting.").

42 *Harbison*, 511 F.Supp.2d at 887.

43 *See* text accompanying *supra* note 40.

44 *How Long Does It Take to Become an EMT? (And Other FAQs)*, INDEED (Mar. 20, 2023), www.indeed.com.

45 *How Long Does It Take to Become a Paramedic? (And More FAQs)*, INDEED (Mar. 3, 2023), www.indeed.com.

46 Declaration of Mark Heath, M.D., *supra* note 39, at 8(j).

47 *Harbison*, 511 F.Supp.2d at 879 (quoting Dr. Mark Dershwitz).

48 *See id.* (noting that the Tennessee Commissioner of Corrections was advised to use executioners who perform the same medical tasks as part of their day job "but conceded that no one who performs these tasks under the new protocol has this experience or these qualifications.").

49 Weil, *supra* note 20.

50 Ty Alper, *Capital Cases: Lethal Incompetence*, 30 CHAMPION MAG. 41, 42 (2006).

51 Transcript of Recorded Interview of Paramedic/Emergency Medical Technician, Okla. Dep't Pub. Safety, The Execution of Clayton D. Lockett (on file with author) ("Question: So could pushing the drug too fast cause [the vein to collapse] or could it cause an IV to back out? Answer: I don't know.").

52 Brief for Amici Curiae Michael Morales, Michael Taylor, Vernon Evans Jr., and John Gary Hardwick Jr., in Support of Petitioners, at 30, Baze v. Rees, 553 U.S. 35 (2008) ("What is particularly disturbing about the California evidence is that execution personnel recorded the vital signs, but were insufficiently trained in anesthesia to recognize the significance of their observations.").

53 Kohler, *supra* note 8.

54 *See* Weil, *supra* note 20.

55 *See* chapter 4, text accompanying note 45.

56 Joel Zivot, *Lethal Injections Are Crueler than Most People Imagine. I've Seen the Evidence Firsthand*, SLATE (Nov. 30, 2022), slate.com (discussing expertise necessary to access a central vein, which cannot be seen or felt, and the danger of puncturing other vessels and/or organs); *id.* ("In a cutdown, the skin is opened with a surgical blade to visualize a vein not otherwise identifiable. Such an act is not in the skill set of an average person and is likely beyond the capabilities of a nurse or an EMT—it requires the skill of a doctor. Cutdowns are rarely used now in a medical setting, as ultrasound—the use of sound waves transmitted through the skin and reflected—has replaced this procedure. A cutdown is within the skill set of an older and experienced doctor."); Mark

Heath, M.D., *US Must End the Use of Paralytic Drugs When Executing Prisoners*, THE GUARDIAN (Jan. 14, 2015) ("Only a subset of physicians—typically intensive care doctors, invasive cardiologists, surgeons, and anesthesiologists—are experienced and proficient in obtaining central intravenous access.").

57 Cary Aspinwall & Ziva Branstetter, *Execution of Clayton Lockett Described as "A Bloody Mess," Court Filing Shows*, TULSA WORLD (Dec. 14, 2014) (quoting Dr. Mark Dershwitz).

58 *Morales*, 465 F.Supp.2d at 979. For a detailed discussion, see Howard Mintz, *San Quentin Execution Team Members Say They Get Little Lethal Injection Training*, EAST BAY TIMES (Nov. 27, 2006).

59 Brief for Amici Curiae Michael Morales, Michael Taylor, Vernon Evans Jr., and John Gary Hardwick Jr., *supra* note 52, at 11.

60 Litigation in Tennessee revealed that the execution team member with the most experience mixing lethal injection drugs learned by watching an executioner do it in Texas. *Harbison*, 511 F.Supp.2d at 897. And a Governor's Commission in Florida convened to study the grossly botched execution of Ángel Díaz cited "failure of the training of the execution team members" as a primary reason for that fiasco. *See The Governor's Comm'n on the Admin. of Lethal Injection* 8 (Mar. 1, 2007), www.floridacapitalcases.state.fl.us; *see also* Weil, *supra* note 20 (discussing "alarming problems with an incompetent execution team" in Missouri, Alabama, California, and Florida).

61 Gavin Lee, *A Painless Cocktail? The Lethal Injection Controversy, in* DEATH PENALTY TODAY 93, 108 (Robert M. Bohm, ed. 2008) (quoting Jay Chapman).

62 Interim Report No. 14 at 105, in the Matter of the Multicounty Grand Jury, State of Okla., Nos. SCAD-2014-70, GJ-2014-1 (May 19, 2016), deathpenaltyinfo.org.

63 Savannah Kumar, *Documents Reveal Confusion and Lack of Training in Texas Execution*, ACLU NEWS AND COMMENTARY (Apr. 21, 2022), www.aclu.org.

64 *Id.*

65 *Id.*

66 *Id.*

67 *Id.*

68 Butler Snow LLP, *Tenn. Lethal Injection Protocol Investigation: Report and Findings* (Dec. 13, 2022), ewscripps.brightspotcdn.com.

69 *Id.* at 38–39.

70 *See* Trial Transcript at 120–121, Evans v. Saar, 412 F.Supp.2d 519 (D. Md. 2006).

71 *See Morales*, 465 F.Supp.2d at 979 (finding that execution team members "almost uniformly have no knowledge of the nature or properties of the drugs that are used.").

72 *See* Trial Transcript, *supra* note 70, at 120–21 (testimony of executioner that second drug will "numb the body" rather than paralyze it); Brief for Petitioners at 8, Baze v. Rees, 553 U.S. 35 (2008) (testimony of warden overseeing executions in

Kentucky that he didn't know that when the paralytic is administered, the inmate could still feel pain).

73 *See* chapter 1, text following note 17.

74 *See* chapter 1, text preceding note 26.

75 Weil, *supra* note 20.

76 Isaac Willour, *America's Changing Death Penalty Debate*, THE DISPATCH (Feb. 25, 2023).

77 Transcript of Recorded Interview of Warden Anita Trammell, Okla. Dep't Pub. Safety, The Execution of Clayton D. Lockett (on file with author).

78 *Harbison*, 511 F.Supp.2d at 891. *See also The Governor's Comm'n on the Admin. of Lethal Injection, supra* note 60, at 8 ("The protocols as written are insufficient to properly carry out an execution when complications arise," noting "failure of the training to provide adequate guidelines when complications occur."). *Id.* ("There was a failure of leadership as to how to proceed when a complication arose in the execution process.").

79 *Morales*, 465 F. Supp. 2d at 979.

80 Leonidas Koniaris et al., *Can Lethal Injection for Execution Really be "Fixed"?*, 369 THE LANCET 352, 352–53 (2007).

6. THE DRUG SUPPLIER SAGA

1 Tom Dart, *Arizona Unveils New Death Penalty Plan: Bring Your Own Lethal Injection Drugs*, THE GUARDIAN (Feb. 15, 2017).

2 *Id.*

3 Emma Marris, *Death-Row Drug Dilemma*, NATURE (Jan. 27, 2011).

4 Press Release, Hospira, Inc., Hospira Statement Regarding Pentothal (Sodium Thiopental) Market Exit (Jan. 21, 2011) (on file with author).

5 Jim Edwards, *Drug Company? Driving School? It's All the Same in the Lethal Injection Business*, CBS NEWS (Jan. 6, 2011). www.cbsnews.com. A picture speaks a thousand words. For the visual, see Kathy Lohr, *Georgia May Have Broken Law by Importing Drug*, NAT'L PUB. RADIO (March 17, 2011), www.npr.org.

6 Michael Kiefer & Dale Baich, *Poorly Executed: The "Golden Age of Executions" Comes to an End*, ARIZ. MIRROR (Apr. 25, 2023).

7 *See* Marris, *supra* note 3.

8 Juliette Jowit, *UK to Ban Export of Drug Approved for Use in US Executions*, THE GUARDIAN, (July 10, 2012).

9 Comm'n Implementing Reg. 1252/2011 of Dec. 20, 2011, amending Council Regulation (EC) No. 1236/2005 of June 27, 2005, Concerning Trade in Certain Goods Which Could Be Used for Capital Punishment, Torture, or Other Cruel, Inhuman or Degrading Treatment or Punishment, Art. 12(2) (criteria for granting export authorizations).

10 Press Release, European Comm'n, Comm'n Extends Control Over Goods Which Could Be Used for Capital Punishment or Torture (Dec. 20, 2011), ec.europa.eu.

11 *Europe's Moral Stand Has U.S. States Running Out of Execution Drugs, Complicating Capital Punishment*, CBS NEWS (Feb. 18, 2014); www.cbsnews.com; *see also* Council Regulation No. 1236/2005 of June 27, 2005, *supra* note 9 (2005 export ban).

12 *Lacking Lethal Injection Drugs, States Find Untested Backups*, NAT'L PUB. RADIO (Oct. 26, 2013), www.npr.org.

13 Jim Salter, *Doctors: US Execution Plan Jeopardizing Hospitals*, ASSOC. PRESS (Sept. 30, 2013).

14 *Europe's Moral Stand Has U.S. States Running out of Execution Drugs*, *supra* note 11.

15 Brief of Amicus Curiae of the Criminal Justice Legal Foundation in Support of Respondents at 5, Glossip v. Gross, 576 U.S. 863 (2015).

16 The United States currently has over thirty trade sanctions programs in effect against other countries. *See Sanctions Programs and Country Information*, U.S. DEP'T OF TREASURY, www.treasury.gov.

17 U.N. Secretary General, Moratorium on the Use of the Death Penalty, ¶ 7, U.N. Doc. A/69/288 (Aug. 8, 2014) ("Approximately 160 of the 193 Member States of the United Nations have abolished the death penalty or introduced moratoriums, either in law or practice.").

18 *See What We Want*, ALLIANCE FOR TORTURE-FREE TRADE, www.torture-freetrade.org.

19 James Gibson & Corinna Barrett Lain, *Death Penalty Drugs and the International Moral Marketplace*, 103 GEO. L.J. 1215, 1222 (2015).

20 Kiefer & Baich, *supra* note 6.

21 Michael Graczyk & Alanna Durkin, *Texas Gives Virginia Lethal Drug for Execution Next Week*, ASSOC. PRESS (Sept. 25, 2015), apnews.com.

22 Marris, *supra* note 3.

23 Rob Stein, *Ohio Executes Inmate Using New, Single-Drug Method for Death Penalty*, WASH. POST (Mar. 11, 2011).

24 *See, e.g.,* Letter from Staffan Schüberg, President, Lundbeck Inc., to Gary C. Mohr, Dir., Ohio Dep't of Rehab. & Corr., files.deathpenaltyinfo.org.

25 Press Release, Lundbeck, Lundbeck Overhauls Pentobarbital Distribution Program to Restrict Misuse (Jul. 1, 2011), investor.lundbeck.com.

26 For a listing, see Lethal Injection Information Center, Controlled Medicines, lethalinjectioninfo.org.

27 *Advertising Slogans and Taglines of Pfizer*, SLOGANLIST, www.sloganlist.com.

28 Matt Ford, *Pfizer v. Lethal Injections*, THE ATLANTIC (May 13, 2016).

29 Erik Eckholm, *Pfizer Blocks the Use of Its Drugs in Executions*, N.Y. TIMES (May 13, 2016).

30 Mary D. Fan, *The Supply-Side Attack on Lethal Injection and the Rise of Execution Secrecy*, 95 B.U. L. REV. 427, 441 (2015) (quoting lawyer for Texas Department of Criminal Justice).

31 Indeed, SLIP appears to have morphed into the Lethal Injection Information Center, "a hub for manufacturers, distributors, and stakeholders interested in preventing the misuse of medicines in lethal injections." lethalinjectioninfo.org/.

32 Lethal Injection Information Center, Industry Statements, lethalinjectioninfo.org/ (Abbott Laboratories, December 2001: "Abbott does not support the use of Pentothal [sodium thiopental] in capital punishment. In fact, [we] communicated with departments of corrections in the United States to request that this product not be used in capital punishment procedures.").

33 Eckholm, *supra* note 29.

34 Mylan has since fallen into line. *See Drug Maker Mylan Takes $70 Million Hit in Battle over Lethal Injection*, NBC NEWS (Oct. 21, 2014), www.nbcnews.com.

35 Brenda Goodman, *Judge Allows Device to Be Used for Monitoring Lethal Injection*, N.Y. TIMES (Apr. 18, 2006).

36 Lauren Gill & Daniel Moritz-Rabson, *Companies Already Ban the Use of Their Drugs for Lethal Injection. Now They're Blocking IV Equipment*, THE INTERCEPT (Sept. 14, 2023), theintercept.com.

37 Letter from Marcelo Fioranelli, Airgas CEO, Re: Executions Using Nitrogen Hypoxia (Jan. 5, 2023); *see also Airgas Will Not Supply Nitrogen for Executions*, EQUAL JUST. INITIATIVE (Jan. 27, 2023), eji.org.

38 Ed Pilkington, *Three Top Nitrogen Gas Manufacturers in US Bar Products from Use in Executions*, THE GUARDIAN (Mar. 10, 2024).

39 West v. Brewer, No. CV-11–1409-PHX-NVW 2011, 2011 WL 6724628, at *9 (Dist. Az. Dec. 21, 2011).

40 *Id.*

41 *Id.*

42 *Id.*

43 Kiefer & Baich, *supra* note 6.

44 *West v. Brewer*, 2011 WL 6724628, at *9.

45 Beaty v. Food and Drug Admin., 853 F.Supp. 2d 30, 35 (2012).

46 West v. Brewer, 2011 WL 6724628, at *9.

47 *Id.*

48 *See* chapter 2, text accompanying note 102 (discussing Heckler v. Chaney, 470 U.S. 821 (1985)).

49 21 U.S.C. § 381(a) (2018) (emphasis added).

50 *Beaty*, 853 F.Supp.2d at 34 (emphasis in original).

51 *Id.* at 43.

52 Cook v. Food and Drug Admin., 733 F.3d 1, 12 (D.C. Cir. 2013). *Cook* and *Beaty* are the same case—the case was restyled as Cook following the execution of the named plaintiff in *Beaty*.

53 That shipment was being delivered by FedEx, and FedEx's policy is to notify federal agencies in advance whenever shipping drugs internationally, so when FedEx learned that the drugs were not authorized for entry into the United States,

it returned the shipment to its sender. Chris McDaniel and Tasneem Nashrulla, *This Is the Man in India Who Is Selling States Illegally Imported Execution Drugs*, BUZZFEED NEWS (Oct. 20, 2015); Tasneem Nashrulla, Chris McDaniel, and Chris Geidner, *Three States Bought Illegal Execution Drugs from Supplier in India*, BUZZFEED NEWS (Oct. 23, 2015) www.buzzfeednews.com.

54 McDaniel and Nashrulla, *supra* note 53; Nashrulla, McDaniel, and Geidner, *supra* note 53; Joe Duggan, *Out $54,400 for Lethal Injection Drugs, Nebraska Wants Its Money Back*, OMAHA WORLD-HERALD (Dec. 11, 2015).

55 Letter from Todd W. Cato, FDA to Texas DOC Representative, at 18 (Apr. 20, 2017), www.fda.gov.

56 Gabrielle Banks, *Texas Prison System Sues Over Execution Drugs Seized by FDA*, HOUSTON CHRONICLE (Jan. 9, 2018).

57 Chris McDaniel, *Texas's Illegal Execution Drugs from India Have Expired. It Plans To Buy More*, BUZZFEED NEWS (June 29, 2017), www.buzzfeednews.com.

58 McDaniel and Nashrulla, *supra* note 53.

59 *Id.*

60 *Id.*

61 *Id.*

62 *Id.*

63 Chris McDaniel and Tasneem Nashrulla, *Texas Almost Bought Execution Drugs from 5 Men from India Who Were Accused of Selling Illegal Party Pills*, BUZZFEED NEWS (Jan. 26, 2017).

64 McDaniel and Nashrulla, *supra* note 53.

65 *Beaty*, 853 F.Supp2d at 42 n.8.

66 *Id.*

67 Prashant Yadav et al., *When Gov't Agencies Turn to Unregulated Drug Sources: Implications for the Drug Supply Chain and Public Health Are Grave*, 58 J. AM. PHARM. ASSOC. 477, 479 (2018). *See also* Patricia J. Zettler & Seemah K. Shah, *Broader Implications of Eliminating FDA Jurisdiction Over Execution Drugs*, 111 AM. J. PUB. HEALTH 1764 (Oct. 2021) (expressing similar concerns).

68 21 U.S.C. § 381(a) (2018).

69 *See Whether the Food and Drug Admin. Has Jurisdiction Over Articles Intended for Use in Lawful Executions* 43 OP. O.L.C. 1 (May 3, 2019), www.justice.gov (signed by Assistant Attorney General Steven A. Engel) [hereinafter "OLC Opinion"].

70 *Id.* at 1–2.

71 21 U.S.C. § 321(g)(1)(2018).

72 *See Thiopental CIII*, U.S. PHARMACOEPIA, store.usp.org; *Thiopental: Compound Summary*, U.S. NAT'L LIBRARY OF MED., pubchem.ncbi.nlm.nih.gov.

73 The OLC concedes this, but says that doesn't stop an agency from changing its mind. *See* OLC Opinion, *supra* note 69, at 22.

74 Memorandum for Attorneys of the Office, Best Practices for OLC Legal Advice and Written Opinions, O.L.C. (May 16, 2005) ("[S]ubject to the President's authority under the Constitution, OLC opinions are controlling on questions of law within the Executive Branch").

75 *See, e.g.,* Trevor W. Morrison, *Stare Decisis in the Office of Legal Counsel,* 110 COLUM. L. REV. 1448, 1464 (2010); Peter L. Strauss, *Overseer or "The Decider"? The President in Administrative Law,* 75 GEO. WASH. L. REV. 696, 739-741 (2007).

76 *See* Office of Legal Counsel, Opinions, www.justice.gov ("Under the Judiciary Act of 1789, the Attorney General was authorized to render opinions on questions of law when requested by the President and the heads of Executive Branch departments. This authority is now codified at 28 U.S.C. §§ 511–513.").

77 Laurie McGinley & Mark Berman, *Justice Department says FDA "Lacks Jurisdiction" over Death-Penalty Drugs,* WASH. POST (May 14, 2019).

78 Dustin Volz & National Journal, *No Drugs, No Executions: Is This Really the End of the Death Penalty?,* THE ATLANTIC (Oct. 28, 2013) (quoting Arkansas attorney general); *See also* William Wan & Mark Berman, *States to Try New Ways of Executing Prisoners. Their Latest Idea? Opioids,* WASH. POST (Dec. 9, 2017) (quoting Kent Scheidegger of the Criminal Justice Legal Foundation saying that compounding pharmacies are a "less than optimal" solution).

79 Kevin Fixler, *Cash Buys, Private Flights, Changing Rules: How Idaho Hides From Execution Oversight,* IDAHO CAPITAL SUN (Jan. 16, 2022).

80 *Compounding and the FDA: Questions and Answers,* U.S. FOOD AND DRUG ADMIN., www.fda.gov.

81 *Consumer and Health Care Professional Information,* U.S. FOOD AND DRUG ADMIN., www.fda.gov; *see also Deaths from Intravenous Colchicine Resulting from a Compounding Pharmacy Error—Oregon and Washington, 2007,* CTR. FOR DISEASE CONTROL & PREVENTION (Oct. 12, 2007); www.cdc.gov (reporting on deaths from compounded IV drug colchicine and the practices that led to them, concluding "these deaths underscore the potentially fatal ramifications of errors by compounding pharmacies, which generally are not subject to the same oversight and manufacturing practices as pharmaceutical manufacturers.").

82 Lincoln Caplan, *The End of the Open Market for Lethal-Injection Drugs,* NEW YORKER (May 21, 2016) ("state oversight [of compounding pharmacies] has been scandalously lax").

83 Edward J. Markey et al., *State of Disarray, How State's Inability to Oversee Compounding Pharmacies Puts Pub. Health at Risk,* HOMELAND SECURITY DIGITAL LIBR. (Apr. 15, 2013), www.markey.senate.gov; *see also* Press Release, Office of Congressman Edward Markey, Compounding Pharmacies Going Untracked, Unregulated, Under-inspected from Coast to Coast (Apr. 12, 2013), www.markey.senate.gov.

84 Markey et al., *supra* note 83, at 3–4.

85 *FDA Report Limited FDA Survey of Compounded Products,* U.S. FOOD & DRUG ADMIN., www.fda.gov.

86 *Id.* (reporting FDA sample that found 34 percent failure rate among compounded drugs); Jennifer Gudeman et al., *Potential Risks of Pharmacy Compounding*, 13 DRUGS R.D. 1, 4 (2013) (reporting Missouri study that found failure rates ranging from 11.6–25 percent, Ohio study finding over 1300 contaminated compounded products, and Texas study that found overall failure rate of compounded drugs of 23 percent).

87 *See generally* Mark G. Klang, *Sterile Preparation Formulation, in* COMPOUNDING STERILE PREPARATIONS 51 (2018) ("This chapter will provide insight into the issues of formulation when applied to compounding sterile preparations. The majority of options discussed in this chapter will involve high-risk compounding.").

88 *Compounding and the FDA: Questions and Answers, supra* note 80.

89 Gudeman et al., *supra* note 86, at 3.

90 Drug Quality and Security Act, Pub. L. No. 113–54, 127 Stat. 587 (2013).

91 Although many states have revised their compounding pharmacy statutes in recent years, they too have focused on nontraditional compounding pharmacies, often revising their statutes to align with the DQSA. It's fair to say that only a handful of states have actually tightened their regulation of traditional compounding pharmacies since the DQSA, so what Congress reported in 2013—that compounding pharmacies were "largely untracked, unregulated and under-inspected"—remains the case today. For a listing of state compounding pharmacy legislation, see *Compounding Pharmacies*, NAT'L CONF. STATE LEGIS., www.ncsl.org.

92 Deborah W. Denno, *Lethal Injection Chaos Post-Baze*, 102 GEO. L. J. 1331, 1366 (2014) ("Further, compounding pharmacies by their very nature run counter to the requirements of *Baze* because the practices they engage in already pose a substantial risk.").

93 Baze v. Rees, 553 U.S. 35, 53 (2008).

94 *See* U.S. Pharmacopeia (USP) Chapter <797> (2022), www.usp.org (describing low-risk, medium-risk, and high-risk sterile compounding preparation, and renaming these as categories 1-3).

95 *See, e.g.*, Garcia v. Collier, 744 Fed. Appx. 231, 232 (5th Cir. 2018) ("using pentobarbital obtained from a compounding pharmacy does not implicate the Eighth Amendment."); Zink v. Lombardi, 783 F.3d 1089, 1102 (2015) (rejecting Eighth Amendment challenge where prisoners relied on "general risks associated with compounding pharmacies").

96 Brief of Amici Curiae Pharmacy, Medicine, and Health Policy Experts in Support of Petitioner at 19–20, Bucklew v. Precythe, 587 U.S. 119 (2019).

97 The reveal came from a late-night talk show. *See Capital Punishment in the United States: Last Week Tonight with John Oliver*, Season 11, Episode 7, aired April 7, 2024, www.scrapsfromtheloft.com. The company denied this, but two other sources confirmed the truth of the story when it broke, with one saying: "They basically bragged about how they built this little home market." Lauren Gill & Daniel Moritz-Rabson, *"Little Home Market": The Connecticut Company Accused of Fueling an Execution Spree*, THE INTERCEPT (April 25, 2024), theintercept. com.

98 Saud Anwar and Joshua Elliott, *No Profit Is Worth A Life*, CONN. INSIDER (April 25, 2024).

99 Lauren Gill & Daniel Moritz-Rabson, *Company Linked to Federal Execution Spree Says It No Longer Produces Key Drug*, THE INTERCEPT (June 22, 2024), theintercept.com. Absolute Standards may not have a choice in the matter. Connecticut has abolished the death penalty, and lawmakers say that the state's businesses have no business supporting the death penalty in other states, drafting a bill to "prevent any Connecticut-based corporation from supplying drugs or other tools for executions." Austin Sarat, *Connecticut May Have Figured Out a Way to Halt Executions in Texas*, SLATE (June 26, 2024), slate.com.

100 Decl. of Larry D. Sasich, Jordan v. Fisher, No. 3:15-cv-00295-HTW-LRA (S.D. Miss., filed June 3, 2015); Brief of Amici Curiae Pharmacy, Medicine, and Health Policy Experts, *supra* note 96, at 19-20 ("To reiterate the obvious, illicit supply channels involve risks that drug products may be substandard, counterfeit or contaminated.").

101 *Compounding from Unapproved (Bulk) Substances in Food Animals*, AM. VETERINARY MED. ASS'N (2023), www.avma.org.

102 Press Release, Am. Pharmacists Ass'n, APhA House of Delegates Adopts Policy Discouraging Participation in Execution (Mar. 30, 2015), www.pharmacytimes. com; Press Release, Int'l Academy of Compounding Pharmacists, IACP Adopts Position on Compounding of Lethal Injection Drugs (Mar. 24, 2015), www. pharmacytimes.com; Am. Society of Health System Pharmacists, ASHP Adopts Policy Opposing Pharmacist Participation in Capital Punishment (Jun. 9, 2015), dpic-cdn.org.

103 Press Release, Am. Pharmacists Ass'n, *supra* note 102.

104 Ed Pilkington, *Georgia Rushes through Executions before Lethal Injection Drugs Expire*, THE GUARDIAN (Feb. 22, 2013).

105 Whitaker v. Livingston, No. 4:13-cv-02901, Plaintiff's Original Complaint (S.D. Tex. filed Oct. 1, 2013). *See* Eric Nicholson, *Texas, Fresh out of Pentobarbital, Begins Experimenting with Execution Drugs*, DALLAS OBSERVER (Oct. 2, 2013) (reporting on lawsuit); Letter from Maurie Levin to the Honorable Eric H. Holder, Attorney General (Mar. 30, 2011), standdown.typepad.com (attorney's letter to U.S. Attorney General reporting incident).

106 Ross Levitt & Deborah Feyerick, *Death Penalty States Scramble for Lethal Injection Drugs*, CNN (Nov. 16, 2013), www.cnn.com.

107 Fixler, *supra* note 79.

108 *Id.*

109 *Id.*

110 *Id.*

111 *See* Collin Reischman, *DOC Hearing Shows Legislative Action on Executions Likely*, MO. TIMES (Feb. 10, 2014); Chris McDaniel, *Pharmacy That Mixed Execution Drugs Is Being Sold after Admitting Numerous Violations*, BUZZFEED NEWS (April 21, 2016).

112 *See* 21 CFR § 1306.11 (2010); *Controlled Substance Guidelines for Missouri Practitioners*, MO. DEP'T OF HEALTH & SENIOR SERVICES, at 12, health. mo.gov. *See also* Ed Pilkington, *Tulsa Pharmacy Faces Questions Over Lethal Drug to Be Used in Execution*, THE GUARDIAN (Jan. 28, 2014).

113 McDaniel, *supra* note 111.

114 Chris McDaniel, *Missouri Fought for Years to Hide Where It Got Its Execution Drugs, Now We Know What They Were Hiding*, BUZZFEED NEWS (Feb. 20, 2018).

115 *Id.*

116 *Id.*

117 *Id.*

118 *Id.*

119 *Id.* In a sworn deposition, the Missouri DOC general counsel was asked: "Did you make inquiry as to whether any professional complaints had been filed against [Foundation Care]?" Counsel's response: "Yes." "And were there any?" he was then asked. He declined to answer. *Id.* Suffice it to say, if he made the inquiry, he knew the answer.

120 Samantha Liss, *Centene Says Subsidiary Will No Longer Provide Drugs for Missouri Executions*, ST. LOUIS POST-DISPATCH (Feb. 20, 2018).

121 Keri Blakinger, *"Struggling with It Ever Since": Former Texas Lethal Injection Drug Supplier Speaks Out*, HOUSTON CHRONICLE (May 3, 2019); Chris McDaniel, *Inmates Said the Drug Burned as They Died. This Is How Texas Gets Its Execution Drugs.*, BUZZFEED NEWS (Nov. 28, 2018).

122 McDaniel, *supra* note 121.

123 Chiara Eisner, *Unmarked Cars and Secret Orders: How a Pharmacy Prepared Drugs for Texas' Executions*, NAT'L PUB. RADIO (July 10, 2024), www.npr.org.

124 Melissa Brown and Josh Keefe, *Who Executes Tennessee's Death Row Inmates? Court Records Provide a True Glimpse—and in Their Own Words*, THE TENNESSEAN (May 25, 2022).

125 *Id.*

126 The Idaho DOC denies that the exchange was made in a Walmart parking lot, calling the claim "absurd and false." But flight records show that the plane did not arrive at the airport until 5:15 p.m., and the pharmacy's hours of operation end at 5:30 p.m., so the pharmacy would have been closed and there is in fact a Walmart parking lot near the pharmacy. Also, it's just hard to fathom making a drug purchase with $15,000 cash by just walking up to the counter. So who knows what actually happened, but it tracks. *See* Kevin Fixler, *Idaho Found Lethal Injection Drugs for an Execution. Here's How Much They Cost Taxpayers*, IDAHO STATESMAN (Dec. 15, 2023).

127 Fixler, *supra* note 79.

128 Alan Blinder, *Georgia Postpones 2 Executions, Citing "Cloudy" Drug*, N.Y. TIMES (Mar. 3, 2015).

129 Chris McDaniel, *Georgia Says "Cloudy" Execution Drug Was Just Too Cold, But Expert Gave a Second Possible Cause*, BUZZFEED NEWS (May 11, 2015).

130 *State-By-State Execution Protocols*, DEATH PENALTY INFO. CTR., deathpenalty-info.org.

131 *See* chapter 2, text accompanying note 86.

132 *See* Butler Snow LLP, Tenn. Lethal Injection Protocol Investigation: Report and Findings, at 23 (Dec. 13, 2022), ewscripps.brightspotcdn.com.

133 Jonathan Allen, *Special Report: How the Trump Administration Secured a Secret Supply of Execution Drugs*, REUTERS (July 10, 2020), www.reuters.com.

134 For the statement, see Jonathan Allen, *Lab That Tested U.S. Execution Drug Will No Longer Accept Lethal Injection Samples*, REUTERS (Jul. 13, 2020) www.reuters.com ("It will be our policy going forward to require a statement from our client indicating their preparation will not be used for execution. Clients that decline to make that declaration will not be allowed to submit their pentobarbital preparations to DYNALABS for testing.").

135 Allen, *supra* note 134.

136 Kimberly Kindy, *Labs That Test Safety of Custom-Made Drugs Fall under Scrutiny*, WASH. POST (Oct. 5, 2013).

137 *Id.*

138 Expert declaration of Dr. Michaela Almgren, Ruiz v. Tex. Dep't of Crim. Justice, No. D-1-GN-22-007149 (Dec. 14, 2022), at 5–6.

139 *Id.*

140 Talia Roitberg Harmon, Michael Cassidy & Richelle Kloch, *Examination of Decision Making and Botched Lethal Injections in Texas*, 64 AM. BEHAVIORAL SCI. 1 (Sept. 13, 2020); McDaniel, *supra* note 121.

141 Expert declaration of Dr. Michaela Almgren, *supra* note 138, at 7.

142 *Id.* at 12.

143 *Id.* at 14. Of note, there was also a fire in the building where the drugs were stored that took 1,500 gallons of water per minute over the course of over four hours to extinguish, and the drugs are extremely susceptible to heat damage. *Id.*

144 *In Re State of Texas ex rel. Ken Paxton*, No. WR-94,432-01 (Texas Court of Criminal Appeals, Jan. 4, 2023). Apparently, Texas received a new shipment of pentobarbital, and thus had an unexpired supply of the drug even as it litigated whether it could use its expired stockpile. It did not inform the court of this material fact, a clear violation of the state attorney's duty of candor to the court. Stephen Cooper, *Texas Lawyers Violated Legal Ethics Over Expired Execution Drugs*, TEXAS OBSERVER (Jan. 30, 2023) (quoting Professor Bruce A. Green, Louis Stein chair and director of the Louis Stein Center for Law and Ethics at Fordham University School of Law, as saying: "All litigators, and especially government lawyers, have a duty of candor to the court. This includes a duty to correct the court's factual misimpressions, especially those the government lawyers and their client created. . . . Here, the state proceeded on the factual premise that it had no choice but to use expired drugs in an execution. When that stopped being true, because the state acquired new drugs, its lawyers had to tell the judge, so that the court could decide whether it still had to decide whether the state could use expired drugs, or whether it should compel the state to use new drugs. The state's lawyers deceived the court by their silence.").

145 *In Re State of Texas ex rel. Ken Paxton, supra* note 144, at 2 (Newell, J., dissenting).

146 Ed Pilkington, *Revealed: Republican-led States Secretly Spending Huge Sums on Execution Drugs,* THE GUARDIAN (Apr. 9, 2021).

147 *Capital Punishment in the United States: Last Week Tonight with John Oliver, supra* note 97. Absolute Standards is discussed at text accompanying *supra* notes 97–99.

148 Robert Anglen, *Arizona Authorities Ask to Expedite 2 Executions, Citing Shelf Life of Lethal Injection Drug,* ARIZONA REPUBLIC (June 23, 2021).

149 Harmon, Cassidy & Kloch, *supra* note 140.

150 Della Hasselle, *In Rush to Find Lethal Injection Drug, Prison Officials Turned to a Hospital,* THE LENS (Aug. 6, 2014), thelensnola.org.

151 *Id.*

152 Tara Culp-Ressler, *State Tricks Hospital into Giving It Hard-to-Find Execution Drugs,* THINKPROGRESS (Aug. 8, 2014), archive.thinkprogress.org.

153 Caplan, *supra* note 82.

154 Verified Complaint for Emergency Injunctive Relief and Return of Illegally Obtained Property, at 4, McKesson Medical-Surgical Inc. v. Arkansas, No. 60CV-17–1921 (Pulaski Cty. Ct. Apr. 14, 2017).

155 *Supplier: Drug Sold to Arkansas Not Intended For Executions,* CBS NEWS (Apr. 14, 2017), www.cbsnews.com (quoting statement issued by McKesson).

156 Verified Complaint, *supra* note 154, at 3.

157 Creede Newton, *Medical Director in Arkansas Could Lose License for Acquiring Execution Drug,* THE INTERCEPT (Apr. 24, 2017), theintercept.com.

158 Verified Complaint, *supra* note 154, at 5; *Supplier: Drug Sold to Arkansas Not Intended For Executions, supra* note 155 (quoting statement issued by McKesson).

159 Mark Berman, *Drug Companies Take Aim at Arkansas Executions and Demand Lethal Injection Drugs Back,* WASH. POST (Apr. 14, 2017).

160 Brief for Fresenius Kabi USA, LLC & West-Ward Pharmaceuticals Corp. as Amici Curiae Supporting Appellee, at 3, State v. McKesson Medical-Surgical, Inc., 2018 Ark. 154 (2018).

161 *Id.*

162 Abstract, Brief, & Addendum of Appellants at *10, Ark. Dept. of Correction v. Shults, CV-17-788, 2017 WL 5891272 (S.C. Ark. Oct. 6, 2017).

163 Temporary Restraining Order, McKesson Med.-Surgical Inc. v. Ark., No. CV-17–1921 (Pulaski Cty., Ark. Apr. 14, 2017).

164 Formal Order, McKesson Med.-Surgical Inc. v. Ark., No. CV-17–31 (Ark. April 20, 2017).

165 Mark Berman, *Drug Companies Don't Want to Be Involved in Executions, So They're Suing to Keep Their Drugs Out*, WASH. POST (Aug. 13, 2018).

166 Complaint for Emergency Injunctive Relief and Return of Illegally-Obtained Property at 1, 24, Alvogen, Inc. v. Nevada, No. A-18–777312-B (Clark County, Nev. Jul. 10, 2018); *id.* at 9 (alleging that Nevada "leveraged the Nevada Chief Medical Officer's license to surreptitiously, evasively, illicitly, and by subterfuge obtain the Alvogen midazolam product").

167 *Id.* at 9, 24.

168 *Id.* at 2–3.

169 Findings of Fact and Conclusions of Law at 37, 39, Alvogen, Inc., v. Nevada, No. A-18–777312-B (Clark County, Nev., Sept. 28, 2018).

170 Complaint, Fresenius Kabi, USA, LLC v. Nebraska, No. 18-cv-3109 (D. Neb. 2018).

171 *Id.* at 5; Richard A. Oppel Jr., *Nebraska Plans First Execution in 21 Years, Not So Fast, Drug Company Says.* N.Y. TIMES (Aug. 9, 2018).

172 Oppel, *supra* note 171.

173 Complaint, *supra* note 170, at 8.

174 Oppel, *supra* note 171.

175 Fresenius Kabi USA, LLC v. Nebraska at *4, No. 18-cv-3109, 2018 WL 3826681 (D. Neb. 2018).

176 Brief of Appellees at 31-32, Fresenius Kabi USA, LLC v. Nebraska, 733 Fed. Appx.871 (8th Cir. 2018) ("Even assuming that Plaintiff's products are at issue here, there is no allegation that the State of Nebraska has publicly disclosed that Plaintiff's products have been purchased by the State for use in an execution. Indeed, it is the Plaintiff that has come forward in this litigation to make known that it believes its products will be used.").

177 Fresenius Kabi USA, LLC v. Nebraska, 733 Fed.Appx. 871 (8th Cir. 2018). See Chapter 3, text accompanying notes 131-34 (discussing botched execution of Carey Dean Moore).

178 Letter from Josh Reid to Hon. Aaron D. Ford, Attorney General, State of Nevada, Re: Demand to Return Hikma Pharmaceuticals USA Inc.'s Ketamine, Cease and Desist Illegal and Tortious Actions, and Preserve Records, at 2-3 (Jun. 24, 2021) (on file with author).

179 *Id.* at 1.

180 *Id.* at 2.

181 Berman, *supra* note 165.

182 *Id.*

183 *Id.*

184 Dave Boucher, *Tennessee Must Rely On "Black Market Drugs" for Executions, Attorney Says*, NASHVILLE TENNESSEAN (June 13, 2018).

185 DEATH PENALTY INFO. CTR., *Secrecy, Execution Methods, and the International Response*, Dec. 20, 2022 (podcast quoting Reprieve Executive Director Maya Foa at 36:53), deathpenaltyinfo.org.

186 For a concise history, *see* David Bernstein, *Freedom of Contract*, George Mason Law & Economics Research Paper No. 08–51 (2016), www.law.gmu.edu.

187 Transcript of Oral Argument at 14, Glossip v. Gross, 576 U.S. 863 (2015).

188 *15 States, Including Arkansas, Side with Nevada over Drugmaker Delay of Execution*, ASSOC. PRESS (Aug. 7, 2018), apnews.com.

189 David Ferrara, *Nevada AG: If Drug Maker Lawsuits Continue, "Death Penalty Is Dead,"* LAS VEGAS REV. J. (2018).

190 Whitepaper filed with Nevada Legislature, *Nevada: Time to Abandon Lethal Injection*, at 2 (Mar. 15, 2021), www.leg.state.nv.us.

191 Amici Curiae Brief in Support of Relator on Behalf of Fresenius Kabi USA, LLC and Sandoz, Inc., at 2–3, State of Ohio, ex rel. Hogal Lovells US LLP and Elizaveth A. Och v. Ohio Dept. of Rehab. and Corr., No. 2016-1776 (Ohio Jul. 10, 2017).

192 Transcript of Oral Argument, *supra* note 187, at 14.

193 *See* Sonja West, *Guerilla Warfare and the Constitution*, WASH. MONTHLY (Jul. 1, 2015) ("Alito's analogy to guerilla warfare suggests that an element of subterfuge is involved. Guerilla warfare brings to mind small groups of fighters who often carry out their missions disguised as civilians. They bypass conventional methods and rely instead on sabotage, ambush, and treachery.").

194 *See supra* text accompanying notes 65-67.

195 Marty Schladen & Randy Ludlow, *Ohio Can't Get Drugs for a New Execution Method, Dewine Admits*, TIMESREPORTER.COM (Jul. 21, 2019), www.timesreporter.com.

196 *Id.*

197 Marty Schladen, *Ohio Ignored Drugmakers on Executions*, COLUMBUS DISPATCH (Sept. 18, 2019).

198 *See* Jason Tashea, *Drugmaker's Lawsuit Could Halt Nebraska's First Lethal Injection*, ABAJOURNAL (Aug. 9, 2018), www.abajournal.com (quoting a letter dated Dec. 16, 2016, from Fresenius Kabi to the Nebraska DOC directing that its drugs not be used in executions, and reminding state that such use "would be an improper use of these products, which are intended to save lives, and could have far-reaching negative consequences on public health due to European Union regulation 1252/2011, which prevents trade in products that could be used for capital punishment or torture.").

199 Memorandum from March S. Inch, Director, Federal Bureau of Prisons to Attorney General Re: Use of Fentanyl in Executions, at 3 (Mar. 7, 2018).

200 Brief of Amici Curiae Pharmacy, Medicine, and Health Policy Experts in Support of Petitioner, *supra* note 96, at 7.

201 *Id.* at 30.

202 *See* Brief for the Ass'n for Accessible Medicines as Amicus Curiae in Support of Neither Party, Bucklew v. Precythe, 587 U.S. 119 (2019).

203 *Current and Resolved Drug Shortages and Discontinuations Reported to FDA,* FOOD & DRUG ADMIN., www.accessdata.fda.gov (listing midazolam, vecuronium bromide, and potassium chloride on its drug shortage list). *See also* Ed Pilkington, *States Are Stockpiling Lethal Injection Drugs That Could Be Used to Save Lives,* THE GUARDIAN (Apr. 20, 2017).

204 Pilkington, *supra* note 203.

205 Asher Stockler, *Health Care Workers Ask States to Hand over Death Penalty Drugs Needed to Fight COVID-19 Pandemic,* NEWSWEEK (Apr. 10, 2020). For the letter, *see* dpic-cdn.org/.

206 The going price for drugs for a single execution is apparently $200,000 as of 2024. *The Expected Cost of drugs for Utah's Execution Jumped from $7K to $200K. Here's Why the State Says It's Worth It,* DEATH PENALTY NEWS (July 27, 2024) deathpenaltynews.blogspot.com.

207 Pilkington, *supra* note 146.

208 Mathew Haag and Richard Fausset, *Arkansas Rushes to Execute 8 Men in Space of 10 Days,* N.Y. TIMES (March 3, 2017).

209 Newton, *supra* note 157.

210 *KY Debated Back-to-Back Executions,* WBKO.COM (Jan. 25, 2011), www.wbko.com.

211 Dave Boucher, *Tennessee Supreme Court Denies AG's Request for 8 Executions by June 1,* USA TODAY (March 15, 2018).

212 Mark Berman, *Missouri Attorney General Wants the State to Produce Its Own Lethal Injection Drugs,* WASH. POST (May 29, 2014); Caplan, *supra* note 82.

213 *See* 21 U.S.C. § 353a(a); § 829(a). *See also* In re Federal Bureau of Prisons' Execution Protocol Cases, 980 F.3d 123 (2020) (finding violation of Administrative Procedure Act where DOJ did not obtain a prescription for its bulk purchase of compounded pentobarbital); Caplan, *supra* note 82 ("no department of corrections could meet a basic requirement for obtaining a drug made by a compounding pharmacy: a medical prescription for an individual patient").

214 Sean Murphy, *Oklahoma Officials Plan to Use Nitrogen for Executions,* ASSOC. PRESS, Mar. 14, 2018. Oklahoma's legislature passed the measure in 2015, as it was waiting for the Supreme Court's decision in *Glossip,* but the DOC didn't announce its turn to the method until 2018. *Id.*

7. THE MEDICAL PROFESSION MANDATE

1 Jim Edwards, *Most People Don't Know America's System for Carrying out the Death Penalty Was Designed by a Holocaust Denier,* BUSINESS INSIDER (Jun. 29, 2015), www.businessinsider.com.

2 *Id.*

3 Atul Gawande, M.D., *When Law and Ethics Collide—Why Physicians Participate in Executions*, 354 NEW ENGLAND J. OF MED. 1221, 1227 (2006). For a deep dive, see Mark A. Hall et al., *Trust in the Medical Profession: Conceptual and Measurement Issues*, 37 HEALTH SERVICES RES. 1419 (2002); Mark A. Hall et al., *Trust in Physicians and Medical Institutions: What Is It, Can It Be Measured, and Does It Matter?* 79 MILBANK Q. 613 (2002); Mark A. Hall, *Law, Medicine, and Trust*, 55 STAN. L. REV. 463 (2002).

4 Stephen Cooper & Joel Zivot, *Stand Up for What's Right: Abolishing the Death Penalty in Alabama and Beyond*, MONTGOMERY ADVERTISER (Nov. 14, 2022).

5 Leon Kass, *Neither For Love Nor Money: Why Doctors Must Not Kill*, 94 PUB. INT. 25, 38 (1989).

6 *Id.*

7 Joel Zivot, *Lethal Injections Are Crueler than Most People Imagine. I've Seen the Evidence Firsthand*, SLATE (Nov. 30, 2022), slate.com.

8 *Ancient Greek Medicine*, NAT'L LIBR. OF MED., www.nlm.nih.gov.

9 Macrina Cooper-White, *Here's the Scary Truth about Science & the Death Penalty*, HUFF. POST (Mar. 13, 2014).

10 Erich H. Loewy, *Healing and Killing, Harming and Not Harming: Physician Participation in Euthanasia and Capital Punishment*, 3 J. CLIN. ETHICS 29, 29 (1992).

11 Joel B. Zivot, *The Slippery Slope from Medicine to Lethal Injection*, TIME (May 2, 2014).

12 Jonathan Groner, *The Hippocratic Paradox: The Role of the Medical Profession in Capital Punishment in the United States*, FORDHAM URB. L.J. 883, 906 (2008); *see also* Jonathan Groner, *Lethal Injection: A Stain on the Face of Medicine*, 325 BMJ 1026, 1028 (Nov. 2002) ("Even without doctors' participation, lethal injection—with its intravenous lines, electrocardiograph monitors, and anesthetic drugs—has a deeply corrupting influence on medicine as a whole.").

13 The landmark article first articulating these harms is William Curran and W. Casscells, *The Ethics of Medical Participation in Capital Punishment by Intravenous Drug Injection*, 302 N. ENGL. J. MED. 226 (1980).

14 Gawande, *supra* note 3, at 1228.

15 Joel Zivot, *Lethal Injection: "Burning as they die"—How Death Penalty Drugs Go Unregulated*, MEDPAGE TODAY (Dec. 7, 2018), www.medpagetoday.com.

16 Brief of Am. Med. Ass'n., Amicus Curiae, in Support of Neither Party, at 14, Bucklew v. Precythe, 587 U.S. 119 (2019).

17 Comment, Travis Case Armstrong, *"Veneer of Medical Respectability": How Physician Participation in Lethal Injections Perpetuates the Illusion of a Humane Execution*, 51 S. TEX. L. REV. 469, 487 (2009).

18 Brief of Am. Med. Ass'n., *supra* note 16, at 3.

19 Chiara Eisner, *The Death Chamber Doctor's Dilemma: A Physician in South Carolina Breaks His Silence*, THE STATE (May 4, 2022), www.thestate.com.

20 Phillip M. Rosoff, *Perspective Roundtable: Lethal Injection*, 358 N. ENGL. J. MED. 2183 (2008) (letter to the editor).

21 Gregory D. Curfman, M.D. et al., *Physicians and Execution*, 358 N. ENGL. J. MED. 403 (2008).

22 Timothy F. Murphy, *Physicians, Medical Ethics, and Capital Punishment*, 16 J. OF CLINICAL ETHICS 160, 168 (2005). *See also* Jerome D. Gorman, M.D. et al., *The Case against Lethal Injection*, 115 VA. MED. 567, 576-77 (1988) (lethal injection "blurs the distinctions between healing and killing, between illness and guilt").

23 United States Holocaust Memorial Museum, *Euthanasia Program and Aktion T4*, HOLOCAUST ENCYCLOPEDIA, encyclopedia.ushmm.org.

24 ROBERT JAY LIFTON, THE NAZI DOCTORS: MEDICAL KILLING AND THE PSYCHOLOGY OF GENOCIDE 15 (1986).

25 *Id.* at 14.

26 *Id.* at 57.

27 *Id.* at 45.

28 *Id. at* 71.

29 Brief of Am. Med. Ass'n., *supra* note 16, at 11.

30 DEATH PENALTY INFO. CTR., *Discussions with DPIC Podcast: Anesthesiologist Dr. Joel Zivot on What Prisoner Autopsies Tell Us about Lethal Injection* (Dec. 9, 2020) deathpenaltyinfo.org.

31 Owen Dyer, *The Slow Death of Lethal Injection*, 348 BMJ 16, 16–17 (Apr. 29, 2014) (quoting Dr. Joel Zivot).

32 N.Y. State Comm'n on Capital Punishment, Report of the Comm'n to Investigate and Report the Most Humane and Practical Method of Carrying into Effect the Sentence of Death in Capital Cases 78 (1888).

33 Ward Casscells and Williams J. Curran, *Doctors, the Death Penalty, and Lethal Injections*, 307 N. ENGL. J. OF MED. 1532, 1532 (1982) ("These firm and well-publicized positions of organized medicine seemed for a considerable time to have stemmed the movement to use lethal injection. No person has been put to death by this method in any of the four states over these years, and 12 other states have rejected lethal injection legislation.").

34 Opinion 2.06 of the Council on Ethical and Judicial Affairs of the American Medical Association: Capital Punishment (1980).

35 American Medical Association, Capital Punishment, Code of Med. Ethics Opinion 9.7.3, code-medical-ethics.ama-assn.org.

36 *Id.*

37 *Amateur Night*, 441 NATURE 2 (May 2006).

38 For a collection of these various position statements, see *Professional Ass'n. Policies*, LETHAL INJECTION INFO. CTR., lethalinjectioninfo.org.

39 World Medical Association, Resolution on Physician Participation in Capital Punishment (Sept. 1981), www.wma.net ("It is unethical for physicians to participate in capital punishment, in any way, or during any step of the execution process, including its planning and the instruction and/or training of persons to perform executions"). For the position statements of 16 state medical associations, see *Professional Ass'n Policies*, *supra* note 38.

40 *NAEMT Position Statement: EMT or Paramedic Participation in Capital Punishment*, NAT'L ASS'N OF EMERGENCY MED. TECHNICIANS (Jan. 26, 2010), www.naemt.org.

41 *Statement on Physician Nonparticipation in Legally Authorized Executions*, AM. SOC. OF ANESTHESIOLOGISTS (Oct. 18, 2006), www.asahq.org.

42 Orin Guidry, *Message from the President: Observations Regarding Lethal Injection*, AM. SOC. OF ANESTHESIOLOGISTS (June 20, 2006), pubs.asahq.org.

43 *Anesthesiologists and Capital Punishment*, AM. BOARD OF ANESTHESIOLOGY (Apr. 2, 2010), www.theaba.org.

44 *Id.*

45 Charles van der Horst, *Doctors Won't Kill for the State*, NEWS & OBSERVER at 9A (May 5, 2009).

46 David J. Rothman, *Physicians and the Death Penalty*, 4 J.L. & POL'Y 151, 153 (1995).

47 N.C. Dep't Corr. v. N.C. Med. Bd., 675 S.E.2d 641, 644-45 (N.C. 2009) (quoting North Carolina Medical Board's Position Statement).

48 *Id.* at 645.

49 For an extended discussion, see Nadia N. Sawicki, *Doctors, Discipline, and the Death Penalty: Professional Implications of Safe Harbor Policies*, 27 YALE L. & POL'Y REV. 107 (2008).

50 For an example, *see* chapter 5, text accompanying note 1.

51 Ben Crair, *Doctors in the Death Chamber*, DAILY BEAST (July 14, 2017).

52 Jonathan Groner, *Lethal Injection: The Medical Charade*, 20 ETHICS & MED. 25, 27 (2004).

53 *See* Gawande, supra note 3.

54 *The Death Penalty in 2023: Year End Report*, DEATH PENALTY INFO. CTR. (Dec. 1, 2023), deathpenaltyinfo.org.

55 In the literature, too, those who favor participation represent a minority view. *See* William Lainer, M.D. et al., *Physician Involvement in Capital Punishment: Simplifying a Complex Calculus*, 82 MAYO CLINIC PROC. 1043, 1043 (2007) (noting that "there is no shortage of medical literature contending that physicians should not be involved in killing" and "a paucity of literature" supporting it); Robert D. Truog et al., *In Reply to Letter to the Editor*, 312 J. AM. MED. ASS'N 1804, 1805 (2014) ("Individual disagreements [as to physician participation in executions] do nothing to call the professional consensus into question").

56 Nolan Clay, *Oklahoma Execution Doctor Paid $15,000 Each Time Death Penalty Carried Out*, THE OKLAHOMAN (Jan. 12, 2022); *Evidence of "Torturous" Fluid in the Lungs, Drug Mislabeling Highlight Federal Trial on*

Constitutionality of Oklahoma Lethal-Injection Protocol, DEATH PENALTY INFO. CTR., (Mar. 10, 2022), deathpenaltyinfo.org ("Dr. Doe received $60,000 for his participation in the four executions, plus $1,000 per day for weekly training sessions and execution-week preparation sessions. Oklahoma has said it intends to schedule as many as 28 executions if the lethal-injection protocol is upheld, meaning Doe stands to make $420,000 for his involvement in the executions and at least another $56,000 in payments for training and preparation sessions.").

57 Michael Kiefer, *Arizona Doctor Earns $18,000 Per Execution*, ARIZ. REPUBLIC (Nov. 22, 2011).

58 Gawande, *supra* note 3, at 1223.

59 *Id.* at 1224.

60 *Id.* at 1225.

61 Transcript of Recorded Interview of Physician, Okla. Dep't Pub. Safety, the Execution of Clayton D. Lockett (on file with author).

62 Kenneth Baum & Julie Cantor, *Doctors Can Ease Suffering, Even in Executions*, N.Y. TIMES (Apr. 30, 2014). *See also* Sandeep Jauhar, *Why It's O.K. for Doctors to Participate in Executions*, N.Y. TIMES (April 17, 2017).

63 *Bad Execution*, 297 SCI. AM. 36, 36 (2007).

64 Rosalyn Stewart & Valerie Hardcastle, *To Cure Sometimes, to Relieve Often, and to Comfort Always*, 19 AM. J. BIOETHICS 66, 66 (2019) ("This quotation has been variously attributed to William Osler, Edward Trudeau, Hippocrates, and anonymous.").

65 Gawande, *supra* note 3, at 1228.

66 *Id.*

67 *Id.* at 1227.

68 Lauren Knapp, *Death Row Doctor*, N.Y. TIMES (Jan. 17, 2017).

69 Groner, *The Hippocratic Paradox*, *supra* note 12.

70 AMER. COLLEGE OF PHYSICIANS, BREACH OF TRUST: PHYSICIAN PARTICIPATION IN EXECUTIONS IN THE UNITED STATES 38 (1994).

71 Gawande, *supra* note 3, at 1229.

72 Dennis Curry, *Lethal Injection and Medical Ethics: Physicians in the Execution Chamber*, 2 HARV. MED. STUDENT REV. 39, 40 (2015).

73 Knapp, *supra* note 68.

74 Brief for Respondents at *49, Baze v. Rees, 553 U.S. 35 (Dec. 3, 2008).

75 *Baze*, 553 U.S. at 59–60.

76 *Id.* at 64 (Alito, J., concurring).

77 *Id. See also supra* text accompanying note 40 (discussing ethical constraints of medical technicians).

78 Ty Alper, *The Truth about Physician Participation in Lethal Injection Executions*, 88 N.C.L. REV. 11, 38 (2009).

79 Bucklew v. Precythe, 587 U.S. 119, 141-42 (2019).

80 Public Joint Appendix at 219–20, Bucklew v. Precythe, 587 U.S. 119 (2019) (Supplemental Expert Report of Joel Zivot). The Justices in *Bucklew* knew full well that medical ethics would prevent prisoners from meeting their required showing. A prior case, *Arthur v. Dunn*, had squarely presented the issue of medical ethics, and the Supreme Court declined to hear it. Arthur v. Dunn, 580 U.S. 1141 (2017) (denying certiorari). *See* Motion for Leave to File Brief of Amici Curiae, Arthur v. Dunn, 1, 4 ("*Amici* are medical professionals, medical ethicists, and university professors with specialized knowledge in medical ethics. . . . This case presents the question whether a district court can require a condemned inmate to produce evidence that medical ethics rules ensure he will not be able to obtain in order to meet that burden."); *id.* at 5 ("Condemned prisoners will not be able to provide that evidence."); *id.* at 22 (arguing that the alternative execution method requirement "requires inmates to produce evidence that medical ethics rules forbid them from obtaining").

81 Brief of Am. Med. Ass'n., *supra* note 16, at 2, 12-13.

82 *Bucklew*, 587 U.S. at 141. The Supreme Court's ruling in *Bucklew* is especially galling in light of the Court's professed concern for "protecting the integrity and ethics of the medical profession" in the context of physician-assisted suicide. Washington v. Glucksberg, 521 U.S. 702, 731 (1997).

83 Deborah W. Denno, *The Lethal Injection Quandary: How Medicine Has Dismantled the Death Penalty*, 76 FORDHAM L. REV. 49 (2007).

84 Ken Ritter, *Doctors, EMTs Pull Out of Consideration for Nevada Execution*, ASSOC. PRESS (Feb. 1, 2022), apnews.com; Katelyn Newberg, *Execution of Quadruple Murderer "Possible but Highly Unlikely,"* LAS VEGAS REVIEW-JOURNAL (Feb. 3, 2022).

85 Newberg, *supra* note 84.

86 Denise Grady, *Three-Drug Protocol Persists for Lethal Injections, Despite Ease of Using One*, N.Y. TIMES (May 1, 2014) (quoting Arthur L. Caplan, Director of Medical Ethics, NYU Langone Medical Center); Peter Lipson, *Botched OK Execution No Surprise*, FORBES (May 1, 2014).

87 Leonidas G. Koniaris et al., *Can Lethal Injection for Execution Really Be "Fixed"?*, 369 THE LANCET 352, 353 (2007).

88 *Ancient Greek Med.*, *supra* note 8.

89 *Ohio Can't Find Doctors to Advise on Executions*, NBC NEWS (Oct. 26, 2009), www.nbcnews.com.

90 Cooper-White, *supra* note 9.

91 Ben Crair, *Exclusive Emails Show Ohio's Doubts about Lethal Injection*, NEW REPUB. (Aug. 17, 2017).

92 *See id.;* Annie Waldman, *Key Expert in Supreme Court Lethal Injection Case Did His Research on Drugs.com*, PROPUBLICA (Apr. 28, 2015).

93 *See, e.g.,* chapter 2, text accompanying note 27 (over 99.999999999999 percent of the population would stop breathing within 60 seconds of receiving overdose of sodium thiopental); chapter 2, text accompanying note 30 (prisoners would go into cardiac arrest within two minutes of receiving injection of third drug, potassium chloride); chapter 2, text accompanying note 50 (two-drug protocol of midazolam-hydromorphone would "knock the patient out and stop his breathing," causing death within a few minutes).

94 Grady, *supra* note 86.

8. THE PRISON PROBLEM

1 Justice Anthony M. Kennedy, Speech at the American Bar Association Annual Meeting (Aug. 9, 2003), www.supremecourt.gov.

2 David Biello, *Reasonable Doubt*, 297 SCIENTIFIC AMERICAN 20, 21 (2007).

3 Alan Greenblatt, *The Capital Punishment Crossroads*, CQ WEEKLY at 530, 537 (Feb. 19, 2007).

4 Deborah W. Denno, *The Lethal Injection Quandary: How Medicine Has Dismantled the Death Penalty*, 76 FORDHAM L. REV. 49, 95 (2007).

5 Jyllian Kemsley, *Botched Executions Put Lethal Injections under New Scrutiny*, CHEMICAL & ENGINEERING NEWS (May 22, 2014), cen.acs.org (quoting Deborah Denno).

6 Deborah W. Denno, *When Legislatures Delegate Death: The Troubling Paradox behind State Uses of Electrocution and Lethal Injection and What It Says about Us*, 63 OHIO ST. L.J. 63 (2002).

7 *See, e.g.*, Ala. Code § 15-18-82.1(a); N.C. Gen. Stat. § 15–188; Fla. Stat. Ann. § 922.105; Okla. Stat. tit. 22, § 1014; S.C. Code Ann. § 24-3-530; Mo. Rev. Stat. § 546.720; Ga. Code Ann. § 17-10-38; Nev. Rev. Stat. Ann. § 176.355.

8 Ty Alper, *Anesthetizing the Public Conscience: Lethal Injection and Animal Euthanasia*, 35 FORDHAM URB. L.J. 817 (2008).

9 Denno, *supra* note 4, at 67 ("Wiseman [the sponsor of Oklahoma's lethal injection bill] and Chapman believed the statute should be vague. Neither of them was certain if or when lethal injection would be implemented or what drugs might then be available. Unfortunately, such stunning unknowns had no impact on Wiseman's confidence in the procedure's potential success."); Brief for the Fordham University School of Law, Louis Stein Center for Law and Ethics as Amicus Curiae in Support of Petitioners at 19, Baze v. Rees, 553 U.S. 35 (2008) (Oklahoma legislators proposed vague statutory language "because they were uncertain how much time would pass before a lethal injection execution would be carried out and thus contemplated that drug technology might advance by that time.").

10 Baze v. Rees, 553 U.S. 35, 40 (2008).

11 *Id.* at 75 (Stevens, J. dissenting).

12 Eric Berger, *Individual Rights, Judicial Deference, and Administrative Law Norms in Constitutional Decision Making*, 91 B.U.L. REV. 2029, 2084 (2011).

13 *See* Alexandra L. Klein, *Nondelegating Death*, 81 OHIO ST. L.J. 923 (2020); Eric Berger, *Death Penalty Administration: A Response to Alexandra Klein's*

Nondelegating Death, 82 OHIO ST. L.J. 9 (2021); Corinna Barrett Lain, *Death Penalty Exceptionalism and Administrative Law*, 8 BELMONT L. REV. 552 (2021).

14 Hobbs v. Jones, 412 S.W.3d 844, 852 (Ark. 2012).

15 *Id.* at 854.

16 Gundy v. United States, 588 U.S. 128, 149 (2019) (Gorsuch, J. dissenting).

17 Deborah W. Denno, *Death Bed*, 124 TRIQUARTERLY J. 141, 160 (2006).

18 *Id.* at 150.

19 Liliana Segura, *"Our Most Cruel Experiment Yet": Chilling Testimony in a Tennessee Trial Exposes LI as Court-Sanctioned Torture*, THE INTERCEPT (Aug. 5, 2018), theintercept.com.

20 *Id.*

21 Eric Berger, *The Executioners' Dilemmas*, 49 U. RICH. L. REV. 731, 758 (2015).

22 *Id.* at 759.

23 Taylor v. Crawford, No. 05–4173-CV-C-FJG, 2006 WL 1779035, at *17 (W.D. Mo. Jul. 25, 2006).

24 *See* Denno, *supra* note 17, at 148 ("Leuchter told me the revelation destroyed his business. No warden would go near him publicly although privately wardens still called him for advice because there was simply no one else available with Leuchter's execution methods expertise.").

25 *See* chapter 1, text accompanying notes 13–14.

26 Segura, *supra* note 19.

27 *See* chapter 1, text following note 13.

28 *See* Ty Alper, *What Do Lawyers Know about Lethal Injection?*, 1 HARV. L. & POL'Y REV. (Mar. 3, 2008) (discussing the "stick a lawyer in the room" litigation strategy); Eric Berger, *Lethal Injection and the Problem of Constitutional Remedies*, 27 YALE L. & POL. REV. 259, 305 (2009) ("By turning over the new protocol to lawyers, Missouri did not consult experts in a meaningful way, but it could claim that the details regarding the new procedure's adoption were subject to attorney-client privilege.").

29 *See* Denno, *supra* note 6.

30 Brief Amicus Curiae of the American Civil Liberties Union, the ACLU of Kentucky, and the Rutherford Institute in Support of Petitioners at 9, Baze v. Rees, 553 U.S. 35 (2008).

31 *See* Denno, *supra* note 17, at 154.

32 *Id.*

33 HUMAN RIGHTS WATCH, SO LONG AS THEY DIE: LETHAL INJECTIONS IN THE UNITED STATES, at 16, n.54 (2006) (Letter dated Jan. 2, 2004, from James L. Hall, Assistant General Counsel, Office of the General Counsel, Texas Department of Criminal Justice to Alberta Phillips, Editorial Department of the Austin-American Statesman), www.hrw.org.

34 *Id.* at 16.

35 See chapter 4, text accompanying note 14.

36 Elizabeth Weil, *The Needle and the Damage Done*, N.Y. TIMES (Feb. 11, 2007).

37 Fernando J. Gaitan, *Challenges Facing Society in the Implementation of the Death Penalty*, 35 FORDHAM URB. L.J. 763, 765 (2008).

38 *Id.*

39 HUMAN RIGHTS WATCH, *supra* note 33, at 20.

40 Jimmy Jenkins, *Arizona Lacks Knowledge and Expertise to Conduct Execution, Governor and Prisons Chief Say*, ARIZ. REPUBLIC (Mar. 16, 2023).

41 *Id.*

42 *Id.*

43 *Id.*

44 Ed Pilkington, *Revealed: Republican-led States Secretly Spending Huge Sums on Execution Drugs*, THE GUARDIAN (Apr. 9, 2021); Jimmy Jenkins, *9th Circuit Affirms District Court's Power to Enforce Arizona Prison Health Care Settlement*, KJZZ—PHOENIX (Jan. 29, 2020), www.kjzz.org.

45 Expert Declaration of Gail A. Van Norman, M.D. at 34, Roane v. Barr (D.D.C., Nov. 1, 2019).

46 Missouri's protocol is available at dpic-cdn.org.

47 Austin Sarat et al., *The Fate of Lethal Injection: Decomposition of the Paradigm and Its Consequences*, 11 BR. J. AM. LEG. STUDIES 81, 110 (2022); Austin Sarat, *"Hear No Evil, See No Evil," State Responses to Botched Executions and the Danger of Indifference*, VERDICT (Feb. 18, 2022), verdict.justia.com.

48 *Tenn. Book Mixes up Execution Protocol*, GAINESVILLE SUN (Feb. 9, 2007), www.gainesville.com.

49 Affidavit of Marvin L. Polk, Warden, at 2, Rowsey v. Beck, No. 5:04-CT-04-BO (E.D.N.C. Jan. 6, 2004).

50 Declaration of Mark Heath, M.D., at 4, Patton v. Jones, No 5:06-cv-00591-F (W.D. Okla. July 27, 2006) (discussing Oklahoma's lethal injection protocol).

51 DAVID GARLAND, PECULIAR INSTITUTION 54 (2010). *See also* Austin Sarat et al., *Botched Executions and the Struggle to End Capital Punishment: A Twentieth-Century Story*, 38 L. & SOC. INQUIRY 694, 697 (2013) ("An execution is meant to be a meticulously choreographed routine that serves not only to extinguish the life of the condemned, but also to reaffirm the legitimacy of the lethal power exercised by the state.").

52 The Honorable Jeremy Fogel, *In the Eye of the Storm: A Judge's Experience in Lethal-Injection Litigation*, 35 FORDHAM URB. L.J. 735, 736 (2008).

53 *Id.* at 740.

54 Morales v. Tilton, 465 F. Supp.2d 972 (N.D. Cal. 2006).

55 Fogel, *supra* note 52, at 743.

56 Mariah Timms, *Tennessee Yet to Release Details on 'Technical Oversight' Delaying Oscar Franklin Smith Execution*, THE TENNESSEEAN (Apr. 25, 2022).

57 *See* Butler Snow LLP, Tenn. Lethal Injection Protocol Investigation: Rep. and Findings at 36 (Dec. 13, 2022), ewscripps.brightspotcdn.com. Shout out to *The*

Tennessean, whose investigative journalists poured through thousands of documents from pending lethal injection litigation in the state and reported on the errors even before the official report was released.

58 *Id.* at 4-5, 34, 37.

59 Josh Keefe and Melissa Brown, *Tennessee Death Penalty: State Didn't Follow Lethal Injection Protocol*, THE TENNESSEEAN (May 26, 2022).

60 Butler Snow LLP, *supra* note 57, at 34.

61 *Id.* at 18. *Records: 2 People in Tennessee Execution Knew Drugs Hadn't Been Tested*, Assoc. Press (May 13, 2022), apnews.com.

62 King v. Helton, No. 3:18-cv-01234, at 1 (M.D. Tenn. May 6, 2022).

63 Kimberlee Kruesi, *Lee: Tennessee High Court Likely Won't Set Executions Soon*, ASSOC. PRESS (Jan. 6, 2023), apnews.com.

64 Butler Snow LLP, *supra* note 57, at 39.

65 Josh Keefe, *Lee's New Prisons Chief Comes From a State That Bungled Executions, Violated Prisoner Rights*, THE TENNESSEEAN (Jan. 12, 2023).

66 Miller v. Hamm, No. 2:22-CV-506-RAH, 2022 WL 4348724, at *15 (M.D. Ala. Sept. 19, 2022).

67 Miller v. Comm'r, Ala. Dep't of Corr., No. 22–13136, at *20 (11th Cir. Sept. 22, 2022).

68 Emergency Application to Vacate Injunction of Execution at 19, Hamm v. Miller, No. 22A258 (S.Ct. Sept. 22, 2022).

69 Smith v. Dunn, No. 2:19-cv-927-ECM, 2021 WL 4396272, at *6-7 (M.D. Ala. Sept. 24, 2021).

70 Andrew Buncombe, *Charles Warner Execution: Oklahoma Inmate's Last Words Are "My Body Is on Fire" as State Carries Out First Death Penalty in Nine Months*, THE INDEPENDENT (Jan. 16, 2015).

71 Press Release, Mary Fallin, Governor Fallin Issues Stay of Richard Glossip Execution while State Reviews Protocol Questions (Sept. 30, 2015).

72 Nolan Clay & Rick Green, *Wrong Drug Used for January Execution, State Records Show*, THE OKLAHOMAN (Oct. 8, 2015).

73 Ariana de Vogue, *Oklahoma Delays Further Executions While System Is Reviewed*, CNN (Oct. 8, 2015), www.cnn.com.

74 Interim Report No. 14, at 1, in the Matter of the Multicounty Grand Jury, State of Okla., Nos. SCAD-2014–70, GJ-2014–1 (May 19, 2016) [hereinafter "Oklahoma Grand Jury Report"], files.deathpenaltyinfo.org.

75 *Id.* at 2.

76 *Id.* at 58.

77 *Id.* at 96.

78 *Id.* at 97.

79 *Id.* at 104.

80 *Id.* at 2 (discussing general counsel Steve Mullins).

81 *Id.* at 68.

82 Sean Murphy, *Grand Jury: Lawyer Backed Use of Wrong Drug in Execution Try*, ASSOC. PRESS (May 19, 2016), apnews.com.

83 Oklahoma Grand Jury Report, *supra* note 74, at 68.

84 *Id.* at 100.

85 Murphy, *supra* note 82.

86 Mark Berman, *Oklahoma Lethal Injection Process Muddled by "Inexcusable Failure," Grand Jury Finds*, WASH. POST (May 19, 2016).

87 Murphy, *supra* note 82.

88 Press Release, *Oklahoma Department of Corrections Prepared to Resume Executions* (Oct. 26, 2021), oklahoma.gov.

89 *See* chapter 2, text accompanying notes 95–96.

90 For the visual, see chapter 4, picture accompanying note 31.

91 *"I was not at all happy," Oklahoma Dept. of Corrections Director Testifies about Execution Transcription Error during Fifth Day of Federal Trial*, OKLAHOMA NEWS 4 (March 4, 2022), kfor.com.

92 *See* chapter 5, text accompanying note 31.

93 Lincoln Caplan, *The End of the Open Market for Lethal-Injection Drugs* at 3-4, NEW YORKER (May 21, 2016).

94 HUMAN RIGHTS WATCH, *supra* note 33.

95 *See supra* text accompanying notes 52-55.

96 *Morales*, 465 F.Supp.2d at 983 n.14.

97 HUMAN RIGHTS WATCH, *supra* note 33, at 9.

98 Transcript of Recorded Interview of Executioner, Okla. Dep't Pub. Safety, The Execution of Clayton D. Lockett (on file with author).

99 Transcript of Recorded Interview of Paramedic/Emergency Medical Technician, Okla. Dep't Pub. Safety, The Execution of Clayton D. Lockett (on file with author).

100 Katie Fretland & Jessica Glenza, *Oklahoma State Report on Botched Lethal Injection Cites Medical Failures*, THE GUARDIAN (Sept. 4, 2014).

101 Segura, *supra* note 19 (reporting on Tennessee lethal injection trial in 2018).

102 Gayle Ray, *Lethal Injection Drug Puts Corrections Employees at Risk*, THE TENNESSEAN (Aug. 6, 2018).

103 Chiara Eisner, *Carrying Out Executions Took a Secret Toll on Workers—Then Changed Their Politics*, NAT'L PUB. RADIO (Nov. 16, 2022), www.npr.org.

104 *Id.*

105 Brief of Amici Curiae Former Corrections Officials Supporting Petitioner, at 6–7, Bucklew v. Precythe, 587 U.S. 119 (2019) (quoting Jerry Givens, Virginia's chief executioner for 17 years).

106 Eisner, *supra* note 103.

107 *Id.*

108 Allen L. Ault, *The Hidden Victims of the Death Penalty: Correctional Staff*, WASH. POST (July 31, 2019).

109 Ed Pilkington, *Prison Officers Traumatized by Rate of Executions in US Death Penalty States*, THE GUARDIAN (April 28, 2024).

110 Austin Sarat, *Oklahoma Judge Tells Execution Staff to "Suck It Up" after Trauma Request*, SLATE (April 1, 2024), slate.com.

111 *Id.* (quoting Judge Gary Lumpkin).

112 For an excellent discussion, *see e.g.,* Michael J. Osofsky et al., *The Role of Moral Disengagement in the Execution Process*, 29 L. & HUM. BEH. 371 (2005). For the bigger picture, see ALBERT BANDURA, MORAL DISENGAGEMENT: HOW PEOPLE DO HARM AND LIVE WITH THEMSELVES (2016); ROBERT J. LIFTON & GREG MITCHELL, WHO OWNS DEATH? CAPITAL PUNISHMENT, THE AMERICAN CONSCIENCE, AND THE END OF THE DEATH PENALTY (2000).

113 Tolly Moseley, *The Enforcers of the Death Penalty*, THE ATLANTIC (Oct. 1, 2014).

114 Brief of Amici Curiae Former Corrections Officials, *supra* note 105, at 4.

115 ROBERT JOHNSON, DEATH WORK: A STUDY OF THE MODERN EXECUTION PROCESS 121 (2nd ed. 2005).

116 *Id.* at 179.

117 Bruce Weber, *Donald Cabana, Warden Who Loathed Death Penalty, Dies at 67*, N.Y. TIMES (Oct. 13, 2013).

118 Rhodes v. Chapman, 452 U.S. 337, 362 (1981) (Brennan, J., concurring).

119 *See* Berger, *supra* note 21, at 745 (prison officials are used to being "insulated from external review" and "fending off suits and other external meddling"); Ty Alper, *The Truth about Physician Participation in Lethal Injection Executions*, 88 N.C. L. REV. 11, 50 (2009) (prisons have a distinct institutional culture, and this culture makes prison officials "institutionally loathe to accede to any intervention in the way they conduct business unless forced to do so by courts").

120 Douglas A. Berman, *Finding Bickel in a Hill of Beans*, CATO SUP. CT. REV. 311, 314 (2006).

121 Transcript of Preliminary Injunction Hearing, at 160, Warner v. Gross, No. 5:14-cv-00665-F (W.D. Okla. Dec. 17–19, 2014).

122 Brad Henry & Andy Lester, *Oklahoma Executions Should Stop until System Is Reformed*, THE OKLAHOMAN (July, 24, 2022).

123 *Id.*

124 Jay Reeves, *Alabama Pausing Executions after 3rd Failed Lethal Injection*, ASSOC. PRESS, (Nov. 21, 2022), apnews.com.

125 *See* Barber v. Ivey, 143 S. Ct. 2545, 2546, 2548 (2023) (Sotomayor, J., dissenting) ("During this review, conducted by the very agency that botched the executions, the State offered no explanations for the failures and reported 'no deficiencies' in its protocols. . . . There was no published report. Instead, the ADOC commissioner [sent a] one-and-a-half page letter to the Governor.").

126 Josh Moon, *Alabama's about to Start Botching Executions Again*, ALABAMA POL. REP. (Feb. 27, 2023).

127 Barber v. Ivey, 143 S. Ct. 2545, 2546 (2023) (Sotomayor, J., dissenting).

128 *Id.* at 2548.

129 *Id.* at 2549.

130 Baze v. Rees, 553 U.S. 35 (2008).

131 Glossip v. Gross, 576 U.S. 863 (2015).

132 Bucklew v. Precythe, 587 U.S. 119, 134 (2019).

133 *Id.* at 141.

134 *Baze*, 553 U.S. at 48; *see also id.* at 94 (Thomas, J., concurring) (arguing that Eighth Amendment protection exists only if the execution method "is deliberately designed to inflict pain"); *Bucklew*, 587 U.S. at 133 (citing *Baze*, and also Justice Thomas's concurring opinion in the case). *See also* Mark Joseph Stern, *The Supreme Court's Conservatives Just Legalized Torture*, SLATE (April 1, 2019), slate.com.

135 Liliana Segura, *When It Comes to the Death Penalty, the Supreme Court Legalized Torture Long Ago*, THE INTERCEPT (April 6, 2019), theintercept.com.

136 *Id.*

137 Transcript of Oral Argument, at 44–45, Bucklew v. Precythe, No. 17–8151, 587 U.S. 119 (2019).

138 Andrew Cohen, *America Is Terrible at Killing People Legally*, POLITICO (Feb. 7, 2014), www.politico.com.

9. THE SECRECY SOLUTION

1 Emergency Motion to Stay Unconstitutional Execution, at 2, Williams v. Hutchinson, No. 5:17-cv-00103 (E.D. Ark. Apr. 24, 2017); Opposition to Plaintiff Marcel Williams's Emergency Motion to Stay Unconstitutional Execution, at 1, Williams v. Hutchinson, No. 5:17-cv-00103 (E.D. Ark. Apr. 24, 2017).

2 Liliana Segura, *Arkansas Justice: Racism, Torture, and a Botched Execution*, THE INTERCEPT, (Nov. 12, 2017), theintercept.com.

3 Austin Sarat, *"Hear No Evil, See No Evil," State Responses to Botched Executions and the Danger of Indifference*, VERDICT (Feb. 18, 2022), verdict.justia.com.

4 *See* chapter 1, text accompanying note 41.

5 *See* chapter 4, text accompanying notes 64–70.

6 Nathan Crabbe, *Warden: Execution Caused No Pain*, GAINSVILLE SUN (Jan. 29, 2007).

7 Tom Dart, *Arizona Inmate Joseph Wood Was Injected 15 Times with Execution Drugs*, THE GUARDIAN (Aug. 2, 2014). "They have not produced one shred of evidence to support that claim," a doctor shot back. Patrick McNamara, *Questions about Arizona's Two-Hour Execution Linger*, ARIZ. DAILY STAR (Feb. 14, 2016).

8 Dart, *supra* note 7.

9 Ed Pilkington & Amanda Holpuch, *Experts Decry "Failed Experiment" with New Death Penalty Drug Combinations*, THE GUARDIAN (July 25, 2014).

10 Corinna Barrett Lain, *The Politics of Botched Executions*, 49 U. RICH. L. REV. 825, 836-37 (2015).

11 Ed Pilkington, *Ohio Officials Insist Dennis Mcguire Execution "Worked Very Well,"* THE GUARDIAN (Feb. 5, 2014); Chapter 2, text accompanying note 56 ("I'm sorry"); *Ohio Says Controversial Execution of Dennis McGuire Was "Humane,"* NBC NEWS (April 28, 2014) ("the inmate was completely unconscious and felt no pain"), www.nbcnews.com.

12 Lawrence Hummer, *I Witnessed Ohio's Execution of Dennis McGuire. What I Saw Was Inhumane*, THE GUARDIAN (Jan. 22, 2014).

13 Elizabeth Bruenig, *Dead to Rights*, THE ATLANTIC (Aug. 14, 2022).

14 *Id.*

15 *Id.*

16 Evan Mealins, *ADOC "Cannot Confirm" If Joe Nathan James Jr. Was Fully Conscious Before His Execution*, MONTGOMERY ADVERTISER (Aug. 17, 2022).

17 *Id.*

18 Bruenig, *supra* note 13.

19 *Id.*

20 *Id.*

21 *Id.*

22 Bryan Lyman, *Dep't. of Corr. Denies Request for Joe Nathan James Jr. Execution Records*, MONTGOMERY ADVERTISER (Aug. 17, 2022).

23 Marco Poggio, *3½ Hour Ala. Execution Was Needlessly Cruel, Suit Says*, LAW360 (May 3, 2023), www.law360.com.

24 *See* chapter 4, text accompanying notes 39-40 (discussing execution of Doyle Lee Hamm).

25 Melissa Brown, *Court Grants Advertiser's Effort to Reveal Alabama Execution Protocol*, MONTGOMERY ADVERTISER (May 31, 2018).

26 *See* chapter 2, text accompanying notes 95-96.

27 Ed Pilkington, *Outcry after Oklahoma Prisoner Vomits and Convulses during Execution*, THE GUARDIAN (Oct. 29, 2021).

28 *Id.*

29 Sean Murphy, *Oklahoma Executes Inmate Who Dies Vomiting and Convulsing*, ASSOC. PRESS (Oct. 29, 2021); *Eyewitnesses Report John Grant Experienced Repeated "Full-Body Convulsions" and Vomited during Execution; Oklahoma Says Execution Was Carried Out "Without Complication,"* DEATH PENALTY INFO. CTR. (Oct. 29, 2021), deathpenaltyinfo.org.

30 Nicholas Bogel-Burroughs, *Oklahoma to Continue Lethal Injections after Man Vomits During Execution*, N.Y. TIMES (Oct. 29, 2021).

31 Carmen Forman, *Details of John Grant's Execution Were "Embellished," Oklahoma Corrections Chief Says*, THE OKLAHOMAN (Oct. 29, 2021).

32 *Id.*

33 Bogel-Burroughs, *supra* note 30.

34 *Id.*

35 @DanSnyderTV, X (Twitter), Oct. 28, 2021, 9:58 p.m., x.com.

36 Max Brantley, *Calls for Investigation Follow Execution of Kenneth Williams, Observed "Lurching" and Moaning during Lethal Injections*, ARK. TIMES (April 28, 2017).

37 Kelly P. Kissel and Andrew DeMillo, Assoc. Press, *Arkansas Inmate Convulses during Deadline-Beating Execution*, THE LEDGER (April 28, 2017).

38 Segura, *supra* note 2.

39 Brantley, *supra* note 36.

40 Phil McCausland, *Arkansas Execution of Kenneth Williams "Horrifying": Lawyer*, NBC NEWS, (April 27, 2017), www.nbcnews.com.

41 Segura, *supra* note 2; Liliana Segura, *"Our Most Cruel Experiment Yet": Chilling Testimony in a Tennessee Trial Exposes LI as Court-Sanctioned Torture*, THE INTERCEPT (Aug. 5, 2018), theintercept.com.

42 McCausland, *supra* note 40.

43 Michael Tarm, *Executioners Sanitized Accounts of Deaths in Federal Cases*, ASSOC. PRESS (Feb. 17, 2021), apnews.com. *See also* Khaleda Rahman, *Donald Trump Executioners May Have Misled Courts, Sparking Calls for Investigation*, NEWSWEEK (Feb. 23, 2021); John Bowden, *Official Reports of Tranquil Federal Executions Don't Match Witness Accounts: AP*, THE HILL (Feb. 17, 2021); Debra Cassens Weiss, *Witness Accounts of Federal Executions Are at Odds with Government Reports on Tranquil Deaths*, ABA JOURNAL (Feb. 19, 2021).

44 For a more fulsome discussion, see Robin Konrad, *Behind the Curtain: Secrecy and the Death Penalty in the United States*, DEATH PENALTY INFO. CTR. (2018) (providing state-by-state examples), deathpenaltyinfo.org.

45 Ruth Brown, *Execution Drug Supplier Secrecy Bill Held in Committee*, IDAHO REPORTS (March 9, 2022), blog.idahoreports.idahoptv.org.

46 *See* chapter 2, text accompanying note 120.

47 Nicholas Bogel-Burroughs and Abbie VanSickle, *Alabama Executes Kenneth Smith by Nitrogen Hypoxia*, N.Y. TIMES (Jan. 25, 2024). This was the line that Alabama officials used to describe the James execution too. *See* introduction, text accompanying note 1.

48 Opposition to Application for a Stay of Execution Pending Petition for Writ of Certiorari and Brief in Opposition at 22, Smith v. Hamm, No. 23A688 (S. Ct. 2024).

49 Nicholas Bogel-Burroughs, *A Select Few Witnessed Alabama's Nitrogen Execution. This Is What They Saw.*, N.Y. TIMES, Feb. 1, 2024.

50 In some states, closing the blinds when something goes wrong with an execution is part of the official protocol. *See State-By-State Execution Protocols*, DEATH PENALTY INFO. CTR, deathpenaltyinfo.org.

51 Morales v. Tilton, 465 F. Supp. 2d, at 972, 978 (N.D. Ca. 2006).

52 Segura, *supra* note 41.

53 Complaint for Temporary Restraining Order and Preliminary Injunction, at 12–13, Nevada Press Ass'n. v. Daniels, 3:21CV00317 (D. Nev. 2002); *Nevada Press Ass'n. Sues to Ensure Access to Execution*, ASSOC. PRESS (Jul. 28, 2021), apnews.com.

54 Austin Sarat et al., *The Fate of Lethal Injection: Decomposition of the Paradigm and its Consequences*, 11 BR. J. AM. LEG. STUDIES 1, 27 (2022).

55 Bruenig, *supra* note 13.

56 In re Kemmler, 136 U.S. 436, 447 (1890) ("Punishments are cruel when they involve torture or a lingering death").

57 Michael Lyle, *ACLU, NV Press Association Sue to Assure NDOC Transparency at Execution*, NEV. CURRENT (Jul. 26, 2021), nevadacurrent.com. For the suit, see *supra* note 53.

58 Complaint, *supra* note 53, at 8; Lyle, *supra* note 57 (quoting executive director of Nevada Press Association).

59 Tarm, *supra* note 43.

60 Kelly Kissel, *New Issue in Executions: Should the Death Chamber Be Silent?*, ASSOC. PRESS (Apr. 26, 2017), apnews.com.

61 *Id.*

62 First Amendment Coal. of Ariz., Inc. v. Ryan, 938 F.3d 1069 (9th Cir. 2019).

63 *Id.* at 1077.

64 *Id.* at 1076–77.

65 Jimmy Jenkins, *Ariz. Republic Denied Request to Serve as Media Witness to Execution for Third Time*, ARIZ. CENTRAL (Nov. 10, 2022).

66 *Id.*

67 Jimmy Jenkins, *Arizona Violates Journalists' Rights to Witness Executions, Attorney Says*, ARIZ. CENTRAL (May 23, 2022).

68 *See* Ianco v. Brunetti, 588 U.S. 388, 393 (2019) ("The government may not discriminate against speech based on the ideas or opinions it conveys."); Rosenberger v. Rector and Visitors of Univ. of Va., 515 U.S. 819, 829-839 (viewpoint discrimination is an "egregious form of content discrimination in which the government targets not subject matter, but particular views taken by speakers on a subject" and is "presumptively unconstitutional").

69 ACLU of Missouri, Missouri Department of Corrections Changes Policy for Witnessing Executions (Nov. 27, 2018), www.aclu-mo.org.

70 Jenkins, *supra* note 65.

71 Ed Pilkington, *Female Journalist Told Skirt Too Short When Reporting on Alabama Execution*, THE GUARDIAN (Aug. 1, 2022).

72 Jenkins, *supra* note 65.

73 Special Hearing Testimony of Annette Viator, Vol. II, at 32, Cain v. Code, No. 138,860-A (Mar. 18, 2003).

74 Ga. Code Ann. §42-5-36 (2014).

75 Order Denying the Department of Corrections Motion to Modify Summary Judgement Order at 17, Indiana Dept. of Corr. v. Toomey, No. 49C01-1501-PL-3142;

Mark Alesia, *Judge Smacks Legislature, Says Retroactive Law Doesn't Prevent Release of Death Penalty Records*, INDIANAPOLIS STAR (Nov. 30, 2018).

76 Indiana Dept. of Corr. v. Toomey, No. 19S-PL-401 (Ind. Feb. 25, 2021).

77 *See* Ark. Code Ann. §5-4-617 (2019).

78 Cover v. Idaho Bd. of Corr., 167 Idaho 721 (2020). *See also* chapter 6, text accompanying note 108 (discussing litigation).

79 Adam Liptak, *After Flawed Executions, States Resort to Secrecy*, N.Y. TIMES (Jul. 30, 2007).

80 Dahlia Lithwick, *The Capital Punishment Cover-Up*, SLATE (Feb. 3, 2015).

81 *Id.*

82 Andrew DeMillo, *Arkansas Lawmakers Advancing More Limits on Public Records*, ASSOC. PRESS. (Mar. 10, 2019), apnews.com.

83 *Id.*

84 Houston Associated Press, *Appeals Court: Texas Must Reveal Execution Drug Supplier*, CBS AUSTIN (May 25, 2017), cbsaustin.com.

85 Michael Muskal, *Judge Strikes Down Oklahoma's Execution Law*, CHI. TRIBUNE (Mar. 26, 2014).

86 Evan Axelbank, *Florida Lawmakers Favor Secrecy in Crucial Part of Lethal Injection Procedures*, FOX 13 (Jan. 25, 2022), www.fox13news.com.

87 Transcript of Oral Argument at 14, Glossip v. Gross, 576 U.S. 863 (2015). For a discussion, see Sam Baker, *Alito: Critics Waging "Guerilla War against the Death Penalty,"* THE ATLANTIC (Apr. 29, 2015).

88 Jonathan Allen, *Special Report: How the Trump Administration Secured a Secret Supply of Execution Drugs*, REUTERS (Jul. 10, 2020); Aamer Madhani, *South Carolina Can't Hold Execution Because No One Will Sell State Lethal Injection Drugs*, USA TODAY (Nov. 20, 2017).

89 Doe v. Reed, 561 U.S. 186, 228 (2010) (Scalia, J., concurring).

90 Tex. Dep't of Criminal Justice v. Levin, 572 S.W.3d 671 (Tex. 2019) rev'ing Tex. Dep't of Criminal Justice v. Levin, 520 S.W.3d 225 (Tex. App. 2017).

91 *Levin*, 572 S.W.3d at 683. For context, the Murrah Federal Building bombing in Oklahoma was the largest domestic terror attack in U.S. history, killing 168 people, and the perpetrator, Timothy McVeigh, used a truck filled with a deadly mix of agricultural fertilizer, diesel fuel, and other chemicals to do it.

92 *Id.*

93 *See* Nooman Merchant & Bailey Elise McBride, *Scant Evidence of Threats to Execution Drugmakers*, ASSOC. PRESS (Apr. 3, 2014), apnews.com.

94 *Id.*

95 *Id.*

96 Death Penalty Due Process Review Project, Am. Bar Ass'n., Report to the House of Delegates, at 12 (2015), www.in.gov.

97 Keri Blakinger, *"Struggling with It Ever Since": Former Texas Lethal Injection Drug Supplier Speaks Out*, HOUSTON CHRONICLE (May 4, 2019).

98 *Levin*, 520 S.W.3d at 234–35.

99 Kelley v. Johnson, 496 S.W.3d 346, 358 (Ark. 2016).

100 Jon Camp, *North Carolina Legislature Passes Bill Limiting Execution Transparency*, ABC11 NEWS (Jul. 29, 2015), abc11.com.

101 Alesia, *supra* note 75.

102 Defendants' Motion for Protective Order and Brief in Support, at 13, Warner v. Gross, No. 14-cv-665, (W.D. Okla. Oct. 14, 2014).

103 First Amendment Coal. of Arizona, 938 F.3d 1069, 1084 (Berzon, J., concurring in part, dissenting in part).

104 *See supra* text accompanying note 87.

105 Renuka Rayasam, *States Try to Obscure Execution Details as Drugmakers Hinder Lethal Injection*, USA TODAY (Mar. 30, 2023).

106 *See* chapter 6, text accompanying note 191.

107 Jimmy Jenkins, *States under Scrutiny for Recent Lethal Injection Failures*, ARIZ. REPUBLIC (Nov. 22, 2022).

108 Deborah Denno, *Lethal Injection Chaos Post-Baze*, 102 GEO. L.J. 1331, 1379 (2014); *See also* Konrad, *supra* note 44, at 24 (concluding that stated reasons for lethal injection secrecy are primarily "a pretext for hiding improper conduct").

109 Lincoln Caplan, *The End of the Open Market for Lethal-Injection Drugs*, NEW YORKER (May 21, 2016).

110 Glossip v. Gross, 574 U.S. 1133 (2015).

111 Chris McDaniel, *Oklahoma's Attorney General Misled Supreme Court about Letter on Execution Drug Availability*, BUZZFEED NEWS (May 13, 2015).

112 *Id.*

113 *See* chapter 6, text accompanying notes 109–10.

114 Ruth Brown, *Execution Drug Supplier Secrecy Bill Held in Committee*, IDAHO REPORTS (Mar. 9, 2022).

115 Konrad, *supra* note 44.

116 *See, e.g., Bucklew*, 587 U.S. 119, 150 (2019) ("Under our Constitution, the question of capital punishment belongs to the people and their representatives, not the courts, to resolve.").

117 Kevin Fixler, *Cash Buys, Private Flights, Changing Rules: How Idaho Hides from Execution Oversight*, IDAHO CAPITAL SUN (Jan. 16, 2022).

118 Austin Sarat, *It's Time to End Death Penalty Secrecy*, THE HILL (Mar. 13, 2022).

119 Fixler, *supra* note 117.

120 Ed Pilkington, *Missouri Ordered to Reveal Pharmacies That Supplied Its Execution Drugs*, THE GUARDIAN (Mar. 22, 2016); FREEDOM FORUM, freedomforum.org ("An independent news media uses its watchdog role to investigate and report on government overreach and wrongdoing and hold those in power accountable for their actions. You can't have democracy without a free press.").

121 Deron Lee, *The First Amendment vs. Death Penalty Secrecy Laws*, COLUMBIA J. REV (Mar. 7, 2014), archives.cjr.org.

122 *Id.*

123 *Id.*

124 Denno, *supra* note 108, at 1379–82.

125 For an excellent discussion, see Eric Berger, *Lethal Injection Secrecy and Eighth Amendment Due Process*, 55 B.C. L. REV. 1367 (2014).

126 The Reporters Committee for Freedom of the Press, Amicus Brief at 8, Indiana Dept. of Correction v. Toomey, No. 19S-PL-401 (Jan. 17, 2020); *After Botched Executions, States Add Secrecy to the Lethal Injection Process*, WASH. POST (Jan. 27, 2015).

127 Lee, *supra* note 121.

128 *Oklahoma Court Rules Lethal Injection Drug Secrecy Law Unconstitutional*, OKLA. NEWS 4, March 26, 2014 (quoting judge's ruling from bench). For the written ruling, see Lockett v. Evans, No. CV2014330, 2014 WL 6809140 (Okl. Dist., Apr. 1, 2014) (finding that state secrecy statute "is an unconstitutional denial or barrier to Plaintiffs' right to access the Courts").

129 Wood v. Ryan, 759 F.3d 1076, 1087 (9th Cir. 2014), vacated by Ryan v. Wood, 573 U.S. 976 (2014).

130 Ryan v. Wood, 573 U.S. 976 (2014).

131 Wellons v. Commissioner, Ga. Dept. of Corrections, 754 F.3d 1260, 1268 (2014) (Wilson, J., concurring).

132 Terrell v. Bryson, 807 F.3d, at 1276, 1282 (2015) (Martin, J., concurring).

133 Lopez v. Brewer, 680 F.3d, at 1084, 1095 (9th Cir. 2012) (Reinhardt, J., dissenting).

134 Brewer v. Landrigan, 562 U.S. 996 (2008).

135 Phillips v. Dewine, 92 F. Supp. 3d, at 702, 717 (S.D. Ohio 2015). Exacerbating the problem is the fact that secrecy prevents prisoners from naming a "feasible and readily implemented" alternative way to execute them, as required by Bucklew v. Precythe, 587 U.S. 119 (2019). How is a prisoner supposed to know what is feasible and readily implemented when the prisoner doesn't have access to the relevant information?

136 *See* Lockett v. Evans, 2014 OK 34, 330 P.3d 488, 491 (2014).

137 *Id.* at 493 (Taylor, J., concurring).

138 Lewis v. Casey, 518 U.S. 343, 354 (1996).

139 Berger, *supra* note 125, at 1429–30.

140 Sepulvado v. Jindal, 729 F.3d 413, 420 (5th Cir. 2013) (emphasis added).

141 Colin Dickey, *An Ugly American Tradition That Dates Back to Our Earliest Settlers: "Civilizing Torture,"* LA TIMES (Nov. 22, 2018) (reviewing W. FITZHUGH BRUNDAGE, CIVILIZING TORTURE: AN AMERICAN TRADITION (2018)). I credit Stephen Cooper's work for bringing this book review to my attention. Stephen Cooper, *Nitrogen Gas Execution: An Abomination in Alabama*, MONTGOMERY ADVERTISER (Sept. 13, 2022).

142 Lee, *supra* note 121.

143 Fixler, *supra* note 117.

EPILOGUE

1 The story of Saul who became Paul on the road to Damascus is told in the Holy Bible, Acts 9.

2 Statement from Shawn Nolan, Attorney for Dustin Honken, www.fd.org. Here is the full statement:

> Dustin Honken was redeemed. He recognized and repented for the crimes he had committed, and spent his time in prison atoning for them. . . . Dustin worked every day at the Catholic faith that was at the center of his life. During his time in prison, he cared for everyone he came into contact with: guards, counselors, medical staff, his fellow inmates and his legal team. Over the years he grew incredibly close to his family, becoming a true father, son, brother and friend. There was no reason for the government to kill him, in haste or at all. In any case, they failed. The Dustin Honken they wanted to kill is long gone. The man they killed today was a human being, who could have spent the rest of his days helping others and further redeeming himself. May he rest in peace.

3 Timothy Lancaster, *We Corrections Officers Know Brian Dorsey Has Changed. Gov. Parson, Don't Execute Him*, KAN. CITY STAR (April 1, 2024).

Index

ABA. *See* American Board of Anesthesiologists

Abbott Laboratories, 148–49, 326n32

Abolitionist movement, 141, 144, 148–49, 168; guerilla war against death penalty, 179–80, 258, 263, 335n193; as justification for secrecy statutes, 258–63, 265; Reprieve, 148–49

abortion, 262–63

Absolute Standards, 163, 167, 172, 330n99

ACLU. *See* American Civil Liberties Union

active pharmaceutical ingredients (APIs), 162–63, 167, 171, 172, 184–85

acute pulmonary edema, 88–97; in autopsy reports, 49, 88–90, 91; cause of, 50, 88–91; etomidate and, 90; frothing and, 92–93, 310n157; in Grant, 52–53, 96, 246; in Gray, 89–90; Greenblatt and, 50, 90, 93–94, 95; litigation defenses of, 92–97; from midazolam executions, 49–52, 88–90, 93–94; non-severe torture and, 52, 85, 95–97; NPR study and, 3, 90; onset of, 93–94; from pentobarbital executions, 90–94; *Roane v. Barr*, 91–94; in Purkey, 92; from sodium thiopental executions, 90; symptoms of, 94–95, 312nn168–69; waterboarding effect of, 3, 50–53, 89–90, 94–96, 245–46, 310n138, 310n157, 312n169

AHFS. *See* American Society of Health System Pharmacists' *Drug Information*

Alabama: botched executions in, 1–2, 57–58, 98, 108, 110, 236–37, 243–45, 248–49; executioners in, 130; hostility to press in, 254; IV insertion problems in, 1, 110–12, 114, 250–51; James execution in, 1, 243–45, 250–51; Smith execution in, 1, 57–58, 248–49; method of execution election forms in, 223–24; nitrogen gas executions in, 1–2, 55–58, 223–24, 248–49; secrecy in, 243–45, 237, 248–49, 250–51; "top-to-bottom review" in, 1, 114, 236–37

Alito, Samuel, 179–80, 204–5, 258, 263, 335n193

Alper, Ty, 31, 199–200, 205, 211

Alvogen, 175–76, 179

AMA. *See* American Medical Association

American Board of Anesthesiologists (ABA), 195, 209

American Civil Liberties Union (ACLU), 137–38, 253, 267

American Medical Association (AMA), 190–94, 206

American Society of Anesthesiologists (ASA), 66–67, *67*, 195

American Society of Health System Pharmacists' *Drug Information* (AHFS), 84, 308nn120–21

American Veterinary Medical Association, 163. *See also* animal euthanasia

amicus briefs: in *Arthur v. Dunn,* 341n80; in *Baze v. Rees,* 122, 127; in *Bucklew v. Precythe,* 182–83, 190–192, 206, 234; in *Glossip v. Gross* (2015), 46, 49, 80–81, 144–45, 298n38; in pharmaceutical company suits, 174, 178, 179–80

About the Author

CORINNA BARRETT LAIN is the S.D. Roberts & Sandra Moore Professor of Law at the University of Richmond School of Law. Before entering legal academia, Professor Lain was a prosecutor, and before that, she was a sergeant in the US Army. Professor Lain is one of the nation's leading authorities on the death penalty, and has published numerous articles, essays, and blog posts about lethal injection over the last decade. Her work has appeared in the most prestigious law journals in the country, and she is a frequent presenter on the death penalty at both national and international conferences. Professor Lain is also one of the leading voices on criminal justice in Virginia more broadly. She is coauthor of the *Virginia Practice Series'* four-volume set of hornbooks on Virginia criminal law, and she lectures on recent developments in the criminal law for the Virginia judiciary and other organizations serving lawyers who practice criminal law in the Commonwealth.

www.ingramcontent.com/pod-product-compliance
Lightning Source LLC
Chambersburg PA
CBHW030150310326
41914CB00099B/1827/J